Jonatan J. Gómez Vilchez

The Impact of Electric Cars on Oil Demand and Greenhouse Gas Emissions in Key Markets

PRODUKTION UND ENERGIE

Karlsruher Institut für Technologie (KIT)
Institut für Industriebetriebslehre und Industrielle Produktion
Deutsch-Französisches Institut für Umweltforschung

Band 27

Eine Übersicht aller bisher in dieser Schriftenreihe
erschienenen Bände finden Sie am Ende des Buches.

The Impact of Electric Cars on Oil Demand and Greenhouse Gas Emissions in Key Markets

by
Jonatan J. Gómez Vilchez

KIT Scientific Publishing

Dissertation, Karlsruher Institut für Technologie
KIT-Fakultät für Wirtschaftswissenschaften

Tag der mündlichen Prüfung: 5. Juni 2018
Erster Gutachter: Prof. Dr. Wolf Fichtner
Zweiter Gutachter: Prof. Dr. Werner Rothengatter

Impressum

KIT Scientific Publishing

Karlsruher Institut für Technologie (KIT)
KIT Scientific Publishing
Straße am Forum 2
D-76131 Karlsruhe

KIT Scientific Publishing is a registered trademark
of Karlsruhe Institute of Technology.
Reprint using the book cover is not allowed.

www.ksp.kit.edu

Print on Demand 2019 – Gedruckt auf FSC-zertifiziertem Papier

ISSN 2194-2404
ISBN 978-3-7315-0914-1
DOI 10.5445/KSP/1000091891

The Impact of Electric Cars on Oil Demand and Greenhouse Gas Emissions in Key Markets

zur Erlangung des akademischen Grades eines

Doktors der Wirtschaftswissenschaften
(Dr. rer. pol.)

von der KIT-Fakultät für Wirtschaftswissenschaften
des Karlsruher Instituts für Technologie (KIT)

genehmigte

Dissertation

von

Jonatan J. Gómez Vilchez

aus Málaga, Spanien

Tag der mündlichen Prüfung: 05.06.2018
Erster Gutachter: Prof. Dr. Wolf Fichtner
Zweiter Gutachter: Prof. Dr. Werner Rothengatter

A mi familia

Abstract

This thesis explores the extent to which electric cars might reduce oil demand and greenhouse gas emissions in key markets: China, France, Germany, India, Japan and the United States. To meet this objective, a dynamic model capable of simulating the market evolution of nine powertrain technologies between 2000 and 2030 is developed.

The model consists of an econometric sub-model, soft-linked with a system dynamics sub-model. The purpose of the time-series econometric sub-model is to project country-specific total car stock. To this end, six single-equation regressions based on autoregressive integrated moving average or autoregressive distributed-lag techniques are estimated. The purpose of the system dynamics sub-model is to represent feedback processes and facilitate policy analysis. The effects of six policy measures are examined: emission standards, energy taxation, electric car purchase subsidies, investment in recharging stations, investment in hydrogen refuelling infrastructure and desired car occupancy. The dynamic hypothesis of the model captures feedback loops that may stimulate the market development of electric cars. The six countries are interlinked to simulate technological progress concerning the electric vehicle battery. In particular, its cost, price and capacity, together with the resulting electric range of the car, are investigated. Two scenarios are constructed: under the Alternative Scenario, the market uptake of electric cars is faster due to a favourable policy package. This leads to a decline in oil demand and direct greenhouse gas emissions as well as to an increase in electricity demand from cars compared to the Reference Scenario.

The methodological linkage of econometrics and system dynamics, together with the endogenisation of the electric vehicle battery price evolution by explicitly modelling six major car markets, is the main contribution of this study. Its major limitations prompt further research on the representation of supply-side aspects (i.e. battery and vehicle manufacturers) using alternative methods such as agent-based modelling.

Table of Contents

List of Figures

List of Tables

List of Abbreviations

Car types and powertrain technologies

AFV	Alternative fuel vehicle
BEV	Battery electric vehicle
CV	Conventional vehicle
D	Diesel car
G	Gasoline car
FC(EV)	Fuel cell (electric vehicle)
FF(V)	Flexible-fuel (vehicle)
EV	Electric vehicle
ICE(V)	Internal combustion engine (vehicle)
NEV	New energy vehicles (EVs in China)
(P)LDV	(Passenger) light-duty vehicle
PHEV	Plug-in hybrid electric vehicle
REEV	Range-extender electric vehicle
SUV	Sport utility vehicle
ZEV	Zero emission vehicle

Countries

BRICS	Brazil, Russia, India, China, South Africa
CN	People's Republic of China (for short, China)
DE	Federal Republic of Germany (for short, Germany)
FR	French Republic (for short, France)
IN	Republic of India (for short, India)

JP	Japan
US	United States of America (for short, US)

Econometrics

ADF	Augmented Dickey-Fuller test
ADL	Autoregressive distributed-lag (also abbreviated as ARDL or AD)
AIC	Akaike information criterion
AO	Additive outlier
AR(MA)	Autoregressive (moving average)
BG(p)	Breusch-Godfrey test of lag order p (see LMSC)
DGP	Data-generation process
DS	Difference stationary
DW	Durbin-Watson
ECM	Error correction mechanism or model
IO	Innovation outlier
JB	Jarque-Bera
KPSS	Kwiatkowski-Phillips-Schmidt-Shin test
LM(SC)	Breusch-Godfrey Lagrange multiplier (serial correlation) test
ML	Maximum likelihood
NID	Normally and independently distributed
OLS	Ordinary least squares
(P)AC	Sample (partial) autocorrelation
(R)MSE	(Root) mean square (forecasting) error
(S)BIC	(Schwarz) Bayesian information criterion
TS	Trend stationary
TSA	Time series analysis

Emissions

CH_4	Methane
CO_2	Carbon dioxide
EF	Emission factor
GHG	Greenhouse gas
GWP	Global warming potential
N_2O	Nitrous oxide

Fuels

(C)NG	(Compressed) natural gas
E85	Ethanol 85 (85% ethanol; 15% gasoline)
H_2	Hydrogen gas
LPG	Liquefied petroleum gas or propane or autogas

Other

ABM	Agent-based modelling
ACE	Agent-based computational economics
AS	Alternative scenario
ASIF	Activity–Structure–Intensity–Fuel
B	Balancing (negative) feedback loop
BAU	Business-as-usual (see RS)
CAFE	Corporate average fuel efficiency standards
DC	Discrete choice
DOE	US Department of Energy
DT	Delta time or time step
EC	European Commission
EIA	US Energy Information Agency

EPA	US Environmental Protection Agency
ETS	Emissions trading system
EU(28)	European Union (28 Member States)
EVB	Electric vehicle battery
EVI	Electric Vehicles Initiative
EVSE	Electric vehicle supply equipment
GDP	Gross domestic product
ICCT	International Council on Clean Transportation
IEA	International Energy Agency
I-O	Input-output
IPAT	Impact–Population–Affluence–Technology
IPCC	Intergovernmental Panel on Climate Change
JC08	Japanese test cycle
LCA	Lifecycle assessment / analysis
M&S	Manufacturing and scrappage emissions
MC	Monte Carlo simulation
NEDC	New European driving cycle
OECD	Organisation for Economic Co-operation and Development
OEM	Original equipment manufacturer
OPEC	Organization of the Petroleum Exporting Countries
R	Reinforcing (positive) feedback loop
R&D	Research and development
RS	Reference scenario
SD	System dynamics
(S)FTP	(Supplemental) federal test procedure
SOE	State-owned enterprise
TCO	Total cost of ownership
TTW	Tank-to-wheel (direct / on-road) emissions

UN	United Nations
UNFCCC	United Nations Framework Convention on Climate Change
VAT	Value added tax
VKT	Vehicle-kilometre travelled
WB	Word Bank
WLTP	Worldwide harmonized light vehicles test procedures
WTT	Well-to-tank (indirect / off-road) emissions
WTW	Well-to-wheel (WTT plus TTW) emissions

Units of measurement of variables

bbl	barrel of crude oil
g	gram
kg	kilogram
km	kilometre
kWh	kilowatt-hour
MJ	megajoule
MPG	miles per (US) gallon
Mt	megatonne
pkm	passenger-km

List of Symbols

Variables

α	intercept (regression) or utility coefficient
β	coefficient (regression) or utility coefficient
γ	utility coefficient
δ	gap (e.g. emissions gap) or utility coefficient
ε	error term (regression) or utility coefficient
ζ	market share
η	elasticity
θ	refinery oil processing gain or utility coefficient
ι	expected loss rate
κ	lifetime
λ	fuel consumption (efficiency / intensity)
μ	mean (expected value)
ν	other costs
ξ	energy use
Δ	differencing (i.e. inverse of summation)
π	profit and other refining, transport and marketing costs
$\hat{\rho}_k$	estimated sample autocorrelation at lag k
Σ	summation
σ	standard deviation (Std. Dev.)
τ	tax (excluding VAT)
χ^2	chi-squared probability distribution
a	powertrain availability
AT	adjustment time

B	government fund
cap	capita
CC	carrying capacity or saturation level
d	order of integration (in an ARIMA model)
DT_t	trend break
DU_t	intercept break
$dmnl$	dimensionless variable
E	energy content
exr	exchange rate
g	fractional growth rate
H_0	null hypothesis
H_A	alternative hypothesis
I	stock of alternative fuel infrastructure (number of stations)
inno	innovation
log	natural logarithm
$l(own)$	log (of own)
own	car ownership
p	order (in AR process) or maximum lag of y (in ADL model)
pop	population or popularity
$Prob$	probability value
$Q(-stat)$	Ljung-Box *Q*-statistic
q	order (in MA process) or maximum lag of x (in ADL model)
r	car scrappage rate
$rgdp$	real GDP
$rfuel$	real gasoline fuel price
$rinc$	real income per capita or real GDP per capita
$roil$	real crude oil price
S	car stock

s	car sales rate
$S.E.$	standard error
T	time series length or sample size
T_B	break date
t_c	critical value
U	utility
$w.r.t.$	with respect to
x	regression independent variables in general
y	regression dependent variable in general (see own)

Subscripts

h	country [COUNTRY in Vensim®]
i	powertrain technology type [TECH in Vensim®]
j	greenhouse gas type
t	time (continuous)
$t-1$	time (discrete, lagged one period)
$t+1$	time (discrete, lead one period)

Superscripts

$*$	target or desired value
agg	aggregate
exp	expected
f	fuel type
$first$	first sales
mid	middle car
new	new car
nom	nominal price

old	old car
$real$	real price
rep	repeat sales
tot	total
TTW	tank-to-wheel
WTT	well-to-tank
WTW	well-to-wheel

Sets

$[t_0, t_{30}]$	closed interval from $t_o = 2000$ to $t_{30} = 2030$
$COUNTRY$	{China, France, Germany, India, Japan, US}
f	{gasoline, diesel, E85, autogas, CNG, electricity, H_2}
GHG	{CH_4, CO_2, N_2O}
$h \in COUNTRY$	h is an element of set $COUNTRY$
$i \in TECH$	i is an element of set $TECH$
$TECH$	{G, D, FF, LPG, NG, HEV, PHEV, BEV, FC}

Acknowledgments and accountability

Diese Doktorarbeit wurde von Herrn Prof. Dr. Wolf Fichtner und Herrn PD Dr. Patrick Jochem vom Lehrstuhl für Energiewirtschaft am Institut für Industriebetriebslehre und Industrielle Produktion (IIP), betreut. Ich bedanke mich herzlich bei meinen beiden Betreuern sowie bei meinem Korreferenten Herrn Prof. Dr. Werner Rothengatter. Ein Dankeschön gilt auch all meinen Kollegen von der Forschungsgruppe „Transport und Energie" für anregende Diskussionen.

I have benefited from exchanges, often in conferences, that are too numerous to mention here. But I would like to express, in particular, my gratitude to two persons: Prof. Pål Davidsen from the University of Bergen in Norway, for having allowed me to visit the Research Group System Dynamics as a guest doctoral student in 2015, and Juan Caro, my teacher of Economics at high school between 2001 and 2003 for his inspiring work.

The work presented in this monograph arose within the context of the inter-disciplinary Helmholtz Research School on Energy Scenarios (ESS). I benefited from a doctoral scholarship for the period 2012-2015, for which I am grateful to the Helmholtz Association. I thank the Helmholtz coordinators and fellow *Stipendiaten* for their support. I am also grateful to the Karlsruhe Service Research Institute (KSRI) for its *Stipendium* in 2016. Finally, I gratefully thank the World Conference on Transport Research Society (WCTRS) for awarding a Young Researcher's Prestige grant in 2016. The prize helped me enrich my library.

I am aware of the gap between what I pursued to achieve at the start of this work and the final result. I hope my effort has reduced this gap to a reasonable size. My own work, my own errors.

Stutensee, im Februar 2017 J. J. Gómez Vilchez

1 Introduction

In this introductory chapter, the main motivation and objective of this study are highlighted (section 1.1). The chapter also describes the research focus and scope, together with the structure of the thesis (section 1.2).

1.1 Motivation and objective

There are three major societal issues under discussion at the time of writing: (i) climate change; (ii) energy transition; and (iii) economic prospects. In its Fourth Assessment Report, the Intergovernmental Panel on Climate Change (IPCC) claimed that global warming is unequivocal (IPCC, 2007c), highlighting possible serious adverse impacts of climate change. Six years later, in its Fifth Assessment Report the IPCC identified human action as a principal cause leading to warming of the climate system (IPCC, 2013). A major influence on climate is exerted by emissions from road vehicles (Uherek *et al.*, 2010), which accounted for around 80% of the more than doubling in transport-related greenhouse gas (GHG) emissions that has taken place since 1970 (IPCC, 2015). In 2010, the transport sector accounted for ca. 23% of total energy-related CO_2 emissions, generating 6.7 $GtCO_2$ of direct emissions worldwide (IPCC, 2015). One sectoral mitigation strategy is road electrification. In the context of the international climate negotiations hosted by the United Nations Framework Convention on Climate Change (UNFCCC), a declaration on electro-mobility and climate change was announced in Paris in December 2015 (UNFCCC, 2015).

The issue of energy transition is related to a shift from fossil-based to non-fossil-based energy supply and use. In 2014, the transport sector accounted for 64.5% of world oil use (IEA, 2016e). Oil represents 93% of world final energy use by the transport sector (IEA, 2016d). Swedish physicist Kjell Aleklett (2012) contends the thesis that peak oil, which refers to the idea that most of the Earth's oil has been found (Deffeyes, 2010), will severely affect transport. The main industrial economies are currently highly dependent on oil. For example, 90% of the crude oil needed in the EU is imported (EC, 2016d). Whereas in the short-term oil importing countries have a high interest in securing access to oil supplies at an affordable price; in the long-term, they have a strong incentive to transition towards a non-oil-based economy. Renewable energy provides an opportunity for this.

Today's major economies are examples of market capitalism, with a mix of public and private sector involvement. In this type of economic system, capital accumulation and innovation are commonly considered two key drivers of positive gross domestic product (GDP) change (i.e. economic growth). From this follows that public policy-makers and private investors favour and promote positive technological change (i.e. technological progress). In general, investments in the development and commercialisation of new products are made, with infant industries emerging and suddenly altering the market status quo, spurring clashes between incumbents and new entrants in the process and leading, eventually, to market losers and winners. Technological progress in the automotive industry is perhaps best symbolised today by the (re-)introduction of electric vehicles (EVs). Its recent emergence has been described by Dijk *et al.* (2013). The losers and winners of this competitive process are yet to be determined.

In terms of systemic risks, climate change and resource scarcity may be seen as examples of a particular type of current threats (cf. Renn (2014)). These three issues, mitigation policy against climate change, energy transition towards renewables and technology-led economic growth, are interlinked. Sperling and Gordon (2009) go as far as identifying electric-drive technology as a key solution in transport. Consequently, the future market development pathway of electric cars and its key implications are of significant interest. From today's perspective, this development is highly uncertain. It is this prospect that motivates this work.

This thesis presents the results of a doctoral study that *aimed* at providing scientifically-sounded orientation on possible evolutions of electric cars as well as on their corresponding energy and emissions impacts until the year 2030 in key markets. The *means* towards it is by carrying out a modelling exercise which entails the development of a computer model that enables the construction of scenarios.

Complex problems, such as the one under investigation, usually require an *interdisciplinary* understanding and there are obvious limits as to whether this can be achieved by a single individual. Given the background knowledge of the author, the main perspective comes from the social sciences.

In 1920, British economist Alfred Marshall ([1920] 2013) [1842-1924] emphasised the practical use of economics, a discipline that helps understand problems, according to British transport economist Kenneth Button (2010). Being a piece of applied research, and as such geared towards solving practical problems (Rogers, 2003), this thesis revolves around the transition from conventional to alternative car technologies in line with the three issues previously introduced. This is supported by international policy goals that aim to upscale the number of electric cars deployed worldwide from 1 million in 2015 (ICCT, 2015) to 20 million by 2020 (EVI, 2015) and to more than 100 million by 2030 (UNFCCC, 2015). But policy goals do not necessarily translate into reality. This thesis sheds light on this uncertain pathway, drawing on insights in matters that concern energy, environmental and transport economics and policy.

The objective is articulated in the following research question:

"*To what extent might electric cars reduce oil demand in key markets?*"

One simple way of answering this question is by accepting that the international policy goals on electric cars deployment are realised and, by assuming that each electric car replaces one average gasoline car, computing the corresponding oil saved. A more elaborated, though not necessarily more accurate, answer than this shall be presented in this thesis. Furthermore, the analysis is complemented by estimating the resulting amount of GHG emissions.

1.2 Focus, scope and structure

Based on the aforementioned objective, this research focuses on four aspects, described in the following.

This work considers one type of motor vehicles: passenger light-duty vehicles (PLDVs) (see section 3.4 for definitions). In particular, it takes the (passenger) car or auto(mobile) as the unit of analysis. In addition, the focus is on a specific technological dimension of cars: the 'powertrain'. This is the term adopted to refer to the propulsion system, drivetrain or driveline (cf. (Lovins, 2013) (p. 18) for definitions). Different kinds of (car) powertrains imply different types of fuels (see Figure 4.1). Currently, most cars are powered by either gasoline or diesel worldwide (IEA/OECD, 2009).

The focus also lies on selected public policies which influence the market penetration of EVs. These policies are usually designed at the country level, commonly arising from the authority of a central or federal government, and are sometimes complemented by a regional or state government. An example is fuel taxation. Besides the focus on policies at the country level, it is argued that a multi-country scope is desirable to model more realistically the future market evolution of electric cars and to compare regulation relevant to the automotive industry across countries. The main reason for this is due to the fact that the automotive sector in general and battery manufacturing in particular have a global nature. Though desirable, a global model represents an extreme case. At the other end of the spectrum, a model may analyse powertrain adoption taking the household as the unit of analysis. From the outset, data availability and resources render this approach as unfeasible for the author. Instead, six major car markets are used as a proxy of the global uptake of electric cars in this work. The disadvantage of having to focus on aggregate variables is partially offset by the international perspective it offers. The countries investigated are China (CN), France (FR), Germany (DE), India (IN), Japan (JP) and the United States (US). These countries meet two criteria: (i) have, or are expected to have in the next years, a large (> 30 million) car stock; and (ii) are currently members of the Electric Vehicles Initiative (EVI), thereby showing publicly commitment to EV deployment (EVI, 2016a). Besides, these countries are major emitters of GHGs and participate in ongoing climate negotiations. Together, these six countries accounted for about 46% of world transport GHG emissions in 2010 ((UNFCCC, 2016); 2012 data for China) and over 60% of global car sales in 2016 (OICA, 2017).

For modelling purposes, a compromise between a rather short time horizon such as 2020, where the impact of alternative powertrains is expected to be low, and a very long time horizon such as 2050, where uncertainty is greatest, was found with a time horizon extending until 2030.

For the sake of clarity, what lies beyond the scope of this work is highlighted:

- Negative effects of car travel, such as accidents, air pollution and congestion, are not considered.
- A comprehensive representation of the supply side, with a focus on the automotive sector, is beyond scope. At the intersection between market and policy, there exist regular reports, such as those by the International Council on Clean Transportation (ICCT) and the Oak Ridge National Laboratory (ORNL), that present in-depth up-to-date market analysis.
- The interactions between personal travel by car and other modes of transport, such as non-motorised and public transport, are beyond scope. In the context of urban mobility, Kelly and Zhu (2016) contend that the solution to foreseeable challenges lies on public transport, not on zero emission vehicles (ZEVs). See also Creutzig *et al.* (2015).
- The implications of car sharing and autonomous cars are not explored. For a recent analysis, see e.g. Chen *et al.* (2016).

These exclusions are motivated by simplification purposes. They also highlight starting points for further research. Specific future research needs are indicated in chapter 7.

The remaining of the thesis is structured as follows. Chapter 2 explores the uncertain market evolution of electric cars from different standpoints. Chapter 3 examines methodological issues, presenting a survey of main research programmes and methods. In chapter 4, the modelling exercise is described. Chapter 5 and chapter 6 show the results of two different scenarios: the Reference Scenario (RS) and the Alternative Scenario (AS), respectively. In chapter 7, conclusions are drawn and limitations identified. Finally, two appendices complement this work.

2 The uncertain market evolution of electric cars

This chapter introduces fundamental ideas (section 2.1), offers a brief historical account (section 2.2) and reviews relevant literature (section 2.3). The chapter concludes with a few remarks.

2.1 Fundamental ideas

There are several long-standing main concepts in economics that are, more implicitly than explicitly, incorporated in this work:

- *Scarcity of resources*: Defined by Robbins ([1932] 2007) as the science connecting human ends with scarce means that have alternative uses, the allocation of scarce resources given competing uses remains the main challenge in economics (Dahl, 2004).

- *Choice*: Marshall ([1920] 2013) pointed out that human wants approach infinity. Hence given scarcity of resources and innumerable wants, humans have to make economic decisions and choices.

- *Opportunity cost*: The concept of opportunity costs is essential to analyse non-renewable resources (Sweeney, 1993). More generally, opportunity costs shape economic decisions, as pointed out by American economist Richard Thaler* (2015)[1].

- *Trade-off and valuation*: Whenever there are alternative uses and opportunity costs involved, trade-offs arise. The action to choose implies judgement (Robinson, 1973). Two important value judgements in our context are: (i) between private or social discounting (cf. Baumol (1968)); and (ii) the role of the 'precautionary principle' (refer to Foster *et al.* (2000)).

---

[1] An asterisk denotes that the author was awarded the Nobel Memorial Prize in Economic Sciences.

- *Incentives*: The structure of economic incentives affects economic behaviour and choices. In the context of climate change, Nordhaus (2013) highlights the power of the incentives structure and claims that a high carbon price is the most effective incentive.

2.1.1 The car and the oil markets

Economic theory helps shed light into the three issues that motive this piece of research (climate change, energy transition and economic prospects). To analyse each of them, it seems wise to consider the economic ideas of externalities, imperfect competition and innovation.

From a microeconomic perspective, analysing the way markets operate is core to economics (Gravelle and Rees, 2004). The market represents an exchange between producers and consumers. In this work, of interest is the car market. Paraphrasing Marshall ([1920] 2013: 283): the supply price of a car is the price at which it will be delivered by car-makers for sale to that group of car purchasers whose demand for it we are considering in the car market From this statement, two strands of analysis emerge: (i) the nature of demand; and (ii) the structure of the market.

Concerning the nature of demand, economic thinkers have since long claimed that the satisfaction of human needs underpins production and exchange. Such a claim can be found in the writings of, among others, Scottish moral philosopher Adam Smith ([1776] 2008) [1723-1790], Austrian economist Carl Menger (2007) [1840-1921] and British economist John Maynard Keynes ([1936] 2015) [1883-1946]. The benefits of possessing a car are generally considered to be increased mobility, convenience and independence (Ponting, 2011). Car ownership may be conceived not only as a useful material good, but also as what Marshall ([1920] 2013) termed an 'immaterial good'. In turn, car ownership may be interpreted as an example of 'conspicuous consumption' (Veblen, 2014), a general idea put forward by Norwegian-origin American economist Thorstein B. Veblen [1857-1929]. In this regard, the car may be understood as a means of acquiring social status. Contemporary observers in wealthy countries may conclude that this remains as valid today for cars as it was for other positional goods in 1899, when Veblen wrote. Thus it can be deduced that there are some psychological or social factors that may play a role in the demand for cars, in addition to the purely economic or material ones. So far, the working of the car market may concisely be described as follows: a person believes (s)he may satisfy her/his mobility and/or immaterial needs by demanding a car which is the result of a production process (i.e. manufactured using raw materials and a mix of human and non-human labour). A voluntary exchange between the consumer and the car-maker, usually via a dealership, takes place at an agreed market price for acquiring/selling a car. Economists such as Canadian economist John K. Galbraith (2015) [1908-2006] and Spanish economist José Luis Sampedro (2010) [1917-2013] identified the presence of an additional mechanism to the exchange process, symbolised by marketing and attempts to shape consumer wants. The results by Kwoka (1993) indicate that sales for a particular car model may grow as a consequence of advertising expenditure. This point shall be taken up later, in the context of market structure. In sum, conditional to money budget constraints and availability of consumer loans that determine a person's ability to pay, (s)he may be willing to pay to own a car. The fact that the car owner faces a high upfront cost, typical of consumer durables, means (s)he is likely to commit to car ownership for several years and has little incentive not to drive the car purchased during that period of time. Although a driving license and insurance are officially required to use it, what is really essential is a source of energy. Disregarding energy inputs in the production process, it is in this way that the car market and the energy market are more visibly linked. Today, the strongest link appears to be between the car market and the oil market. In economic terminology, the internal combustion engine (ICE)-car and gasoline fuel are complementary goods. A weaker link has been established, via first-generation biofuels or 'agrofuels', between the car market and the food market. Currently, a new link between the car market and the electricity market is emerging. It is thus unsurprising that EVs are often promoted by electric utilities (Wolf, 2009).

Figure 2.1 represents a hypothetical situation in the oil market, using the scientific device known as *ceteris paribus* (Marshall, [1920] 2013). Let us assume the shift of the demand curve from D_t to D_{t+1} due to increased vehicle registrations in emerging economies. Given the shapes of the demand and supply curves (inelastic and linear, for simplicity), the market price increases as a result (moving from point A to B). Thus a temporarily high oil price economically justifies the deployment of more expensive extraction techniques (e.g. hydraulic fracturing and directional drilling) and an increase in supply is initiated, which takes time to materialise. If demand remains at that level, once the additional supply comes into the market (the supply curve shifts from S_t to S_{t+2}), the price changes abruptly (from B to C). Figure 1 is a simple example of economic analysis, and admittedly static. Nevertheless, this figure highlights graphically three issues: (i) a crucial concept in economics, that of stable equilibrium, between demand and supply; (ii) the effects of changes given the nature of oil demand, or more precisely, of one of its refined products: gasoline; and (iii) the role of time lags. In the oil market, three principal sources of sudden changes (i.e. shocks) can be identified: nature or resource-driven affecting availability of supply, human-driven on the supply side and human-driven on the demand side. In 2008, Hamilton suggested an increasing role to be played by scarcity rent in the oil market. See also Hall and Hall (1984).

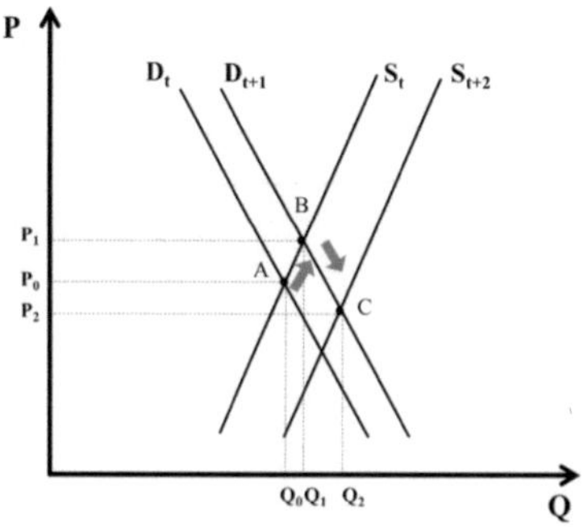

Figure 2.1: Oil supply and demand curves
Source: Own work [the electronic version of this thesis contains coloured figures]

The market structures mentioned above are generally considered by economists as examples of market failure, which create welfare losses. Two additional sources of market failure are: (i) information asymmetry (see Akerlof

(1970) for an example in the secondary car market by American economist George Akerlof*); and (ii) external effects termed 'externalities', such as GHG emissions.

Given that the nature of car demand, including its external effects (see Parry *et al.* (2007)), and the structure of the car market lead to a market failure, the optimal allocation of resources is not guaranteed (cf. sections on welfare in manuals such as Johansson (1991) and Varian (1992)). Whenever the actions of an *economic* agent directly affects the well-being of another *economic* agent, an externality occurs (Mas-Colell *et al.*, 1995). Although the market structure is important, a concern of greater importance in this work is GHG emissions, an externality that affects a number of agents as large as people inhabit planet Earth, with negative consequences for most of them. In situations where an externality affects a large number of people, the solution of direct negotiation and voluntary agreement is unlikely to succeed (Baumol and Oates, 1988). Market failures suggest that the government may play a role (Johansson, 1991). Hence government intervention is, in such cases, justified by standard economic theory. However, the possibility of 'government failure', as stressed by e.g. Wolf (1993) and proponents of public choice theory, should not be excluded. A proportion of economists propose market-based incentives, as opposed to regulations (also known as command and control (CAC), see Turner *et al.* (1994)), to mitigate externalities such as GHG emissions. For example, the design and implementation of an emissions trading system (ETS), such as the EU ETS in 2005, whereby a carbon market is created and a carbon price determined, is motivated by the idea of the externality being caused by a missing market. In general, economists tend to favour the internalisation of external costs, by reflecting these costs in the market price. Ideally, a Pigouvian tax (see Pigou [1920] 2013) equalling the social marginal cost should suffice. In reality, measuring the social marginal damage is unfeasible (Baumol and Oates, 1971).

After externalities and imperfect competition, the third fundamental idea briefly examined is innovation. Since its beginnings, the automotive industry has run a long knowledge race, with examples of just-in-time and *Jidōka* concepts originating in Japan (Rawlinson and Wells, 1996). The automotive sector is currently undergoing an intense process of product development. Mitchell *et al.* (2010: 3) speak of the new 'auto deoxyribonucleic acid (DNA)' with electrically driven, intelligent and interconnected cars. With regards to e-mobility (electro-mobility or electric mobility), the governments of EVI countries invested more than 3 billion dollars in EV battery and fuel cell research and development (R&D) over the period 2008-2012 (EVI, 2013). To Ederer and Ilgmann (2014), e-mobility represents the application of planned economy ideas in transport policy. In the EU, the automotive sector is the largest private investor in R&D (EC, 2016a), investing 44.7 billion euros per year, ca. 5% of the industry's total turnover (ACEA, 2016). Governments protect intellectual property rights by issuing patent laws (Chang, 2010: 60; 122). In 2012, car-makers featured among the main recipients of US patents (Auto Alliance, 2016). Two examples of government involvement and support: the German State of Lower Saxony holds a 20% share in Volkswagen (VW, 2016); the US Department of Energy, under the Loan Programs Office, issued a low-interest loan of 465 million dollars to Tesla Motors in 2010 (DOE, 2016a), which was repaid by the firm (Tesla, 2016). Governments tend to consider the automotive a strategic sector. Whereas regions like the EU pursue to maintain their leading position as vehicle manufacturer (EC, 2016b), countries like China aim at gaining from developing a new industry, see WB (2011). This new industry, if successful, may shift the centre of gravity not only from the 'construction-oil-car' to the 'information-electrochemical-car' conglomerate but also between manufacturing world regions, possibly altering trade balances.

The car market per se is likely to be an excessively limited framework of analysis for it only focuses on the supply, demand and market price for cars. A broader perspective may perhaps be offered by introducing the idea of a system. After all, road traffic is not a matter of counting the number of cars on the road but a *system* that requires management (Bertalanffy, [1968] 2003). The term 'ecosystem' is used to refer to 'innovation systems' (Mazzucato, 2015) and the more specific 'car ecosystem' shall be adopted often in this thesis to convey the idea that the car market is changing, through powertrain innovation, and being increasingly influenced by its surrounding environment. In the context of sustainability, the need not only for technical but also for socioeconomic and institutional innovation is stressed by Grunwald and Kopfmüller (2006). Admittedly, this term may be subject to criticism, for the prefix 'eco-' has ecological connotations.

2.1.2 On complex systems, uncertainty and scenarios

"*A system may be defined as a set of* elements *standing in* interrelation *among themselves and with* environment" (Bertalanffy, [1968] 2003: 252) [emphasis added]. Meadows and Wright (2008) make this definition more complete by stressing that any system serves a *function* or *purpose*. What is the function of the car ecosystem? A basic distinction is between an *intended* function and an *actual* function, and these may not necessarily be the same at all times. It can be argued that the intended function of the car ecosystem is mainly the long-term satisfaction of people's mobility needs, defined as accessibility to destinations spatially distant from the point of origin. If this is also the actual function, it can be said that the actual function of the system is determined by the demand side. In this way, car-makers are thought to anticipate people's mobility needs and act in accordance with business criteria such as increasing sales and profits. If, however, the actual function of the system over time shifts and becomes determined by the supply side, a mismatch between the intended function and the actual function appears. For example, a car-maker may increase its short-term profits by carrying out malpractices that may negatively affect personal mobility in the long-term. In the presence of such a divergence between intended and actual functions, the system may not work as envisaged. In such a case, intervention in the system (whether a system may be successfully controlled, managed or, at least, influenced is another issue) may be helpful to restore its original purpose and ensure its functioning.

A particular system may be seen from a different perspective as a sub-system, as being part of a wider system (Laszlo, 1996). For instance, the car ecosystem may be seen as a sub-system of the transport system. One step further, one may conceive the transport system as a sub-system of the social system. This hints at some concept of nested systems and system hierarchy. A system combines a physical structure (e.g. engines and vehicles) and a less visible system structure (e.g. driving rules) (Bossel, 2007a). The system of interest in this work can be characterised as a socio-technical system, in the sense that the system integrates the natural environment and people with their artefacts (Miser and Quade, 1985). As highlighted by Simon (1984), by 'artefacts of man' such as cars one usually understands 'technology', but technology is not simply things: it also refers to knowledge. Socio-technical systems are characterised by complexity properties (Miser and Quade, 1985). Whereas Forrester (1971) pointed out that social systems are more complex than technical systems, Boulding (1988) went a step further and asserted that they are the most complex systems. A complex social entity such as the economy (Heilbroner, 1999) can be understood through complexity analysis. For example, Randall Wray (2015a: 16) views economics as "*the science of extraordinarily complex social systems* [...] *subject to interdependence, hysteresis, cumulative causation, and "free will" influenced by expectations*" (see also section 3.1.3). Complex systems and nonlinear dynamics are associated with chaos, which emerged as a new science in the 1970s (Gleick, 2011). Complexity may be regarded as one dimension of the car ecosystem.

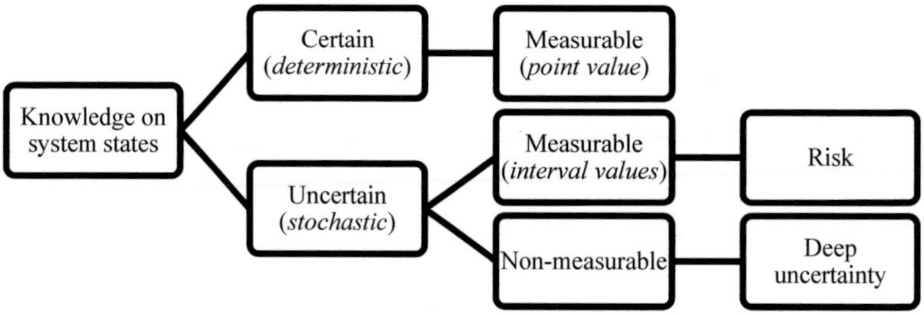

Figure 2.2: Concepts related to systems uncertainty
Source: Adapted from Gómez Vilchez *et al.* (2016)

In addition to complexity, the second dimension of interest related to systems is uncertainty. Walker *et al.* (2003) define uncertainty as any deviation from absolute determinism. By equating 'certainty' with 'determinism' and 'uncertainty' with 'nondeterminism' or 'stochastic', a working taxonomy is proposed and illustrated in Figure 2.2. Terms commonly found in the literature related to the concept of 'deep uncertainty' include 'Knightian', 'Keynesian', 'fundamental', 'irreducible', 'radical uncertainty' or, to some, even 'ambiguity' (cf. Lavoie (2014)). In the context of the economics of climate change, Weitzman (2009) speaks of 'fat-tailed structural uncertainty' or 'deep structural uncertainty'. In essence, deep uncertainty refers to a level of uncertainty that is so high that it cannot be even measured. For an elaborate description of deep uncertainty, see Lempert (2003) and Walker *et al.* (2013). In economics, thought about uncertainty has a long tradition. For example, Lawson (1988) highlights the accounts of American economist Frank H. Knight [1885-1972], J. M. Keynes and those of the subjectivist and rational expectations traditions. As commonly understood, what distinguishes risk from deep uncertainty is the suitability of applying probability theory. As indicated by Hoover in Mills and Patterson (2007), prominent economists such as Mill, Marshall and Robbins thought that probability distributions could not be successfully applied to economics because of the complexity of social interactions.

Figure 2.3 shows a representation of the possible combination of these two system dimensions. Each axis may be understood as consisting of different layers or levels. At one extreme lies 'facts', with a low level of complexity and a low level of uncertainty; at the other extreme, 'speculations', characterised by a high level of complexity and a high level of uncertainty. 'Scenarios', broadly defined as including 'projections' and 'explorations', can be seen as dealing with medium to high levels of complexity and uncertainty. As Dieckhoff *et al.* (2014) point out, the boundaries of the definition of 'scenarios' are not clear and the following terms are often found in the literature with a similar meaning: 'prognosis', 'visions', 'roadmaps' or 'projections'. In any case, they are all dealing with statements about the uncertain future. The inconvenience is that, because of this, they can be interpreted by people in different ways. Therefore, an asymmetry between the intentions of scenario producers (e.g. modellers) and the interpretation by scenario consumers (e.g. policy-makers or other users) may arise. The view that scenarios are neither forecasts nor predictions has been stated by e.g. Common (2005), Zurek and Henrichs (2007), IPCC (2007a) and Dieckhoff (2011). Some authors refer to scenarios as hypothetical stories about the future and distinguish between projections and forecasts, with the latter conveying a greater sense of likelihood (WBCSD, 2004). Deep uncertainty may be broadly interpreted as fluctuating between projections and speculations.

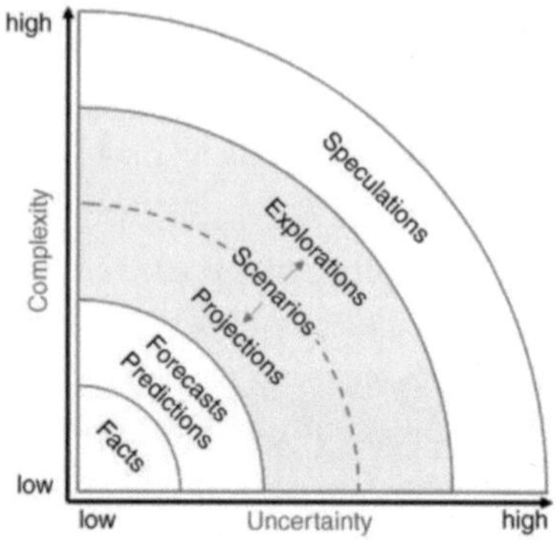

Figure 2.3: Projections, scenarios and explorations | Source: (Zurek and Henrichs, 2007: 1284)

In terms of forecasting energy prices, energy economist Carol Dahl (2004: 33; cf. Fig. 2-4) acknowledges that this activity has not been very successful. To Taleb (2010), who uses oil prices as an example, the problem is the unawareness of such forecasting errors. To Clements and Hendry (1998), forecast failure hints at the occurrence of unanticipated changes.

Cullenward *et al.* (2010) argue that it is unlikely that energy and economic systems, dynamic by nature, are predictable. This brings time, which may be added as a third dimension in our conceptualisation, onto the canvas. Although chaotic systems are considered to be deterministic, predicting their behaviour for long time horizons is unlikely to be possible (Sterman, 2000). "*The line that separates the possibly predictable future from the unpredictable distant future is yet to be drawn*" (Kahneman, 2013: 221). That line perhaps underscores the fact that predictability may be not absolute, but a matter of degree. Makridakis and Taleb (2009) speak of 'low levels of predictability', which is interpreted as deep uncertainty here. Perhaps a new attitude towards forecasting is needed to deal with the future (Makridakis *et al.*, 2009). Broadly speaking, there may be three possible attitudes today towards the prospect of EV market uptake: (i) radically sceptical; (ii) over-optimistic (conversely, over-pessimistic); or (iii) moderately sceptical. These attitudes may be reformulated into the view endorsed by American philosopher John Dewey ([1910] 1997: 108-109) [1859-1952]: "*taken merely as a doubt, an idea would paralyze inquiry. Taken merely as a certainty, it would arrest inquiry. Taken as a doubtful possibility, it affords a standpoint, a platform, a method of inquiry*". The merit in the third option leads to a moderately sceptical position that sees rapid EV market uptake as a doubtful possibility.

Swedish economist Gunnar Myrdal* (1990) [1898-1987] contended that a 'system' does not exist in the real world, but can nevertheless be used as an analytical device to analyse social phenomena. Systems theory (see Boulding (1956) and Bertalanffy ([1968] 2003)) or systems thinking (see Meadows and Wright (2008)) is useful in this work in at least two respects: (i) as an analytical application that facilitates public policy analysis (Walker, 1978); and (ii) as a modelling tool that allows scenario analysis (Swart *et al.*, 2004). These authors distinguish between the 'participatory' and the 'problem-oriented' approach in scenario analysis. The emphasis of this work is on the latter. A practical way of conducting scenario analysis is by first defining a simple analytical framework, considered in turn.

2.1.3 Analytical framework

The skeleton of the modelling exercise is formed by an accounting principle expressed as an identity. The role of identities is clarified by e.g. Hendry (1995) and Common (2005). The research question posed in chapter 1 indicates that the dependent variable is oil *use* (past *consumption* and future *demand*). This can be formulated at a more specific level, in terms of gasoline and diesel use, or at a more general level, in terms of energy use from car travel. Thus by extension, other relevant types of fuels available in the market may be included. Energy use can be thought of as an environmental impact for oil has to be extracted from Earth. Chertow (2000) credits Commoner, Ehrlich and Holdren with having identified key factors that cause environmental impacts. This was captured in an identity known as IPAT ('Impact',

'Population', 'Affluence' and 'Technology') (Commoner *et al.*, 1971). As can be seen, Eq. 2.1 is of a multiplicative nature. If the interest lies in the rates of growth, the logarithmic transformation may be applied as an approximation, which results in the additive formulation shown in Eq. 2.2.

$$\mathrm{I} \equiv \mathrm{P} * \mathrm{A} * \mathrm{T} \tag{2.1}$$

$$\ln\mathrm{I} \equiv \ln\mathrm{P} + \ln\mathrm{A} + \ln\mathrm{T} \tag{2.2}$$

Once energy demand has been derived, it can be relatively easy to calculate their corresponding direct emissions and relatively difficult to estimate their associated indirect emissions. In the context of the Assessment Reports by the IPCC, the IPAT identity has been reformulated as the Kaya identity (Kaya (1990) in IPCC (2000)). In transport research, another well-known variant of these equations is ASIF ('Activity', 'Modal Structure', 'Modal Energy Intensity' and 'Carbon Content of Fuels'), introduced by Schipper and Marie-Lilliu (1999). ASIF is the most applied framework to analyse transport CO_2 emissions (ADB, 2010).

$$gasoline_{h,t} \equiv S_{h,t} * \mathrm{VKT}_{h,t} * \lambda_{h,t} \qquad \forall h,t \tag{2.3}$$

[litre/year] [car] [(km/car)/year] [litre/km]

$$\mathrm{GHG}_{h,t}^{TTW,f} = \xi_{h,t}^{f} * \mathrm{EF}_{h,t}^{TTW,f} \qquad \forall h,t \tag{2.4}$$

[CO_2/year] [MJ/year] [CO_2/MJ]

Let us focus on $S_{h,t}$ in Eq. 2.3, which can be interpreted as a stock variable affected by a sales inflow $s_{h,t}$ and a scrappage outflow $r_{h,t}$, as in Eq. 2.5.

$$S_h(t) = \int_{t_0}^{t} [s_h(t) - r_h(t)]dt + S_h(t_0) \tag{2.5}$$

[car] [car/year] [car/year] [car]

As long as there are cars being powered by different sources of energy, the interest in this work must be in the car stock disaggregated by technology, not only in the aggregate car stock. Following a general framework suggested by Chatfield (2003), two possible ways of working with $S_{h,t}$ can be applied:

Top-down approach:

$$s_{h,i,t} \quad = \zeta_{h,i,t} \quad * \quad s_{h,t}^{agg} \qquad \forall h,i,t \qquad (2.6)$$

[car/year] [dmnl] [car/year]

where: ζ is dimensionless (dmnl), $\sum_{i=1}^{9} \zeta_i = 1$ and *i* represents technology.

Bottom-up approach:

$$s_{h,t}^{agg} \quad = \sum_{i=1}^{9} s_{h,i,t} \qquad \forall h,t \qquad (2.7)$$

[car/year] [car/year]

The top-down approach may be more flexibly updated with new projections of $S_{h,t}^{agg}$. For this reason, it is the preferred approach in this thesis. This choice is *a posteriori* reinforced by the results of the literature review and data screening. Each of the terms in Eq. 2.3-2.6 is consistent with objects or substances that can be observed and/or measured in the real world. Therefore, these variables may be quantified and empirical testing conducted. The applied data is shown in section 3.4.

2.2 Historical perspective

The importance of history to economics has been notably stressed, among others, by Austrian-born American economist Joseph A. Schumpeter (1954) [1883-1950] and J. K. Galbraith. For it is not by ignoring the past that the present may be understood (Galbraith, 1991).

French engineer N. L. Sadi Carnot [1796-1832], whose path-breaking work in 1824 initiated the science of thermodynamics (Gribbin, 2011), credited Savery, Newcomen, Smeaton, Watt, Woolf, Trevithick, and others, as the inventors of the steam engine (Carnot, [1824] 1986). A steam engine powered the drilling rig used by Edwin L. Drake when he famously found oil in the US state of Pennsylvania in 1859 (Aleklett, 2012). Two years later, Nikolaus A. Otto [1832-1891] received a patent for his internal combustion engine (ICE); in 1867, he built a first four-stroke engine; in 1893, Rudolf

Diesel [1858-1913] developed the first diesel engine (Wolf, 2009). As British economist Kenneth E. Boulding (1988) [1910-1993] noted, the availability of oil and advances in gasoline refining soon filled the niche that had emerged for cars. Around a century and a half later, it is not uncommonly acknowledged that cars are "*the lynchpin of the Second Industrial Revolution*" (Rifkin, 2011: 122), "*one of the great industrial success stories*" (Sperling and Gordon, 2009: 1), and "*the new product that had the greatest industrial and social impact in the twentieth century*" (Ponting, 2011: 329). Part of the success stems from technical but also organisational improvements. For instance, few years before American industrialist Henry Ford [1863-1947] doubled the wage most of his factory employees received (Raff & Summers, 1987), he had managed to run his business in a way that reduced automobile prices from 2,000 dollars in 1906 to 700 dollars in 1907 (Wolf, 2009). In 1911, Frederick Winslow Taylor [1856-1915] published his influential 'Principles of Scientific Management', whose analysis of efficiency in manufacturing greatly influenced technology and business (McClellan and Dorn, 2006). Society's perception of the car transmuted from novelty to familiarity in a decade (Yergin, 2012). In the US, the economic boom of the 1920s was emblematically symbolised by the success of General Motors (Ahamed, 2009), the same car-maker that introduced in 1996 the electric car known as EV1 (Sell, 2015).

Although in many ways, EVs are a new product (Urban *et al.*, 1996), the history of electricity-powered vehicles is long (see e.g. Mom (2013)). Building on the previous work by Italian physicist Luigi Galvani [1737-1798], Alessandro Volta [1745-1827] invented in 1800 the pile (i.e. battery), which could store electricity (McClellan and Dorn, 2006). Almost one century later, EVs found their first commercial application in the New York City's taxi fleet, nine years after Andreas Flocken [1845-1913] built the first four-wheeled electric car in Germany (EVI, 2013). The recognised advantages of the electric car over the steam car comprised cleanness, low noise and efficiency. In contrast, the dependence on batteries with very low energy density and slow recharging remained a serious disadvantage (Serra, 2013). Besides steam, gasoline and pure electric, a fourth type of propulsion combining thermal and electric energy sources co-existed: the hybrid car. The history of the hybrid powertrain is basically as old as the electric (Mom, 2013). For key historical dates for cars, see Sperling and Gordon (2009: 17). The competition among the steam, electric and gasoline car ended for all practical purposes by 1905 (Yergin, 2012). One of the disadvantages of the gasoline car was ultimately removed thanks to the invention in 1911 of an engine-starting device by Charles F. Kettering [1876-1958], for which he received the US1150523A patent (Kettering, 1915).

The benefits of the car to its users are offset by its costs to society. When first introduced, the car was perceived not only to be faster than the horse but also cleaner (Ponting, 2011). At that time, nobody expected they would become decades later the main source of urban pollution (Commoner, 2014). Odum (2013: 215) speaks of the "*wasteful automobile culture*". As already indicated, economic theory suggests that perfectly competitive markets are efficient and do not require government intervention, with the exception of providing a working legal framework for private (including intellectual) property and market exchange (see also Barr (2012)). The idea of self-regulated private markets was studied and dismissed by Hungarian-American economist Karl P. Polanyi (2001) [1886-1964], for whom regulation and markets jointly emerged. Mazzucato (2015) suggests that car diffusion was enabled by the government, besides the prominent role played by the market. Government involvement has historically served various functions in the car ecosystem, described next.

With regards to mitigation of the negative effects of cars, the US government granted French engineer Eugène J. Houdry [1892-1962] the US2742437A patent for his catalytic converter (Houdry, 1956). The US Clean Air Act to control air pollution was enacted in 1963 (EPA, 2016). Underpinning this legislation was the 'polluter-pays-principle', whose application the OECD encouraged to its members, with some exceptions, in 1972. By this principle, "*the cost of these* [pollution prevention and control] *measures should be reflected in the cost of goods and services which cause pollution in production and/or consumption*" (OECD, 1972: online; unpaged). Shortly after this idea was under discussion, the first oil crisis took place (see Issawi (1978)), with the average crude oil price climbing from 3.29 to 11.58 current dollars per barrel (bbl) between 1973 and 1974 (BP, 2016). According to Ganser (2013), the dollar crisis was a key contributor to the oil crisis. As a reaction, the US enacted fuel economy standards in 1975. Test cycles were implemented in Europe, Japan and the US in the late 1960s and early 1970s (see Fig. 2.58 in Giakoumis (2016)).

The acting of government as regulator means that compliance on part of the regulated agent is required by law. Two recent real-world cases of non-compliance in Europe may be found by looking at the communications by the Spanish *Comisión Nacional de los Mercados y la Competencia* (CNMC), whose sanctions in 2015 for anti-competitive practices, including cartel formation, were: 131 million euros imposed on car-makers and 32 million on oil corporations (CNMC, 2016).

Part of what is extraordinarily taken from industry as a result of punishment (via fines) for economic misbehaviour may be extraordinarily given back to industry by means of financial support (e.g. for ecological innovations). In periods of economic crisis, unemployment generally rises. The idea of government intervention during crises to achieve faster economic recovery belongs to the realm of what is generally known as 'Keynesianism'. The most recent developments are to be framed in the context of the global financial crisis and the present stagnation in the Eurozone. As a result of the 2007-2008 financial crisis, the US government implemented the Automotive Industry Financing Program (AIFP) with the aim of preventing a major disruption of the US automotive sector. Through the AIFP, the Treasury provided 81 billion dollars (Treasury, 2012). From the initial investment of 51.0 billion dollars that was conceded to one major US car-manufacturer, 39.7 billion dollars was recovered (Treasury, 2016). The phenomenon of 'privatizing profits and socializing losses' can be traced, in the context of banking, to US president Andrew Jackson (Doorman, 2013).

Today, economic recovery in many regions is not complete and changes in the automotive marketplace, in terms of new powertrain availability, are happening. In addition to the revival of EVs, plans to introduce commercial hydrogen fuel cell cars in the market have been announced (Rifkin, 2003) and have very recently become reality (Toyota, 2016). As a result of the ZEV mandate by the US state of California in 1990, not only awareness of the EV1 but also of the fuel cell electric vehicle raised (Yergin, 2011). Given persistent energy efficiency and emissions concerns, Yergin (2011) expects that today's transport system will change dramatically in the next decades. Clô (2008) considers the required penetration time of battery electric and fuel cell to be excessively long. In 2009, Sperling and Gordon expressed confidence that the market will in the future be dominated by battery electric and fuel cell vehicles, with some share probably accorded to biofuels. In the same year, Service (2009) summarised the position by the expert community: it will take at least 20 years to see the impact of alternative vehicles, with only battery electric and fuel cell technologies providing solutions in the long-run.

2.3 Techno-economic aspects of electric cars

This brief section is devoted to the main techno-economic aspects of EVs, with a focus on the European market. Admittedly, the details exposed here risk at becoming quickly outdated, as advancements in this sector are taking place at a high pace. EVs have features that are unique, compared to their ICE counterparts. In a stylised manner, Figure 2.4 shows the main differences among conventional vehicles (CVs), hybrid electric vehicles (HEVs), plug-in hybrid electric vehicles (PHEVs), range-extender electric vehicles (REEVs), battery electric vehicles (BEVs) and fuel cell (FC) vehicles.

REEVs are not explicitly modelled in this work. Two types of EVs are examined here: BEV and PHEVs. In addition, FC cars are considered. As can be seen, the most prominent component of these powertrains is the battery and the fuel cell system, respectively. At their current stage of development, these components have a large impact on the price tag of these technologies. Figure 2.5 gives an overview of purchase prices by type of powertrain and segment (excluding luxury (F), sport coupés (S) and multi-purpose (M)) in Germany in early 2017. Segments can be used as a proxy for car size, with A and B representing small cars and C medium-sized cars. EVs in these segments were priced below 40,000 EUR. As expected, larger cars tended to be more expensive. Large PHEVs cost a minimum of 40,000 EUR. In the executive (E) and sport utility vehicles (SUV) (J) segments, FC cars and BEVs with very large battery capacities (100 kWh) display prices exceeding 65,000 EUR, which are well above the prices of the rest of the cars shown in that figure.

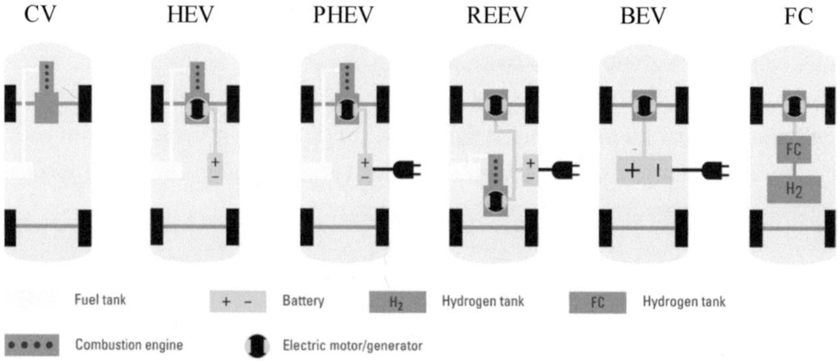

Figure 2.4: Types of car, by powertrain | Source: Adapted from e-Mobil BW (2011)

The purchase price is however only one, though the most important, of the multiple factors that need to be taken into account to perform a total cost of ownership (TCO) analysis (see Gómez Vilchez *et al.* (2013a)). To date, incentives have been offered in various markets to increase the attractiveness of EVs, thus altering the TCO. For a list of incentives in Norway, the most successful EV market in terms of sales market share so far, see Figenbaum *et al.* (2015).

Compared to the ICE, the electric motor (e-motor) is more efficient. Two types of e-motors are currently used in EVs: induction and permanent magnet motors. The latter require rare earth elements such as dysprosium and neodymium, which have been affected by price volatility in the past and have been ranked by Moss *et al.* (2013) as critical metals. Greater efficiency can exert some influence on the TCO but it remains unclear how much more efficient e-motors may become over the next years. The composition and durability of the battery influences the TCO, especially for BEVs. Battery technology is complex and still evolving. The present work dramatically oversimplifies. For HEVs, nickel–metal hydride (Ni-MH) batteries are widespread, though this is expected to change. Some PHEVs, such as the BYD Qin, have a lithium iron phosphate (LFP or LiFePO4) battery. Lithium-ion (Li-ion or LIB) batteries are common in BEVs and different types of LIBs co-exist in the market: mainly lithium iron phosphate (LFP), nickel-cobalt-aluminum oxide (NCA) and nickel-manganese-cobalt oxide (NMC). These batteries vary in their chemical mix and properties, with NMC batteries relying more on a key resource: cobalt. Deterioration of the battery can occur through utilisation (e.g. how often and with how much power it is recharged) and ageing. Some OEMs have offered a battery warranty of eight years. If EV owners seek to keep their cars for much longer, a replacement of the battery is likely to be needed.

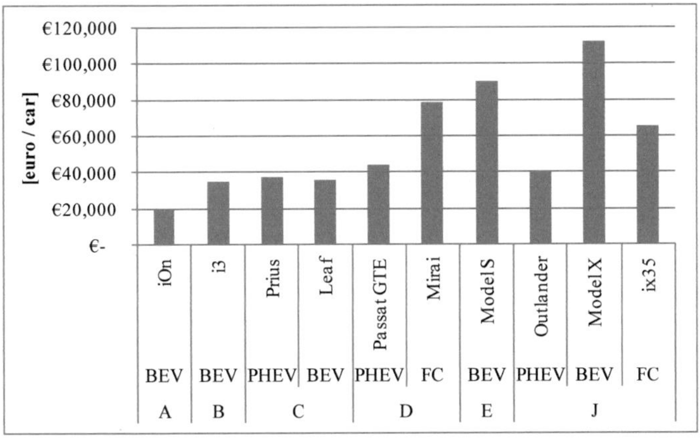

Figure 2.5: Prices of selected powertrains in Germany in 2017
Source: Own calculation using original equipment manufacturers' (OEMs) websites and catalogues. Prices may vary depending on the configuration (e.g. extras) of the car.

In the absence of an effective battery leasing or swapping programme, this comes at a future expense, to some extent offset by the prospects of selling the old battery for stationary purposes (a second-hand market that is yet to be fully established). In terms of the capacity of the battery, it affects not only the purchase price but also the electric range (e-range) of these cars. Based on

EAFO data from early 2017, an average battery capacity of 10 kWh and 33 kWh was calculated for PHEVs and BEVs, respectively. Fig. 2.6 casts light on the correlation between these two variables for a sample of 64 EV models (of which 34 were BEVs).

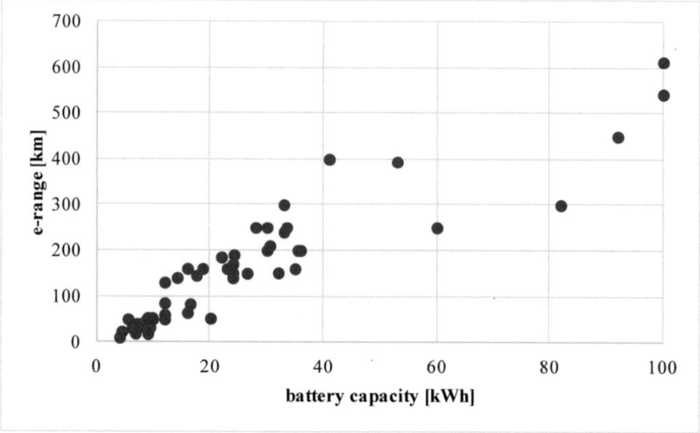

Figure 2.6: Battery capacity and electric range
Source: Own analysis using data from EAFO (2017)

The batteries of EVs may be recharged using several types of recharging equipment and infrastructure. In the European Union (EU), Directive 94/2014 distinguishes between 'normal power' and 'high power' recharging points. Whereas the former is defined as power greater than 3.7 kW and up to 22 kW, the latter is reserved for infrastructure providing power greater than 22 kW. In the Directive, the technical specifications of each, in terms of types of current and connectors supported, are outlined (see annex II in EC (2014)). For fast recharging, three standards are currently under competition: the combined charging system (CCS), the *CHArge de MOve* (CHAdeMO) and the Tesla Supercharger. While fast recharging at 50-70 kW is common, the next generation of ultra-fast recharging stations are expected to enable charges above 150 kW and even 350 kW. The possibility of successful commercialisation of inductive recharging cannot be completely ruled out at this stage.

For EV drivers, when it comes to paying for the electricity they consume to recharge their car's battery, several business models have been put to test. For instance, FASTNED (2017) offers two main pricing options for making use of their fast recharging network in the Netherlands: pay-as-you-go and a monthly rate.

Finally, it is worth stressing that the number of models available can influence the car market. Based on an understanding of the EAFO database, the following aspects can be identified: (i) the number of BEV models in the A and B segment is larger than in the rest of the segments, (ii) there are virtually no PHEVs and FCs commercialised in the segments of small cars, (iii) for FCs, only large cars have been launched into the market to date. It can be expected that the recent trend towards increasing the number of EV models and variants available in the market will continue over the next years.

2.4 Previous research

E-mobility is currently a very active topic of research and media attention. The literature available is growing fast, especially if grey literature and news are not disregarded, which limits coverage of the whole spectrum of studies. The variables highlighted in Eq. 2.3-2.6 have been used to organise this review into four strands: car ownership modelling, choice of type of car, car travel demand and car-related fuel intensity and emissions policies. This section summarises the outcome of the literature review and is deliberately short, for a review of key studies and additional surveys of methods and models have been presented by the author elsewhere (see in particular Jochem *et al.* (2018)).

The first strand of literature considered is car ownership modelling. Car ownership models have been reviewed and compared by e.g. de Jong *et al.* (2004) and Anowar *et al.* (2014). Figure 2.7 shows an overview of projections of global vehicle stock. A significant amount of the available studies conclude that high growth in car ownership is to be expected in non-OECD countries, particularly in Brazil, Russia, India, China, South Africa (BRICS countries). This seems to be an unsurprising consequence of greater affluence and the 'demonstration effect' (Button *et al.*, 1982).

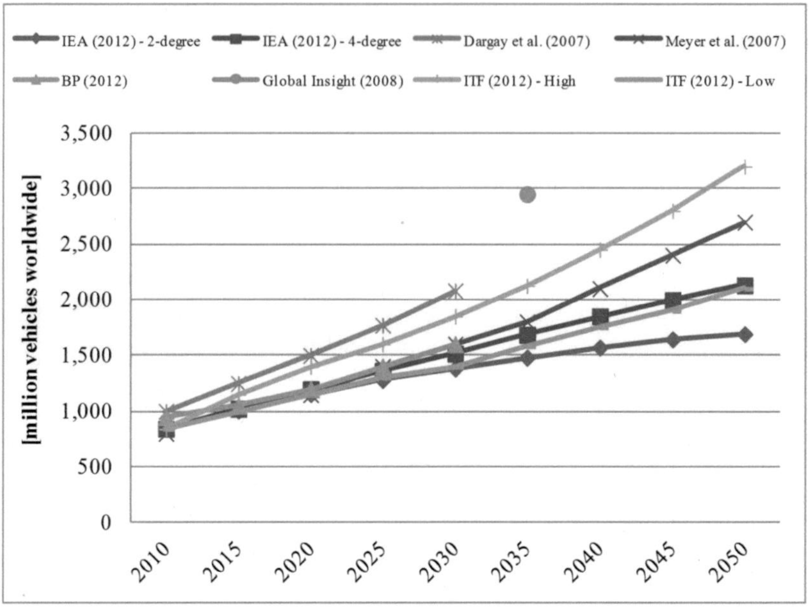

Figure 2.7: Overview of projections of the global vehicle stock
Source: Adapted from Gómez Vilchez *et al.* (2013b)

Most of these projections seem to be based on the assumption of unlimited or unconstrained growth over the projection period. A common distinction is made between unlimited growth, often modelled with an exponential function, and limited growth, popularly represented by an S-shaped function. The list of S-shaped curves commonly applied include the Verhulst or logistic (by Shell, cf. Figure 42 in Dörner (2003)), power growth (Tanner, 1977) and Gompertz (by the *Deutsche Institut für Wirtschaftsforschung* (DIW), cf. Figure 42 in Dörner (2003)). Growth functions differ in their estimates of origins, slopes and ceilings (Griliches, 1957). For this type of nonlinear function, the determination of the saturation level is crucial (as discussed by Button *et al.* (1982)).

The previous studies have an aggregate focus and do not provide information on the types of car in use. A second strand of literature more in line with the choice of car powertrain technology, either from the point of view of the market (diffusion) or from the perspective of the individual consumer (adoption), has developed (see also Table 4.1 in Gómez Vilchez *et al.* (2014)). Concerning technology diffusion, innovation theory has been used to partition the market into various segments (see Rogers (2003)) and trace the diffusion over time of new products (Bass, 1969) (Bass, 2004), (Mahajan *et al.*, 1991). In applied work on vehicle technology uptake, the structure of the Bass model has been used by e.g. Wansart (2012) (see also Al-Alawi and Bradley (2013)). With regards to adoption of new car technology, a vast literature that takes individuals as the unit of analysis and assumes that their choices are discrete has emerged. This literature stresses heterogeneity of car options and consumer preferences. Notwithstanding, these studies contain models based on two distinct frameworks: (i) statistical models resulting from discrete choice analysis; and (ii) simulation models based on agent interaction and the emergence of macro behaviour. Discrete choice studies have usually made use of stated preference data, which is of hypothetical nature (see Hensher (2010); other data issues are mentioned in section 3.4). Moreover, given its statistical basis, differences between sample and population are likely to appear (see Table 1 in Hackbarth and Madlener (2016)). As a result, it is not unusual to find a divergence between the simulated market shares and the actual market shares of new cars. As an example, Shepherd *et al.* (2012) apply a scaling factor of value 6/20 to the estimates by Batley *et al.* (2004). This example also illustrates the division of labour in modelling car technology uptake: whereas some researchers conduct choice analysis and estimate discrete choice models, others apply the results of the former in simulation models that take into account other aspects of relevance (see a list of studies in, respectively, Table 3.2 and Table 4.1 in Gómez Vilchez *et al.* (2015)). The link between discrete choice and diffusion models has recently been investigated by Jensen *et al.* (2016). In terms of simulation of adoption by agents, Mueller and de Haan (2009) developed an agent-based model at the household level using data from Switzerland. They assumed bounded rational decision-makers to simulate car choice. A review of this type of studies is given by Gnann (2015).

The third strand of literature of interest is car travel demand. Elasticity analysis represents a fruitful way of investigating this. The importance of transport elasticities has been highlighted by Wohlgemuth (1997). Button (2010) shows the effect, with an adjustment lag, between sharp increases in gasoline prices and improvements in car miles per gallon (MPG) in the US (see his Table 8.3 in p. 272). Evidence supports the idea that the elasticity of car fuel demand with respect to (w.r.t.) fuel prices is inelastic, even in the long-run Johansson and Schipper (1997) (for a comprehensive review of transport elasticities, see also Goodwin (1992) and Litman (2013)). With regards to the price elasticity of demand w.r.t. to the electricity price, sufficient evidence has not accumulated yet, but based on theoretical considerations, it is expected to be also inelastic. This is due to the fact that electricity costs represent a smaller proportion of operating costs for an electric car than fuel costs for a conventional car. In the future, given the possibility of EV and electricity demand growth, the structure of the electricity market may become, for transport analysis, a very important economic issue.

Lastly, the four strand of literature refers to policies that affect car-related fuel intensity and emissions. By car-related fuel intensity it is meant the fuel economy or fuel efficiency of new cars. Small (2012) and Tran *et al.* (2013) contain a list of policies of interest. This includes fuel economy programmes, whose impacts are hard to predict (Anderson *et al.,* 2011). Using a discrete choice model, Goldberg (1998) found evidence suggesting that California's Corporate average fuel efficiency standards (CAFE) incentivised the development of more efficient vehicles. The ZEV mandate was analysed, from the perspective of car-makers with a focus on ZEV credits, by Walther *et al.* (2010). By assuming a risk neutral agent, Sallee *et al.* (2016) cautiously conclude that fuel economy is valued by consumers. However, Larrick and Soll (2008) have highlighted the problem of consumer perception in the US when the metric MPG is used. An alternative to regulation by means of fuel economy standards is the market-based mechanism known as 'feebate' or bonus-malus schemes (Greene *et al.*, 2005). de Haan *et al.* (2009) updated their aforementioned Swiss model to simulate feebates, of which an earlier example, albeit using a different method, was offered by Ford (1995) for the state of California, concluding in Ford and Sun (1995) that a feebate system can be controlled by planners without requiring accurate EV sales forecasts. System dynamics was applied in that work, which was updated in BenDor and Ford (2006) with a model extension that enabled the exploration of scrappage programmes. The system dynamics method has proved useful to examine the market evolution of new vehicle technology (see Shepherd (2014) and Table 4.2 in Gómez Vilchez *et al.* (2014)). Finally, Tsang *et al.* (2012) identify barriers to EV adoption and policy interventions.

In addition, there is a set of studies that are highly relevant to the topic of this thesis that rely on computer models that contain features of the different strands. They range in their geographical boundary and level of aggregation of the car stock from global and highly aggregated (some of them are multi-country, if not strictly speaking global) to country-specific and relatively disaggregated. In the social sciences, world models are the most ambitious (Bunge, 2015). An acknowledged problem with world models in general, and Integrated Assessment Models (IAMs) in particular, is the representation of behaviour. McCollum *et al.* (n.d.) recently propose a framework to improve this. Four examples of IAMs are DNE21+, GCAM, MERGE, and WITCH (see Aldy *et al.* (2016) for details and also Schwanitz (2013)). For an overview of some global models of interest, see Table 3.1 in Gómez Vilchez *et al.* (2015). Country-specific, and in some cases regional (e.g. US state) models typically represent the car stock in much greater detail than multi-country models do (see a list with main features in Table 6 in Jochem *et al.* (2018)). See also the review by Linton *et al.* (2015).

Finally, one practical way of dealing with uncertain future developments is by means of scenario analysis. There is a tradition for developing supply-side energy scenarios that dates back to the 1970s, prepared by oil corporations (see e.g. Shell (2016)). In recent years, scenarios studies focusing on renewable energy have also been published by campaigning organisations (see e.g. Greenpeace (2016)). In contrast, demand-side scenarios are less common, as pointed out by Wietschel *et al.* in Dieckhoff (2011)). Since transport is an end-user of energy, a scenario study that focuses on the transport sector, such as the one presented in this thesis, may be understood as an example of a demand-side energy scenario study. Transport or mobility scenarios are also becoming increasingly available. Rijkee and van Essen (2010) provide a review of transport scenarios.

2.5 Concluding remarks I: Modelling tasks

Three key ideas on the car market prevail: (i) it is subject to market failure caused by a structure with a less than optimal degree of competition and by the presence of externalities; (ii) these provide an economic justification for the intervention of government which also, together with the private sector, promote industrial innovation; and (iii) the car market should not be seen in isolation, but interlinked with other markets as part of a wide system. Hence the suggested emphasis is on car ecosystems, not on car markets.

Government intervention in the car ecosystem generally arises on various grounds: as an initial facilitator, including guarantor of intellectual property, of an infant industry; as a regulator concerned with negative effects; as a supporter of a mature industry in periods of downturns and weak demand. In terms of mitigating negative impacts, the concern about pollution preceded the concern about oil scarcity, which preceded the concern about climate change. New car powertrain technology is today seen by many governments as a necessary means to reduce GHG emissions in transport and as a desirable compromise between society's needs and producers' requests. EVs are making a comeback in the market, in a better yet possibly still fragile shape than in the past. On technology hypes or fads, particularly of the car industry, see Bakker (2010).

The research question stated in section 1.1 has been framed in terms of a possibility ("*might*"), not of a very likely ("*will*") or certain outcome (cf. the scenario typology by Börjeson *et al.* (2006)). This is in line with the view that the car ecosystem under study is highly complex and uncertain, and can consequently hardly be forecasted. If the successful market penetration of a particular car powertrain depends on user acceptance, energy prices and technological development and these cannot be forecasted, it follows that the uptake of that powertrain cannot be forecasted either. This problem arises when assessing the chances of the electric car, as it depends on the price evolution of the battery price, a rather uncertain development. Against this backdrop, the scenarios approach may be more appropriate than the forecasting/prediction approach to answer the research question.

Based on the analytical framework applicable to the construction of scenarios, four broad strands of research were identified. When selectively combined, these strands provide the basis for most of the system models of interest in this work. The adjective that better describes these model-based studies is diversity. For even if some of them are based on the same method, they use different numerical assumptions and structures as well as give alternative weights to the ideas of the various strands of literature.

The main four modelling tasks to be accomplished (see chapter 4) based on theory (concepts) and evidence (historical observation) are:

(i) Projection of car ownership and the resulting aggregate car sales
(ii) Simulation of the market shares by car technology
(iii) Estimation of travel demand by car and energy use
(iv) Calculation of corresponding GHG emissions

Before proceeding to tackling these modelling tasks, chapter 3 describes the methodology, whereby suitable methods are identified and selected. In that chapter, the content-related trade-off between width and depth is noticeable, whereby the author deliberately errs on the former. This is despite admittedly risking oversimplification. The perceived advantage of this choice of exposition is the setting of a relatively plural methodological background that facilitates, it is hoped, the comprehension of chapter 4.

3 Methodological considerations for dynamic modelling

In section 1.2, the endeavour to develop a model that meets the research objective was indicated. Since modelling entails methodological decisions (Boland, 2014), it may be salutary to briefly reflect on the 'methodology', which arguably encompasses the 'method'. These are respectively described in section 3.1 and section 3.2. Computer models are considered in section 3.3. In section 3.4, data issues are given treatment. Finally, section 3.5 outlines the chosen method and the modelling stages.

3.1 Economic methodology

The distinction between economic methodology and economic method is highlighted by Boumans *et al.* (2010) who define economic methodology as the philosophy of science for the economics discipline. First, patterns of scientific reasoning in economics are outlined. In section 3.1.2, positive and normative economics are briefly examined. The diversity of economic research, at an institutionalised level, is sketched in section 3.1.3.

3.1.1 Scientific reasoning in economics

British philosopher Bertrand Russell (2004: 486) [1872-1970] concluded that the founding fathers of modern science possessed a combination of "*immense patience in observation, and great boldness in framing hypotheses*". He regarded Copernicus [1473-1543], Kepler [1571-1630], Galileo [1564-1642], and Newton [1642-1727] as forerunners in forging science. German economist Hermann Heinrich Gossen (1854: VI) [1810-1858] perceived the merits of his own work to be comparable to those of Copernicus'. From the inception of modern economics in 1776 (*communis opinio* relates it to the publication of Adam Smith's seminal work), economists have found inspiration in the work of scientific pioneers. Since the age of the scientific discoveries made by Galileo and Newton, economic scientific reasoning has polarised into the positivist-inductive and the abstract-deductive views (Palazuelos, 2000). These two types of reasoning were contrasted by British economist William S. Jevons (1874) [1835-1882] as follows: while the process of going from less general towards more general truths is induction, the contrary is deduction.

Russell (2004) acknowledged that British philosopher Francis Bacon [1561-1626] is the father of modern inductivism, which has had a great influence on the methodology of science (Lakatos, 1971), especially in those social sciences that are more analytically-oriented (Ortúzar and Willumsen, 2001). A precursor in empirical economics was the Briton William Petty [1623-1687] (Palazuelos, 2000) (cf. chapter 1 of '*Verbum Sapienti*' by Petty ([1664] 1963). More than a century later, British political economist Thomas R. Malthus ([1798] 2008) [1766-1834] emphasised the importance of experiment or experience in confirming theories. From the work by these two economists, two methodological issues stick out: the importance of empirical information (i.e. statistical data) and the role of experiments.

In contrast, French philosopher René Descartes [1596-1650] opposed the inductive approach proposed by Bacon, attempting instead to deduce the consequence from the cause (McClellan and Dorn, 2006). To Palazuelos (2000), the apriorist approach was initiated in economics by Adam Smith and virtuously developed by David Ricardo. Economic data is imperfect and, in contrast to the natural sciences, controllability of experiments in economics is seldom possible. Furthermore, Austrian-British philosopher of science Karl Popper (2007: 4) [1902-1994] highlighted 'the problem of induction', that is, "*the question whether inductive inferences are justified, or under what conditions*". For these reasons, a proportion of economists leans towards (abstract) deduction and downplays the importance of induction. In economics, two famous 'method disputes' may be mentioned: the first one is considered next, the second is postponed to section 3.1.2.

In 1891, British economist John Neville Keynes [1852-1949] published his work on economic methodology in an attempt to reconcile the opposing views that were at the core of the '*Methodenstreit*' that took place during the 1880s between Carl Menger, from the Austrian School, and German economist Gustav von Schmoller [1838-1917], who represented the German Historical School (Blaug, 2008). J. N. Keynes (1891) understood that economics, regardless of the use of deduction, starts and ends with observation. According to Dewey ([1910] 1997), an act of thought is complete when it involves both induction and deduction. By the end of the nineteenth century, the inductive and the deductive approaches were both considered to be complementary (Spanos, 2006). With origins in the Vienna Circle in the 1920s (Hahn *et al.*, 1929), the logical positivist movement endorsed the view that scientific knowledge has two sources of inference: inductive from data and deductive from axioms (Hoover in Mills and Patterson (2007)). Logical positivists regarded mathematics, logic and the natural sciences in very high esteem (Okasha, 2002). By the 1950s, the positivist vision was widely accepted, both in the natural and in the social sciences (Caldwell, 1980).

As indicated by Blaug (2008), the view that the natural and the social sciences share the same methodology is known as methodological monism. He contrasts methodological monism with methodological dualism, which relates to the view that the social sciences may employ a different methodology. To Reardon (2009), pluralism represents the antithesis of monism. The difference between natural and social sciences was highlighted by Austria-Hungary-born economist Friedrich A. von Hayek* [1899-1992] and, some fifty years earlier, by Marshall. Whereas the latter had emphasised the nature of human behaviour (Marshall, [1920] 2013); the former stressed the complexity arising from the actions of a large number of individuals (von Hayek, 1975).

So far, the discussion has been pitched at a generic level. In transport modelling, positivism, in its various variants, is the most common philosophy (Timms, 2008). He links positivism with instrumentalism, in particular with the prediction accuracy relevant to naïve instrumentalism. This leads to American economist Milton Friedman* [1912-2006], who put forward the 'as if' behavioural hypothesis (Friedman and Savage, 1948), a defense of the adoption of unrealistic assumptions in economic analysis (see Friedman (1953)). This position was termed by American economist Paul Samuelson*

[1915-2009] the 'F-Twist' (called by Blaug (2008) the 'irrelevance-of-assumptions' thesis), a methodological stance Samuelson regarded as harmful to empirical research (see Archibald *et al.* (1963)).

It can be argued that, in opposition to the underlying monism of logical positivists, two alternatives are represented by pragmatism and realism, in its various forms. Pragmatism is usually linked to the ideas of American philosophers Charles S. Peirce [1839- 1914], William James [1842-1910] and John Dewey (Robson, 2011). Concerning realism, a particular strand of this methodological position of interest to economics is 'causal' realism, with its pursuit towards discovering causal factors (Timms, 2008) and its emphasis on cause-effect relationships (Boumans *et al.*, 2010). The variant known as 'transcendental' or 'critical' realism has found its niche in economics through the work by Lawson (2006) (see also Holt *et al.* (2009)).

The scientific status of economics has been examined by many authors. In the view of Schumpeter (1954), 'scientific economics' is the result of conducting economic analysis that is based on four techniques: statistics, theory, '*Wirtschaftssoziologie*' (economic sociology) and, most importantly, history. Boulding (1988) understood economics as a multi-faceted (social) science. To Marshall ([1920] 2013), economics is a pure and applied science. The role of economics as a policy science has been stressed by e.g. Blaug (2008) and Boumans *et al.* (2010). The latter links this with the original name of economics (i.e. political economy). Foley (2009: xv) rejects the idea that economics is a deductive or inductive science. He speaks of 'the Adam's fallacy' and regards economics as "*speculative philosophical discourse*". For J. M. Keynes, economics was a moral science based on value judgements and introspection (Keynes and Skidelsky, 2015). Max-Neef and Smith (2014) underscore the fact that Adam Smith, J. M. Keynes and Myrdal considered economics to be a moral science. If economics may in fact be better described as a moral science, normative aspects cannot be completely ignored. Argentine philosopher of science Mario Bunge endorses the common distinction between positive and normative economics, examined in the next section, and concludes that the status of scientific, semi-scientific or pseudo-scientific may in principle apply to normative economics, but also to positive economics (Bunge, 2015). He concludes that the economic discipline is today a semi- or proto-science. Keen (2011) holds the slightly less optimistic view that economics is still at the stage of being a pre-science.

3.1.2 Positive and normative economics

J. N. Keynes (1891) demarcated a clear line between political economy and its application. Today, the distinction is referred to as positive economics and normative or welfare economics, with the latter encompassing value judgements related to the desirability of changes in the economy (Johansson, 2008).

Scottish philosopher David Hume [1711-1776] had famously distinguished between 'is' and 'should', a distinction German sociologist Max Weber [1864-1920] strongly emphasised. He was involved in the '*zweiten Methodenstreit*' (second method dispute) or '*Werturteilsstreit*' (value judgement dispute) (see Pierenkemper (2012)) and recommended that social scientists strive for objectivity and avoid making judgements of value. In his view, this was a logical consequence of separating empirical knowledge and value judgements (Weber, 2010). It is important to remark that in the social sciences the 'should' may become the 'is' over time. Bunge (2015) describes two types of predictions in the social sciences: passive and active. The latter type is made to guide human action, and it can be linked to the idea of a self-fulfilling prophecy. He also discusses economic 'laws', which he considers have permanent properties, and economic trends, which have temporary properties and may be reversed by human action. In our context, it is important to understand the annual rate of GHG emissions as a trend, not as an economic law. In contrast, the Carnot cycle relates to a scientific law, in this case a thermodynamic law. The law of supply and demand is seen as the quintessential example of an economic law (cf. Figure 2.1).

John Locke [1632-1704], George Berkeley [1685-1753] and David Hume are considered representatives of British empiricism, the philosophy that ruled in the eighteenth century. The last of the three arrives at the conclusion that a rational belief does not exist. German philosopher Immanuel Kant [1724-1804] sought to refute this idea (Russell, 2004). Sedlacek and Havel

(2013) highlight Kant's antiutilitarianism. Bunge (1979) identifies three rival conceptions of the nature of society: individualism (atomism or reductionism), holism (collectivism) and systemism. Barr (2012) distinguish between libertarian, collectivist and liberal theories, with the latter grounded in the utilitarian philosophy. Today, utilitarianism, based on the ideas by British Jeremy Bentham [1748-1832], James Mill [1773-1836] and his son John Stuart Mill [1806-1873], is regarded as a major theory of ethics (Faber and Manstetten, 2007). The need for economists to take ethics into account in their work was highlighted by e.g. Marshall ([1890] 2013) and Boulding (1988). Indian economist Amartya Sen* (1991) laments the increasing distance that separates economics and ethics.

British economist Joan Robinson [1903-1983] described economics as a mixture of science and ideology (Robinson, 1973). She and Myrdal are perhaps the economists who have more strongly emphasised the need to make values explicit in economics (Pasinetti, 2010). That ideology affects the social sciences, in particular economics, is an acknowledged fact (Bunge, 2014). In particular, the connection between economics and politics has been highlighted by e.g. economists Albert O. Hirschman (2013) [1915-2012] and Joseph E. Stiglitz* (2016). Finally, Bunge (2015) encourages economists to declare their value judgements in normative economics because, in his view, the act of hiding them is dishonest.

3.1.3 Research programmes in economics

Once the main approaches to scientific reasoning and the dichotomy positive-normative economics have been introduced, a collection of research programmes and school of thought active in the discipline are presented. These emerge at a more institutional level than previously discussed. It can be argued that the introduction of schools of thought in economics is desirable due to four main reasons: (i) the larger the number of schools indicated, the fuller the picture of options in economic research; (ii) underpinning each school is a particular philosophy; (iii) the policy recommendations from each school in most cases differ; and most importantly, (iv) embracement of the core ideas of a certain school is likely to determine the type of methods that may be applied to answer a research question in economics. For example, logical positivism may be regarded as the philosophy that mainly underpins econometrics (Hoover in Mills and Patterson (2007)). Econometrics is assessed differently by several schools of thought. For instance, it is favoured by neoclassical economists, partially accepted by Post-Keynesian economists and, since it is the result of blending empiricism and mathematics, methodologically rejected by Austrian economists. For differences in modelling transport futures by various schools of thought, see Creutzig (2016).

3.1.3.1 Research programmes: orthodox and heterodox economics

Hungarian philosopher of science Imre Lakatos [1922-1974] understood science as competing programmes with their own 'hard core' (i.e. essential propositions) (Hoover in Mills and Patterson (2007)). Lakatos *et al.* (1980) distinguished between successful 'progressive' and unsuccessful 'degenerating' problemshifts or research programmes. Lavoie (2014) uses the terms research programmes, research traditions and paradigms interchangeably. He identifies two research programmes in economics, which he calls the 'orthodox' and the 'heterodox' programmes. Today, the orthodox programme is exemplified by neoclassical economics, which is also the main school of thought in economics. In contrast, the heterodox programme comprises various schools of thought, understood as alternatives to neoclassical economics.

3.1.3.2 Schools of thought in economics

A set of schools of thought in economics are introduced below (see also Figure 3.1). The goal of this section is not to judge and determine which school is the best, but to identify salient features of each of them that are in principle relevant to the research question posed in this study. This list is not exhaustive (for instance, Marxist economics is not included, admittedly due to insufficient exposure by the author). For a more comprehensive view, see also e.g. Figure 1 in Radzicki (2003), chapter 18 in Keen (2011) and Table 1.2 in Lavoie (2014).

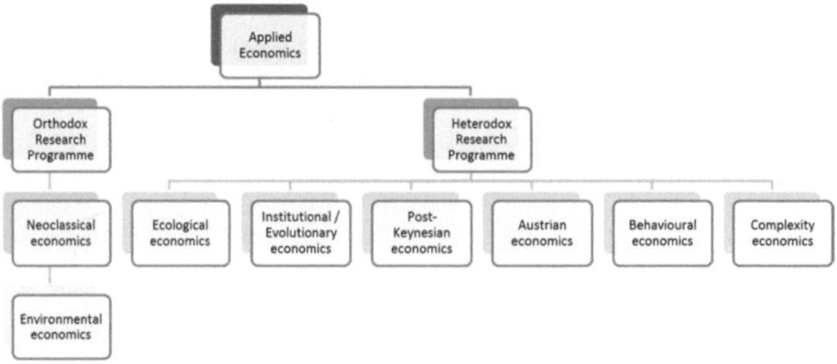

Figure 3.1: Overview of schools of thought in economics
Source: Own work based on the references cited in the main text

Neoclassical economics: Jevons, Menger and French economist Léon Walras [1834-1910] are recognised as leaders of the marginal revolution and fathers of neoclassical economics (Pierenkemper, 2012), a term seemingly coined by Veblen (Czech, 2013). Before focusing on the environmental branch of interest, two general methodological features of neoclassical economics are highlighted: (i) the reliance on 'methodological individualism', which strongly emphasises individual behaviour as the foundation for representing social phenomena (Blaug, 2008) (cf. Austrian economics below); and (ii) the assumption of rational choice behaviour (cf. behavioural economics below). The former led to the idea of 'microfoundations', viewed by e.g. Nelson (1984) as an attempt to shrink macroeconomics into microeconomics. In order to arrive at aggregate behaviour from individual behaviour in economic models, the strategy of the 'representative agent' is the preferred choice of neoclassical economists (Hoover, 2010). The main disadvantage of such assumption, especially when it comes to empirical testing, has been pointed out by e.g. Kirman (1992). The linkage between macro behaviour and micro behaviour, adopting the assumption of the representative agent, has been under debate for years (see e.g. Colander (2006), King (2012), Vroey (2016) and also section 3.2.5). The branch of neoclassical economics dealing with the environment is known as *neoclassical environmental economics* (henceforth, for short, *environmental economics*) and may be further divided into a sub-branch that focuses on natural inputs or resources (known as *natural resource economics*) and a sub-branch that focuses on problems associated with waste or pollution resulting from economic activity. From early contributions by Jevons (1866), Gray (1914) and Hotelling (1931), environmental economics has become a major branch of economics (Pearce, 2002). From the perspective of environmental economics, efficiency and optimality in the use of environmental services are to be framed not only in a static (intra-temporal) but also in a dynamic (inter-temporal) dimension (Perman, 2011). As an example of intertemporal calculation of the costs and benefits of climate action, Nordhaus (2013) usually applies in his own studies a discount rate that reflects an annual real rate of return on capital of ca. 4% or greater. Lower discount rates were used in the prominent 'Stern Review' (Stern, 2007). The assumption of a higher or lower discount rate in economic research leads to different conclusions and policy implications concerning the desirability of public investment to mitigate emissions. This difference becomes significant in the calculation of sustainable development, where a long time horizon is accounted. The general policy implication of this school is that optimal government intervention, partially justified as a result of market failure arising from the presence of externalities, can be precisely defined. Often, this leads to the conclusion that little government involvement is desirable.

Ecological economics: British Frederick Soddy [1877-1956], who was awarded the Nobel Prize in Chemistry in 1921, Romanian economist Nicholas Georgescu-Roegen [1906-1994] and K. E. Boulding are generally regarded as the precursors of ecological economics. Soddy's work constitutes an early effort to connect energy and ecology with economics (Daly, 1991). Georgescu-Roegen's 'bioeconomics' (term superseded by 'ecological economics' (see Mayumi and Martinez-Allier (2001))) represents a strong critique to neoclassical economics (Bonaiuti in Georgescu-Roegen (2003)) (Carpintero and Redondo, 2006). Boulding wrote an essay (Boulding in (Jarrett, 2013)), where he contrasted the open with the closed economy, which influentially paved the way to ecological economics (Pearce, 2002). This pluralistic and interdisciplinary school (Jusmet and Martinez-Alier, 2013) pays attention to the interactions between the environment and the economy (Shmelev, 2011). Following Martinez-Alier in Rosser *et al.* (2010), a striking difference between mainstream and ecological economists lies in their view of whether the economy is an open or a closed system. Whereas from the perspective of environmental economists, the focus is generally on value and its associated cost-benefit analysis; from the point of view of ecological economists, the focus is on managing resources and ecosystems (Naredo, 2015). Costanza (1989: 4) distinguishes between 'technological optimism' and 'technological pessimism', linking the latter with current economic thinking working under the assumption of unlimited economic growth. Ecological economists attach utmost importance to the laws of thermodynamics (Georgescu-Roegen, 1971). As Carnot ([1824] 1986) had understood, the motive power of combustibles could not be utilised in full. Ecological economists also draw a line between economic scarcity (recall section 2.1) and physical scarcity, with the latter determined by entropy (Daly, 1991). The view that the man should be the master of nature, promoted from opposite directions by Bacon and Descartes (McClellan and Dorn, 2006), is not entirely shared by ecological economists (see Becker *et al.* (2005)). According to Faber (2008), two normative aspects (nature and justice) and one methodological (time) are the basic characteristics of ecological economics. The general policy implication of this school is that public planning and management of natural resources is desirable to attain sustainability (i.e. to ensure the long-term preservation of Earth and its inhabitants).

Institutional economics (IE: Original IE, not to be confused with Neoinstitutional) / *Evolutionary economics*: Schumpeter (2014) acknowledged the contribution of the German Historical School in spreading the 'evolutionary' and the 'organic' points of view, stressing that economics cannot be divided into a collection of isolated economic agents. Nevertheless, Veblen contended that economics was in 1898 still at a pre-evolutionary stage (Veblen, 1898). Evolutionary biology was for him the adequate methodological model in economics (Foley, 2009). Early leaders of IE were Henry C. Adams [1851-1921], Charles H. Cooley [1864-1929], who also contributed to transport theory (see Cooley (1894)), Veblen and Wesley C. Mitchell [1874-1948] (Hamilton, 1919). Jr (1967) credited John R. Commons [1862-1945] with having explained how the economy *evolves*. As noted by Hamilton (1970), institutionalism is evolutionary and Darwinian, not mechanistic and Newtonian. Culture, whose dynamic aspect is technology, is the focus of the institutionalist (Hamilton,

1970) and the point of departure of analysis using 'circular and cumulative causation' (O'Hara, 2008) (see also section 3.5). Radzicki (1990) considers that IE bases its philosophy on the pragmatic instrumentalism of Dewey and its methodology in the pattern-modelling approach (see section 3.5). The general policy implication of this school is that it is desirable to understand institutions and control them in a manner that leads to a well-functioning economy.

Post-Keynesian economics: Taking the work of J. M. Keynes as seminal, several strands of Post-Keynesian economics have flourished (see King (2002)). In general, Post-Keynesians remain suspicious of key assumptions made in neoclassical models (see a list in JPKE (1978: 3-4)) and particularly stress the frequent presence of fallacies of composition in orthodox economic analysis (see Table 1.4 in Lavoie (2014)). For a list of nine distinctive features of Post-Keynesian economics, see Pasinetti (2010: 195-209). Post-Keynesian economics attaches due importance to the principle of effective demand (i.e. demand-led models) and monetary macroeconomics (Godley and Lavoie, 2016). In the view of Post-Keynesians, the *eigendynamics* of the economic system lead to instability but policies may stabilise it (Minsky, 2008). In the context of energy and environmental issues, Post-Keynesians dismiss economic analysis based on perfect foresight premises that result in long-run Pareto-optimal allocations as misguided policy formulations (JPKE, 1978). The general policy implication of this school is that it is desirable that the government plays a major role in the economy, proactively to reduce financial instability as well as reactively in periods of economic downturns.

Austrian economics: Menger is regarded as the father of the Austrian School of economics, which has an earlier antecedent in the Spanish School of Salamanca. Two major Austrian thinkers were Ludwig von Mises [1881-1973] and von Hayek. The key differences between neoclassical and Austrian economics are listed by Soto (2012) in his Table 1.1. Palazuelos (2000) contrasts two main 'marginalists' groups: those economists (British, Swiss, Swedish and Americans) preferring the use of mathematics versus (vs.) those Austrian economists opposing mathematical economics and favouring a logico-deductive approach. As first defined by Schumpeter

(1908: 3), methodological individualism "*bases certain economic processes on the actions of individuals*". The methodology of the Austrian School is 'praxeology' (see Dolan and Studies (1976)). According to Blaug (2008), modern Austrian economists deny the possibility of prediction in economics and the validity of empirical testing, a view he dismisses. Two additional methodological issues worth remarking are: (i) the time dimension (Garrison, 1984); and (ii) disequilibrium processes (see chapter 1 in Rizzo (1979)). Austrian economists attach due importance to these. For a description of Austrian environmental economics in the context of climate change, see Dawson (2012), who argues that neoclassical environmental economics is not compatible with individual freedom, as understood by classical liberals. To him, climate change is not a market failure, but an illustration of interpersonal conflict arising from competition for resources. In his view, Austrian economics accords no role to public policy in dealing with climate change. The general policy implication of this school is that laissez-faire is desirable, so that government does not diminish individual freedom.

Behavioural economics (including *experimental economics*): Avineri (2012) argues that neoclassical economics underpins mainstream transport policy-making. Although the assumption of maximising behaviour is widespread in economic modelling (Boland, 2014), it has been subjected to criticism both internally and externally. The internal critique refers to the one put forward by a proportion of economists who defend the conception of the economic agent as an 'animal spirit'. As pointed out by American economist Robert J. Shiller* (2015: xvi), this term, popularised by J. M. Keynes, relates to "*the fluctuations in the basic driving force in human actions*". External criticism has come mainly from psychologists. The differing views held by neoclassical economics and psychology are highlighted by McFadden (1999) (see his Table 1 for a list of cognitive anomalies), who contrasts the Chicago-man model (Lucas, 1986) (Becker, 1993) (also known as *homo oeconomicus* or economic man) with the Kahneman-Tversky (K-T) man. German philosopher Nida-Rümelin (2011) speaks of the *homo oeconomicus* ideology. Furthermore, the original work by Muth (1961) has served as a basis for rational expectations modelling. Blanchard (1983) found evidence supporting intertemporal optimisation with rational expectations in the US car industry, at least in the context of inventory management. However, the hypothesis of rational expectations is currently under debate, as it is being increasingly perceived as unsound (Kirman, 2014) and a weakness of neoclassical economics (Foley, 2009). The application of expected utility theory as a description of economic behaviour under risk was criticised by Israel-born psychologists Amos Tversky [1937-1996] and Daniel Kahneman*, who suggested an alternative: prospect theory (Kahneman and Tversky, 1979), which is capable of integrating risk and ambiguity (Wakker, 2010). Cognitive economics, represented by Kahneman and Tversky's work, and experimental economics, by the work of American economist Vernon L. Smith*, originally developed independently (Motterlini and Piattelli Palmarini in Kahneman *et al.* (2012)). Fehr in Rosser *et al.* (2010) speaks of the satisfactory union between behavioural and experimental economics. Thaler (2015) defines the relatively new field of behavioural economics as economics with a dose of other social sciences, prominently psychology. As forerunners of Kahneman and Tversky, he cites Swiss mathematician Daniel Bernoulli [1700-1782] and American economists Herbert Simon* [1916-2001] and Thomas Schelling* [1921-2016]. With regards to method, experiments play a crucial role in behavioural economics. The general policy implication of this school is that social 'nudges' (cf. Sunstein and Thaler (2012)) may be a desirable option to improve decision-making. Some behavioural economists advocate the idea of 'libertarian paternalism' (Thaler and Sunstein, 2003).

Complexity economics: Holt *et al.* (2011) contend that a new era of complexity economics has replaced the neoclassical era. Notorious complexity ideas include: 'tipping points', '(path) dependence', 'discontinuity', 'fractals' and 'emergence'. Complexity economics strives for applying these ideas to economic analysis, especially in the context of quantitative finance. "*Complexity portrays the economy not as deterministic, predictable, and mechanistic, but as process dependent, organic, and always evolving*" (Arthur, 1999: 107). Complexity science (cf. Johnson (2009)), and complexity economics in particular, are very active areas of research (see e.g. Goodwin (1990), Metcalfe and Foster (2007), Arthur (2014) and Faggini and Parziale (2014)). On 'tipping points' and 'critical' points, thresholds or transitions, see Scheffer *et al.* (2009). Polish-born French and American mathematician

Benoît Mandelbrot [1924-2010] developed fractal theory and suggested that dependence and discontinuity effects are part of markets (Mandelbrot and Hudson, 2010). Axtell in Colander (2006) pointed out that 'emergence' is closely related to 'self-organisation' and to the economic ideas of the 'invisible hand' (Smith, [1776] 2008) and 'spontaneous order' (Hayek, 1966). The general policy implication of this school is that a complex adaptive system can be influenced, but not controlled. As opposed to the 'standard policy frame', Colander and Kupers (2014: 31) speak of "*"activist laissez-faire" policy*" as part of the 'complexity frame'.

Boumans *et al.* (2010) attribute the aforementioned first method dispute to competition between different schools of thought. As a matter of fact, the research schools highlighted above may compete or cooperate. Neoclassical economics is contested for its insistence on *inter alia*: equilibrium (by Austrian and Post-Keynesian), the representative agent (by institutional and complexity), perfect rationality (by behavioural), conceptualising the economy as a circular system (by ecological). Even if environmental and ecological economists give due attention to the role of the environment, they conceptually differ as the latter adopt the view that the economy is an open, not a closed and circular system. German-American economist Karl William Kapp [1910-1976], who was an example of work on institutional and ecological economics, lamented that the economic idea of externalities, first proposed by Marshall, was being used excessively to analyse environmental problems (Kapp, 1978). Martinez-Alier in Rosser *et al.* (2010) credits him with the insight of understanding an externality as a cost-shifting success, and not as a market failure (an idea in consonance with the prevailing conventional wisdom). Given the differences between the two research programmes, cooperation seems feasible for only a subset of the schools that are part of the heterodox programme (see also the discussion by Lavoie (2014)). As an example, although Swedish economist J. G. Knut Wicksell [1851-1926] was an intellectual source of inspiration for Austrian economists and J. M. Keynes (Wolf, 2014), the general policy recommendations derived from Austrian and Post-Keynesian economic analyses can hardly be more distant. Hence it would be naïve to expect fruitful cooperation for most schools from the heterodox programme. However, for some of them, a certain form of synthesis may be accomplished over time by cooperating. The intellectual link between Post-Keynesian and ecological economics has recently been explored by Holt *et al.* (2009) and the idea of 'green Keynesianism' is gaining attention. Although Post-Keynesian and ecological economists methodologically agree on the role of irreversibility and dynamics, they have virtually opposing views on the need for economic growth and thus challenges remain. The link between Post-Keynesian and institutional economics has been suggested by e.g. Radzicki in Harvey and Garnett (2008: chapter 9) (see also section 3.5 for an example of actual collaboration). It has crystalized in Post-Keynesian Institutionalism (PKI), which synthesises the work of Commons and J. M. Keynes (Whalen, 2008) and highlights the role of evolution in the macroeconomy (Zalewski and Whalen, 2010).

3.2 Economic methods

At a general level, an economic method reflects *how* economic analysis is undertaken. Since there are many possible ways of doing this, there are many methods that can be potentially used in economic analysis. In this section, only a few of them, not ranked in accordance with their perceived importance but listed in chronological order, are briefly surveyed. For a more detailed treatment of methods, with a focus on EV market penetration, see the work by the author and colleagues (Jochem *et al.*, 2018)). For exposition, the choice of methods was: (i) motivated by *a priori* considerations of the potential usefulness of the method to answer the research question (because of this, Austrian economics represented no longer an option); (ii) guided by Table 3.1 (see section 3.2.1); and (iii) influenced by the result of the literature review (section 2.3). Although the initial attitude of the author towards the choice of method was generally open and conditional to an assessment of strengths and weaknesses, there have been four main exceptions: neuroeconomics, econophysics, game theory and IAM. Background knowledge has prevented the author from getting on time anything close to the method practiced by neuroeconomists and econophycisists. Neuroeconomics can be understood as the investigation of the biological factors of human behaviour, both individual and social (Fehr in Rosser *et al.* (2010)) (cf. Smith (2007), especially chapter 14, and Glimcher and Fehr (2013)). It can be argued that econophysics (see Buchanan (2013)) and agent-based modelling (see section 3.2.5) may be seen as being part of the complexity research programme. However, Gallegati in Rosser *et al.* (2010) highlights differences between them in terms of tools. Econophysics rely on tools from the realm of statistical mechanics and theoretical physics (Mantegna and Stanley, 1999). Besides, the recent (for many, still present) economic crisis has been too important to ignore issues of method in academic economics. In particular, scepticism on the usefulness of the type of macroeconomic modelling known as dynamic stochastic general equilibrium (DSGE) for economic policy has notably increased lately (see Caiani *et al.*, (2016) for key criticisms). In this respect, Bezemer (2009) lists a number of economists who anticipated the financial crisis with success. Incorporating some of their ideas in this doctoral work seems to be opportune. Game theory, owing to the minimax theorem by Hungarian-American mathematician John von Neumann [1903-1957] (Luce and Raiffa, 2012), may, despite its name, also be considered a method. The possibility of applying game theory in this work has been excluded primarily on the grounds that it is largely static (Neumann and Morgenstern, 2007), more theory-focused, and not suitable to answer the research question adequately. Admittedly, game theory shapes real-world strategic behaviour of transnationals (e.g. car-makers) at the industry level as well as governments at the international arena (e.g. foreign policy, climate negotiations). However, it requires a level of abstraction and rationality on part of the modelled agent that lies far from what is judged to be practically admissible in the dynamic context of this work. Not only DSGE models embrace general equilibrium theory, but also IAMs, which combine knowledge on human and natural systems, often rely on them, particularly those whose focus is on policy optimisation (see e.g. Weyant *et al.* in Bruce *et al.* (1996: chapter 10)). Given the partial scope of this thesis, a truly general, global approach is unattainable. Veblen drew a line between high prestige and low practical knowledge (esoteric) and low prestige and high practical knowledge (exoteric) (Galbraith, 1991). This work leans towards the latter. The existence of a unique, perfect and objective method has been questioned by Blaug (2008). See Bunge (2014: 68-69) for his proposal of the key ingredients that generally constitute successful scientific research.

3.2.1 Quantitative methods in applied economics

As a preliminary step, research methods may be categorised as qualitative or quantitative. Swart *et al.* (2004) distinguish between qualitative and quantitative scenario analyses as well as a combination of them ('integrated scenarios'). An approach to combine qualitative and quantitative scenarios is 'story and simulation' (SAS) (Alcamo, 2008) (see also Weimer-Jehle *et al.* (2016)). Trutnevyte *et al.* (2014) introduced a two-step approach to link qualitative narratives (storylines) with multiple models. The advantage of quantitative analysis, from a mathematical perspective, is that it by definition conveys a qualitative result, expressed as the direction of a change of a certain variable (Chiang and Wainwright, 2005). In the case presented in this thesis, the first words of the research question ("*To what extent…*") already signal the need for obtaining magnitudes. Hence the methods considered in this work are of a quantitative nature. Furthermore, contemporary computers facilitate the task of applying quantitative methods and building quantitative models. In this thesis, the use of mathematics and the computer should be seen as a means to answering the research question, not as an end in itself. Therefore mathematics and the computer are to be interpreted in this thesis as tools and, as such, they possess advantages and disadvantages.

Two French minds were pioneers in mathematical economics: mathematician Antoine Augustin Cournot [1801-1877], with his focus on pure theory, and engineer-economist Jules Dupuit [1804-1866], with his interest in applications (Touffut, 2007). In the twentieth century, British economist John Hicks* [1904-1989] and American economists Paul Samuelson and Kenneth Arrow* made economics substantially more mathematical (Thaler, 2015). W. S. Jevons ([1879] 2013) had expressed the view that only a mathematical treatment of economics could render it a science, at the same time acknowledging that a mathematical treatment of the subject does not necessarily mean the attainment of truth. Boulding (1988) warned of the power and danger of using mathematics in economics: simplicity and formalism. The application of quantitative methods using computers in economics is generally known as computational economics. With caveats (see section 3.3), the pros of using computers in principle exceed its cons.

Table 3.1: Methods in energy, transport and ecological economics

Energy	Transport	Ecological
Econometrics	Demand allocation	Environmental input-output analysis
Energy balances	Matrix estimation	Life cycle assessment
Game theory	Regression analysis	Multicriteria decision aid
Input-output analysis	Simulation	Optimisation
Network modelling	Time series analysis	Simulation
Optimisation	-	-
Simulation	-	-
Time series analysis	-	-

Source: Based on Dahl (2004: 23) for energy, Bell and O'Flaherty (1997: 110) for transport and Shmelev (2011: 134) for ecological economics

Meadows in Randers (1980) examined four methods to model social systems: econometrics, input-output analysis, system dynamics and optimisation. The first three, together with linear programming, were listed by Walker (1978) as being popularly applied in policy analysis studies.

Table 3.1 gives an overview of methods commonly applied in energy, transport and ecological economics, as identified by authors from these fields. As noted in section 3.1.3, two radically different schools of thought in economics dealing with environmental issues co-exist at present time. In Table 3.1, only the usual methods of ecological economics are shown, for much of environmental economics is based on neoclassical methods that are usually found also in the fields of energy and transport. Since Table 3.1 shows a selection, other methods are missing: the noticeable absence, though perhaps implicit in simulation, is agent-based modelling.

In energy economics, a categorisation of models into top-down and bottom-up, arising from the application of different methods, is common (cf. Sensfuss (2008) and Herbst *et al.* (2012)). In the context of personal transport, Schafer and Victor (1999) concluded at the turn of the millennium that the methods available to researchers are not suitable for making long-term projections of personal transport. Dargay (2008) distinguishes between two main types of studies on personal transport choice, each based on different methods: (i) those focusing on the attributes of the transport system; and (ii) those focusing on the characteristics of the individuals. Whereas the former tend to be based on dynamic models that rely on aggregate data; the latter require disaggregate survey data. McFadden (2007) considers three levels at which travel behaviour has been modelled: (i) physical analogies (e.g. gravity model); (ii) models using rational behaviour theory; and (iii) models using the results of other social sciences that do not assume the level of rationality of (ii).

In the remainder of section 3.2, four methods are briefly presented: (i) econometrics; (ii) input-output analysis; (iii) system dynamics; and (iv) agent-based modelling. For each method, the sequence of exposition covers historical background, main features and examples. It is common to distinguish between macroeconomics and microeconomics and this, in turn, is mirrored in econometrics, with a separation between macroeconometrics and microeconometrics (Greene, 2011).

3.2.2 Econometrics

Economic analysis along the lines of econometrics had existed before this method was institutionalised in the 1930s through the creation of Econometric Society and the *Econometrica* journal. In its first editorial, Norwegian economist Ragnar Frisch* (1933: 1) [1895-1973] asserted that the object of econometrics was "*a unification of the theoretical-quantitative and the empirical-quantitative approach to economic problems*". Prominent developers of the econometric method by mid-century were Dutch economist Jan Tinbergen* [1903-1994], Dutch-American economist Tjalling C. Koopmans* [1910-1985], Norwegian economist Trygve Haavelmo* [1911-1999] and American economist Lawrence R. Klein* [1920-2013] (see e.g. Christ (1994)). Early scepticism towards econometric models was notably expressed by J. M. Keynes (1939) and the critiques by American economists Robert Lucas Jr.* (1976) and Christopher A. Sims* (1980) influenced later developments. According to Morgan (1992), the founding ideal of econometrics had collapsed by the 1950s. Today, several approaches to econometrics co-exist (see e.g. Pagan (1987), Hoover (2005) and Kennedy (2008)). Furthermore, decision analysts and statisticians have differing views on the philosophical foundations of their disciplines (Raiffa, 1968). Unsurprisingly, this situation applies to econometrics, with common distinctions between classical or frequentist and subjectivist or Bayesian econometrics as well as between parametric estimation and others. For an overview of the purposes of econometrics, see Intriligator (1983).

3.2.2.1 Dynamic econometrics

Macroeconometrics is also known as aggregate econometrics, dynamic econometrics or time-series econometrics. This method is distinct from time series analysis (TSA) (Newbold and Granger, 1989), in either its time-domain or frequency-domain variant. Both dynamic econometrics and TSA are statistical methods (Clements and Hendry, 1998) but reflect the scientific tension between abstraction and observation (recall section 3.1.1). At one extreme, economists use data to fit their theoretical models and assign a minor role to the statistical properties of data. At the other extreme, statistically-minded economists attach little weight to economic theory. The time-domain TSA approach is best illustrated by the set of models popularised by British statisticians George E. P. Box [1919-2013] and Gwilym M. Jenkins [1932-1982] (Box and Jenkins, 1976). This set includes autoregressive moving average (ARMA) and autoregressive integrated moving average (ARIMA) models. An alternative is represented by autoregressive distributed-lag (ADL) models, which seek to integrate econometric theory in the statistical model. In line with the latter, an econometric approach known as the London School of Economics (LSE) approach (see Gilbert (1986); (1989)) originated from the work by British economists J. Denis Sargan [1924-1996], Clive Granger* [1934-2009] and David F. Hendry (see Sargan (1964) in Hendry and Wallis (1984)) and Davidson *et al.* (1978)).

It has been operationalised into the general-to-specific (GETS) modelling approach, in contrast to the specific-to-general or simple-to-general approach (cf. Lütkepohl (2007)).

3.2.2.2 Discrete choice analysis

A variant of microeconometrics, or disaggregate econometrics, of special interest is qualitative choice analysis, more commonly known today as discrete choice (DC) analysis. American economist Daniel McFadden* has been instrumental to its development (see e.g. Manski (2001)).

The fact that many decisions in transport can be characterised as being indivisible (Glaister, 1981) means that a discrete representation of individual choices may be appropriate (Manski and McFadden, 1981). In those cases, logit analysis, or logistic regression, complements ordinary regression analysis (Cramer, 2003). In a discrete choice setting, the set of alternatives is assumed to be finite, exhaustive and the alternatives mutually exclusive (Train, 2009). Furthermore, the maintained assumption of measurability of utility is needed (Hensher, 2010). DC models include an error term and are thus considered probability models (Gujarati and Porter, 2009). Depending on the assumptions imposed on the error term, different types of DC models may be estimated (see e.g. Ben-Akiva and Lerman (1985)). A more recent type of DC model is the mixed logit (Hensher and Greene, 2003). Besides, though DC models traditionally relied on the random utility maximisation (RUM) assumption, the alternative hypothesis of random regret minimisation (RRM) has gained attention in recent years (see Chorus *et al.* (2008), Chorus (2012) and Hensher *et al.* (2013)).

In principle, the advantage of the DC method is its ability to predict the demand for new goods (Beggs *et al.*, 1981). For this reason, the method has been popularly applied in the context of vehicle choice. An early example is provided by Train (1986). More recently, the market introduction of EVs has been vastly investigated using DC analysis (recall section 2.3). In practice, the *ex ante* estimates derived from state-preference surveys may be different from the actual values. Using the new San Francisco Bay Area Rapid Transit (BART) as a real-world case, McFadden and Talvitie (1977) examined successfully disaggregate travel demand models based on DC (see Part II, chapter 3 for a comparison of pre-BART and post-BART model estimates).

3.2.3 Input-output analysis

Russian-origin American economist Wassily W. Leontief* [1906-1999] developed in the early 1930s, with colleagues at Harvard University, the input-output (I-O) method whose application resulted in I-O tables. As described by his founder, the method was a new attempt to combine economic theory with empirical facts (Leontief, 1986). Since the purpose of I-O analysis is to understand interdependences in the industrial economy, it is also known as interindustrial analysis (Miller and Blair, 2009).

I-O analysis, which is closely related to linear programming, is an example of linear economics (Dorfman *et al.*, 1988). There has been a historical development from linear I-O models, static or dynamic, to nonlinear I-O models (cf. Zhang (2001)). See Rose and Casler (1996) for the evolution of the I-O method towards I-O structural decomposition analysis (SDA).

I-O analysis is a method widely applied in economics (Miller and Blair (2009) citing Baumol (2000)) and perhaps the most popular method for regional analysis, in part due to its versatility (Rose and Miernyk, 1989). Regarded as a powerful method by ecological economists (Jusmet and Martinez-Alier, 2013), I-O analysis has been applied in the field of energy (including future scenarios (Blair, 2013)) and the environment (see respectively chapters 9-10 in Miller and Blair (2009)). Carter (1974) analysed the impacts of new energy technologies on economic growth using a closed dynamic I-O model. Another example is provided by Baumol (2000).

I-O analysis is also not uncommonly applied in combination with other methods, such as econometrics. An example is the model known as PANTA RHEI, which includes several car technologies (see e.g. Meyer (2005)).

3.2.4 System dynamics

The system dynamics (SD) method was founded by American electrical engineer Jay W. Forrester [1918-2016] at Massachusetts Institute of Technology (MIT) in 1957. Initially known as 'industrial dynamics' for its focus on corporate and industrial problems, it was later renamed 'system dynamics' after a wider field of applicability was recognised (Forrester, 1971).

The representation of feedback processes (servomechanisms, information-feedback or feedback-control systems) is at the core of the method (Forrester, [1961] 2013). Specifically, Forrester (1971: 110) understood social systems as "*multi-loop nonlinear feedback systems*". Wheat (2007) shows an example of how feedback processes may be represented in SD based on the economic hypotheses of Walras and Marshall. Some feedback structures are so common that they have been called 'generic structures' or 'system archetypes' (see appendix 2 in Senge (2010)).

Although feedback processes are conceptualised as closed systems (Forrester, [1961] 2013) and SD stresses the 'endogenous point of view' (Richardson, 2011), most SD models of the socio-economy are open (Radzicki and Tauheed, 2009), include sources and sinks that reflect the model boundaries, and may be driven by exogenous factors.

Radzicki (1990) highlighted the similarities between SD and institutional economics. More recently, he identified synergies between SD and Post-Keynesian, institutional, ecological and behavioural economics (Radzicki in Meyers (2009)). Rather than a method, Lavoie (2014) has classified SD as a school of thought. For contributions of SD to economics, see Radzicki in Meyers (2009). The strengths and weaknesses of SD for transport modelling were assessed by Abbas and Bell (1994). Twenty years later, Shepherd (2014) reviewed SD applications in the transport field. A prominent example of SD modelling in transport is the ASsessment of TRAnsport Strategies (ASTRA) model (Schade, 2005) (Krail, 2009) (Fiorello *et al.* (2010)). With regards to the market penetration of alternative vehicle technologies, SD has been applied vigorously in recent years (recall section 2.3).

3.2.5 Agent-based computational economics

Agent-based modelling (ABM) is commonly regarded as a method and known in economics as agent-based computational economics (ACE) (Hamill and Gilbert, 2016). Still considered a new research method (Gallegati in Rosser *et al.* (2010)), it has gained popularity in the late decades. ACE highlights agent interaction in dynamic economic systems (Tesfatsion in Colander (2006)). In ACE, an economic agent is an autonomous and adaptive entity (Guerci and Hanaki, 2012). Agents are assumed to possess limited information, which leads to satisficing but not optimal choices (Gallegati, 2016). Agent interaction takes place via rules that are prescribed (Farmer and Foley, 2009), without the need for a central coordinator (Caiani *et al.*, 2016). Page (2008) summarises the four main characteristics of ABM: (i) heterogeneity; (ii) learning; (iii) externalities; and (iv) networks. Machine learning allows agents to react to the changing environment (Junges and Klügl, 2013). The unclear connection between network structure and economic macro-behaviour (Kirman and Zimmermann, 2012) may be clarified by ABM, which can elicit emerging macro structure from individual or micro behaviour (Gilbert, 2008), for individual action may result in surprising collective or macro behaviour (Schelling, 2006). The critique by Lucas (1976) was influential in encouraging models with microfoundations (see section 3.1.3.2 above). Currently, ABM represents the alternative modelling approach to microfoundations to the dominant DSGE (Gallegati, 2016). ABM enables the modelling of agent interaction, which is required in truly microfounded models (Gallegati in Rosser *et al.* (2010)).

ABM are computer simulations (see e.g. Miller and Page (2009)) found useful in energy and transport research: see Sensfuß and Ragwitz in Möst (2008) for an example of the electricity sector and Eppstein *et al.* (2011) for the simulation of the PHEV market uptake. Kieckhäfer *et al.* (2014) show how ABM may be jointly applied with SD to simulate EV market penetration.

3.3 Dynamic models for decision support

According to Bell and O'Flaherty (1997: 103), "*models are simplified representations of reality which can be used to explore the consequences of particular policies or strategies*". Models are contextual (Rodrik, 2015), problem-oriented and viewpoint-dependent (Ortúzar and Willumsen, 2001).

Models can be classified in accordance with several dimensions (see e.g. Bossel (2007a: 24-25)). Four relevant dimensions examined in this section are: (i) mental vs. computer models; (ii) linear vs. nonlinear models; (iii) optimisation vs. simulation models; and (iv) discrete-time vs. continuous-time dynamic models.

To support decision-making under uncertainty, a choice between the use of the mental model of the decision-maker and a computer model, which may in turn enrich the original mental model, must be made (Sterman, 2000). The mental model is neither complete nor precisely stated. In contrast, the computer model must be made explicit (Forrester, 1971). By computer model it is meant the application of a methodology, based on one or more methods, using a computer and historical data for a certain purpose. According to Knight (2012: 16), "*the aim of science is to predict the future for the purpose of making our conduct intelligent*". To improve economic decision-making, future-oriented thinking is likely to be helpful. An important task of scientific policy advice is to construct model-based scenarios (Acatech, 2015). When decisions are complex and important, computer models tend to be preferable. For example, the European Commission encourages the use of 'model-based decision support tools' (see e.g. EC (2015)), interpreted as scientifically-sounded computer models that inform policy-making. Unfortunately, computer modelling is not exempt from the 'garbage in-garbage out' problem (Foley, 2009). The use of computers allows a more efficient development of large-scale and complex models. However, this is not without its own perils, for it significantly increases the efforts needed to trace and understand the connections between model input and output. In the context of mobility scenarios until 2030, Kuhnimhof *et al.* in Hülsmann and Fornahl (2013) lament the pretension of exactness that model-based projections create, an exactness that Marshall ([1920] 2013) had long argued is less achievable in the sciences that deal with humans. No pretension of exactness in this work is made and the recommendation by Manski (2013) on the need to move policy analysis from incredible certitude (point prediction) to credible interval prediction is seriously taken. But arguably the advantages of making computer model-based numerical statements about the future offset its potential disadvantages. Two of these advantages are recognised: (i) it enables experiments (Ruth and Hannon, 1997); and (ii) it facilitates the quick visualisation of indirect (side and far-reaching) effects (Dörner, 2003).

The second dimension of interest relates to the distinction made long ago in economics by Malthus ([1798] 2008) between arithmetic (linear) and geometric (nonlinear) relationships, in particular growth. Nonlinearity in economics conveys the idea of an economic limit or level of saturation. By 1879, Jevons (2013) recognised that linear functions are seldom, if ever, a feature of economics, a reality increasingly perceived by economists (Baumol, 1970). More generally in social systems, nonlinearity is not the exception (May, 1976). Whereas linear systems can be subjected to the principle of superposition, most nonlinear systems cannot be solved analytically (Strogatz, 2014: 8; see also Fig. 1.3.1 on p. 10). When Jevons wrote, computers were not available. Analytical tractability of a given economic problem was a necessity. Fortunately, today computers provide us with a way of representing nonlinearities, thereby helping us tackle at least one level of complexity in social systems. Hence this represents another rationale for using computer models.

In broad terms, models may be primarily based on one of the following modelling techniques: (i) optimisation; (ii) simulation; or on a mixture of both. At the core of economic analysis lies optimisation (Lancaster, 1987). For three purposes of simulation, see Gilbert and Troitzsch (2005: 4-5). Optimisation models, which are methodologically more challenging, generally allow less dynamic complexity than simulation models (Moxnes in Rahmandad *et al.* (2015)). The choice of technique largely depends on the purpose of the model. On the application of optimising procedures in the context of energy scenarios, Grunwald (2011) has sounded a note of caution. Models may also contain a mixture of optimisation and simulation, thereby complementing each other, as illustrated by three examples: (i) econometric models may result from minimisation of least squares and simulation of future values over a certain lead time; (ii) system dynamics models are inherently simulation models but may also incorporate the outcomes of calibration or policy optimisation; (iii) a modelling exercise may be based on an optimisation pathway replicated by a simulation pattern (see an example in Haasz *et al.* (2018)). Typically, the simulation pattern is portrayed on a Cartesian plane where the variable 'time' is shown in the abscissa. *Ergo* simulation is often understood as dynamic simulation.

In economics, Swiss economist de Sismondi [1773-1842] was a precursor of dynamics (see e.g. Schumpeter in Sismondi (2011)). Conceptualising EV market uptake as an evolving process is an invitation to adopt the system (recall section 2.1.1) view and to consider two key aspects of any system: its state description and its dynamics (Boulding, 1988). More specifically, interest in how the system changes over time leads to consideration of dynamic(al) system theory (Bertalanffy, [1968] 2003). Since the computer model developed in this thesis explicitly takes time into account, the question of how time is mathematically treated consequently arises. The distinction is between discrete-time and continuous-time dynamic models. In economics, the former are specified as difference equations and the latter as differential equations (Lancaster, 1987). Though some economists in the 1950s argued that a continuous representation of economic systems is more accurate, discrete-time models became the norm (see Richardson (1991)). To Marshall ([1890], 2013), nature determines that time is continuous. The assumption of time continuity was rejected by Mandelbrot and Hudson (2010), who proposed a more flexible approach to time (termed 'time deformation'). In addition, a distinction between logical time and historical time can be made (see Robinson (1980)). The pros and cons of differing interpretations of the element of time are summarised in section 3.5. Finally, Shone (2002) highlights the importance of dimensionality in economic dynamics.

3.4 Data availability, collection and quality

In the modelling exercise, data is needed for two reasons: (i) to feed the model; and (ii) to evaluate the model results in view of the empirical evidence, thereby validating the model. The analytical framework described in section 2.1.3 helps identify data requirements. Three data issues are considered next: (i) data availability; (ii) data collection; and (iii) data quality.

Economic data is the main window to the observation of economic behaviour (Griliches, 1986), but modelling requires not only numerical data (Forrester, 1980). Ford and Flynn (2005) point out at the spectrum of information available to model builders, including social system data. Social measurements in general, and economic data in particular, is mainly non-experimental (i.e. observational) (Spanos, 1999), related to unique phenomena (Morgenstern, 1963) and either discrete or continuous (Greene, 2011) (see also Stevens (1946)). Following section 1.2, this study requires data related to policy at the country level. This indicates a rather high level of aggregation, closer to the 'macro' model (which deals with the interplay between policy-makers and economic agents (Greene, 2011)) than to the 'micro' model in the widespread distinction in economics between the 'micro', 'meso', and 'macro' levels. The inevitability of data aggregation is highlighted by Hendry (1995) and its opportunities and risks pointed out by Button (2010). More specifically, low-frequency (annual) time series is the preferred data for the dynamic model to be developed. Seasonality is excluded from this analysis. For some aspects, analysis would require more disaggregated data but this is often not available (see Pasaoglu *et al.* (2014) for an example in the context of driving and recharging profiles for electrically-driven vehicles in the EU). Today, the Internet provides availability to a substantial amount of aggregated data from secondary sources (see chapter 4). On the negative side, missing data points in those sources is not unusual. To partially compensate for this, the set of available information has been increased, with caveats, by judgementally considering the grey literature.

With regards to data collection, Button (2010) highlights two pertinent issues: (i) confidentiality if data collection is undertaken by a commercial firm, which reduces the level of transparency available to the modeller; and (ii) in the context of transport statistics, the fact that most of the data collected relates to the physical aspects of transport systems and is of limited value for economic analysis of travel behaviour. As noted by Leontief (1986), there is a natural time lag between data gathering and availability.

Perhaps, the most critical issue relates to data quality, which is influenced by data availability and collection and in turn affects the quality of the model results. The presence of large errors in economic statistics was acknowledged by Belarus-born American economist Simon S. Kuznets* [1901-1985] (see Kuznets (1950)). Three brief examples of issues encountered in this study that affect data quality are worth mentioning (the problematic matter of stated preference data was highlighted in section 2.3). The first example relates to the temporal and spatial consistency of statistical definitions. Table 3.2 shows the example of the term LDV, which encompasses different sets of vehicles depending on the institution responsible for collecting the data. Besides, light trucks are more often used for passenger activities in the US compared with other countries (ORNL, 2016), and this is hard to disentangle from available statistics. The second example concerns the co-existence of two datasets from seemingly reliable sources showing very different historical evolutions of the same variable (defined in both sources as 'passenger car stock / cars in use') in Japan (see Figure 3.2). This discrepancy has a large effect on the model output (estimation of total car-related oil use and GHG emissions). The third example relates to the availability of car-related data disaggregated by powertrain. In EVI data, there is a slight discrepancy between the cumulative sales and the total EV stock. Lack of evidence of sales prior to 2008 does not mean evidence of absence of EVs. As long as different sources for each powertrain are used, the possibility of a mismatch between the sum of these and aggregate data from another source appears. The other possibility is to use only one source, but this is unfortunately not feasible. For instance, the German *Kraftfahrt-Bundesamt* (KBA) does not provide online separate data for FF, PHEV and BEV (KBA, 2016). It remains to be seen whether it shall also show separate data for FC in the future.

Table 3.2: LDV, as defined by various institutions

Term	IEA/OECD*	EU**	US DOE***
Light-duty vehicle (LDV)	Automobiles, SUVs, mini-vans, light trucks	Cars, vans	Cars, vans, SUVs, pickups

Source: *IEA/OECD (2009: 113); **Eurostat (2016); ***AFDC (2015)

Five final remarks concerning data: (i) data conversions to the standard scientific IS format (e.g. from miles per US gallon (MPG) to litre/km) are made; (ii) the units of measurement of data are shown in this work inside square brackets; (iii) given data availability (partially influenced by the language skills of the author) and quality, the data collected for the European countries and the US appear to be more satisfactory for analysis than the ones obtained for the Asian countries; (iv) the data gathered is summarised and stored in a suitable format, so that it may be readily used to feed the model (see appendix I); and (v) the data issues considered in this section have implications for the selection of method, considered next.

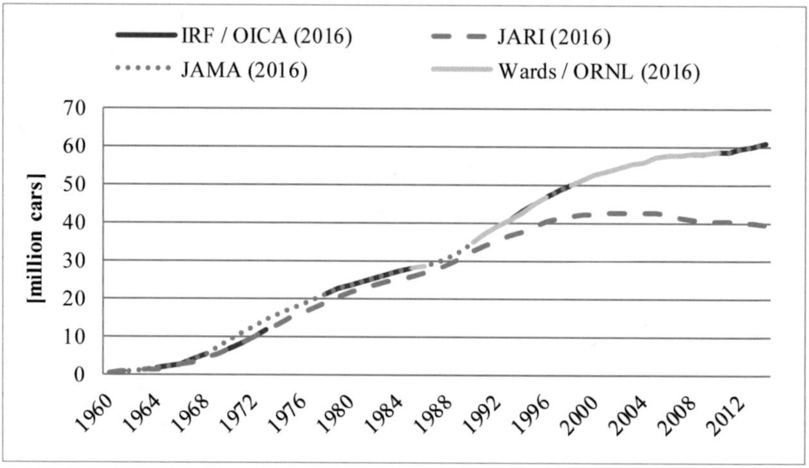

Figure 3.2: Data discrepancy for Japan
Source: Based on the sources indicated in the legend (see appendix I)

3.5 Concluding remarks II: Method assessment and selection

In the previous sections, methodological traditions related to schools of thought and methods in economics were introduced. The schools often differ not only in method but also in their policy recommendations (prominently, on the desirable degree of government intervention in economic issues). In sum, conventional car market downfall and electric car market uptake (henceforth 'car market upturn') may be modelled with ideas from different schools of thought. Some tentative hypotheses are: by assuming that the choices of individual consumers are based on a purely rational TCO basis (neoclassical economists' view); by modelling car purchasers as rationally bounded and incorporating additional psychological factors (behavioural economists' view); by emphasising the role of government policy to promote the energy transition in the automotive sector (e.g. 'green Keynesianism' adopting the Post-Keynesian view); by considering in-market competition of different niches along Darwinian lines (evolutionary economists' view); by stressing energy flows, taking into account physical constraints and acknowledging the desirability to reduce car usage (ecological economists' view). That any methodology has its own limits was a point suggested by Austrian philosopher of science Paul Feyerabend ([1975] 2010) [1924-1994]. All the methods presented in section 3.2 have three features in common: (i) are quantitative methods; (ii) may be implemented in computer software; and (iii) are regarded as *a priori* suitable for answering the research question of this thesis.

A clearer statement of the model purpose is due before the selection of the method is elucidated. Boland (2014) distinguishes between pure or abstract models and applied models, the latter being divisible into explanatory models and models that provide policy recommendations. The purpose of the model developed in this thesis is to facilitate policy analysis in the context of car market upturn. Manski (2013) highlights three relevant issues related to policy analysis: (i) its goal is the provision of information necessary to policy-making; (ii) the prediction of policy outcomes is hard; and (iii) an honest communication of imperfect knowledge is desirable. The policy analysis based on the developed model shall support the exploration, adopting the 'what-if' device, of policy options that contribute to the car market upturn. For this, the set of information found useful concerns the policy options shown in section 4.3. This does not necessarily mean that the model shall deliver definite answers to policy issues, but it may instead offer, in line with the idea suggested by Colander and Kupers (2014), visions to policy.

Ultimately and as a result of the method selection, the model should enable its user to obtain responses to the following four modelling questions:

1. What are the projected aggregate car stock and annual sales?
2. What are the possible market shares and resulting car-mix?
3. What is the estimated demand for energy?
4. What are the corresponding GHG emissions?

These questions are based on the previously identified modelling tasks (recall section 2.4). Although projections and forecasts are needed to attain this (modelling question 1), forecasting is by no means the purpose of the model.

With regards to the selection of method, this decision requires the assessment of the methods identified in section 3.2 and the consideration of these steps: (i) choice on the preferred modelling approach; (ii) choice between a single-method and a multi-method model. If a multi-method model is favoured, justification on the feasibility and desirability of linking the selected methods is needed.

The first choice is between a bottom-up and a top-down modelling approach. A third alternative is the development of a hybrid model that integrates both approaches. It is argued that dynamic econometrics, I-O analysis and SD may be classified as top-down modelling approaches. The crucial decision is whether methodological individualism shall be pursued or not. Because of the purpose of the model and the need to keep complexity at a manageable size, which is constrained by data availability and requires a high level of aggregation, the answer is negative. Hence a top-down approach is preferred and disaggregate econometric and ABM methods shall not be applied.

The second choice is that between a single method and a multi-method top-down model. The risk of an inflexible methodological stance is highlighted by Buongiorno (1996). See also Jick (1979) for the idea of 'triangulation'. Since the modelling exercise was partitioned into different modelling tasks (recall section 2.4), a multi-method approach appears feasible, provided that each method is *a priori* suitable for one or more modelling tasks. In principle, it is desirable to use the same method to answer modelling questions 2-3, for they are closely related and call for a method capable of simulating the system-wide effects of policy. But consistent with Eq. 2.6 (section 2.1.3), modelling question 1 may be answered using a distinct method, compatible with the generation of projections. This represents an opportunity for developing a model that draws from two different methods.

The need for a dynamic model that captures the complex aspects of the car ecosystem reverts to consideration of: (i) historical time; (ii) cumulative causation; and (iii) feedback processes. Historical time leads to causality (Pasinetti, 2010). Norwegian-born statistician Herman Wold [1908-1992] emphasised that: (i) causality is an indispensable concept in science (Wold, 1954), and (ii) simultaneity is absent in economic relationships for they are always characterised by a time lag between cause and effect (Charemza and Deadman, 1997). The notion of 'cumulative causation' was mentioned by Veblen and expanded ('*circular and* cumulative causation') by Myrdal and Hungarian economist Nicholas Kaldor [1908-1986] (see Veblen (1898), Myrdal (1944: appendix 3) and Berger (2008)). The application of this notion demonstrates that collaboration between economists that hold views consistent with the institutional and Post-Keynesian schools is a possibility. Economists working under the heterodox programme accord due importance to storytelling (Lavoie, 2014), "*a method of theorizing that binds together facts, low-level generalizations, high-level theories, and value judgements in a coherent narrative*" (Blaug, 2008: 251). Pattern modelling, a term coined by American philosopher Abraham Kaplan [1918-1993], is storytelling carried out in a systematic manner, which seems adequate to analyse situations shaped by a multiplicity of factors (Wilber and Harrison, 1978). The formalisation of these ideas in quantitative terms occurs by modelling feedback processes with the aid of computers. By the late 1980s, Boulding (1988) perceived that the idea of positive and negative feedback was steadily spreading in economics. Richardson (1991) offers a historical account of the development of feedback thought in the social sciences and identifies two major conceptual threads: cybernetics and servomechanism (see Wiener ([1948] 1961) and Brown and Campbell (1948), respectively). An interesting early example of implicit feedback modelling was given by German-born physicist Albert Einstein, winner of the Nobel Prize in Physics in 1921, when writing on the 1930 economic crisis (Einstein, [1949] 2005). Richardson (1991) concludes that only two methods consistent with the concept of mutual causality (circular and cumulative causation and feedback) may help analyse dynamic social systems: econometrics and SD. Among the various approaches to econometrics (recall section 3.2.2), there is one (the aforementioned LSE approach that emerged in Britain) that explicitly models feedback processes, highlighting the close link between servomechanisms and error correction terms (Hendry *et al.*, 1984).

Based on the previous discussion, the conclusion that the joint consideration of the econometric and the SD method represents an adequate means of inquiry is reached. Consequently, econometrics and SD are the two methods selected for the modelling exercise. Specifically, dynamic econometrics is used to answer modelling question 1 and the SD method is applied to develop the main model that delivers answers to the modelling questions 2-4. Data issues also influenced this decision, because dynamic econometrics requires long time series for each of the countries analysed, which are only available for variables such as population, GDP and total car stock.

Once the selection of methods has been made, the coherence of their philosophical underpinnings requires at least a brief consideration. Sommer (1984) examines the methodological "tensions" and possibly conflicting co-existence of econometrics and SD. He rightly indicates that econometrics and SD suffer from a paradigm conflict, a conclusion that had also been reached by Meadows in Randers (1980). In fact, when the 'Limits to Growth' report, perhaps the most well-known example of SD modelling, was released (Meadows *et al.*, 1972), it faced strong criticism (see e.g. Nordhaus (1973) and Beckerman (1974)). Whereas logical positivism underpins econometrics (recall section 3.1.3), pragmatic instrumentalism influences SD (Forrester, 1985). A list of arguments by proponents of the econometric and SD used to defend their own methods is collected in Gómez Vilchez (2016b). In particular, it can be argued that the modelling assumptions of discrete time and white noise (econometrics) as opposed to, respectively, continuous time and pink noise (SD) can hardly be reconciled. Notwithstanding, Sommer (1984) also points out that a certain problem might require the application of both methods. The author is in agreement with this statement and, despite the differences in philosophies, the reliance of both methods on the empirical approach can be contested with immense difficulty (see e.g. Hendry (1995: 4) and Forrester ([1961] 2013: 18)). Moreover, Richardson (1991) places both methods in the servomechanism thread. Apel *et al.* (1978) indicate that there are situations in modelling complexity where econometrics may be more advantageous than SD. Finally, there is evidence that the two methods may be combined (see the studies by Buongiorno (1996) and Smith and van Ackere (2002) on forestry and health, respectively).

The sole purpose of the dynamic econometric sub-model is to deliver key projections for the main model. This sub-model is stochastic and, being of a statistical nature, it is a descriptive (Bunge, 2015) 'black-box' (von Hayek in Bunge (1964)) (see also Bossel (2007a)) that cannot imply causation (*cum hoc ergo propter hoc*). Furthermore, this sub-model is the result of solving difference equations and hence the estimated values are prone to alterations due to unexpected changes (Boulding, 1988). Blanchard (2008) recalls the Lucas critique condemning that established relationships between variables can break down in the presence of policy regime shifts. In practice, a single-equation regression sub-model is estimated for each country using dynamic econometrics. For this, the software employed is EViews®.

As Hicks (1995) suggested, the introduction of policy variables in a model opens the door to analysis beyond econometrics. SD, which is an example of pattern modelling (Radzicki, 1990), facilitates policy analysis and design (SDS, 2014). The SD sub-model (main model) is essentially deterministic, but noise may be added. In practice, the developed SD sub-model is based on a system of equations that comprises the six countries. The software used is Vensim® DSS, which facilitates the modelling of stock and flow structures and dimensional analysis, two crucial aspects in dynamic modelling.

A final methodological question remains: Does a model connection (soft linkage) suffice or is a model integration or combination (hard linkage) needed? It is argued that a soft linkage between models is adequate. Sterman (2000: 438) provides reasons for not integrating regression equations into SD models.

The development of the model and how the two sub-models, each being the result of a different method, are connected are explained in the next chapter.

It remains to be seen at the end of this thesis whether the methodological linkage of econometrics and system dynamics is one of the main contributions of this study.

4 Model development

In this chapter, a description of the developed model is given, with an emphasis on the model assumptions (section 4.2).

4.1 Overview

4.1.1 Model description

As indicated in section 1.1, the variables of ultimate interest in this thesis are *energy use* and *GHG emissions*, which correspond to the *final* model output. For this, *intermediate* model output concerning the *car-mix* (recall modelling question 2 in section 3.5) is needed. Determination of the possible *car-mix* should be interpreted as a means to generate the final model output, not as the goal of modelling. The sets of car technologies (nine elements) and energy sources (seven elements) included in the model are shown in Figure 4.1. Only PHEVs are assumed to be powered by two different energy sources: gasoline and electricity. Admittedly, these relationships do not exhaust all present and future technical possibilities, but they represent a reasonable approximation to what consumers can expect from the market in the near future.

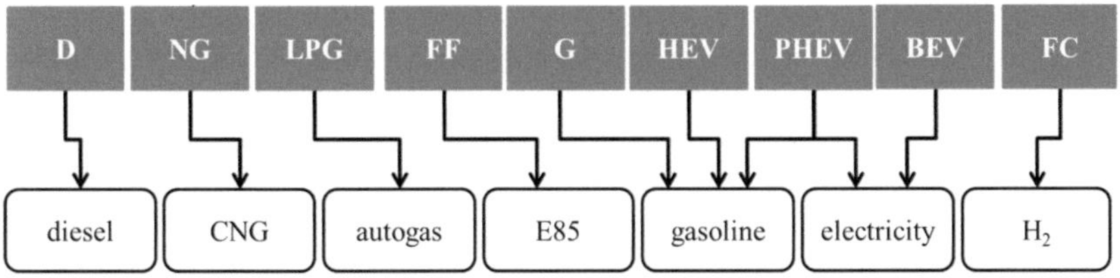

Figure 4.1: Car technologies and energy sources linkages | Source: Gómez Vilchez (2016a)

First of all, three model subscripts are created: h for country, i for technology and j for the type of GHG emission. In addition, a t subscript denotes time. In the econometric part, time is treated in a discrete fashion; in the SD part, time is conceptually continuous and computationally approximated in a discrete manner.

4.1.1.1 Modules

Next, a modular approach is implemented with the following nine modules: *Population-GDP, Car Stock, Travel Demand by Car, Infrastructure, Attributes, Market Behaviour, Energy, Emissions* and *Policy*. Using the 'multiple view' capability of Vensim®, each module is embedded in one or more 'views' and the modules are interlinked using 'shadow variables' (defined in other views (Vensim, 2016)). Figure 4.2 illustrates the modular structure of the model.

In the remainder of this section, each module is concisely introduced:

1. *Module Population-GDP*: The aim of this module is to incorporate the external projections on population and GDP. Here, *income per capita* (intermediate output) is derived from *population* and *GDP* (inputs). Other macroeconomic variables are used to translate money values from nominal to real.

2. *Module Car Stock*: The aim of this module is to fulfil the modelling task 1 (i.e. projection of car ownership and the resulting aggregate car sales) and part of the modelling task 2 (i.e. simulation of the market shares by car technology). Thus the module contains the results of the econometric sub-model. It generates the intermediate model output and sends this information to *Energy* and *Emissions*.

3. *Module Market Behaviour*: This module aims at partially fulfilling modelling task 2. The module comprises the model's main behavioural assumptions.

4. *Module Travel Demand by Car*: This module seeks to partially fulfil modelling task 3 (i.e. estimation of travel demand by car and energy use). The module contains three alternative ways (expected, simulated and desired) of representing travel demand by car.

5. *Module Infrastructure*: The goal of this module is to partially fulfil modelling task 2. The module relates policy variables to the deployment of public refuelling and recharging infrastructure.

6. *Module Attributes*: The aim of this module is to partially fulfil modelling task 2. The module is divided into three broad classes of car attributes: *Technical Features*, *Production Costs* and *Consumer Costs*, each with its own view.

7. *Module Energy*: This module consists of: *Energy Prices*, *Electricity Mix* and *Energy Use*, each embedded in a separate view. The goal of each sub-module is respectively: (i) to accommodate the assumptions concerning the price evolution of the different energy sources; (ii) to reflect assumptions on power generation by source; and (iii) to fulfil the modelling task 3.

8. *Module Policy*: The goal of this module is to attain the model purpose: to facilitate policy analysis. It hosts the decisions, to be determined by the model user, that affect the policy variables of the model. Hence the module represents the core of the modelling exercise and affects the rest of the modules.

9. *Module Emissions*: This module consists of six sub-modules: *Emission Factors*, *New Car Emissions*, *Manufacturing and Scrappage*, *Tank-to-Wheel (TTW)*, *Well-to-Tank (WTT)* and *Lifecycle*. In sum, this module seeks to fulfil modelling task 4 (i.e. calculation of corresponding GHG emissions).

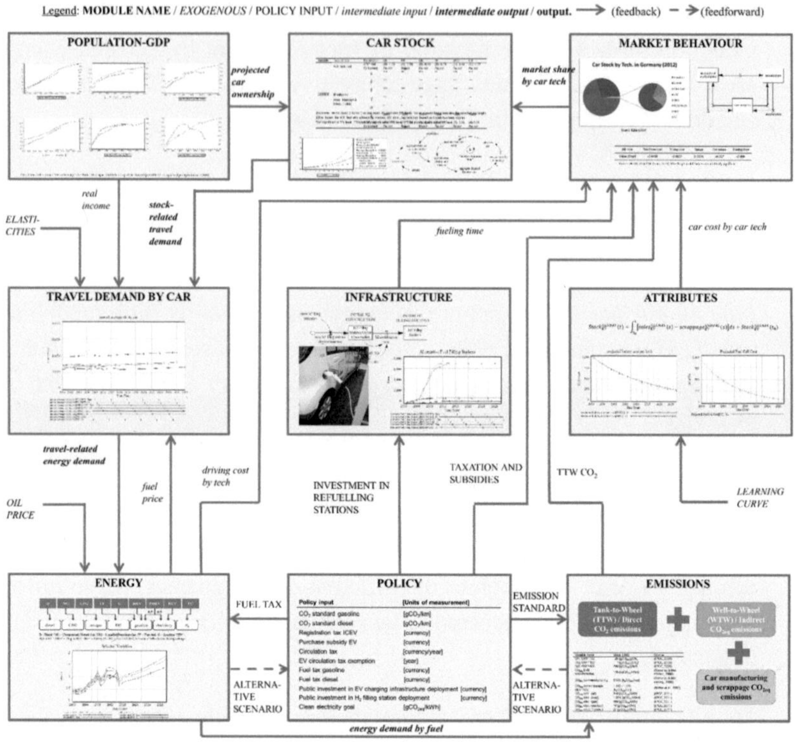

Figure 4.2: Overview of the developed model
Source: Adapted from Gómez Vilchez *et al.* (2016)

4.1.1.2 Variables

Economic variables may be expressed as either:

(i) "Flows *through time* [...] *or* stocks *at a moment of time*" (Baumol, 1970: 127). This distinction is crucial in a dynamic model. Stocks are also known as state variables. In economics, flows and stocks are respectively known as rates and levels (Sterman, 2000). In Vensim®, flow variables are represented by the icon ⧖ and stock variables by a box. Clouds symbolise sources and sinks, located beyond the system boundaries.

(ii) Exogenous or endogenous. This distinction is important in a model that provides policy recommendations (Boland, 2014). For the econometric sub-model, the terminology independent and dependent variables is preferred for customary reasons.

In addition, there is a third important distinction concerning the model variables that should be taken into account:

(iii) Desired or actual state variables. The advantage of differentiating between the desired states (decision-makers' goals) and the actual states of the system has been stressed by Sterman (2000). For example, whereas the model variable 'projected aggregate total car stock' would represent the desired state, the variable 'aggregate car stock' would represent the actual state of the system. Drawing from Gilboa (2009), any model user that attempts to make rational choices should distinguish between those model variables (s)he may control and the rest (in this case, between the desired and actual states).

In the *Car Stock* module, it is important to differentiate between the car market share and the car-mix (cf. modelling question 2 in section 3.5). By *market share* it is meant the configuration of the annual car *sales* by powertrain, expressed in percentage terms (e.g. 0.6 or 60% market share of gasoline denotes that 60% of the new cars sold in a market are gasoline). The term *car-mix* is borrowed from the literature of the energy field, where it is common to speak of the electricity-mix. By *car-mix* it is meant the configuration of the car *stock* by powertrain in a particular year, expressed in percentage terms (e.g. a value of 0.4 or 40% share of diesel cars in the car-mix denotes that 40% of the car stock is powered by diesel cars). Both variables are dimensionless [dmnl], and they are attached to variables with different dimensions. The *market share* variable is associated with the flow variable *aggregate sales rate*, measured in [car/year]. The *car-mix* variable is linked to the stock variable *aggregate car stock*, measured in [car].

Table 4.1: Model boundary chart: variables included, by type

	Model input: Exogenous variables		Model (intermediate and final) output: Endogenous variables
	Data / projections / own assumptions	*Policy inputs*	
Constants	Learning curve based on battery cost reduction fraction [dmnl]	Value added tax [%]	Effect of learning experience on battery cost [dmnl]
	Utility coefficients [dmnl]	Target load factor [passenger/car]	
Variables	Population [passenger]	Emission standards [gCO_2/km]	New car sales [car/year]
	Gross domestic product [dollar]	Target PKM per cap [pkm/passenger]	Car stock [car]
	PKM per cap [pkm/passenger]	Car taxes [dollar/car]	EVB cost based on capacity [dollar/battery]
	Car average lifetime [year]	Energy taxes [dollar/unit]	Market share by technology [dmnl]
	Car prices [dollar]	Carbon intensity electricity mix [gCO_{2eq}]	Vehicle-km travelled [km]
	Number of stations [station]		**Energy use [unit]
	Energy prices [dollar/unit*]		**GHG emissions [gCO_{2eq}]
	Emission factors [gCO_{2eq}/unit]		

* Unit = per unit of fuel / ** Energy use and emissions from car travel.

Two types of model input are identified: (i) (historical) data and projections, which are obtained from external sources (e.g. international organisations or forecasting firms), and own assumptions (assumptions made by the modeller based on his judgement, motivated by the lack of reliable data); and (ii) policy inputs (in this case, the controllable variables). Whereas the former are assumed by the modeller, the latter are to be determined by the model user. In this thesis, the author has acted as both modeller and model user, for the purpose of developing the model and conducting scenarios, respectively. With the exception of the module *Policy*, each module may be affected by exogenous variables or variables (exogenous and/or endogenous) from other modules. Furthermore, two types of quantities are considered: constants and variables. A summary of the main variables included in the model, and their nature, as well as the variables excluded from the model, for reasons of either boundary or level of aggregation, is shown in Table 4.1 and Table 4.2.

Table 4.2: Model boundary chart: variables excluded, by reason

DUE TO BOUNDARY	**DUE TO AGGREGATION**
Road infrastructure (e.g. network length)	Car size (e.g. B or C segment)
Traffic congestion	Engine displacement / horsepower
Speed	Alternative modes of transport (e.g. bus)
Travel time	Type of recharging plugs
Value of travel time savings (VTTS)	Population by age and gender
Generalised cost of travel	Number of driving license holders
Car inventories held by manufacturers	Car travel demand by purpose of the trip
International oil market dynamics	Vehicle-km travelled by powetrain
Trade tariffs (e.g. car import duties)	Emissions credits and penalties

An example of how some of these variables are conceptually connected is shown in the next section, where the core dynamic hypothesis of this model is sketched.

4.1.2 Dynamic hypothesis

As mentioned in section 2.4, various studies based on SD models have examined the market uptake of new car technologies. This thesis attempts to demarcate from them by highlighting the following dynamic hypothesis, implemented in the SD model. Whereas positive signs in causal links (arrows) denote positive polarity, negative signs indicate negative polarity. Whereas the letter *R* denotes a reinforcing (positive) feedback loop, *B* means balancing (negative) feedback (see chapter 5 in Sterman (2000)). For example, the higher the EV battery price, the lower the EV sales, and the higher the EV sales, the lower the EV battery price (at least at the current stage of development, where cost reductions are dependent on the volumes of batteries manufactured). This circularity, *ceteris paribus*, is captured by a reinforcing feedback loop *R*.

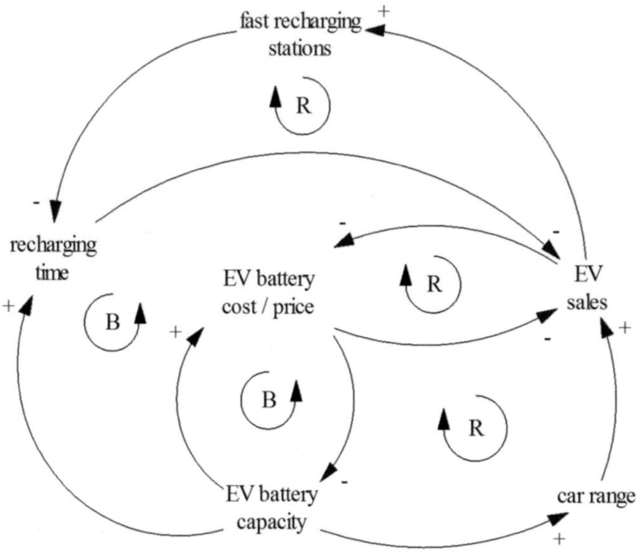

Figure 4.3: Dynamic hypothesis | Source: Own work using Vensim®

Hence this dynamic hypothesis seeks to capture the basic feedback loop between quantity and price as well as additional feedback processes. In particular, it shows the mutual causality between the number of electric cars sold and the price of the battery (at present, the main cost component in BEVs). As opposed to the available studies, the variable 'EV sales' is modelled jointly for China, France, Germany, India, Japan and the US. To the best knowledge of the author of this thesis, this feedback process had not been modelled by explicitly considering the main EV markets until now.

4.1.3 Stages in model building

For each of the methods applied in this work, there are standard descriptions of the modelling process (i.e. stages or phases in model building). For example, see Patterson (2000) for dynamic econometrics and Sterman (2000) for SD. Although the exposition of the modelling process is sequential, in reality it is iterative. In addition, this modelling exercise requires a description of the method linkage.

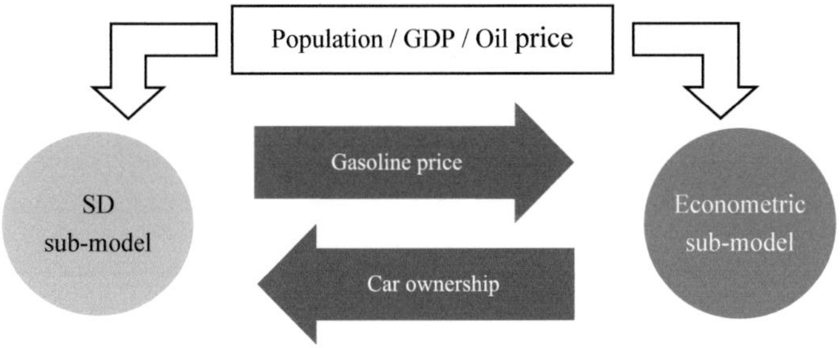

Figure 4.4: Information exchange between sub-models | Source: Own work

Firstly, assumptions concerning *population*, *GDP* and *crude oil price* are adopted. These assumptions are maintained throughout the modelling exercise. Then the SD model is used to generate the assumption of the gasoline fuel price per country. This information may be used to feed the econometric sub-model. The output of the econometric sub-model (i.e. car ownership) is then fed into the SD model. The stylised iterative process is shown in Figure 4.4.

Following section 3.5, the model connection, thereby harmonising both methods, is illustrated by the feedback loop shown in Figure 4.5. Given the divergence in values between the econometric aggregate total car stock and the simulated (SD) aggregate car stock, primacy is given to the former. Hence the econometric projections are re-interpreted as desired values. Then, a correction is forced onto the SD sub-model, which attempts to replicate the dynamic behaviour of the econometric projection. In essence, this reflects a stock management problem (see chapter 17 in Sterman (2000)). As a result of the negative feedback and the presence of time delays, there is the risk that the system displays oscillating behaviour. To avoid that, the appropriate decision rule must be found (see sections 4.2.9.3 and 5.2.2).

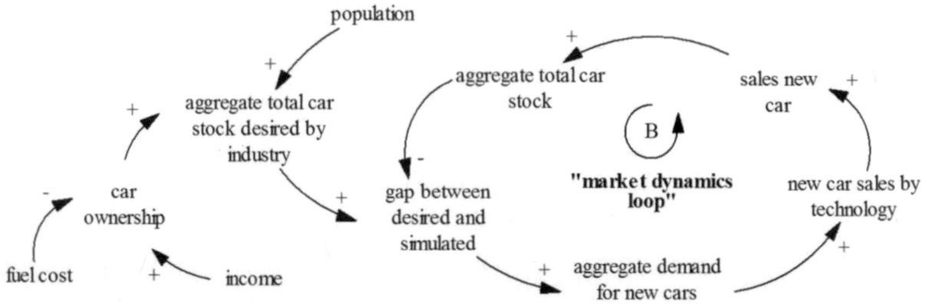

Figure 4.5: The 'market dynamics' feedback loop | Source: Own work using Vensim®

4.2 Assumptions

This section describes the modeller's assumptions, namely equations and numerical values. The assumptions listed in each sub-section relate to the most important variables of the model (see also appendices I and II). The simplifications described in the next sections are motivated by the purpose of the model and the need to keep assumptions at a manageable level. Some of the strongest assumptions are, if not fully relaxed, at least tested in chapter 5.

4.2.1 Population

Population can be differentiated by gender and age and this could be captured by a complex ageing stock-and-flow structure that models birth, mortality and net migration rates. In addition, data on the proportion of the population that is unemployed and holds a driving license might be exploited. Population is simplified in this model by considering only *total population*.

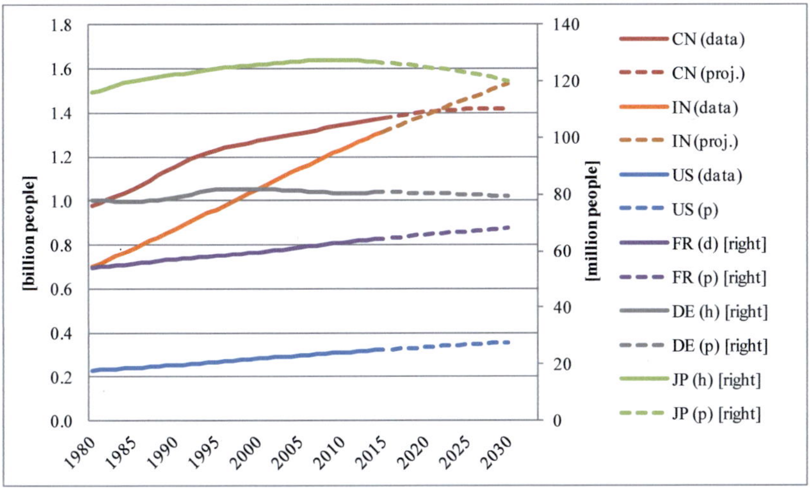

Figure 4.6: Population: data and projections
Source: Data (1950-2015) and projections (2016-2030) from UN (2016)

Figure 4.6 shows total population in each of the six countries analysed, based on historical data (data or d) (solid lines) and projections (proj. or p) (dotted lines) from UN (2016). The values for the projections are taken from the scenario termed 'medium fertility variant'. France, Germany and Japan are on the right-axis. China and India are the two most populous countries in the world. They accounted for ca. 37% of the world population in 2015. Together, the six countries analysed accounted for ca. 45% of world population. In the same year, the total population of France and Germany represented ca. 28% of the total EU28 population. For these two countries, a few historical values slightly differ from those reported by Eurostat (2016).

4.2.2 Gross domestic product

An indication of economic wealth for each country, captured by the size of the economy as measured by the variable *gross domestic product* (GDP), is needed. In the model, this is expressed in per capita, nominal and real terms.

Figure 4.7 shows country-specific historical data and assumed future values for the *real GDP change rate*, in these cases *real GDP growth*, expressed as percentage per year. The base year, for this and the rest of real variables, is 2005 for Japan, 2009 for the US, 2011 for India and 2010 for the rest. The historical data and part of the projected values (2016-2021) are from IMF (2016). For the period 2022-2030, absence of information led the author to apply his own assumption, namely a martingale, where the best projection of a variable is its antecedent outcome (Hendry, 1995). For many economic time series, this type of naïve model (Simon, 1959) provides satisfactory results (Hyndman and Athanasopoulos, 2012).

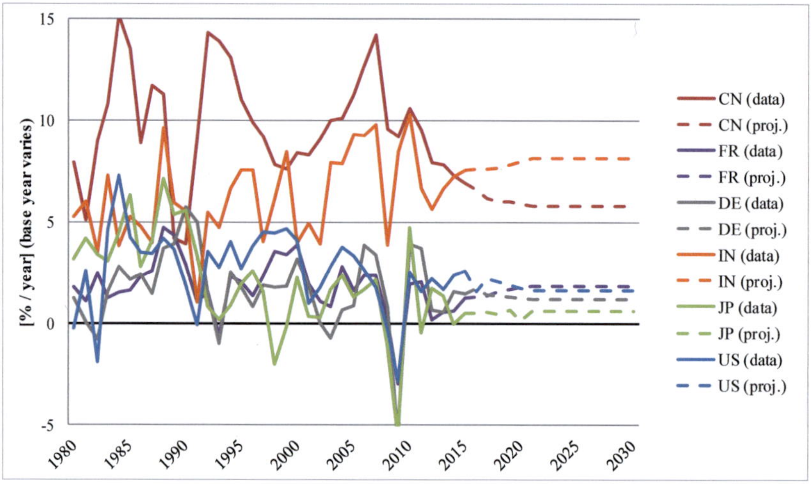

Figure 4.7: Real GDP change rate: data and projections
Source: Data (1980-2015) and projections (2016-2021) from IMF (2016) and own assumptions (2022-2030)

Based on the assumed future values from the previous figure and knowledge of initial values of *real GDP* [country currency], the behaviour over time of *real GDP* in each country currency (abbreviated as 'currency' in the equations) can be calculated. Recall from the white arrows in Figure 4.4 that these assumptions affect both the econometric and SD sub-models. The actual calculations to derive *real GDP* are different (see Eq. 4.1 for the econometric sub-model and Eq. 4.2 for the SD sub-model).

$$GDP_{h,t+1}^{real} \quad = \quad \frac{GDP\ change\ rate_{h,t+1}^{real}}{100} * GDP_{h,t}^{real} + GDP_{h,t}^{real} \tag{4.1}$$

Adopting a stock-and-flow structure in the SD sub-model, the assumptions of fractional rate of change, *real GDP change rate* [year^{-1}] (Figure 4.7), and the initial value of the stock variable *real GDP* [country currency] are used to determine the inflow variable *real GDP rate* [country currency/year].

$$GDP_h^{real}(t) = \int_{t_0}^{t} \left[\left(\frac{GDP\ change\ rate_h^{real}}{100} * GDP_h^{real} \right)(t) \right] dt + GDP_h^{real}(t_0) \tag{4.2}$$

[currency] [year^{-1}] [currency] [currency]

As a result of the different treatment each method gives to time, there is a discrepancy in the calculated values, unimportant for the modelling purpose. The results are shown, based on the SD values, in Figure 4.8.

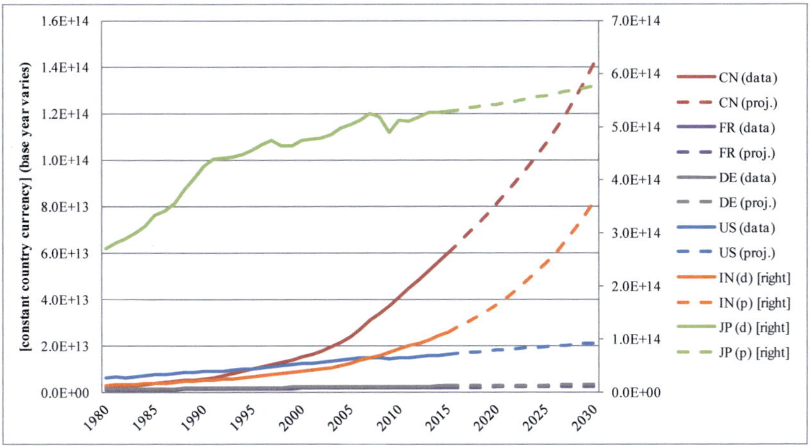

Figure 4.8: Real GDP: data and projections
Source: Data (1980-2015) and projections (2016-2021) from IMF (2016) and own assumptions (2022-2030)

These projections deliver an optimistic picture: no economic crisis is in sight during the model time horizon. The assumed overall trend shows economic growth. Ecological economics is the only school mentioned in section 3.1.3 with proponents of zero economic growth (i.e. steady-state economy; see Daly (1991)) or de-growth. No attempt has been made in this work at analysing the financial system. These projections are pragmatically adopted to proceed with the modelling exercise. In addition to considering economic indicators in real terms, such as $GDP_{h,t}^{real}$ [country currency], as needed for the econometric sub-model, it is of interest for the SD sub-model to work with variables in nominal as well as in dollar terms (i.e. $GDP_{h,t}^{nom}$ [dollar]).

4.2.3 Price level and exchange rates

Given the purpose of the model, the target model user is supposed to undertake policy analysis at the country level. In this modelling exercise, it is desirable to work with prices in dollar as well as in the currency units of the country where the economic policy is examined, both in nominal and real terms. The latter is done by considering the price level. The concept of purchasing power parity (PPP) is not applied. If country comparisons are needed, e.g. in the context of panel data econometric estimation, the consideration of PPP values becomes important. This is not the case in this work.

With regards to the price level, two common measures are the GDP deflator and the consumer price index (CPI), which often move closely (Blanchard, 2008). The assumptions concerning the price level, measured as annual *inflation* using the *GDP deflator* (abbreviated *GDP def*) [%/year] are shown in Figure 4.9. Using values from, the author calculated the assumed price level following Eq. 4.3.

$$inflation_{h,t} = \begin{cases} \left(\frac{(GDP\ def_{h,t+1} - GDP\ def_{h,t})}{GDP\ def_{h,t}}\right) * 100; & t < 2021 \\ inflation_{h,2020} & ; t \geq 2021 \end{cases} \tag{4.3}$$

Adopting these assumptions for the future price level, the implications for the GDP deflator [index] for each country are derived using the same type of formulae as in Eq. 4.1 and 4.2 for respectively the econometric and the SD part. The results, this time based on the dataset used for the econometric sub-model, are shown in Figure 4.10.

$$GDP\ def_{h,t} = \frac{price_{h,t}^{nom}}{price_{h,t}^{real}} \qquad \forall h, t \qquad (4.4)$$

Note that the GDP deflator reflects the assumption shown in Eq. 4.4 (see Blanchard (2008)). With this information, prices can thus be translated from real into nominal terms using Eq. 4.5.

$$price_{h,t}^{nom} = price_{h,t}^{real} * GDP\ def_{h,t} \qquad \forall h, t \qquad (4.5)$$

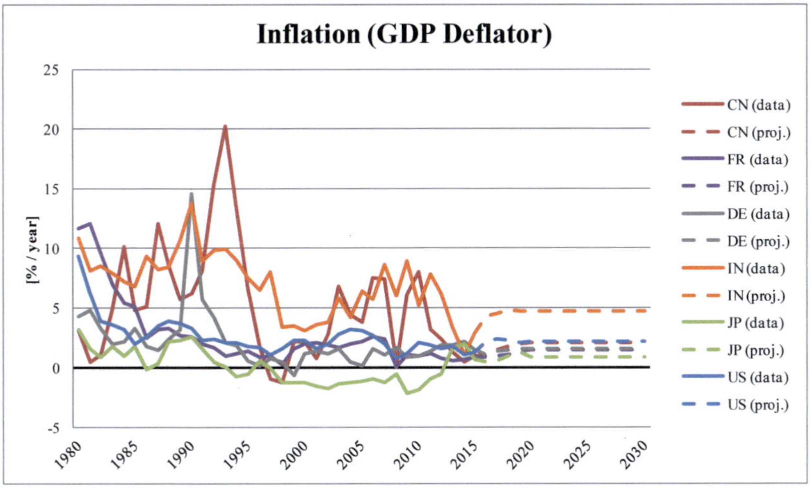

Figure 4.9: Price level: data and projections
Source: Own calculation (1980-2021) using IMF (2016) and own assumptions (2022-2030)

Two main variables are usually reported in dollar currency: oil price and the battery price. The price of a barrel is quoted in the international oil market in

US dollars [$] (see section 4.2.5), for which no adjustment is necessary if we are dealing only with the US market. However, for non-US countries the selection of the appropriate currency is required. This means that for China, France and Germany, India and Japan we are interested in expressing the relevant variables in their own currencies, respectively in yuan (renminbi) [¥], euro [€], rupee [₹] and yen [¥].

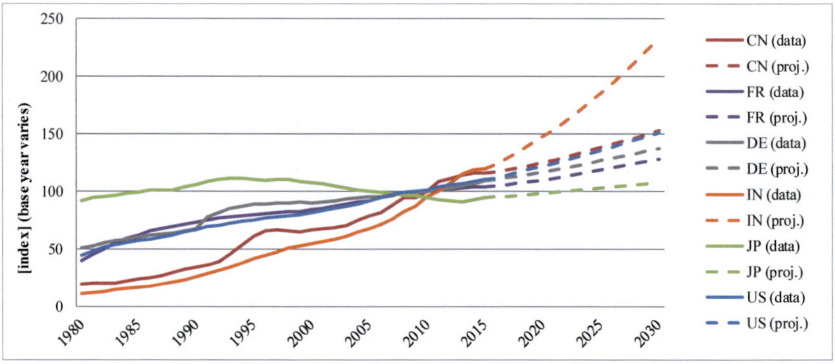

Figure 4.10: GDP deflator: data and projections
Source: Own calculation (1980-2021) using IMF (2016) and own assumptions (2022-2030)

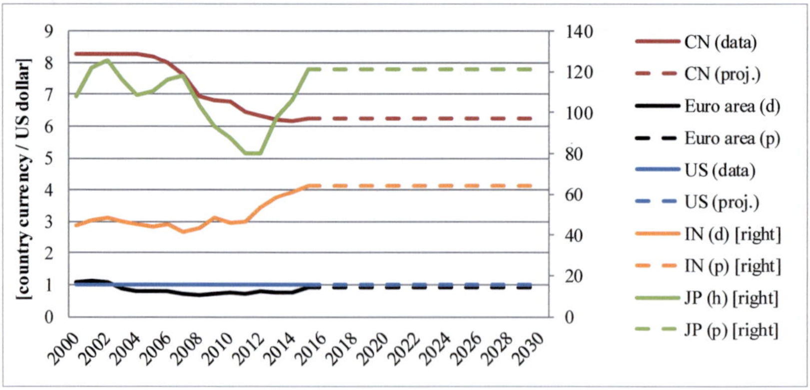

Figure 4.11: Exchange rates: data and projections
Source: Data (2000-2015) from WB (2016) and own assumptions (2016-2030)

In the model, there are two units used to denote currency: dollar and country currency. In the process of translating prices from dollars to other country currencies, an explicit consideration of the exchange rate is needed, for such a rate reflects the country price per unit of foreign currency (Eichengreen, 2008). The assumptions concerning the official nominal exchange rates ($exr_{h,t}^{nom}$), needed only for the SD sub-model, are shown in Figure 4.11.

As can be seen, stability in exchange rates is assumed. Moreover, it is implicitly assumed that France and Germany continue to be part of the monetary union. Successful model-based forecasts of exchange rates in a floating system have not been generated yet (Wray, 2015b). The assumed exchange rates shall be used to translate the oil price into country currencies.

4.2.4 Income per capita

GDP per capita is used as a proxy for disposable income per capita. The examination of income distribution and its impact on car ownership is desirable but beyond the scope of this work. Instead, the simplifying assumption of the average income per capita is adopted.

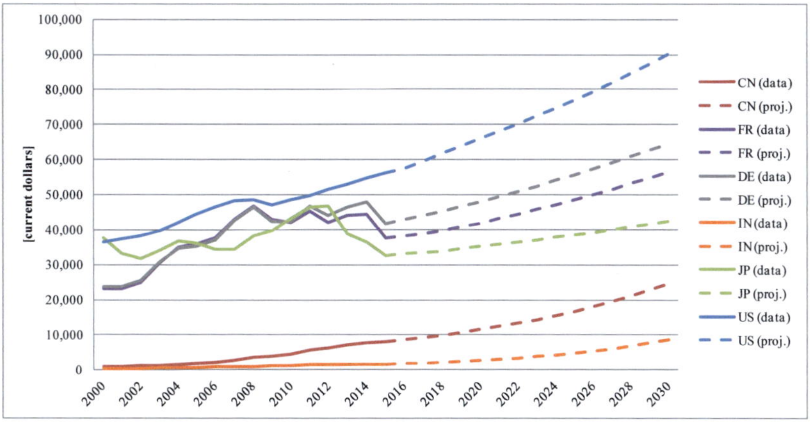

Figure 4.12: Nominal income per capita: data and projections
Source: Own calculation (2000-2021) using IMF (2016), WB (2016) and own assumptions (2022-2030) using UN (2016).

Based on the assumed values of real GDP, GDP deflator, exchange rates and population shown in the previous sections, the variable GDP per capita can be derived and expressed in real and nominal terms. Figure 4.12 shows *nominal income per capita in dollars*. Figure 4.13 shows *real income per capita*, expressed in relative terms taking the year 2000 as reference.

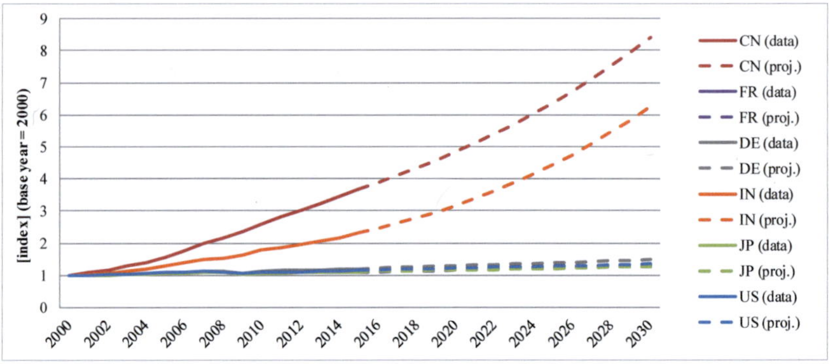

Figure 4.13: Real income per capita, indexed: data and projections
Source: Own assumptions based on IMF (2016) and WB (2016)

4.2.5 Conventional fuel prices I: crude oil prices

By conventional fuel it is meant the type of oil-based fuel that powers conventional cars, namely gasoline and diesel fuels. By conventional cars it is meant gasoline (G) and diesel (D) cars. The fuel price refers to the retail or end-user price that can be seen by drivers at the pump or fuel dispenser located in a refuelling station. The modelled fuel price consists of: (i) a tax part and (ii) the rest (i.e. non-tax). The tax part is usually expressed in the same unit of account of the retail price (i.e. [country currency/litre]). In contrast, the main component of the non-tax part is defined by the international oil market and is expressed in dollars per barrel of oil [dollar/bbl]. Calculations are needed to bring these components to a consistent unit of measurement (e.g. country currency/litre in Eq. 4.6, which shows the example for diesel).

The tax part is described in section 4.2.6, the terms $oil_{h,t}^{nom}$ and $v_{h,t}^{nom}$ are examined in this section. Whereas $oil_{h,t}^{nom}$ refers to the nominal price of crude oil; $v_{h,t}^{nom}$ denotes other costs, such us transport, refining, retailing (including marketing) and profit margins.

$$diesel_{h,t}^{nom} = \underbrace{oil_{h,t}^{nom} + v_{h,t}^{nom}}_{\text{non-tax}} + \underbrace{\tau_{h,t}^{nom} + VAT_{h,t}^{nom}}_{\text{tax}} \qquad \forall h,t \tag{4.6}$$

Figure 4.14 shows the historical data for oil_{t}^{nom}, expressed in terms of dollar/bbl. The barrel of reference is Brent. It also depicts three scenarios for future prices. These refer to the scenarios termed 'low oil price', 'reference case' and 'high oil price' by EIA (2016a).

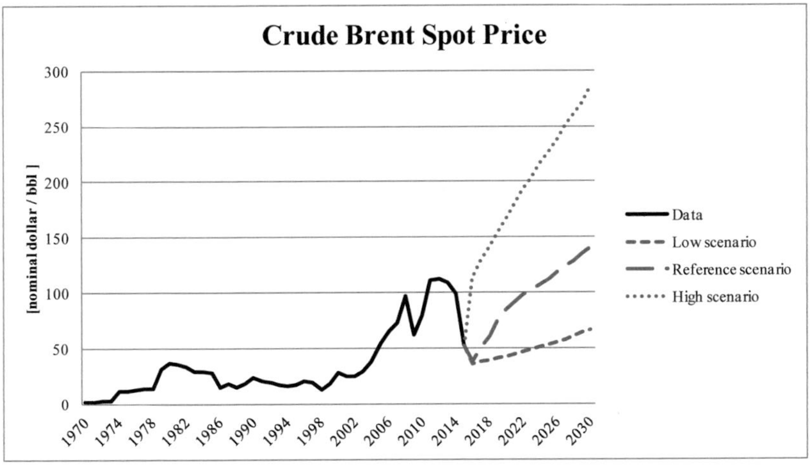

Figure 4.14: Oil price: data and scenarios
Source: Data (1970-2015) from (BP, 2016) and scenarios (2016-2030) from (EIA, 2016a)

As it currently stands, there is a mismatch of units in Eq. 4.6 if $oil_{h,t}^{nom}$ is measured in dollar/bbl. Hence there is a need to express this variable in country currency/litre. To achieve unit consistency, the following formulations (Eq. 4.7-4.8) are implemented in the SD sub-model.

$$oil_{h,t}^{nom,diesel} \quad = \quad exr_{h,t}^{nom} \quad * \quad \frac{oil_{h,t}^{nom}}{(159*(1+\theta_{h,t}^{diesel}))} \quad \forall h,t \qquad (4.7)$$

[currency/litre] [currency/dollar] [(dollar/bbl)/((litre/bbl)*dmnl)]

$$price_{h,t}^{nom} = price_{h,t}^{real} * GDP\ def_{h,t} \qquad \forall h,t \qquad (4.8)$$

One barrel is assumed to contain 159 litres of oil. The assumed constant average refinery oil processing gain is determined by θ, which reflects a value of 6%. As a reference, the 2000-2014 average for the US was 6.5% (DOE, 2016b). Again, exr denotes the official exchange rate.

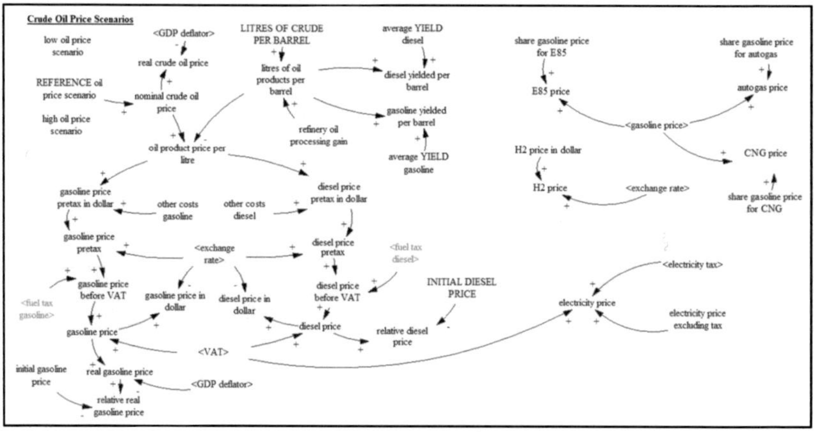

Figure 4.15: Overview of the sub-module 'Energy prices' | Source: Own work using Vensim®

4.2.6 Conventional fuel prices II: energy taxes

The tax part of the conventional fuel price can be split into: the *value added tax* (VAT) and the non-VAT concept. The assumptions concerning VAT from section 4.3.2 apply here. In this field, the non-VAT concept is commonly referred to as *energy tax* (e.g. the *taxe intérieure de consommation sur les produits énergétiques* (TICPE) (former *taxe intérieure de consommation sur les produits pétroliers* (TIPP)) in France and the *Energiesteuer* (former *Mineralölsteuer* in Germany). The International Energy Agency (IEA) names the non-VAT part of the tax *excise tax* (IEA, 2016b). In this work, the variables *fuel tax gasoline*, *fuel tax diesel* and *electricity tax* are chosen to represent non-VAT taxation of respectively gasoline, diesel and electricity. The introduction of an *eco tax* for conventional fuel, in addition to the *fuel tax*, has been suggested in policy debates. Although this may be motivated by public acceptability issues (the idea of 'framing' in behavioural economics comes into mind), the introduction of an *eco tax* can, from a modelling perspective, simply be represented in the model as higher values of the *energy tax*.

The assumptions concerning the tax part of energy prices can be amended by the policy inputs examined in sections 4.3.2 and 4.3.3.

Below Figures 4.16-19 show the historical and simulated price evolution of conventional fuels, expressed in nominal dollars, in China, India, Japan and the US. Historical data, available on a bi-annual basis, is taken from GIZ (2016). For France and Germany, annual data is available from IEA (2016b). Because of the assumptions concerning the exchange rates, the values of each source for the European countries vary slightly. Figures 4.20-21 show the historical and simulated price evolution of conventional fuels, expressed in nominal euros, in France and Germany.

For the period 2016-2030, the values of the reference scenario in Figure 4.14 are used to calculate the conventional fuel prices in each country. This can be appreciated in the French and German series.

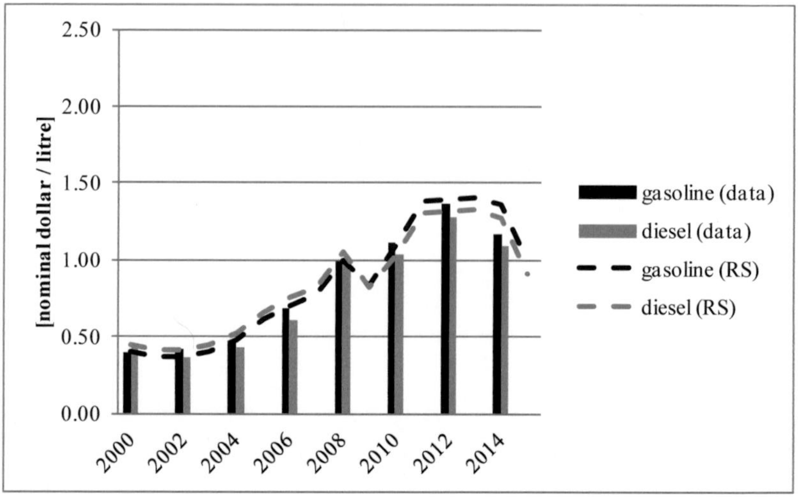

Figure 4.16: Fuel prices in China: data vs. simulations
Source: Data (2000-2014) from GIZ (2016) and own simulations (2000-2015) based on BP (2016) and IEA (2016b)

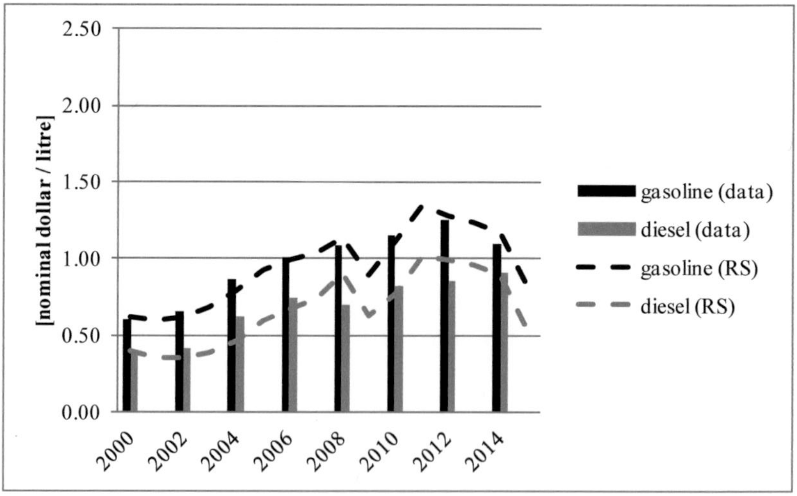

Figure 4.17: Fuel prices in India: data vs. simulations
Source: Data (2000-2014) from GIZ (2016) and own simulations (2000-2015) based on BP (2016) and IEA (2016b)

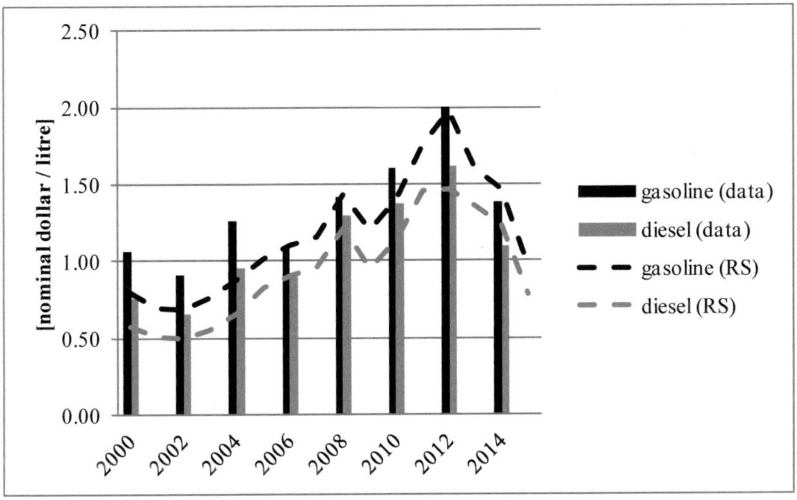

Figure 4.18: Fuel prices in Japan: data vs. simulations
Source: Data (2000-2014) from GIZ (2016) and own simulations (2000-2015) based on BP (2016) and IEA (2016b)

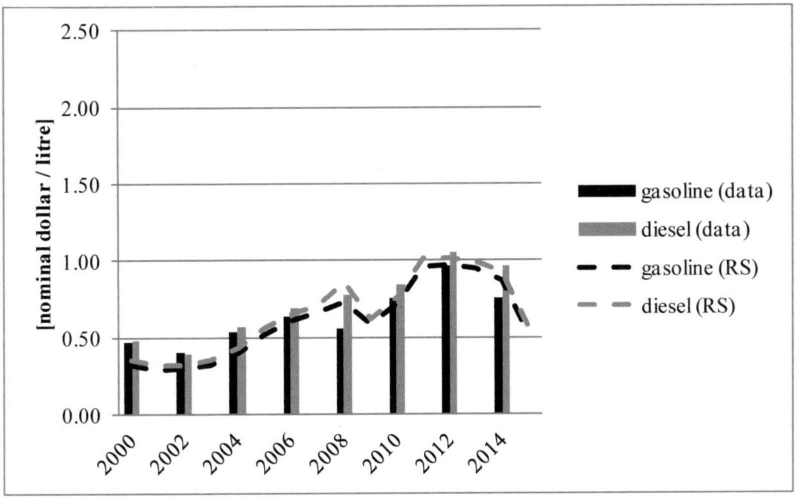

Figure 4.19: Fuel prices in US: data vs. simulations
Source: Data (2000-2014) from GIZ (2016) and own simulations (2000-2015) based on BP (2016) and IEA (2016b)

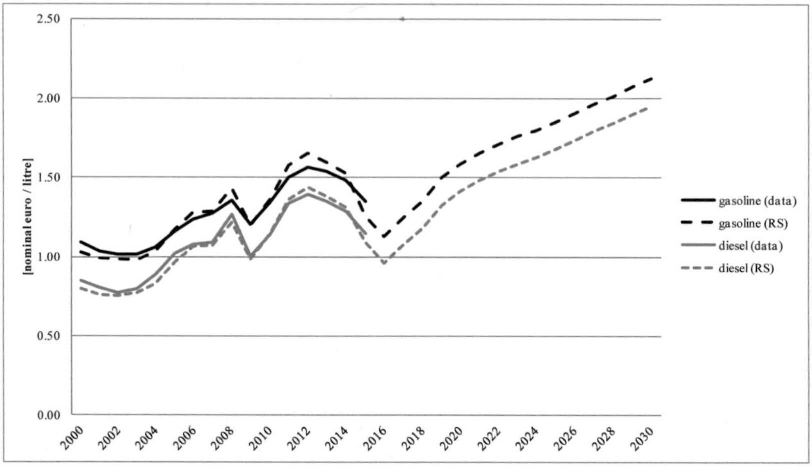

Figure 4.20: Fuel prices in France: data and scenarios
Source: Data (2000-2015) from IEA (2016b) and own simulations (2016-2030) using Fig. 4.14

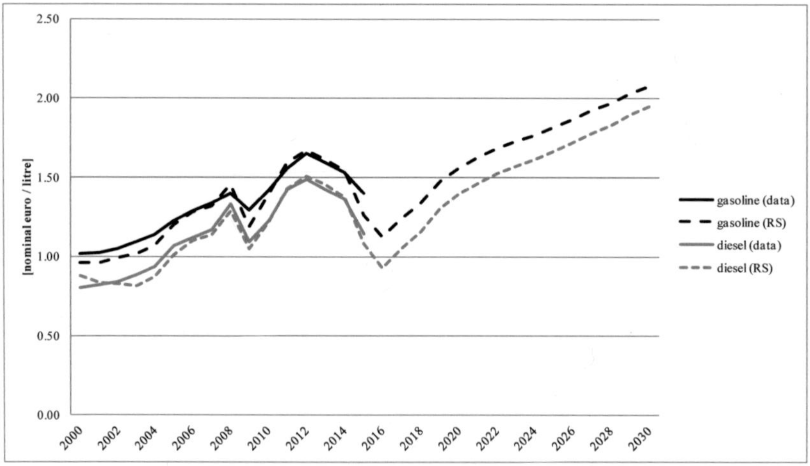

Figure 4.21: Fuel prices in Germany: data and scenarios
Source: Data (2000-2015) from IEA (2016b) and own simulations (2016-2030) using Fig. 4.14

4.2.7 Alternative fuel and electricity prices

In addition to the two types of conventional fuels mentioned in the previous sections, two types of alternative fuels are considered in this work: (i) liquids such as ethanol 85 (E85) and autogas (also known as propane in the US); and (ii) gases such as CNG and hydrogen (H_2). Finally, electricity completes the set of seven energy sources incorporated in the model. Three types of energy units are appropriate: litre, kilogramme [kg] and kilowatt-hour [kWh]. They are used to express the price of alternative fuels and electricity (see Figure 4.22). Taken collectively, conventional fuel, alternative fuel and electricity prices reflect the modelled energy prices. These assumptions are part of the *Energy Prices* sub-module of the *Energy* module. The prices of electricity, conventional and alternative fuels influence the choice of powertrain by the market. For EV drivers, the electricity price is thought to be the end-user price displayed in a recharging column or smart meter and billed by the electric utility.

E85 is one main type of biofuel (see Magdoff (2008) for others). Its inclusion in the model is motivated by recent policy discussions concerning the role of biofuels along two lines: (i) as a source of competition between food and vehicle fuel (Hill *et al.*, 2006) (Magdoff and Foster, 2011); and (ii) as an instrument to mitigate emissions (Scharlemann and Laurance, 2008) (see section 4.2.13).

The assumed fuel price is used to estimate travel demand tentatively. For the econometric sub-model, considered next, the assumed *fuel price* (again gasoline only, for simplicity) is used as a potential explanatory variable for France, Germany and the US. For the rest, given the absence of reliable historical data, the assumed *oil price* is used as a proxy.

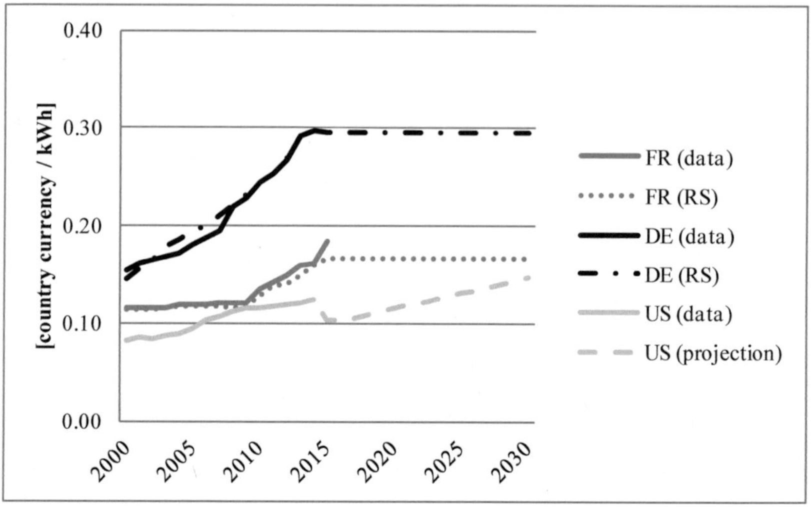

Figure 4.22: Electricity prices for households: data and simulations
Source: Data (2000-2015) from IEA (2016b), projection for the US from EIA (2016a) and own simulations (2016-2030)

4.2.8 Car ownership

Notwithstanding that forecasting is not the purpose of the model (recall section 3.5), it is desirable to have acceptable forecasts of key variables. It is argued that *car ownership* is, in this regard, the most crucial variable of the modelling exercise. It is common in the literature to measure *car ownership* (own) as the ratio between *aggregate total car stock* (car) and *population* (pop), typically expressed in *car ownership per capita* [car/person] (often scaled to ownership per 1,000 people [car/thousand people]). The convention is followed here. For the US, this variable excludes minivans, pick-up trucks and SUVs. As a result, no conclusions should be drawn on the number of passenger vehicles in this country. The reason for this exclusion is because these three types of vehicles have higher fuel consumption than passenger cars, which requires significant additional modelling efforts. The Japanese *kei* cars represent another example, at the opposite extreme.

Economic theory provides clues about the multiple factors that determine the demand for cars (see e.g. Gómez Vilchez (2016a)). The information set available to the author at the time of writing conditions the econometric exercise. Access to reliable data for most of the a priori variables of interest is pending.

Previous econometric research on car ownership has been surveyed by the author elsewhere (see section 2 in Gómez Vilchez (2016a)). Worth mentioning is the GETS modelling approach adopted by Romilly *et al.* (1998) and Romilly *et al.* (2001). For the UK, Romilly *et al.* (1998) found that only three of the eight explanatory variables they examined were statistically significant: real personal disposable income per capita, real motoring cost index, real bus fare index. Here, the real fuel price (the real oil price, given lack of data, for CN, IN, JP) is used as a proxy for the real motoring cost. They also found a co-integrating relationship between car ownership per capita and the three explanatory variables using a sample of 42 observations.

ARIMA modelling typically requires a minimum of 50, and preferably 100, observations (Box and Jenkins, 1976). Unit root and co-integration testing is also subject to small-sample bias. The available series of y contain: 35 (CN), 55 (FR), 46 (DE), 34 (IN), 56 (JP), 55 (US) historical observations. This is, however, the longest series, and other variables are characterised by $T = 35$. As a result, this piece of applied work is not fully unproblematic (see section 7.2). Since this work proceeds with a small sample, it is therefore pertinent to ask whether an appropriate approximation of the underlying data-generation process (DGP) of the analysed series is possible with the available information.

This section focuses on the econometric results of modelling car ownership. In what follows, six single-equation models are introduced. Along the way, brief detours to describe specific modelling issues in each sub-section are offered. As part of the econometric exercise, some pre-testing has been carried out. The presentation of the outcomes of these tests is postponed to section 5.2.1, devoted to testing. The interested reader may prefer to read that section now, before checking the estimated equations.

4.2.8.1 Car ownership in China

In addition to analysing the levels of the series, it is desirable to inspect changes and relative changes after applying suitable transformations (Kirchgässner *et al.*, 2012). A common one is the economic approximation illustrated by Brandt and Williams (2007). First differencing helps remove the trend and the log transformation can stabilise the variance (Lütkepohl and Krätzig, 2004). In addition, the latter can be usefully exploited in the presence of an exact unit root and cointegration (Banerjee *et al.*, 1993).

The time plots of own and Δown as well as their counterparts expressed in natural logarithms (henceforth, for short logs) are shown for CN in Figure 4.23.

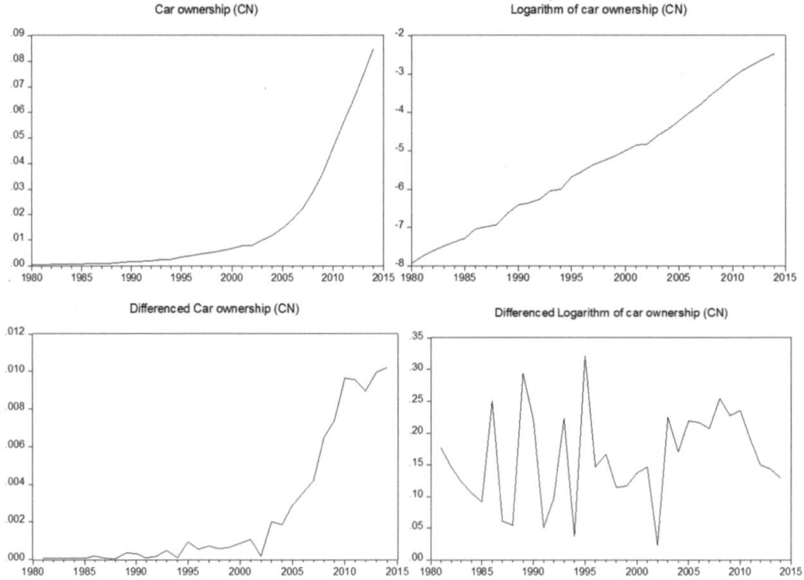

Figure 4.23: Key time plots for China
Source: Own work using EViews® (see appendix I for dataset sources)

The visual conclusion is that the variable of interest is nonstationary. Nonstationarity may be investigated by means of fractionally integrated processes, discrete shifts in the time trend (Hamilton, 1994) or, as in this work, unit root tests. In the next sections, this property of the series is examined more carefully (formal tests are illustrated in section 5.2.1).

The value of $\hat{\rho}_{k=1}$ for the natural log of own ($lown$) is 0.913. The correlogram of $lown$, which provides information on the sample autocorrelation (AC) and sample partial autocorrelation (PAC), is shown in Figure 4.24.

At this point, two possible modelling paths emerge: ARIMA or ADL modelling (recall section 3.2.2.1).

From the perspective of this work, one unsatisfactory feature of ARIMA models is that they are statistical, not economic models (Vogelvang, 2004). Economic theory suggests a relationship between consumer durables and income, which in the literature appear to have unit roots. For this reason, this work attempts to embrace the ADL alternative. Notwithstanding, it is still desirable to estimate ARIMA models so that model comparisons can be made and their respective forecasts evaluated (see section 5.2.2). A final remark before embarking on model specification and estimation: EViews® has a feature that enables automatic selection of ARIMA and ADL models; by applying it, models with lower forecasting errors than the ones reported in this thesis may be found.

As suggested by economic theory, the variable *real income per capita* ($rinc\_country$) is used in the econometric sub-model. For this, the assumptions highlighted in section 4.2.4 are adopted. Figure 4.25 shows a time plot of this series in logs.

Autocorrelation	Partial Correlation		AC	PAC	Q-Stat	Prob
		1	-0.093	-0.093	0.3195	0.572
		2	-0.015	-0.024	0.3284	0.849
		3	0.171	0.169	1.4880	0.685
		4	0.043	0.077	1.5635	0.815
		5	-0.144	-0.134	2.4409	0.785
		6	0.045	-0.011	2.5310	0.865
		7	-0.144	-0.169	3.4689	0.839
		8	-0.052	-0.039	3.5956	0.892
		9	-0.062	-0.064	3.7812	0.925
		10	0.007	0.031	3.7836	0.957
		11	0.042	0.093	3.8782	0.973
		12	-0.081	-0.089	4.2412	0.979
		13	-0.043	-0.073	4.3505	0.987
		14	0.136	0.065	5.4789	0.978
		15	0.101	0.151	6.1316	0.977
		16	-0.078	-0.031	6.5486	0.981

Figure 4.24: Correlogram of $\Delta lown$ for China | Source: Own work using EViews®

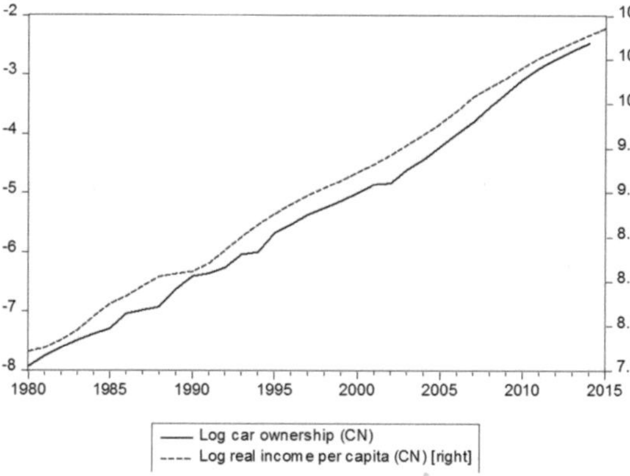

Figure 4.25: Car ownership and real income in China
Source: Own work using EViews® (see appendix I for dataset sources)

The second modelling path entails the specification and estimation of ADL equations. Firstly, a static linear regression or ADL(0,0) is specified in logs as in Eq. 4.9.

$$lown_t = \beta_0 + \beta_1 lrinc_t + \varepsilon_t \tag{4.9}$$

The results of estimating such a relationship for China are shown in Table 4.3. This output hints at problematic issues that shall be examined in this section and in section 5.2. Suffice to state here that the fact that R^2 is greater than the Durbin-Watson (DW) statistic is a signal that the regression may be spurious (Granger and Newbold, 1974). Using time series to estimate a static regression results in a model affected by residual autocorrelation because it omits dynamics (Hendry, 1995). To avoid this, two main steps can be followed: (i) specify and estimate the general, unrestricted ADL model; and (ii) test restrictions (Charemza and Deadman, 1997).

Table 4.3: First static regression on Chinese *lown*

Dependent Variable: LOWN_CN
Method: Least Squares

Sample: 1980 2010
Included observations: 31

Variable	Coefficient	Std. Error	t-Statistic	Prob.
C	-22.09397	0.214207	-103.1432	0.0000
LRINC_CN	1.822443	0.023732	76.79193	0.0000

R-squared	0.995106	Mean dependent var	-5.703227
Adjusted R-squared	0.994938	S.D. dependent var	1.413748
S.E. of regression	0.100589	Akaike info criterion	-1.693200
Sum squared resid	0.293428	Schwarz criterion	-1.600685
Log likelihood	28.24461	Hannan-Quinn criter.	-1.663043
F-statistic	5897.001	Durbin-Watson stat	0.988593
Prob(F-statistic)	0.000000		

Source: Own work using EViews®

What about including additional explanatory variables? An available candidate is the log of the real oil price ($lroil$). The effect of adding this variable to the previous regression is illustrated in Table 4.4.

In addition to the problems pointed out for the results shown in Table 4.3, the estimated parameter for $lroil$ in Table 4.4 has a sign that is contrary to theoretical expectations.

Table 4.4: Second static regression on Chinese *lown*

Dependent Variable: LOWN_CN
Method: Least Squares

Sample: 1980 2010
Included observations: 31

Variable	Coefficient	Std. Error	t-Statistic	Prob.
C	-22.52347	0.298744	-75.39382	0.0000
LRINC_CN	1.841796	0.024673	74.64784	0.0000
LROIL_CN	0.062482	0.031709	1.970451	0.0587

R-squared	0.995702	Mean dependent var	-5.703227
Adjusted R-squared	0.995395	S.D. dependent var	1.413748
S.E. of regression	0.095934	Akaike info criterion	-1.758543
Sum squared resid	0.257694	Schwarz criterion	-1.619770
Log likelihood	30.25741	Hannan-Quinn criter.	-1.713306
F-statistic	3243.531	Durbin-Watson stat	1.115349
Prob(F-statistic)	0.000000		

Source: Own work using EViews®

To add dynamism to the regression, a lagged dependent variable $lown_{t-1}$ (in EViews® $lown(-1)$) is now included (see Eq. 4.10). The estimated output is shown in Table 4.5.

$$lown_t = \beta_0 + \beta_1 lown_{t-1} + \beta_2 lrinc_t + \varepsilon_t \qquad (4.10)$$

Though appropriate for ARIMA modelling, the *Q*-stat should not be used for residuals of a stochastic difference equation (Harvey, 1990). To test for serial correlation, the Breusch-Godfrey Lagrange multiplier serial correlation LMSC test, or BG(p) test, is used (Breusch, 1978) (Godfrey, 1978). The null hypothesis is that there is no autocorrelation up to the predefined lag order p. For Eq. 4.10, a value of $p = 2$ is selected, that is, testing for second-order autocorrelation. The following decision rule applies: if prob-values are close to zero, then reject the null; otherwise, do not reject. In this case, the BG-test stat (Obs*R-squared) is 2.03 and its associated probability value (Prob), based on $\chi^2(p)$, is 0.36 or 36%. Hence, do not reject the null.

Table 4.5: Dynamic regression on Chinese *lown*

Dependent Variable: LOG(OWN_CN)
Method: Least Squares

Sample (adjusted): 1981 2010
Included observations: 30 after adjustments

Variable	Coefficient	Std. Error	t-Statistic	Prob.
C	-5.329780	3.210324	-1.660200	0.1084
LOWN_CN(-1)	0.763419	0.145966	5.230133	0.0000
LRINC_CN	0.456193	0.261940	1.741591	0.0930

R-squared	0.997342	Mean dependent var	-5.628924
Adjusted R-squared	0.997145	S.D. dependent var	1.374974
S.E. of regression	0.073469	Akaike info criterion	-2.289257
Sum squared resid	0.145739	Schwarz criterion	-2.149137
Log likelihood	37.33886	Hannan-Quinn criter.	-2.244432
F-statistic	5065.108	Durbin-Watson stat	2.183791
Prob(F-statistic)	0.000000		

Source: Own work using EViews®

A normality test is the Jarque-Bera (JB), which tests the null that the residuals are normally distributed (see EViews (2016) for details). Figure 4.26 shows the results of this test for Eq. 4.10. Hence the normality assumption is not rejected.

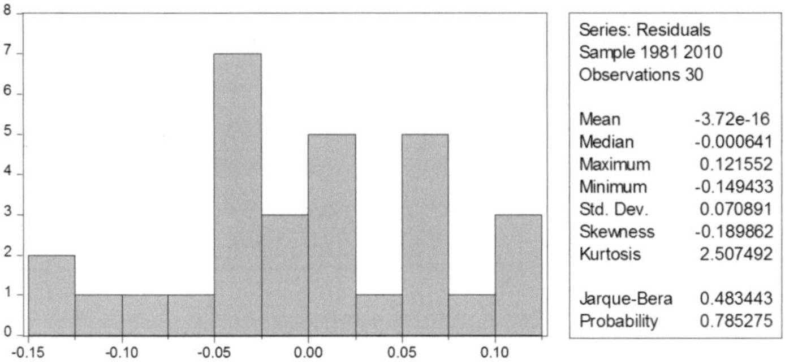

Figure 4.26: Jarque-Bera test on Chinese dynamic regression | Source: Own work using EViews®

When the equation includes lagged dependent variables, dynamic simulation is used to derive forecasts (see EViews (2016) for details). Based on Eq. 4.10, a forecast, together with standard error (S.E.) bands, is generated (see Figure 4.27). The quality of this projection is assessed in section 5.2.2.

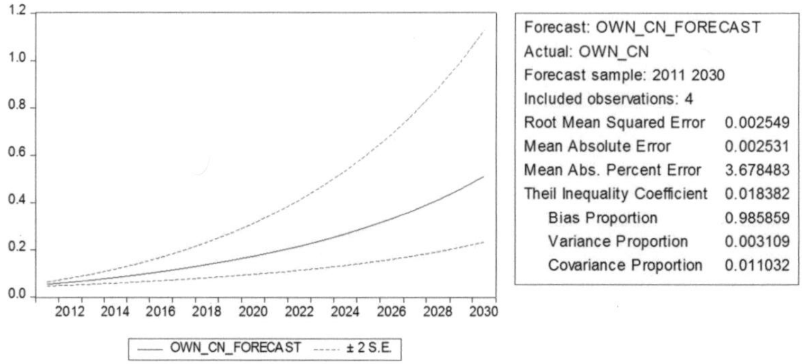

Figure 4.27: Projections of car ownership in China | Source: Own work using EViews®

The historical data and assumed future values for population and GPD per capita were shown in, respectively, section 4.2.1 and 4.2.4. In addition, the assumptions concerning crude oil and fuel prices were mentioned in sections 4.2.5 and 4.2.6.

4.2.8.2 Car ownership in France

Figure 4.28 shows own, $lown$, Δown and $\Delta lown$ for the French series.

ARIMA models are a powerful way of representing the past behaviour of a series under the assumption that it is, or in some cases can be made, stationary (i.e. $y \sim I(0)$). This means that the series' distribution is independent from time (Stock and Watson, 1988) and "*the process remains in* equilibrium *about a* constant mean level" (Box and Jenkins, 1976: 7).

The goal is to find an ARIMA model of $lown$ that shows no residual autocorrelation and contain few p and q statistically significant terms. The choice of these terms is guided by the information shown in the correlograms

(Figures 4.29-4.30) (see Figure 1.7 in Box and Jenkins (1976) for their proposed stages in ARIMA model building).

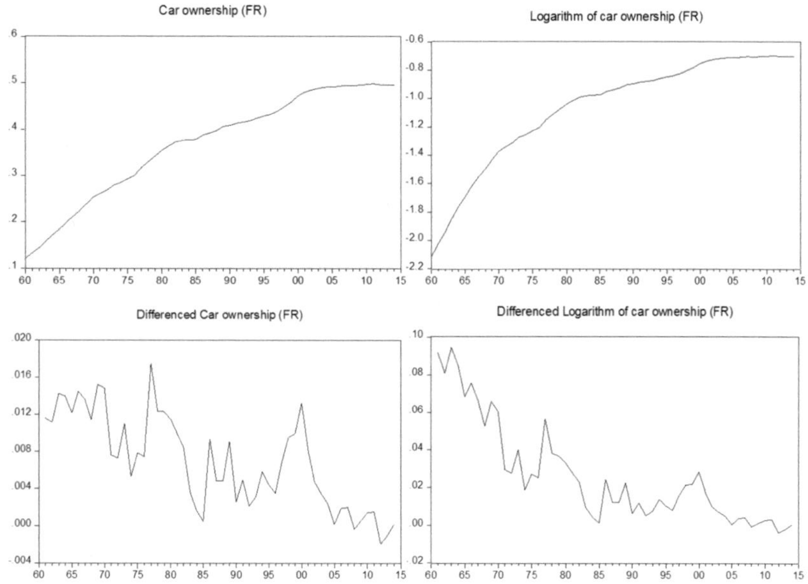

Figure 4.28: Key time plots for France
Source: Own work using EViews® (see appendix I for dataset sources)

For France, the value of $\hat{\rho}_{k=1}$ for $\boldsymbol{lown}$ is 0.918. The correlogram of $\boldsymbol{\Delta lown}$ can be seen in Figure 4.29. This information can be used to inform initial model specifications.

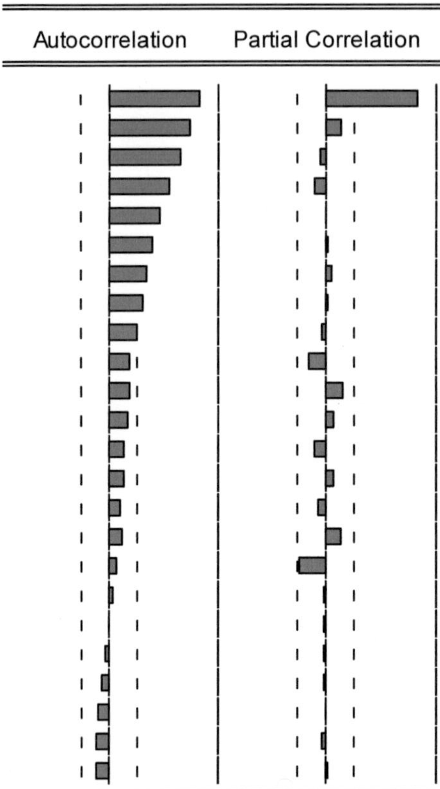

Lag	AC	PAC	Q-Stat	Prob
1	0.854	0.854	41.640	0.000
2	0.771	0.152	76.208	0.000
3	0.675	-0.053	103.19	0.000
4	0.569	-0.101	122.77	0.000
5	0.486	0.004	137.35	0.000
6	0.412	0.010	148.07	0.000
7	0.359	0.043	156.38	0.000
8	0.317	0.024	163.00	0.000
9	0.272	-0.034	167.97	0.000
10	0.197	-0.158	170.65	0.000
11	0.189	0.164	173.16	0.000
12	0.174	0.069	175.34	0.000
13	0.133	-0.114	176.65	0.000
14	0.135	0.067	178.03	0.000
15	0.105	-0.071	178.88	0.000
16	0.125	0.149	180.12	0.000
17	0.066	-0.249	180.48	0.000
18	0.027	-0.021	180.54	0.000
19	-0.007	-0.009	180.54	0.000
20	-0.039	-0.015	180.68	0.000
21	-0.075	-0.019	181.20	0.000
22	-0.104	-0.006	182.23	0.000
23	-0.117	-0.030	183.56	0.000
24	-0.130	0.015	185.27	0.000

Figure 4.29: Correlogram of $\Delta lown$ for France | Source: Own work using EViews®

Because the SACF tappers off slowly and the probabilities (Prob) associated with the Q-statistic are zero, the hypothesis that this French series is $\Delta^2 lown$ may be conjectured. The correlogram in second differences is shown in Figure 4.30.

Autocorrelation	Partial Correlation		AC	PAC	Q-Stat	Prob
		1	-0.316	-0.316	5.5889	0.018
		2	-0.104	-0.226	6.2072	0.045
		3	0.169	0.067	7.8708	0.049
		4	0.017	0.094	7.8871	0.096
		5	-0.172	-0.112	9.6819	0.085
		6	-0.061	-0.199	9.9136	0.128
		7	0.087	-0.064	10.395	0.167
		8	-0.149	-0.148	11.827	0.159
		9	0.211	0.209	14.789	0.097
		10	-0.075	0.023	15.174	0.126
		11	0.062	0.090	15.443	0.163
		12	0.024	-0.004	15.485	0.216
		13	-0.015	-0.034	15.502	0.277
		14	0.160	0.231	17.408	0.235
		15	-0.340	-0.241	26.252	0.035
		16	0.140	-0.003	27.796	0.033
		17	0.031	0.019	27.874	0.046
		18	-0.057	0.003	28.143	0.060
		19	0.013	0.154	28.159	0.080
		20	0.088	-0.000	28.840	0.091
		21	-0.035	-0.074	28.949	0.115
		22	0.020	0.074	28.986	0.145
		23	0.083	-0.046	29.659	0.159
		24	-0.138	0.093	31.571	0.138

Figure 4.30: Correlogram of $\Delta^2 lown$ for France | Source: Own work using EViews®

In the case of France, the analysis so far suggests that an $ARIMA(p, 2, q)$ model is appropriate. An ARIMA model is specified as in Eq. 4.11.

$$\Delta^2 lown_t = \beta_0 + \varepsilon_t + \beta_1 \varepsilon_{t-1} \qquad (4.11)$$

Table 4.6 shows the corresponding estimates of the ARIMA(0,2,1) model. The estimator used to estimate the ARIMA model is maximum likelihood (ML) (see any of the cited econometric textbooks and EViews (2016) for details). The ARIMA model requires that the roots of the polynomial lie outside the unit circle (Charemza and Deadman, 1997).

Table 4.6: ARIMA model for French *lown*

Dependent Variable: D((LOG(OWN_FR)),2)
Method: ARMA Maximum Likelihood (OPG - BHHH)

Sample: 1962 2010
Included observations: 49
Convergence achieved after 32 iterations
Coefficient covariance computed using outer product of gradients

Variable	Coefficient	Std. Error	t-Statistic	Prob.
C	-0.001808	0.000946	-1.910971	0.0623
MA(1)	-0.384128	0.172781	-2.223201	0.0312
SIGMASQ	0.000104	1.51E-05	6.864628	0.0000

R-squared	0.130083	Mean dependent var	-0.001809
Adjusted R-squared	0.092260	S.D. dependent var	0.011040
S.E. of regression	0.010519	Akaike info criterion	-6.208829
Sum squared resid	0.005089	Schwarz criterion	-6.093003
Log likelihood	155.1163	Hannan-Quinn criter.	-6.164885
F-statistic	3.439300	Durbin-Watson stat	1.985430
Prob(F-statistic)	0.040550		

Inverted MA Roots	.38

Source: Own work using EViews®

A value of 0.38 is reported for the inverted MA roots, which meets the criterion that the inverted roots lie within the unit circle (Vogelvang, 2004) (see Figure 4.31).

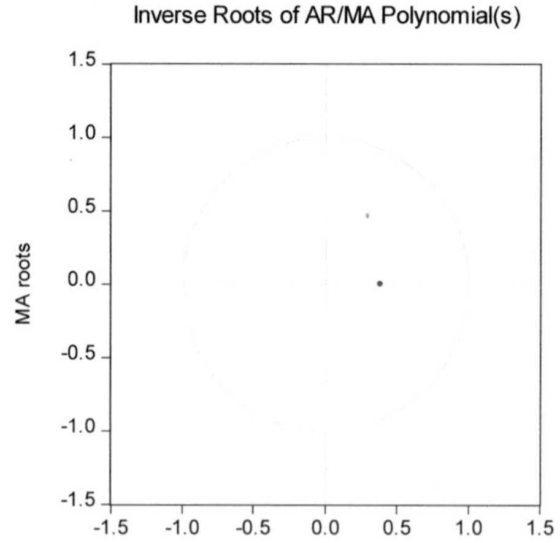

Figure 4.31: Roots of the French ARIMA(0,2,1) model | Source: Own work using EViews®

The Ljung-Box Q-statistics test specifies the null that there is no autocorrelation at lag k. That is, the Q-stat values indicate whether the residuals are white noise up to order k (see EViews (2016) for details). The correlogram of the residuals, which includes Q-stat, from Eq. 4.11 is shown in Figure 4.32. The null of white noise residuals up to order 16 cannot be rejected.

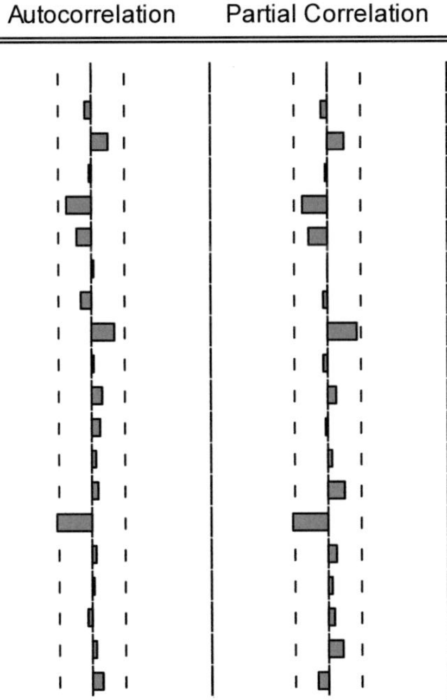

	AC	PAC	Q-Stat	Prob
1	-0.002	-0.002	0.0001	
2	-0.055	-0.055	0.1582	0.691
3	0.147	0.147	1.3350	0.513
4	-0.017	-0.021	1.3509	0.717
5	-0.226	-0.215	4.2442	0.374
6	-0.126	-0.158	5.1734	0.395
7	0.013	-0.003	5.1839	0.520
8	-0.083	-0.031	5.6069	0.586
9	0.196	0.251	8.0011	0.433
10	0.022	-0.030	8.0335	0.531
11	0.089	0.069	8.5576	0.575
12	0.080	-0.013	8.9900	0.623
13	0.034	0.025	9.0693	0.697
14	0.065	0.138	9.3744	0.744
15	-0.304	-0.298	16.182	0.302
16	0.034	0.077	16.267	0.365
17	0.018	0.025	16.292	0.433
18	-0.034	0.051	16.388	0.497
19	0.035	0.124	16.488	0.559
20	0.089	-0.094	17.167	0.579

Figure 4.32: Correlogram of the residuals for France | Source: Own work using EViews®

Figure 4.33 shows the French *lrinc* and *lown* series. As indicated in section 5.2.1, the possibility of a cointegration relationship between these two series is not formally investigated.

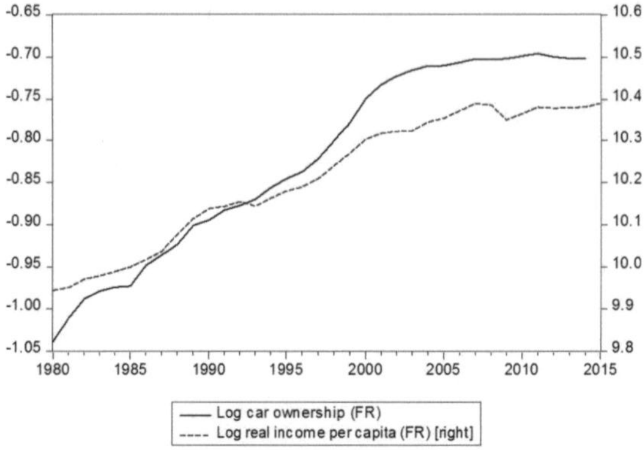

Figure 4.33: Car ownership and real income in France
Source: Own work using EViews® (see appendix I for dataset sources)

Using the estimated ARIMA(0,2,1) model, projections for the French car ownership series are computed (see Figure 4.34).

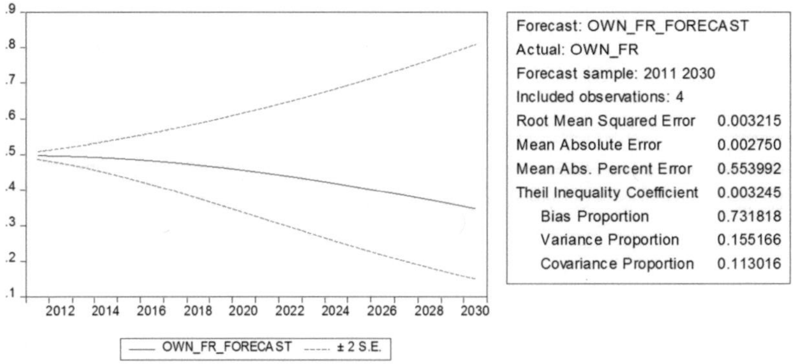

Figure 4.34: Projections of car ownership in France | Source: Own work using EViews®

4.2.8.3 Car ownership in Germany

For Germany, the time plots of own, $lown$, Δown and $\Delta lown$ are shown in Figure 4.35. For this series, the presence of a temporary change in level is obvious. The possibility of structural breaks is examined in section 5.2.1.

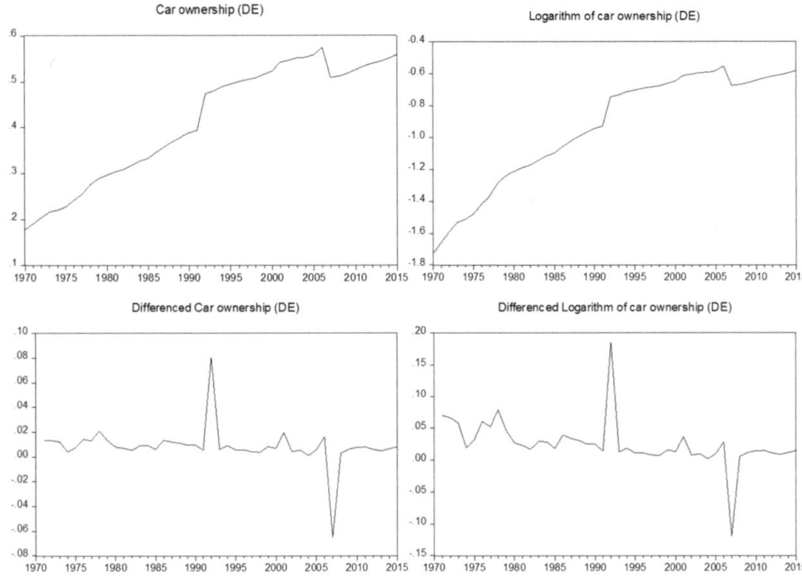

Figure 4.35: Key time plots for Germany
Source: Own work using EViews® (see appendix I for dataset sources)

A value of $\hat{\rho}_{k=1}$= 0.925 is obtained for $lown$. Figure 4.36 shows the correlogram of this series in first differences. Figure 4.37 illustrates the dynamic behaviour of $lown$ and $lrinc$. The effect of the recent economic crisis on income per capita is visible.

The possibility of two breaks is included in the estimation process. For that, a dummy (*dum*) variable that takes the value of 1 from 1992-2006 is created.

Autocorrelation	Partial Correlation		AC	PAC	Q-Stat	Prob
		1	0.137	0.137	0.8993	0.343
		2	0.158	0.142	2.1322	0.344
		3	0.109	0.074	2.7323	0.435
		4	0.110	0.070	3.3594	0.500
		5	0.162	0.123	4.7486	0.447
		6	0.107	0.050	5.3660	0.498
		7	0.105	0.043	5.9777	0.542
		8	0.081	0.023	6.3510	0.608
		9	0.117	0.064	7.1525	0.621
		10	0.008	-0.060	7.1567	0.711
		11	0.021	-0.031	7.1840	0.784
		12	-0.002	-0.038	7.1844	0.845
		13	0.048	0.026	7.3353	0.884
		14	0.194	0.178	9.9001	0.769
		15	-0.283	-0.365	15.546	0.413
		16	0.071	0.120	15.912	0.459
		17	-0.023	0.007	15.950	0.527
		18	-0.068	-0.106	16.317	0.570
		19	0.011	0.046	16.327	0.635
		20	0.009	0.072	16.334	0.696

Figure 4.36: Correlogram of $\Delta lown$ for Germany | Source: Own work using EViews®

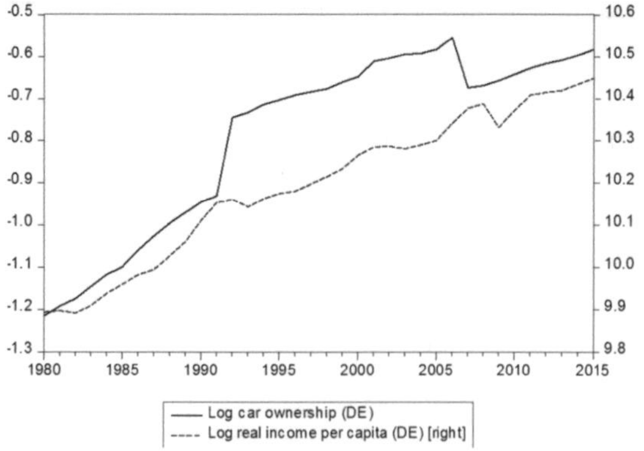

Figure 4.37: Car ownership and real income in Germany
Source: Own work using EViews® (see appendix I for dataset sources)

Table 4.7: Dynamic regression on German *lown*

Dependent Variable: LOWN_DE				
Method: Least Squares				
Sample (adjusted): 1981 2010				
Included observations: 30 after adjustments				
Variable	Coefficient	Std. Error	t-Statistic	Prob.
C	-8.000563	1.037753	-7.709504	0.0000
LOWN_DE(-1)	0.268687	0.079822	3.366093	0.0024
LRINC_DE(-1)	0.725367	0.095632	7.585004	0.0000
DUM	0.114996	0.012339	9.319944	0.0000
R-squared	0.992353	Mean dependent var		-0.803207
Adjusted R-squared	0.991471	S.D. dependent var		0.210070
S.E. of regression	0.019401	Akaike info criterion		-4.923455
Sum squared resid	0.009786	Schwarz criterion		-4.736628
Log likelihood	77.85182	Hannan-Quinn criter.		-4.863687
F-statistic	1124.709	Durbin-Watson stat		1.222879
Prob(F-statistic)	0.000000			

Source: Own work using EViews®

A dynamic model is specified following Eq. 4.12. The estimator used to estimate the ADL model is ordinary least squares (OLS) (see any of the cited econometric textbooks and EViews (2016) for details). The relevant output is shown in Table 4.7.

$$lown_t = \beta_0 + \beta_1 lown_{t-1} + \beta_2 lrinc_{t-1} + dum + \varepsilon_t \qquad (4.12)$$

The estimated model yields statistically significant parameters. Both the assumptions of normality and no serial correlation cannot be rejected. Projections of car ownership in Germany based on this model are made. The future values of this series are depicted in Figure 4.38.

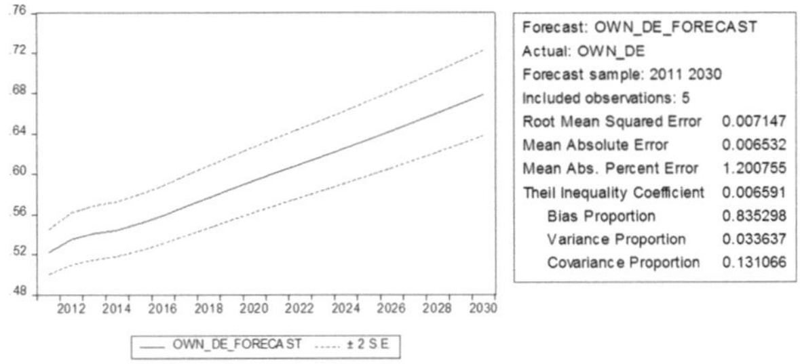

Figure 4.38: Projections of car ownership in Germany | Source: Own work using EViews®

4.2.8.4 Car ownership in India

Figure 4.39 shows the dynamic behaviour of own, $lown$, Δown and $\Delta lown$ for India.

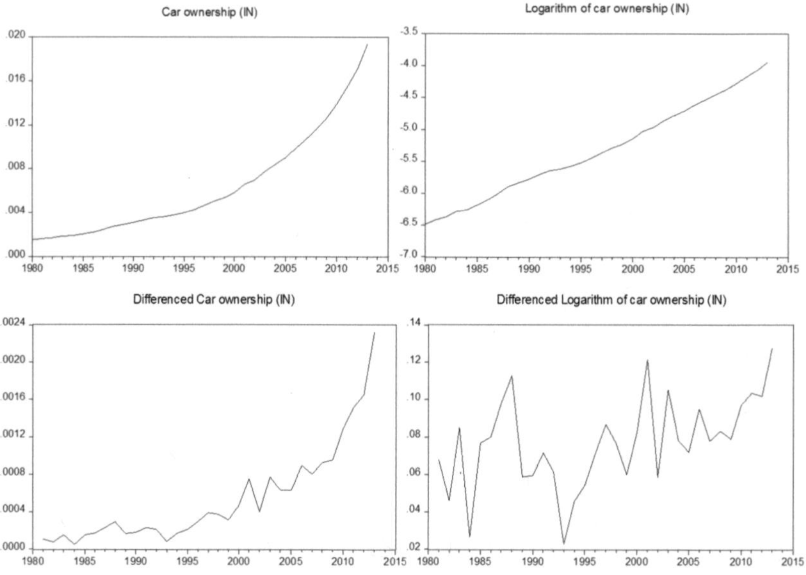

Figure 4.39: Key time plots for India
Source: Own work using EViews® (see appendix I for dataset sources)

Before continuing with the exposition of the estimated equations, a brief detour is appropriate. In empirical time-series econometric modelling, almost every type of single-equation model is captured by the autoregressive distributed-lag model ADL(1,1) (cf. Table 7.1 in Hendry (1995), which shows a general typology; compare with section 2 in Ajanovic *et al.* (2012), which focuses on its application to transport-related fuel demand estimation). Following Hendry (1995) and expressing Eq. 4.9 in logs:

$$y_t = \beta_1 x_t + \beta_2 y_{t-p} + \beta_3 x_{t-q} + \varepsilon_t \tag{4.13}$$

where ε_t is an uncorrelated error, an innovation in which normality and homoscedasticity are assumed. That is, $\varepsilon_t \sim NID(0, \sigma_\varepsilon^2)$. From this general ADL(p,q) model, an ADL(1,1) can be derived. From such an ADL(1,1) model, several models can be empirically identified (see Hendry and Richard (1983) and Hendry *et al.* (1984)). Two models commonly used in economics, as a result of applying parameter restrictions, are shown in Figure 4.40.

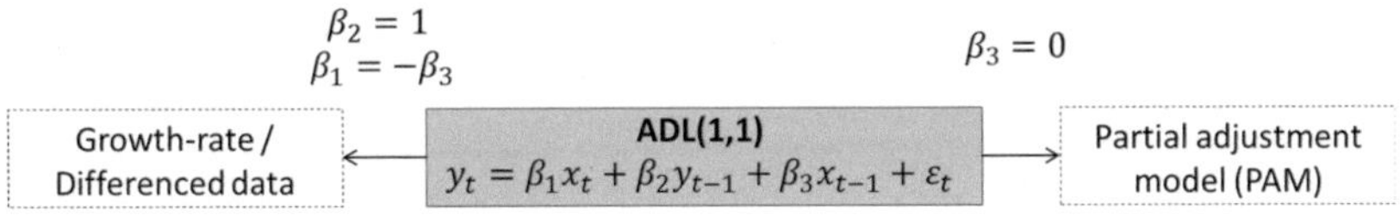

Figure 4.40: General ADL(1,1) and two specific models
Source: Own interpretation of Hendry (1995)

Using Monte Carlo simulation techniques, Hendry (1995) examines the goodness of fit of the standard error in nine models that arise from the general ADL(1,1) model, identifying ‘growth-rate or differenced-data’, ‘partial adjustment’, ‘common factor’ (COMFAC) and ‘equilibrium correction’ models as the most desirable ones by this measure. In line with the discussion in section 3.2.1, some of these models are more consistent with economic theory than others.

For the Indian series, the value of $\hat{\rho}_{k=1}$ for $lown$ is 0.906. For $\Delta lown$, the correlogram is shown in Figure 4.41.

Figure 4.42 represents a time plot of $lown$ and $lrinc$. Both series appear to move in the same direction.

A static regression that includes an explanatory variable other than real income per capita is specified according to Eq. 4.14.

$$lown_t = \beta_0 + \beta_1 lrinc_t + \beta_2 lroil_t + \varepsilon_t \tag{4.14}$$

Autocorrelation	Partial Correlation		AC	PAC	Q-Stat	Prob
		1	0.260	0.260	2.4328	0.119
		2	0.264	0.210	5.0237	0.081
		3	0.162	0.060	6.0386	0.110
		4	-0.040	-0.157	6.1031	0.192
		5	0.038	0.029	6.1613	0.291
		6	-0.092	-0.079	6.5206	0.367
		7	-0.061	-0.017	6.6877	0.462
		8	-0.092	-0.061	7.0778	0.528
		9	0.214	0.338	9.2897	0.411
		10	0.148	0.080	10.385	0.407
		11	0.035	-0.151	10.450	0.490
		12	0.124	-0.013	11.292	0.504
		13	0.048	0.099	11.426	0.575
		14	-0.053	-0.155	11.594	0.639
		15	0.027	0.040	11.641	0.706
		16	-0.066	0.044	11.933	0.749

Figure 4.41: Correlogram of $\Delta lown$ for India | Source: Own work using EViews®

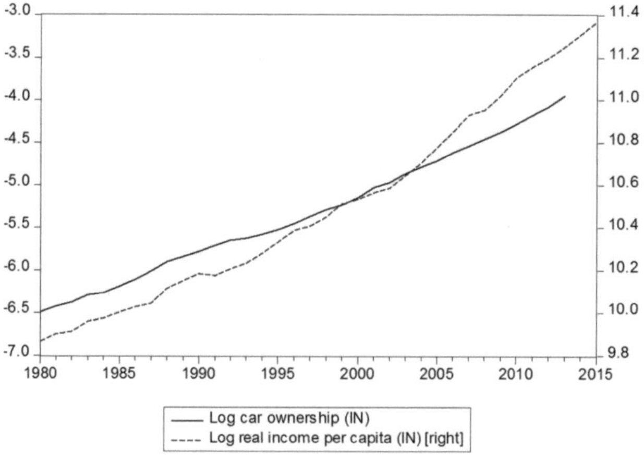

Figure 4.42: Car ownership and real income in India
Source: Own work using EViews® (see appendix I for dataset sources)

The results of estimating such a static regression are shown in Table 4.8. The estimated parameters are statistically significant. Moreover, the sign of the coefficient attached to the real oil price matches, as opposed to the one estimated for the Chinese series, the theoretical expectation. However, this model is discarded as it is seriously affected by serial correlation.

Table 4.8: Static regression on Indian *lown*

Dependent Variable: LOG(OWN_IN)				
Method: Least Squares				
Sample: 1980 2010				
Included observations: 31				
Variable	Coefficient	Std. Error	t-Statistic	Prob.
C	-23.09067	0.338047	-68.30607	0.0000
LRINC_IN	1.739188	0.029001	59.97029	0.0000
LROIL_IN	-0.093968	0.016159	-5.815051	0.0000
R-squared	0.994290	Mean dependent var		-5.444870
Adjusted R-squared	0.993882	S.D. dependent var		0.662470
S.E. of regression	0.051818	Akaike info criterion		-2.990393
Sum squared resid	0.075183	Schwarz criterion		-2.851620
Log likelihood	49.35110	Hannan-Quinn criter.		-2.945157
F-statistic	2437.671	Durbin-Watson stat		0.670483
Prob(F-statistic)	0.000000			

Source: Own work using EViews®

By dropping *lroil* from Eq. 4.14, a new equation is estimated. The resulting residuals are saved. Then the unit-root test is performed on the new residuals series. The value of the ADF *t*-stat obtained is -1.20. Since $H_0\colon y \sim I(1)$, it is concluded that no cointegration relationship between the Indian *lown* and *lrinc* holds.

Alternatively, the same dynamic regression employed for China is estimated here for the Indian series. The results are shown in Table 4.9. As can be seen, *lrinc* turns out not to be statistically significant under this specification. Notwithstanding, the results of the JB and BG tests contribute to conclude that the assumptions of non-normality and serial correlation can be rejected. In the absence of a more satisfactory model specification, forecasts are computed. The results are shown in Figure 4.43.

Table 4.9: Dynamic regression on Indian *lown*

Dependent Variable: LOG(OWN_IN)				
Method: Least Squares				
Sample (adjusted): 1981 2010				
Included observations: 30 after adjustments				
Variable	Coefficient	Std. Error	t-Statistic	Prob.
C	-1.681077	1.286429	-1.306777	0.2023
LOWN_IN(-1)	0.936314	0.053515	17.49643	0.0000
LRINC_IN	0.135177	0.095639	1.413397	0.1690
R-squared	0.998975	Mean dependent var		-5.410039
Adjusted R-squared	0.998899	S.D. dependent var		0.644278
S.E. of regression	0.021379	Akaike info criterion		-4.758153
Sum squared resid	0.012341	Schwarz criterion		-4.618033
Log likelihood	74.37230	Hannan-Quinn criter.		-4.713328
F-statistic	13154.80	Durbin-Watson stat		1.840029
Prob(F-statistic)	0.000000			

Source: Own work using EViews®

As can be seen, car ownership in India is projected to grow rapidly.

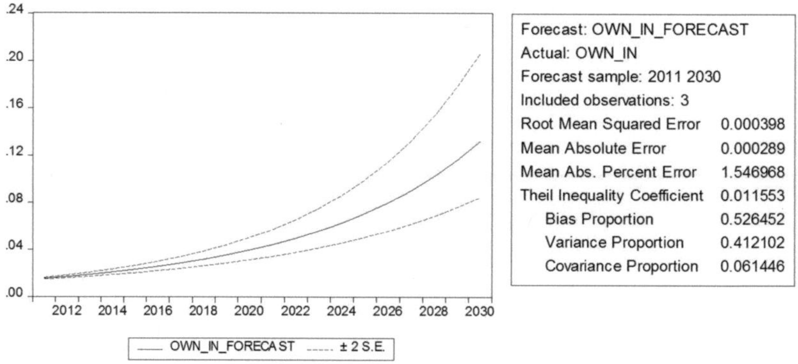

Figure 4.43: Projections of car ownership in India | Source: Own work using EViews®

4.2.8.5 Car ownership in Japan

The own series, expressed in first differences and logs ($lown$, Δown and $\Delta lown$) are shown for Japan in Figure 4.44.

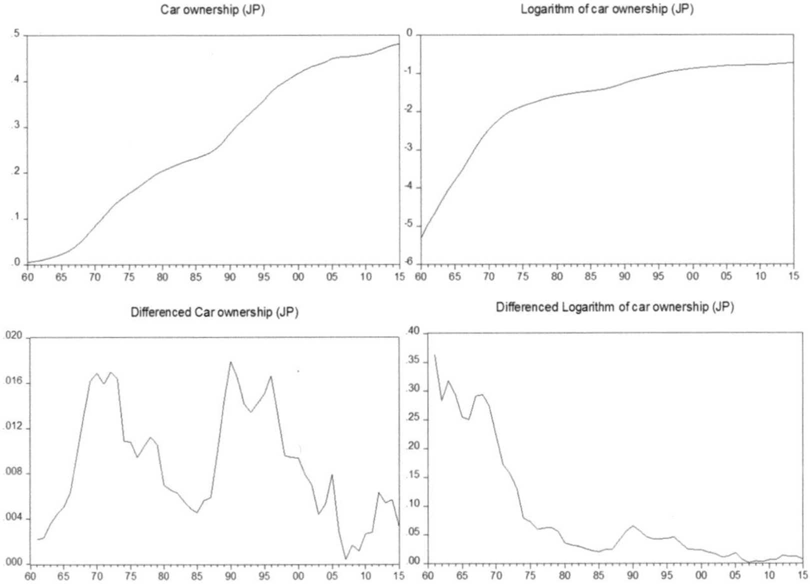

Figure 4.44: Key time plots for Japan
Source: Own work using EViews® (see appendix I for dataset sources)

The series $lown$ displays a value of 0.904 for $\hat{\rho}_{k=1}$. As in the case of France, it is desirable to plot the series in second differences. The correlogram of $\Delta^2 lown$ can be seen in Figure 4.45.

However, when the possibility that the Japanese $lown$ series can be characterised as having a unit root is tested (see section 5.2.1), such assumption cannot be rejected. In view of this, it is explored whether a cointegration relationship between $lown$ and $lrinc$ can be established. In order to do that, a static regression is first estimated (see Table 4.10). Following the procedure described in the previous section, a unit root test is performed on the residuals of this static regression. The numerical outcome is an ADF t-stat approaching -2.58. Based on the values provided by Hamilton (1994) (Case 1 in his Table B.9), the null can be rejected only at the 10% level of statistical significance. Tentatively, it is held that the Japanese $lown$ and $lrinc$ may be cointegrated. When cointegration is present, the error correction model

(ECM) is an adequate type of ADL(1,1) model (Hendry, 1995). Hence, finding a cointegration relationship opens up the opportunity to estimate an ECM. Thus if 'car ownership' and 'income per capita' are indeed cointegrated (see the formal test in section 5.2.1), their relationship can be expressed in terms of an ECM. In economics, cointegration analysis is exploited in e.g. cliometrics (Greasley and Oxley, 2011).

Autocorrelation	Partial Correlation		AC	PAC	Q-Stat	Prob
		1	0.132	0.132	0.9881	0.320
		2	0.038	0.021	1.0715	0.585
		3	0.112	0.106	1.8125	0.612
		4	0.130	0.105	2.8367	0.586
		5	-0.028	-0.064	2.8868	0.717
		6	0.046	0.044	3.0205	0.806
		7	-0.085	-0.123	3.4820	0.837
		8	0.095	0.122	4.0741	0.850
		9	0.250	0.245	8.2875	0.505
		10	0.091	0.039	8.8539	0.546
		11	0.023	0.011	8.8926	0.632
		12	0.140	0.050	10.309	0.589
		13	-0.087	-0.188	10.870	0.622
		14	-0.018	-0.000	10.894	0.694
		15	-0.062	-0.075	11.188	0.739
		16	-0.094	-0.040	11.888	0.752
		17	-0.086	-0.046	12.496	0.769
		18	-0.001	-0.069	12.496	0.821
		19	-0.054	-0.024	12.749	0.851
		20	-0.038	-0.071	12.874	0.883
		21	0.042	0.044	13.032	0.907
		22	0.052	0.118	13.290	0.925
		23	0.022	0.052	13.336	0.944
		24	-0.075	-0.066	13.907	0.949

Figure 4.45: Correlogram of $\Delta^2 lown$ for Japan | Source: Own work using EViews®

The formal link between cointegration and error correction occurs thanks to the Granger Representation Theorem (Banerjee *et al.*, 1993), put forward by Granger (1981) (see the proof in e.g. Granger and Weiss (1983) in Karlin *et al.* (2014)) and also Engle and Granger (1987)).

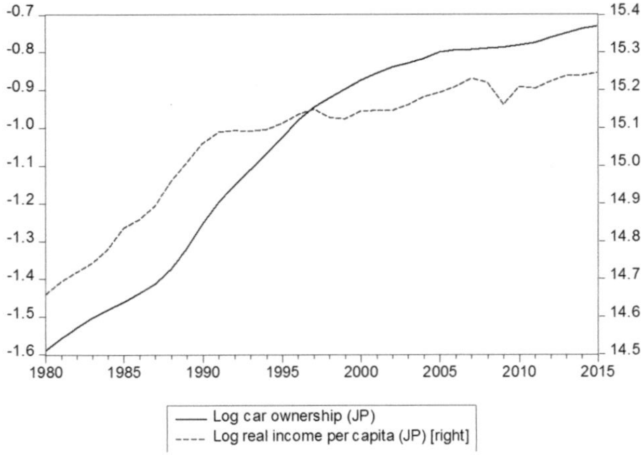

Figure 4.46: Car ownership and real income in Japan
Source: Own work using EViews® (see appendix I for dataset sources)

As shown in Figure 4.40, one option is a growth-rate model. However, this type of model discards potentially useful information. In contrast, ECMs retain information about long-run relationship between variables, expressed in terms of levels (Hendry in Engle and Granger (1991)). That is, not only short-run but also long-run relationships can be examined by employing ECMs (Pickup, 2014). Engle and Granger (1987) in Engle and Granger (1991) mention the work by Phillips (1957) and Sargan (1964) as early examples of the ECM, a type of model that has found, as they note, wide use in economics.

Table 4.10: Static regression on Japanese *lown*

Dependent Variable: LOG(OWN_JP)
Method: Least Squares

Sample: 1980 2010
Included observations: 31

Variable	Coefficient	Std. Error	t-Statistic	Prob.
C	-24.54926	1.455403	-16.86767	0.0000
LOG(RINC_JP)	1.559005	0.096763	16.11164	0.0000

R-squared	0.899510	Mean dependent var	-1.101849
Adjusted R-squared	0.896045	S.D. dependent var	0.286608
S.E. of regression	0.092409	Akaike info criterion	-1.862853
Sum squared resid	0.247641	Schwarz criterion	-1.770338
Log likelihood	30.87422	Hannan-Quinn criter.	-1.832695
F-statistic	259.5851	Durbin-Watson stat	0.151748
Prob(F-statistic)	0.000000		

Source: Own work using EViews®

Following Vogelvang (2004), an ECM model for the Japanese series is estimated. Table 4.11 shows summary information. The estimated parameters, including the error correction, are statistically significant (however, $lown_{t-2}$ at the 10% level).

Table 4.11: ECM regression for Japan

Dependent Variable: D(LOWN_JP)
Method: Least Squares

Sample (adjusted): 1983 2010
Included observations: 28 after adjustments
White heteroskedasticity-consistent standard errors & covariance

Variable	Coefficient	Std. Error	t-Statistic	Prob.
C	0.009429	0.002465	3.825471	0.0009
D(LOWN_JP(-1))	1.035830	0.219338	4.722523	0.0001
D(LOWN_JP(-2))	-0.341604	0.183678	-1.859794	0.0758
D(LRINC_JP(-2))	-0.108168	0.045487	-2.377978	0.0261
RESID_CO	-0.070979	0.019197	-3.697494	0.0012

R-squared	0.926941	Mean dependent var	0.026704
Adjusted R-squared	0.914235	S.D. dependent var	0.017492
S.E. of regression	0.005123	Akaike info criterion	-7.549881
Sum squared resid	0.000604	Schwarz criterion	-7.311987
Log likelihood	110.6983	Hannan-Quinn criter.	-7.477154
F-statistic	72.95336	Durbin-Watson stat	2.019203
Prob(F-statistic)	0.000000	Wald F-statistic	57.67342
Prob(Wald F-statistic)	0.000000		

Source: Own work using EViews®

The estimated equations shown in Table 4.10 and Table 4.11 can be written as follows:

Static: $lown_t = -24.55 + 1.56lrinc_t + \varepsilon_t$ (4.15)

ECM: $\Delta lown_t = 0.01 + 1.04\Delta lown_{t-1} - 0.34\Delta lown_{t-2} - 0.11\Delta lrinc_{t-2} - 0.07\varepsilon_{t-1}$

(4.16)

Whereas Eq. 4.15 can be interpreted as the non-spurious long-run equilibrium relationship, Eq. 4.16 reflects its associated short-run ECM. The latter, whose constant term represents the level of equilibrium (Hendry, 1995), introduces past disequilibrium as an explanatory variable (Maddala and Kim, 1998).

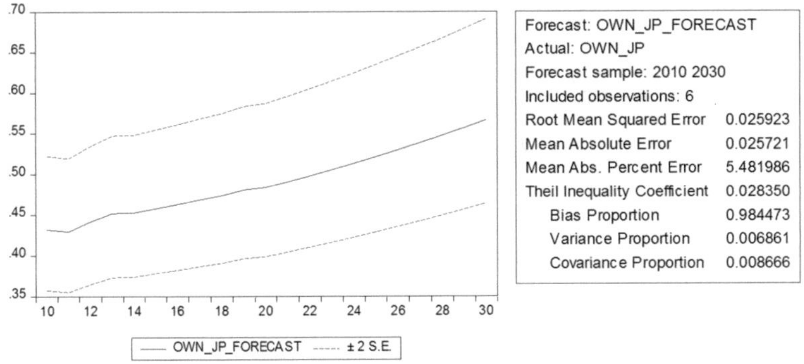

Figure 4.47: Projections of car ownership in Japan | Source: Own work using EViews®

Figure 4.47 shows the Japanese car ownership projections based on the estimated long-run equation.

4.2.8.6 Car ownership in the US

Figure 4.48 shows the time plots of own, $lown$, Δown and $\Delta lown$ using US data. Two declines, in 1990 and 2009, are remarkable (see section 5.2.1). It is worth reminding the reader that this series excludes SUVs.

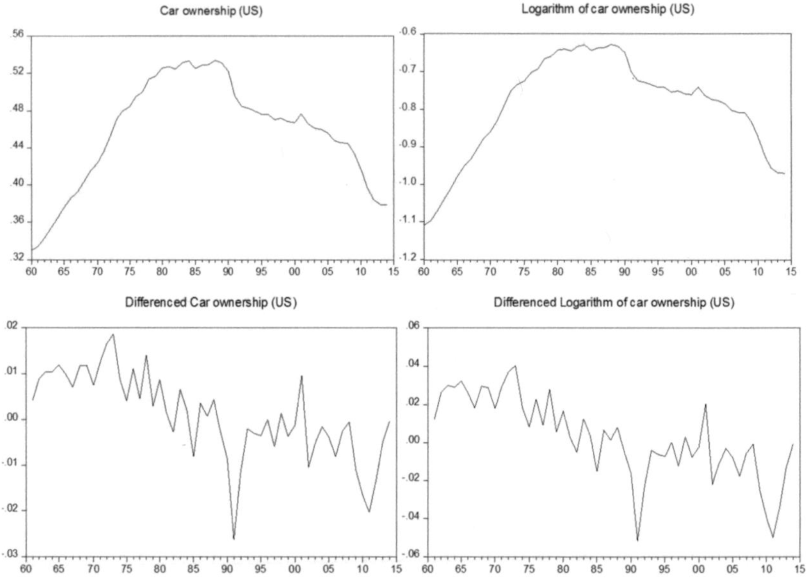

Figure 4.48: Key time plots for the US
Source: Own work using EViews® (see appendix I for dataset sources)

The $\hat{\rho}_{k=1}$ value of $lown$ equals 0.919. The possibility that the US series is also $\Delta^2 lown$ is considered (see Figure 4.49).

Autocorrelation	Partial Correlation		AC	PAC	Q-Stat	Prob
		1	-0.243	-0.243	3.3063	0.069
		2	-0.127	-0.198	4.2322	0.121
		3	-0.024	-0.121	4.2657	0.234
		4	-0.106	-0.194	4.9349	0.294
		5	-0.016	-0.150	4.9512	0.422
		6	0.076	-0.042	5.3128	0.504
		7	0.016	-0.027	5.3299	0.620
		8	0.026	0.009	5.3728	0.717
		9	-0.034	-0.031	5.4503	0.793
		10	-0.013	-0.013	5.4623	0.858
		11	-0.052	-0.068	5.6520	0.896
		12	0.100	0.069	6.3654	0.897
		13	-0.154	-0.157	8.0922	0.838
		14	-0.001	-0.108	8.0923	0.884
		15	0.198	0.122	11.114	0.744
		16	-0.132	-0.076	12.494	0.709
		17	-0.039	-0.089	12.615	0.762
		18	0.069	-0.005	13.008	0.791
		19	-0.196	-0.213	16.288	0.638
		20	0.207	0.096	20.074	0.453
		21	0.165	0.218	22.541	0.369
		22	-0.137	-0.020	24.310	0.331
		23	-0.093	-0.095	25.147	0.343
		24	-0.022	-0.055	25.194	0.395

Figure 4.49: Correlogram of $\Delta^2 lown$ for the US | Source: Own work using EViews®

Figure 4.50 shows the behaviour of the US series for income and car ownership. The drop in income in 2008-2009 was followed by a sharp decline in car ownership. As noted in section 5.2.1, the possibility of a cointegration relationship between these two series is not examined.

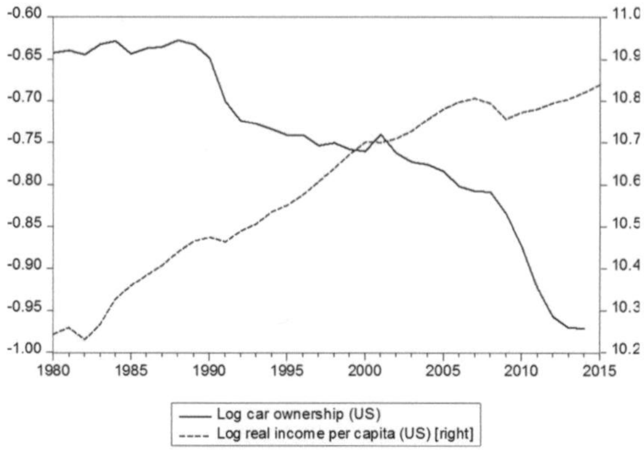

Figure 4.50: Car ownership and real income in US
Source: Own work using EViews® (see appendix I for dataset sources)

A key distinction related to the persistence of shocks or innovations is between 'short' and 'long' memory processes. In the former, an original shock to the series has basically no impact on its present values (Engle and Granger, 1991). In the latter, persistence is greater (Patterson, 2000). Beran *et al.* (2013) credit Granger with having discovered long memory processes in economics. Whereas white noise can be considered a representation of short memory, a random walk is a way of expressing a long memory process. Sterman (2000) warns against the use of white noise in SD models and contests that in real systems shocks are persistent.

Table 4.12 provides info on the estimated regression equation for US *lown*. The original inclusion of real income and the fuel price led to poor estimates. Dummies have been included to reflect the dramatic drop in the series values in 1991 and 2009. Based on these results, the hypothesis of no serial correlation cannot be rejected. Also, the normality assumption cannot be rejected using the JB test.

Table 4.12: Dynamic regression on US *lown*

Dependent Variable: LOWN_US
Method: Least Squares

Sample: 1980 2010
Included observations: 31

Variable	Coefficient	Std. Error	t-Statistic	Prob.
C	0.023244	0.023441	0.991572	0.3302
LOWN_US(-1)	1.037688	0.032929	31.51273	0.0000
DUMMY	-0.050424	0.011003	-4.582709	0.0001
@YEAR>2008	-0.024496	0.008613	-2.844150	0.0084

R-squared	0.980017	Mean dependent var	-0.721421
Adjusted R-squared	0.977797	S.D. dependent var	0.071359
S.E. of regression	0.010633	Akaike info criterion	-6.129787
Sum squared resid	0.003053	Schwarz criterion	-5.944756
Log likelihood	99.01169	Hannan-Quinn criter.	-6.069471
F-statistic	441.3865	Durbin-Watson stat	2.192004
Prob(F-statistic)	0.000000		

Source: Own work using EViews®

Finally, the projections of car ownership in the US using the regression in Table 4.12 are shown in Figure 4.51. Following the downwards trend displayed by the last available observations, the projected trajectory leads to a strong decline in car ownership.

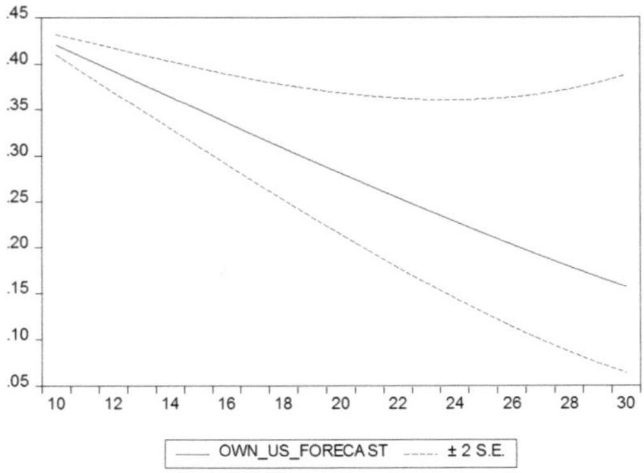

Forecast: OWN_US_FORECAST	
Actual: OWN_US	
Forecast sample: 2010 2030	
Included observations: 5	
Root Mean Squared Error	0.008581
Mean Absolute Error	0.007053
Mean Abs. Percent Error	1.820908
Theil Inequality Coefficient	0.010939
Bias Proportion	0.010736
Variance Proportion	0.350648
Covariance Proportion	0.638616

Figure 4.51: Projections of car ownership in the US | Source: Own work using EViews®

4.2.9 Car stock

The future values of *car ownership* estimated in this section can be treated as forecasts. In conjunction with the population assumptions mentioned in section 4.2.1 (see Eq. 4.17), these values represent the *projected aggregate total car stock.*

$$S^{agg}_{h,t} \quad = \quad y_{h,t} \quad * \quad pop_{h,t} \qquad \forall h,t \qquad (4.17)$$

[car] [car/people] [people]

As a result of the econometric output outlined in the previous section, the following projections of the car stock in each country are derived (see Figure 4.52).

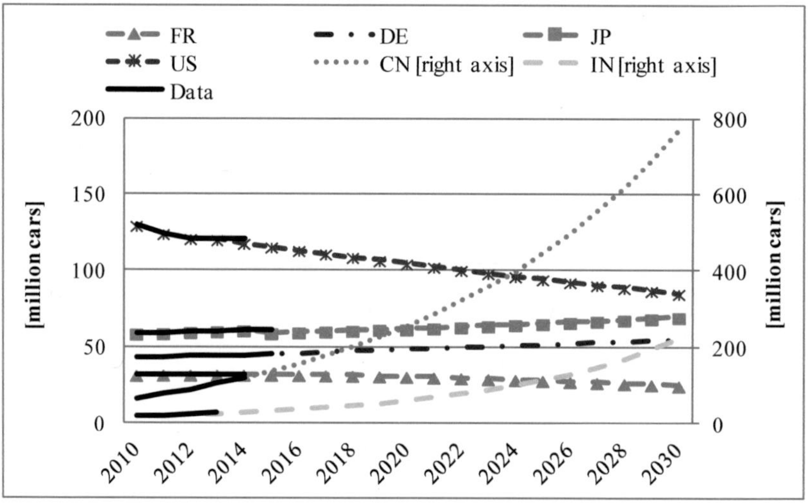

Figure 4.52: Car stock by country: data and projections
Source: Own work using EViews® (see appendix I for dataset sources)

Clearly, the projections concerning China and the US appear to be contrary to expectations (see section 5.2.2). In particular, the results for China are largely determined by the optimistic GDP growth assumptions adopted in the exercise. The Chinese car stock projection would entail a number of annual car sales for an extended period that is hard to conceive. Because of this, the econometric results from China are not inserted in the SD sub-model. Instead, a cap to annual car sales is imposed, so that the initial exponential development is succeeded by a period of decelerated growth in Chinese car stock. With regards to the US values, the effect of the US financial crisis in the last available observations is difficult to counteract. For simplicity, a recovery in the car stock level, as opposed to the extrapolation of the recent trend, is modelled. The result of implementing these amendments in the SD sub-model can be seen in Figure 4.53. For China, there is a persistent gap between the data and the simulation values, due to computational issues, and a change in the growth rate around 2015-2016.

As a product, the car is highly heterogeneous. Two main rationales for product differentiation are technical specifications set by regulation and market segmentation motivated by marketing strategies. The types of car available in the market differ in e.g. makes and variants, footprint, weight, power and other features. This model simplifies this level of complexity by assuming a hypothetical average car and focusing on the powertrain and age aspects.

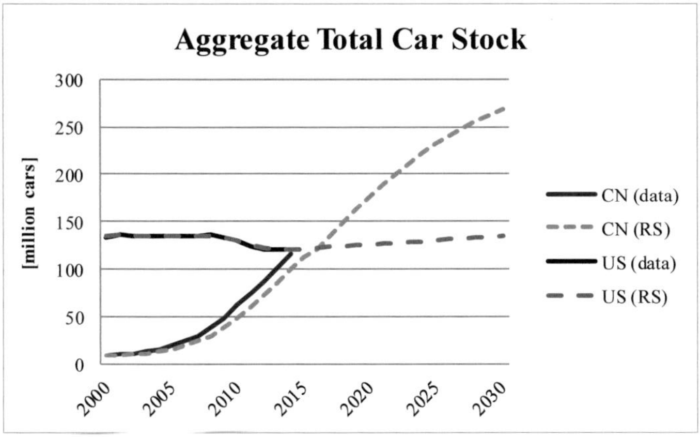

Figure 4.53: Car stock in China and the US: data vs. Simulations
Source: Own work using Vensim® (see appendix I for dataset sources)

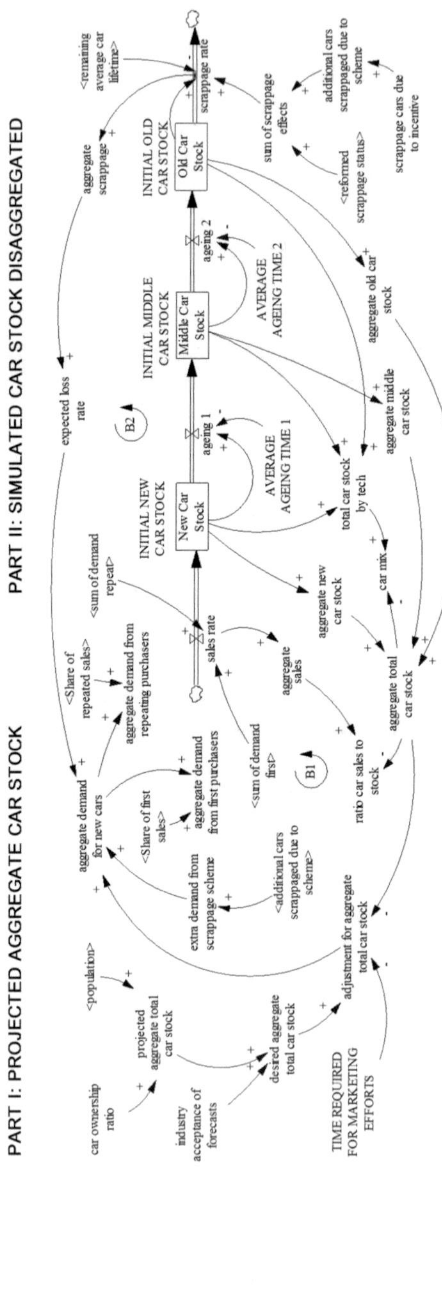

Figure 4.54: Overview of the module ‘Car Stock’ | Source: Own work using Vensim®

The car stock is implemented in the SD model using a stock-and-flow structure with three main components: state variables, scrappage rates and sales rates. Two balancing (i.e. negative) feedback loops (B1 and B2) are represented (see Figure 4.54). The initial values of key variables are shown in section 5.1.

4.2.9.1 State variables

The state variables of the stock-and-flow framework are based on an ageing chain (see chapter 12 in Sterman (2000)) consisting of three stocks . These are called *new car stock* ($S_{h,i,t}^{new}$), *middle car stock* ($S_{h,i,t}^{mid}$) and *old car stock* ($S_{h,i,t}^{old}$). The sum of these stocks results in *total car stock*. Each stock is disaggregated by powertrain technology, denoted i. In terms of initial values, whereas $S_{h,i,t}^{new}$ reflects previous car sales, a 60:40 split of the remaining car stock between $S_{h,i,t}^{mid}$ and $S_{h,i,t}^{old}$ is assumed.

In principle, there is no explicit distinction between the primary car market and the secondary car market (used or second-hand cars). Some readers might find it useful to re-interpret the $S_{h,i,t}^{old}$ as the secondary car market.

4.2.9.2 Scrappage rates

Meadows and Wright (2008) point out that humans tend to underestimate the role of outflows in a stock-and-flow structure. In the model, the variable car *scrappage rate* is an outflow from $S_{h,i,t}^{old}$. As Sterman (2000) notes, for consumer durable products such as cars, a first-order process does not usually approximate well the discard rate. One possibility is to assume yearly values of the scrappage rate. Another one is to derive probability distributions such as Weibull. Yet another possibility is to assume an average car lifetime value that remains constant throughout the simulation period. The last option is preferred for simplicity. However, this assumption shall be tested for the German case. The theorem by Little (1961) may be applied to a stock-and-flow structure in dynamic equilibrium. This is a useful approximation in saturated car markets and has been employed by e.g. Wansart (2012) and Thies *et al.* (2016). Based on survival rates, Davis *et al.* (2010) point out that the average car lifetime in the US is 17 years. In the model, a value of

16 years is assumed for all countries. In addition, for Germany the impact of the 2009 scrappage scheme (see section 4.3) is also modelled.

4.2.9.3 Sales rates

The variable car *sales rate* (s), an inflow to $S^{new}_{h,i,t}$, is causally linked to the variable *aggregate demand for new cars.* This variable translates the adjustment mechanism that connects the econometric output and the SD sub-model (this is visible in Figure 4.54) into a flow variable.

Already in 1938, de Wolff (1938) distinguished between 'the demand for first purchase' and 'the demand for replacement'. If the modelled market is saturated, there appears to be little need to make this distinction. However, since this work includes fast-growing Asian markets, the distinction proposed by de Wolff (1938) is retained.

Consequently, Eq. 2.6 becomes Eq. 4.10.

$$s_{h,i,t} = \left(\zeta^{first}_{h,i,t} * s^{first}_{h,t}\right) + \left(\zeta^{rep}_{h,i,t} * s^{rep}_{h,t}\right) \quad \forall h,i,t \qquad (4.18)$$

[car/year] [dmnl] [car/year] [dmnl] [car/year]

where: $first$ refers to first sales, rep means repeated sales and $\sum_{i=1}^{9} \zeta_i = 1$.

The terms in Eq. 4.18 are explained in the next two sections.

4.2.10 Market segmentation

Before tackling choice, it is useful to introduce the idea of market segmentation, a pillar in marketing science (see chapter 9 in Kotler *et al.* (2008)). In this model, the market is divided into two groups, first-time car purchasers and repeating car purchasers, each of which is in turn further divided into four sub-groups: habit(-oriented), innovators, low-cost buyers and utility maximisers (see Figure 4.55).

It is implicitly assumed that whereas innovators are high-income consumers, low-cost buyers have low-income. One might associate the habit sub-group with loyalty. However, this would be misleading. Although *brand loyalty* appears to be a feature of the car market, *powertrain loyalty* is less clear to date. The utility maximisers sub-group includes consumers who basically behave in line with the assumption of economic rationality.

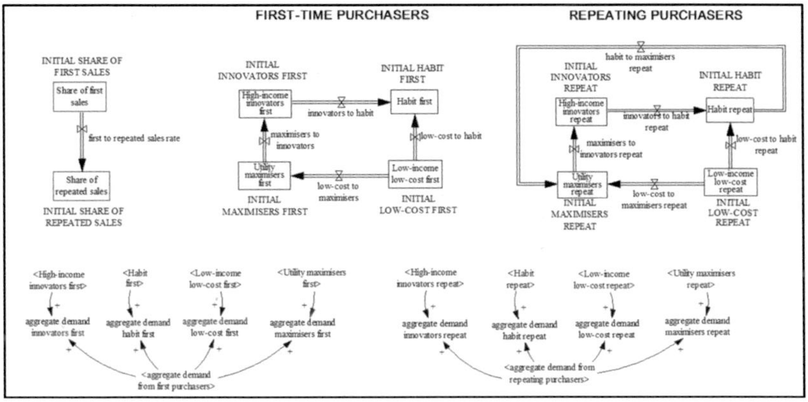

Figure 4.55: Overview of the sub-module 'Market Segmentation'
Source: Own work using Vensim®

Table 4.13 shows the initial values of each sub-group for a particular market. Given the lack of data for these variables, two approaches were considered: (i) performing an internal calibration of the SD sub-model using a plausible range of values; or (ii) making theoretical assumptions informed by the literature. The second approach was adopted. The justification for the assumed values is the following. For the first-time car purchasers: (i) all of them are thought to be low-income people (i.e. they are not innovators who can afford the most expensive technology but, instead, buy the powertrain with the lowest purchase price); and (ii) since it is the first time they buy a car, habit plays no role. For repeating car purchasers, (i) experience basically clusters them in either the habit or utility maximisers segments; (ii) in line with innovation theory (see Figure 1.2 in Mahajan *et al.* (2000)), high-income innovators represent a small fraction of the market; and (iii) assuming that the first car purchase takes place at the age of 18-20 and a car has an average lifetime of 16 years, repeating purchasers are assumed to buy their second and third cars at the age of ca. 35 and 51 years, respectively. By that time, it is likely that those purchasers have accumulated sufficient working experience not to receive a low-income salary.

Table 4.13: Market segmentation, values (%) in 2000 in France

Type of purchase	Habit	High-income innovators	Low-income low-cost	Utility maximisers
First purchasers	0	0	100	0
Repeat purchasers	74	1	5	20

Source: Own assumptions

The initial values in Table 4.13 differ by country. Furthermore, the proportion of each sub-group within a market does not necessarily remain constant over the simulation period. It is implicitly assumed that, as alternative powertrains become more visible (e.g. media, roads), the size of the habit sub-group decreases and the number of utility maximisers grows. Thus as the car choice becomes more complex due to the increased availability of powertrains, a larger number of factors is incorporated in the decision-making process of prospective car purchasers (in essence, a flow from the habit to the utility maximisers sub-groups takes place).

4.2.11 Technology choice

The question of how technology is selected leads to an explicit mathematical representation of human choice behaviour. This is not a trivial issue, especially when choice behaviour has to be depicted *over time*. In such a dynamic context, is stability of consumer preferences a reasonable assumption? Intertemporal optimisation breaks down if preference stability does not hold (Thaler, 2015). Veblen provided the insight that, in a dynamic context, the assumption that tastes are given does not hold (Boulding, 1988).

Depending on the degree of economic rationality assigned to consumers, two extreme cases appear: choice is the result of either intuitive feeling or of a thorough TCO analysis. The latter can be rendered to monetary quantification. When the future has to enter the TCO calculation, as that happens with prospective prices, strong assumptions are required. One such assumption is rational expectations (as indicated in section 3.1.3.2). The adoption of such assumption in the context of this work would imply that the prospective car purchaser has perfect foresight (Hommes, 2013) and knows the future evolution of energy prices and batteries, anticipating policy. In reality, common experience dictates that car purchasing decisions involve a mix of intuitive feeling and reasoning. And, after all, *errare humanum est.* The ability to learn is also a human characteristic. In SD, expectations are generally modelled as adaptive learning processes (Sterman, 1987).

In this thesis, technology choice relates to the selection of a particular car powertrain by the car purchasers, grouped as shown in Table 4.13. Ben-Akiva and Lerman (1985) categorise decision rules in four classes: dominance, lexicographic, satisfaction and utility. Inspired by this classification, Table 4.14 shows the decision rules assumed in the model. As with the values in Table 4.13, the choice of decision rules is based on theoretical considerations and motivated by a lack of data. Empirical evidence on car technology choice exists, but it mainly originates from DC studies assuming that only the utility rule applies. In the model, (i) low-cost buyers purchase the powertrain with the lowest purchase price, initially represented by the gasoline car; (ii) once a new powertrain becomes commercially available, its degree of innovativeness becomes highest, which appeals to innovators; (iii) habit-oriented consumers replace their car without switching to other powertrains; and (iv) utility maximisers make their choice after taking into account a range of powertrain attributes.

For the segment that is assumed to make purchase decisions based on the utility maximisation rule, a crucial variable is the expected use of the car, measured in km, which leads to explicit consideration of travel demand. As PHEVs can be powered by gasoline and electricity, a 50% split in VKT (i.e. half of the mileage run by a PHEV is on gasoline and the other half on electricity) is assumed in the model. The attributes influencing attractiveness are shown in section 4.2.17.

Table 4.14: Decision rules and technology choice

Market segment	Decision rule	Technology choice
Low-income low-cost	Dominance	The powertrain with the lowest purchase price is chosen
High-income innovators	Lexicographic	The powertrain with the highest degree of innovativeness is chosen
Habit	Satisfaction	The current powertrain is chosen again
Utility maximisers	Utility	The powertrain that offers the maximum level of utility is chosen

Source: Own assumptions

4.2.12 Travel demand by car

Travel demand by car can be understood in terms of two metrics: as an indicator of performance based on passenger-km (PKM) travelled, and as an indicator of vehicle usage based on vehicle-km travelled (VKT). This section focuses on car usage and the key variable is defined as annual average VKT by car (also referred to as mean driving distance, or simply mileage), expressed in [(km/car)/year]. Three ways of representing this variable are included in the model: as *expected*, *simulated* or *desired* values, denoted respectively $VKT_{h,t}^{exp}$, $VKT_{h,t}$ and $VKT_{h,t}^{*}$. The latter is examined in section 6.2.6. The simplest approach is to assume a constant expected value. Given the lack of data for China and India, this is not a totally unjustified approach. Moreover, any prospective car purchaser is likely to have an expectation of the annual distance (s)he may drive by car. For simplicity, it is assumed that the *expected average car service life* has a value of 200,000 km. In addition, recall from section 4.2.9 that the total *average car lifetime* is 16 years. The expected annual average VKT by car value can be calculated as in Eq. 4.19. For mature car markets for which data is available, this approach is extremely simplistic.

$$VKT_{h,t}^{exp} = \frac{service\ life_{h,t}^{exp}}{\kappa_{h,t}} = \frac{200{,}000}{16} = 12{,}500 \quad \forall\, h,t \tag{4.19}$$

[(km/car)/year] [km/car] / [year] [(km/car)/year]

The second approach is based on simulating $VKT_{h,t}$ using the economic concept of elasticity. As noted in chapter 2, the literature on transport elasticities is abundant. Using US data for the period 2000-2006, the elasticities w.r.t. real GDP per capita and w.r.t. real gasoline price were simply derived using a logarithmic functional form. No comparable data after 2006 is available (recall section 3.4). The estimated values are respectively 1.13 and -0.13. These are in line with values found in the literature (see e.g. Table 4 in Johansson and Schipper (1997)). Since the model formulated was static, these values reflect the long-run elasticities. Eq. 4.20 captures how this information was formulated in the SD sub-model. Figure 4.56 shows the simulated behaviour of US VKT over time. The sharp decrease in the oil price in recent years results in an increase in simulated annual average VKT by car. Implicitly assumed is the idea that the US government does not correct gasoline taxes for future inflation.

$$VKT_{h,t} \quad = \quad VKT_{h,t_0} \quad * \left(\left(\frac{rinc_{h,t}}{rinc_{h,t_0}}\right)^{\eta_{rinc}}\right) * \left(\left(\frac{rfuel_{h,t}}{rfuel_{h,t_0}}\right)^{\eta_{rfuel}}\right) \qquad (4.20)$$

[(km/car)/year] [(km/car)/year] [dmnl] [dmnl]

The problem with using elasticities as exponents is that growth is unconstrained and this again becomes an unrealistic feature for the Chinese and Indian variables. The proposition that travel demand by car is unbounded is rather weak. There are physical limits as to how much time people can daily spend on travelling, particularly by car using congested roads (see e.g. Metz (2012) and the review by Mokhtarian and Chen (2004)). For these two countries, the first approach is therefore preferred and retained. Better data is expected to shed light about this issue in the next years. An alternative modelling approach, not examined here, would be to analyse passenger-km (PKM) per capita and cap $VKT_{h,t}$ accordingly.

Furthermore, in France and Germany there is a sizeable difference between the annual average VKT by gasoline car and the annual average VKT by diesel car. However, this difference is minor for the US (see Figure 4.57). For Japan, this data was not available. The main pro of having VKT values disaggregated by powertrain for France are Germany becomes visible when energy use by type of fuel is estimated; the cons relate to the inherent difficulties that this disaggregation entails for simulating the market choices of technologies. Therefore, the use of an average values represents a pragmatic approach to model the choice of powertrain.

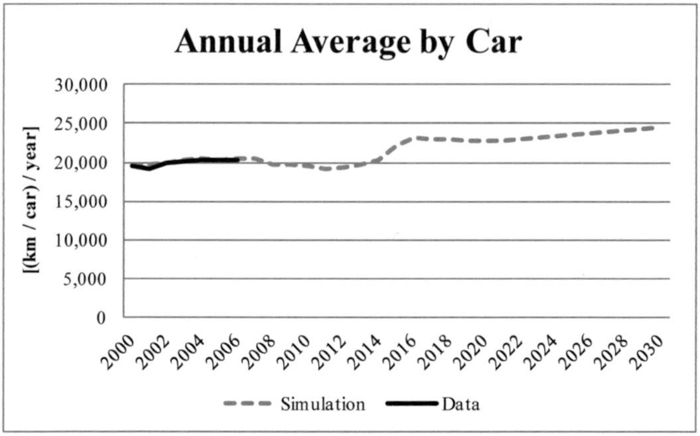

Figure 4.56: Travel demand (VKT) in the US: data vs. simulation
Source: Own estimation (see appendix I for dataset sources)

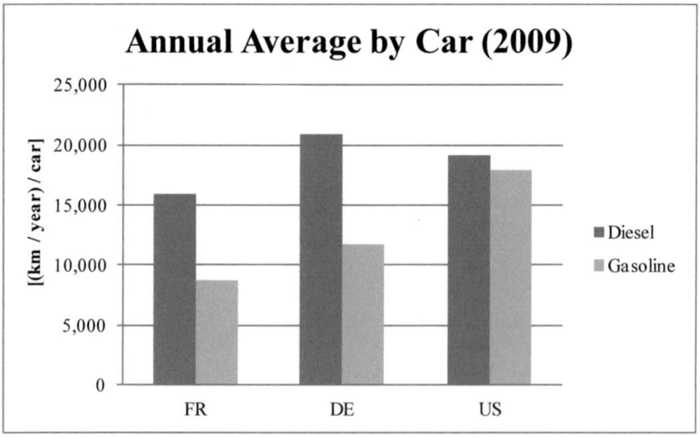

Figure 4.57: Travel demand (VKT) by powertrain and country
Source: (SOeS, 2016) (VIZ, 2016) and (NHTS, 2009)

Figure 4.58 provides an overview of this module, as implemented in the SD software.

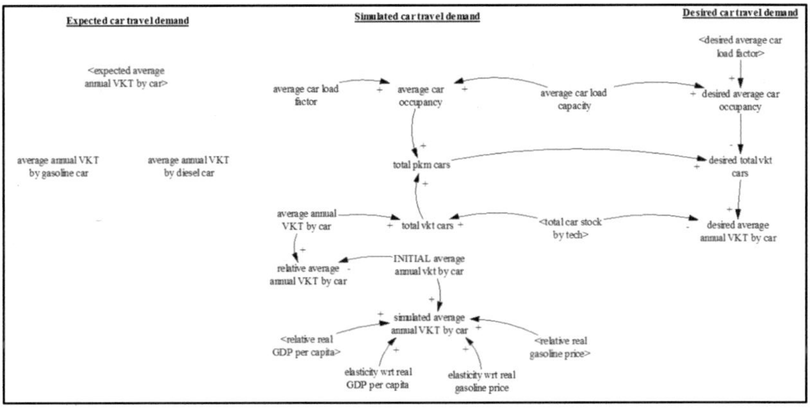

Figure 4.58: Overview of the module 'Travel Demand by Car' | Source: Own work using Vensim®

4.2.13 Infrastructure

Travel demand by car presupposes fuel availability, achieved through a network of refuelling infrastructure with a certain number of stations (i.e. nodes interconnected by road links). Admittedly, the spatial aspects of infrastructure are not given due treatment in this work. The length of roads plays no role in the model. Instead, the analysis is simplified by considering only the number of stations in operation in each country.

The deployment of refuelling infrastructure can be conceived as a growth process reaching a saturation level. From the generalised logistic curve, various main growth models can be derived (see e.g. section 4 in Tsoularis and Wallace (2002)). Computational numerical methods facilitate the task of simulating any type of nonlinear growth behaviour (Sterman, 2000). In the model, the user has the possibility to change the assumptions concerning the deployment of refuelling infrastructure for BEVs and FCs (see section 4.3.5). For PHEVs, a simplifying assumption is adopted: potential car purchasers do not pay attention to recharging infrastructure, as they can use conventional stations to fill the tank. Refuelling infrastructure for CVs, HEVs and PHEVs is represented by the variable *conventional fuel filling stations*, which relies on historical information. For CN and IN, it is assumed that there are respectively 150,000 and 100,000 stations selling gasoline and diesel by 2030. For the rest of the countries, the future values are assumed to remain constant at 11,356 (FR), 14,151 (DE) and 156,100 (US) stations. For the alternative fuels E85, autogas and CNG, see Eq. 4.21. An example is shown in Figure 4.59. These assumptions are maintained throughout the modelling exercise.

$$I_h(\mathrm{t}) = \int_{t_0}^{t} [g_h * I_h * (1 - \frac{I_h}{CC_h})(t)]dt + I_h(t_0) \qquad (4.21)$$

[station] [year^{-1}] [station] [dmnl] [station]

where I denotes the stock of alternative fuel infrastructure (i.e. number of E85, autogas and CNG stations), g the fractional growth rate and CC the assumed carrying capacity or saturation level.

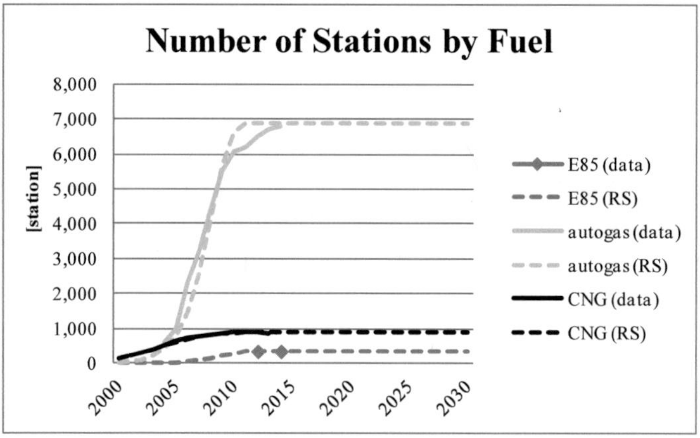

Figure 4.59: Evolution of refuelling infrastructure in Germany
Source: Own assumptions based on ADAC (2016), Autogastanken24 (2016), MWV (2016) and dena (2016)

The expectation of refuelling infrastructure installed capacity and thus fuel availability influences car production, deployment and commercialisation.

The relationship between refuelling infrastructure and car powertrain market uptake is commonly framed in the literature as a 'chicken-and-egg' problem. In the model, two basic extreme conditions apply: an absolute one and a relative one. The absolute condition can be formulated as follows: if there are zero stations for a certain fuel, then there are no car sales of the type of powertrain that *only* uses that fuel (emphasis added because this does not apply to PHEVs). Note that the reverse does not hold. For example, the fact that private registrations of LPG cars in Japan is non-existent does not necessarily mean that there are no autogas stations in that country, because other types of vehicles such as taxis may be running on autogas and therefore demand the fuel. The logic of this formulation is challenged when a distinction between public and private refuelling infrastructure is made. The notable case is electric vehicle supply equipment (EVSE). Even if public EVSE is non-existent, some people may choose to buy an EV if they have their own private recharging point. The key message is that, from a modelling perspective, it is hard to capture how refuelling infrastructure affects powertrain choices. In an attempt to simplify the modelling task, a relative condition is established: the market considers the possibility of purchasing a certain powertrain, depending on the fuel availability in stations, relative to the most popular one (i.e. gasoline). This is reflected in the variable *relative station coverage*. The module can be seen in Figure 4.60.

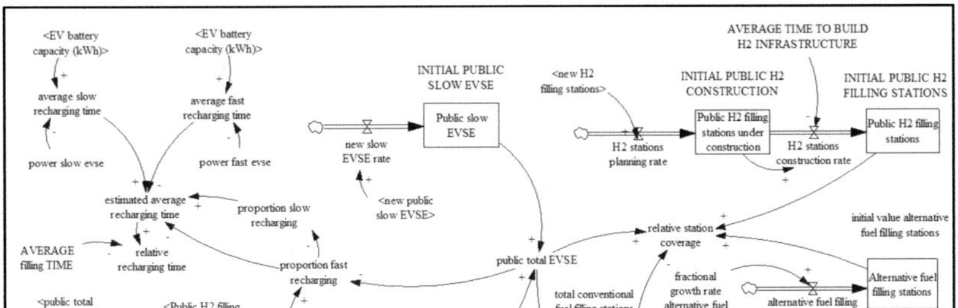

Figure 4.60: Overview of the module 'Infrastructure' | Source: Own work using Vensim®

4.2.14 Fuel intensity, battery capacity and range

In addition to infrastructure coverage and recharging time for BEVs, other attributes that affect the choice decision of the utility maximisers segment include: purchase price, usage cost, (driving) (e-)range and CO_2 emissions (it is implicitly assumed that prospective consumers judge the environmental performance of the car solely in terms of this regulated source of GHG emission). How the values of these attributes are derived is the topic of this and the next sections. The sub-module 'Technical Features' covers the fuel intensity of the car stock, the capacity of the EVB and the corresponding (electric) range by powertrain. Figure 4.61 shows this sub-module.

To model fuel efficiency of the car stock over time, three fuel intensity stocks are created, using a coflow structure (see chapter 12 in Sterman (2000)). This is consistent with the ageing chain formulation of the car stock. The initial values of each fuel intensity stock are given in the dataset. The future values affecting the fuel efficiency of new conventional cars are determined by the model user through the policy input targeting emission and car efficiency standards (see section 4.3.1).

The assumptions on the average car fuel consumption, together with the assumed size of the tank per powertrain determine the range, expressed in km. For PHEVs, the range on gasoline is for simplicity selected for the purchase decision, thus implicitly assuming that PHEV drivers are not affected by range anxiety. However for BEV drivers, this issue is critical. Therefore, the capacity of the EVB is used. In the developed model, the variables related to the battery apply to PHEVs and BEVs, but there is no explicit consideration of the different types of batteries. Instead, the metric of interest is simply 'price per kWh'. For example, an EVB priced at 7,200 dollars reflects the assumption of a 24 kWh battery pack at 300 dollars per kWh.

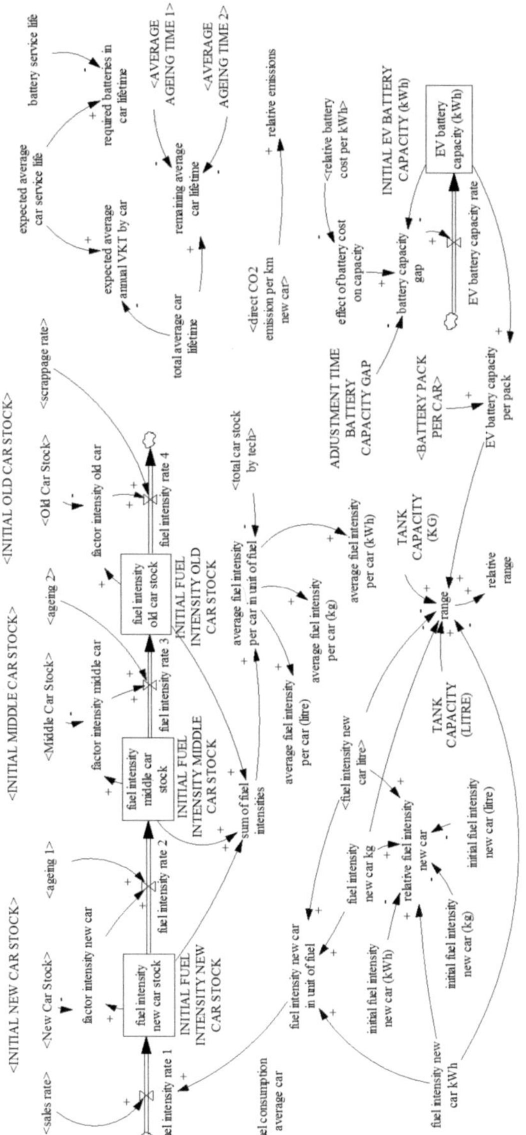

Figure 4.61: Overview of the sub module 'Technical Features' | Source: Own work using Vensim®

As can be seen in Figure 4.62, when the assumed EVB cost goes below a certain threshold, a sharp increase in the capacity of the battery that features in the EV takes place (the timing is scenario-dependent). In this case, the figure shows that the rise is from 8 kWh to 16 kWh and from 24 kWh to 30 kWh for PHEVs and BEVs, respectively. This is consistent with the recent offering of a 30 kWh EVB for the Nissan Leaf, which previously had a 24 kWh pack. In sum, through a mechanism that relates reductions in the cost of EVBs to increases in size (kWh per pack), the capacity of the EVB is time-variant in the simulations. The main rationale for adding extra EVB capacity is to increase e-range. However, this benefit is offset by an increase in the purchase price of the EV.

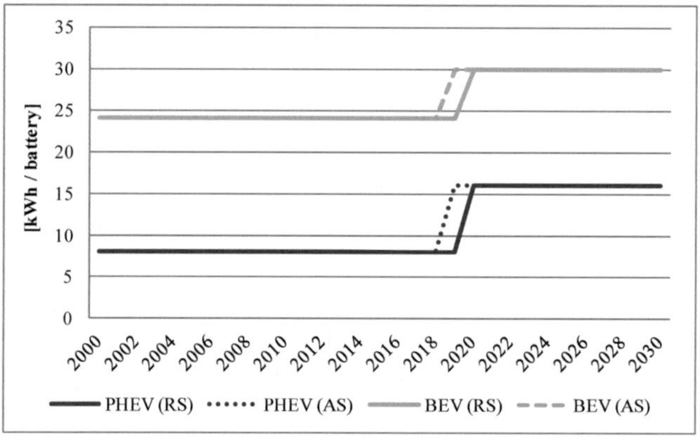

Figure 4.62: Evolution of electric vehicle battery capacity | Source: Own work using Vensim®

Recall the feedback loops in section 4.1.2. The EVB price does not only affect technology attractiveness and choice via the PHEV and BEV purchase price. It also influences the battery capacity, which in turn affects e-range. This involves a simultaneous feedback loop. In the SD sub-model, simultaneity is prevented after introducing a delay by modelling battery capacity as a stock variable. For simplicity, it is implicitly assumed that the energy density of the battery remains constant. In the future, research on new materials may generate very high energy density batteries that become a disruptive technology.

4.2.15 Production costs

A key model variable is the purchase price by type of powertrain. This is assumed to be the result of market prices (production or manufacturing costs plus profits) and taxation, respectively determined by car-makers and government. Car manufacturing cost comprises the cost of labour and raw materials for multiple components, such as chassis and engine. The complexity of car manufacturing and its broader supply chain activity is neglected in this work. Also in reality, trade barriers can lead to significant price differentials for certain powertrains, at least temporarily. Examples include relatively high import tariffs of foreign hybrid cars in China and India. If there is no domestic production of the powertrain, such tariffs are expected to alter the choice of technology by the market. Tariffs are not modelled, but their possible existence should be borne in mind by the reader interpreting the model results. To simplify matters, a reasonable price for a medium size gasoline (G) car is chosen, and the VAT is deducted to reflect its production cost. It is implicitly assumed that this production cost already includes the car-maker's profit. The G car is powered by the spark-ignition (SI) engine (commonly, Otto) and this also applies to FF, LPG and CNG cars. For convenience, these are assumed to be dedicated, as opposed to bi-fuel (cf. Figure 4.1), and no distinction is made between direct and port injection SI engines. In contrast, the compression-ignition (CI) engine (commonly, Diesel) powers the diesel (D) car. Compared to gasoline cars, an extra cost of only 100 dollars is required for FFVs and at least 2,000 dollars for diesel engines and CNG cars (Sperling and Gordon, 2009). Conversions, illegal or not, of gasoline cars to FF, LPG or even CNG in the after-sales market are possible in the real world but ignored in the modelling exercise for simplicity. The conventional (non-plug-in) hybrid technology (i.e. HEVs) is thought to be mature and therefore its battery cost component is not explicitly modelled. Instead, it is assumed that this powertrain has a slightly higher price than CVs due to the small battery. For EVs, the non-battery components are less expensive than for CVs. Conversely, two components are added to the production process of EVs and substantially alter their purchase price: the electric vehicle battery (EVB) for PHEVs and BEVs, and the fuel cell for FCs. Figure 4.63 offers an overview of this sub-module.

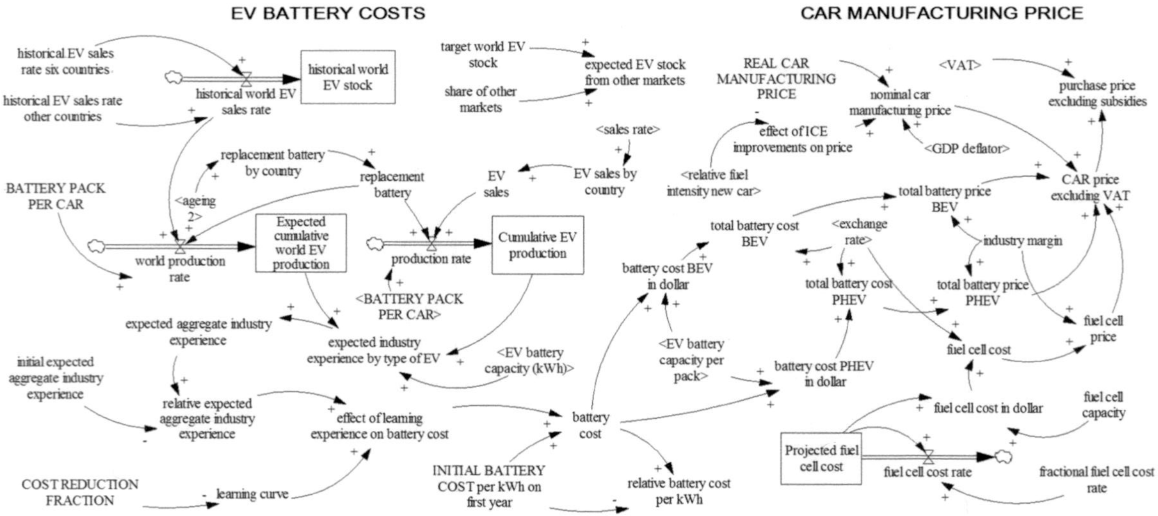

Figure 4.63: Overview of the sub-module ‘Production Costs’ | Source: Own work using Vensim®

This distinction between cost and price is important, especially in the context of batteries and fuel cells. A realistic model representation of this process would incorporate decision rules that attempt to capture car-manufacturers' strategies concerning R&D and desired return on investment (ROI) for batteries. But this approach is beyond scope. Production costs and purchase prices depend not only on powertrain but also on the size of the car and targeted consumers. For example, SUVs and luxury cars are more expensive than a compact car, because they are more costly to manufacture and are marketed and priced for high-income drivers. Arguably, whereas production costs may decrease over time, this does not necessarily translate into lower purchase prices. An example is a situation where manufacturers consider that consumers can still bear the prevailing prices. The manufacturers' price setting process is not explicitly modelled. Instead, a mark-up is assumed. Figure 4.64 shows the assumed nominal car manufacturing price for technologies relying on the ICE (with the exception of HEVs and PHEVs) for Germany.

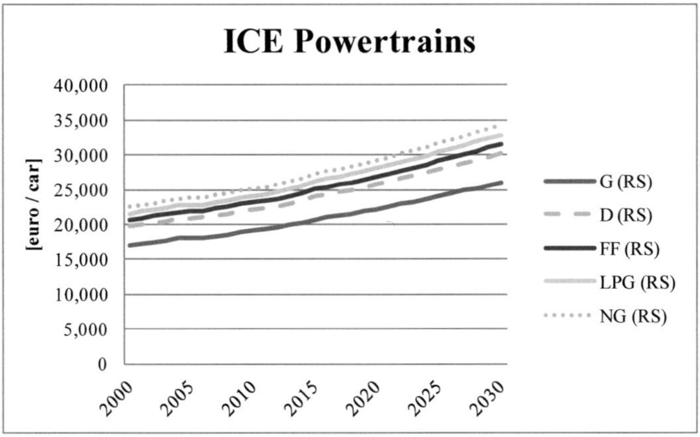

Figure 4.64: Evolution of car prices in Germany | Source: Own work using Vensim®

4.2.16 Consumer costs

In this work, the two streams of costs faced by prospective buyers of a certain powertrain are: ownership and usage. Figure 4.65 shows how these streams are organised. To simplify, depreciation does not enter the economic calculation of costs. Since the insurance premium is assumed not to vary across powertrains, it has also been disregarded. The two components of usage cost are the driving cost and the maintenance cost. The usage cost is calculated over the entire assumed lifetime of the car.

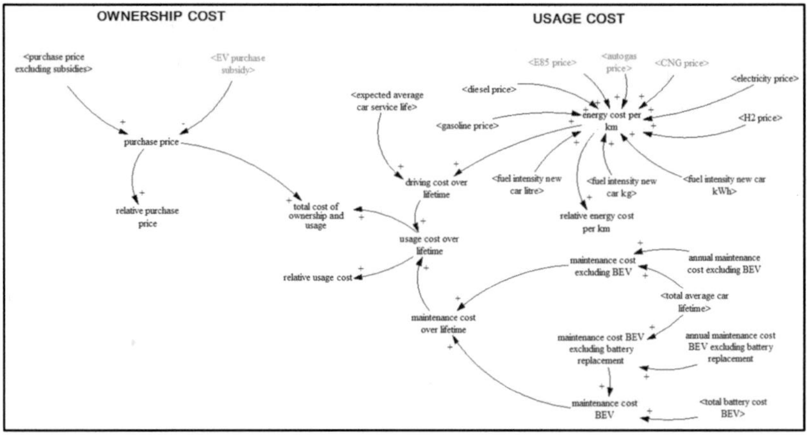

Figure 4.65: Overview of the sub-module 'Consumer Costs' | Source: Own work using Vensim®

The driving cost is influenced by the efficiency of the powertrain and the corresponding energy price. With regards to the maintenance cost, the same value is used for all the powertrains, with the exception of BEVs. Since the model assumes that the service life of the EVB is 100,000 km, a battery replacement needs to take place after 8 years of the date the BEV was purchased. Since the assumed average car lifetime is 16 years, one battery replacement is necessary over the car lifetime. This entails an additional cost for those consumers characterised in this work as utility maximisers. This extra cost is added as part of the calculation of maintenance costs, for it represents the cost these consumers face if the wish to *maintain* the usability of their purchased BEV. Figure 4.66 shows the assumed values for the US market at certain years. As can be seen, whereas the value reflecting the maintenance cost for the gasoline car remains constant, the value capturing the maintenance cost for the BEV decreases over time. This is caused by the price evolution of the EVB.

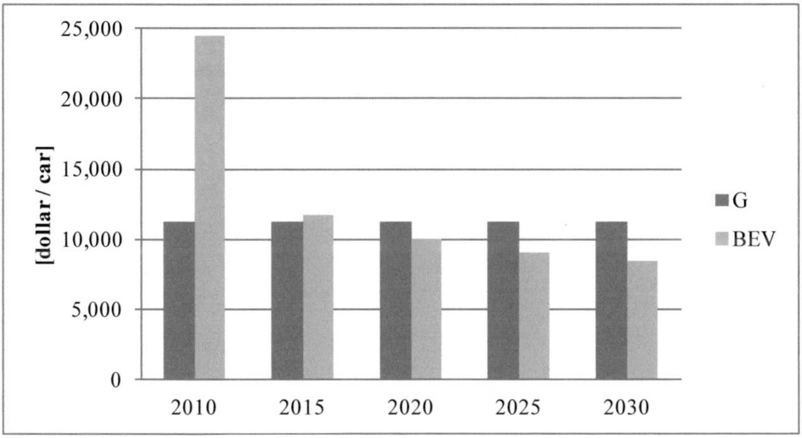

Figure 4.66: Evolution of maintenance costs in the US | Source: Own assumption

4.2.17 Powertrain attractiveness

It seems reasonable to assume that consumers can choose what is available or will soon be available in the market. Examples include: the recent market commercialisation of FC cars and the pre-orders for the Tesla Model 3. It is uncertain when these new products will be introduced in other countries. Interestingly, the aforementioned BEV branded Nissan Leaf is expected to be introduced in the Indian market in 2018. That is, around 8 years after it was first successfully commercialised in its domestic Japanese market. Also, there is preliminary empirical evidence of correlation between the number of models/makes of a powertrain available in the market and sales of that powertrain. But this mainly depends directly on private business decisions, not governments. The exceptions are perhaps State-owned enterprises (SOEs), such as the major Chinese car manufacturers. Examples of car-makers with a mixed stock ownership by family, government and foreign capital can be found in Europe (Groupe PSA and Volkswagen AG). Since the model does not account for models/makes, this correlation cannot be taken into account.

In the model, choice is influenced by a measure of 'powertrain attractiveness', which differs by market segment (see section 4.2.11). Attractiveness can be constrained by powertrain availability, which is determined by the year in which the powertrain technology was introduced in the market. For instance, electric cars are not available in the market at the beginning of the simulation and hence the attractiveness of these powertrains is constrained to zero. Figure 4.67 shows the sub-module 'Attractiveness'. The model assumptions encapsulated in this sub-module are applicable to the innovators and utility maximisers segments.

For the innovators sub-group, the higher the degree of perceived innovativeness, the higher the attractiveness and, in turn, the market share of the powertrain. The *degree of innovativeness* is modelled as a stock variable, affected by the inflow *gaining innovativeness* and the outflow *losing innovativeness*. Whereas the inflow is determined by the timing of the market introduction of a given powertrain in each country, it is assumed that the degree of innovativeness can fade away using a 5-year constant. Between 2015 and 2030, BEVs are simulated to have the highest degree of perceived innovativeness. Because the degree of innovativeness is not a function of the simulated policies, the values do not differ between scenarios.

For the utility maximisers sub-group, the choice of technology, attractiveness is determined in a more elaborated way. In a first step, a vector of country-invariant coefficients is chosen, thereby characterising the six attributes considered: purchase price, usage cost, range, recharging time, emissions and station coverage (see Eq. 4.22). The default coefficients are shown in Table 4.15. In interaction with the simulated values of the attributes, which differ across countries, a measure of utility for each attribute is obtained. In this context, the powertrain of reference is the gasoline car. Alternative specific constants have not been included. By imposing an additive formulation, unrestricted attractiveness is derived.

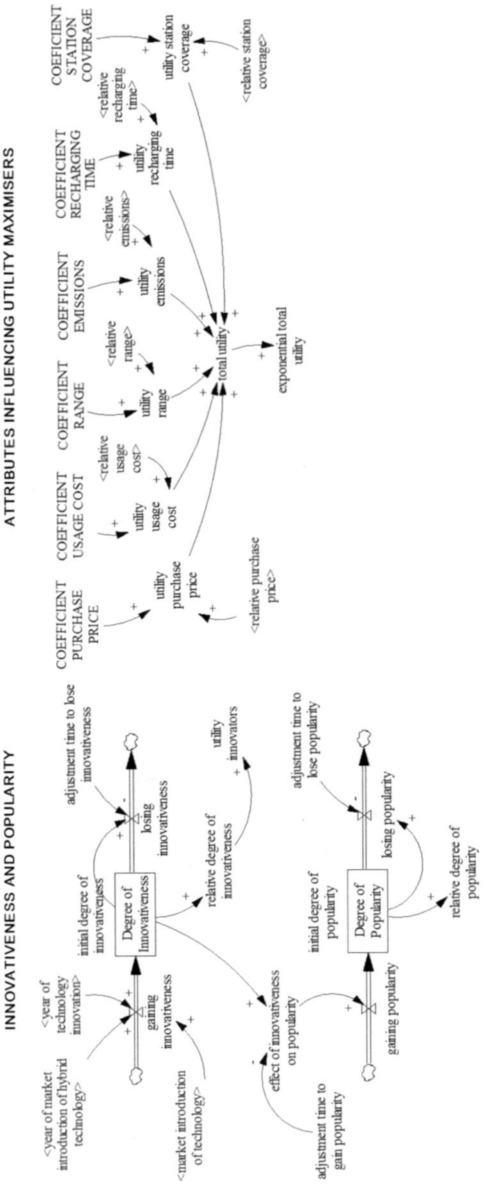

Figure 4.67: Overview of the sub-module 'Attractiveness' | Source: Own work using Vensim®

In a subsequent step, attractiveness is restricted in two ways: (i) by powertrain availability, which prevents that a certain powertrain (e.g. FC) is chosen if availability is zero (e.g. because there are no H_2 filling stations); and (ii) by a measure of popularity (Eq. 4.23). The latter is represented by the stock variable *degree of popularity* (*pop*), which can be altered by the inflow *gaining popularity* and the outflow *losing popularity* (Eq. 4.24). The inflow is influenced by the aforementioned *degree of innovativeness*, to which an adjustment time (AT) ranging from 3 to 9 years is added. In other words, a popularisation effect through which powertrains that are perceived as innovative (i.e. recently introduced in the market) become popular after some years is modelled. Given the decision rules assumed for each sub-group (recall Table 4.14), such popularisation effect can shape the choice of only the utility maximisers sub-group. Similar to the degree of innovativeness, the degree of popularity can erode over time. In this case, a time lag with a value equal to 10 years is assumed to define the outflow. As expected, BEVs are the most popular powertrain in all the countries in 2030. Because popularity is modelled as a function of innovativeness, the simulated values again do not change between scenarios. However, powertrain attractiveness as perceived by the utility maximisers sub-group does change between scenarios. The reason for this being that the simulated policies have an impact on the powertrain attributes.

$$U_{hit} = e^{(\alpha_{it}*price_{hit})+(\beta_{it}*cost_{hit})+(\gamma_{it}*range_{hit})+(\delta_{it}*time_{hit})+(\varepsilon_{it}*emission_{hit})+(\theta_{it}*coverage_{hit})} \quad (4.22)$$

$$attractiveness_{h,i,t} = a_{h,i,t} * U_{h,i,t} * pop_{h,i,} \quad \forall h,i,t \quad (4.23)$$

[dmnl] [dmnl] [dmnl] [dmnl]

$$pop_{h,i}(\mathrm{t}) = \int_{t_0}^{t} [(\frac{gaining_{h,i}}{AT_{h,i}^{inflow}})(t) - (\frac{losing_{h,i}}{AT_{h,i}^{outflow}})(t)]dt + pop_{h,i}(t_0) \quad (4.24)$$

[dmnl] [dmnl/year] [dmnl/year] [dmnl]

Table 4.15: Utility coefficients, by attribute

Purchase price	Usage cost	(e-)Range	Recharging time	Emissions	Station coverage
(α)	(β)	(γ)	(δ)	(ε)	(θ)
-0.5	-0.5	0.1	-0.1	-0.05	0.05

Source: Own assumptions

Figure 4.68 shows the dynamic behaviour of the variables *degree of innovation* (*inno*) and *pop*, in relative terms, for gasoline and electric cars in Japan (in this market diesel cars remain unpopular). The perceived innovation and popularity of gasoline cars starts declining after the commercialisation of EVs. The market introduction of PHEVs has a temporary adverse impact on the perceived innovation of BEVs. However this powertrain recovers quickly under the assumption that better batteries with greater e-range are perceived by the market as a series of innovative steps. The behaviour of PHEVs could be interpreted as a representation of fads. Due to the assumed time lags between innovation and popularisation, whereas the innovativeness of BEVs exceeds that of gasoline cars in 2012, the former become more popular than the latter only in 2019.

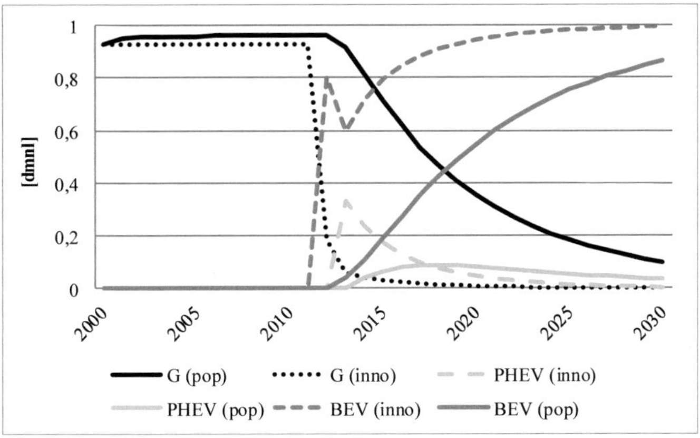

Figure 4.68: Simulated relative degree of popularity in Japan | Source: Own work using Vensim®

With regards to the remaining two market segments, attractiveness is defined as follows: for the habit sub-group, the powertrain scrapped yields the highest level of attractiveness; for the low-cost sub-group, the cheapest powertrain (i.e. the one with the lowest purchase price at the year the choice is made) yields the greatest attractiveness.

4.2.18 Electricity generation

China, which has become the world's largest generator of electricity, and India display a trend towards increased electricity generation. The rest of the analysed countries have a relatively stable level of electricity generation activity, with a recent dip caused by the financial crisis. This may change as a result of EV uptake, as it will be shown later.

Currently, across the countries analysed in this work the degree of market concentration varies. In France and China, concentration is high: State-owned *Électricité de France* (EDF) is the main French electric utility and the Chinese market is split in two electric utilities: *Guójiā Diànwǎng Gōngsī* (State Grid Corporation of China (SGCC)), the largest in the world, and *Zhōngguó Nánfāng Diànwǎng* (China Southern Power Grid Company Limited (CSG)). Regional players are present in Germany and Japan, where the electricity market continues to be shaped by the Fukushima nuclear disaster in 2011 (the short-term impact of this event is visible in Figure 4.73). In India, the market consists of public sector undertakings (PSUs), state-level corporations and private firms. The latter play a major role in the US, an early example of electricity market liberalisation. The trend towards decentralisation of electricity generation is not examined in this work. Figures 4.69-4.74 show how the utilities of these countries chose to generate electricity in the past using the energy sources available to them: oil, coal, natural gas, nuclear and renewables. Only in Japan does oil still hold a non-negligible share. There is an overall growing trend, at different paces in each country, for renewables. Coal dominates production in China and India. The mix is more diversified in Germany and the US. In France, nuclear energy reigns. Nuclear phase-out is underway in Germany, with inactivity in German nuclear power plants to be expected by 2022.

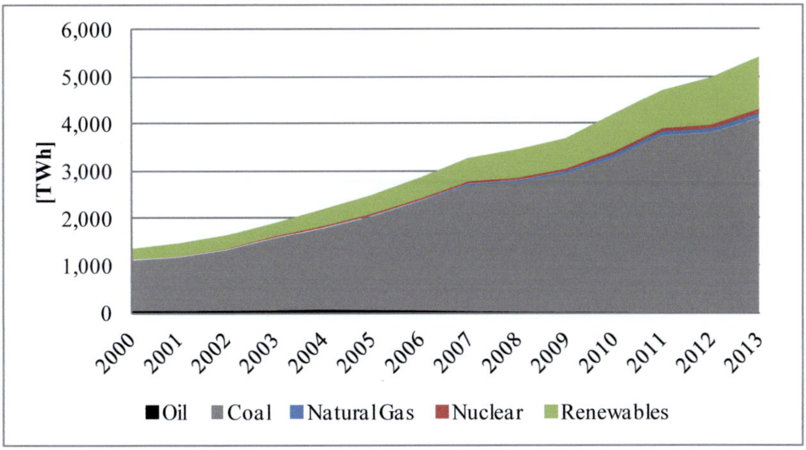

Figure 4.69: Electricity generation in China by source
Source: Data (2000-2013) based on IEA (2016a)

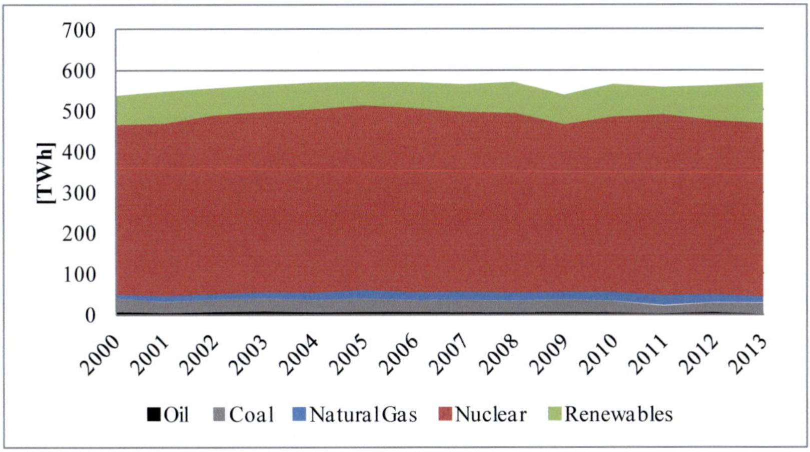

Figure 4.70: Electricity generation in France by source
Source: Data (2000-2013) based on IEA (2016a)

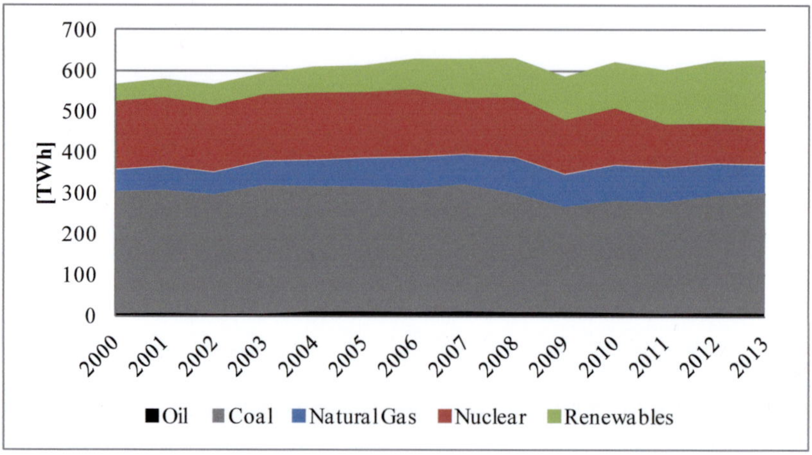

Figure 4.71: Electricity generation in Germany by source
Source: Data (2000-2013) based on IEA (2016a)

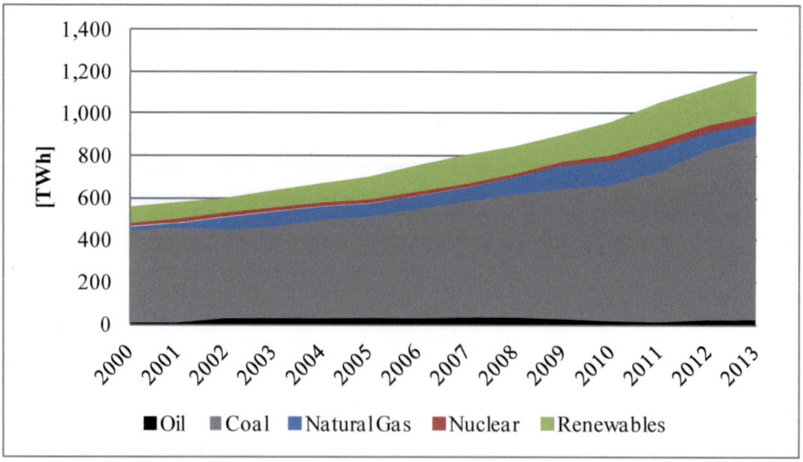

Figure 4.72: Electricity generation in India by source
Source: Data (2000-2013) based on IEA (2016a)

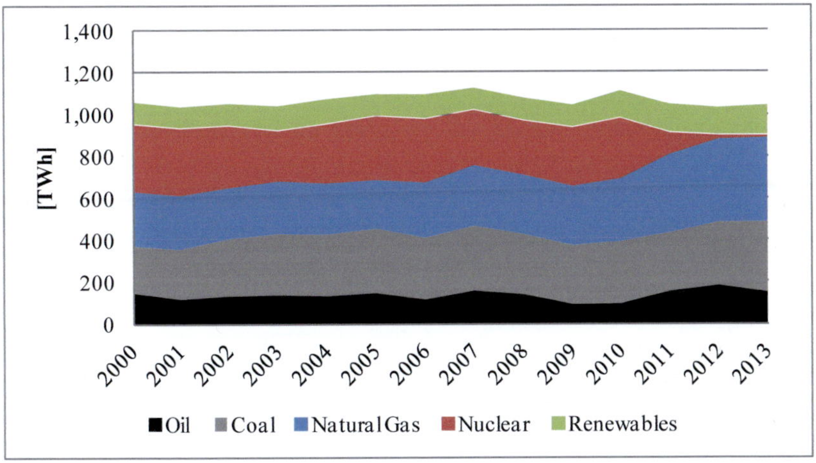

Figure 4.73: Electricity generation in Japan by source
Source: Data (2000-2013) based on IEA (2016a)

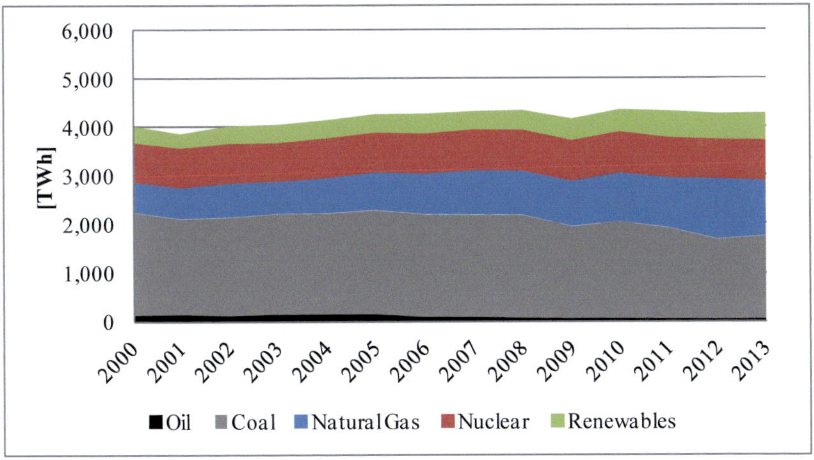

Figure 4.74: Electricity generation in the US by source
Source: Data (2000-2013) based on IEA (2016a)

Assuming that the planned nuclear and renewables targets materialise (the extent to which the new US government reverses the policy pledges of the previous administration has not been taken into account), two types of scenarios for 2030 can be generated by giving different weights to coal and natural gas generation. In a hypothetical *gas* scenario, gas would fulfil the required electricity needs with gas turbine power plants gaining market share at the expense of alternatives. In the *coal* scenario, coal-fired power plants would continue to play an important role. This last scenario is the one adopted for reporting in this thesis. The assumed country-specific electricity mix is shown in Figure 4.75. It is assumed that oil will play no role in electricity generation in the future. The implications of neither merit-order situations nor emission trading schemes have been modelled. Simply, a trade-off between marginal cost (low for carbon, higher for natural gas) and carbon intensity (high for carbon, lower for natural gas) underpins the selected scenario.

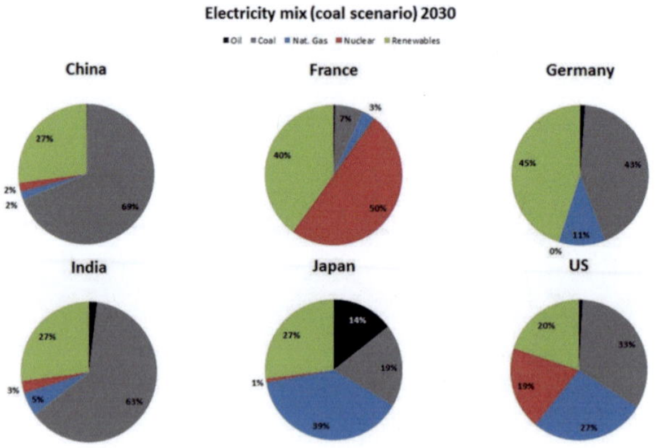

Figure 4.75: Electricity mix (coal scenario) by country in 2030 | Source: Own assumptions

4.2.19 Energy use

Figure 4.76 gives an overview of the 'Energy Use' sub-module. As can be recalled from section 4.2.12, the analysis of energy use may be framed in terms of expected travel demand or simulated travel demand. In the exposition, expected travel demand is chosen.

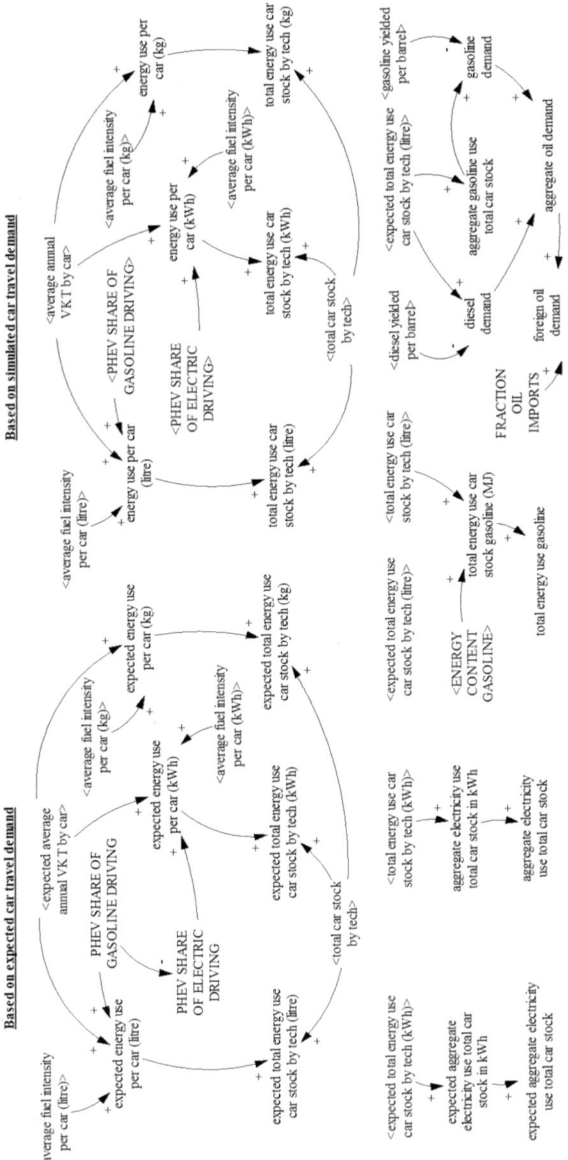

Figure 4.76: Overview of the sub-module ‘Energy use’ | Source: Own work using Vensim®

4.2.20 Emissions

Three types of emissions are included in this modelling exercise: CH_4, CO_2 and N_2O. Because these gases are long-lived and have a global impact, the emission metric known as global warming potential for a hundred-year horizon (GWP-100) is conventionally adopted. But the choice of emission metric and time horizon is still under scientific debate (for a discussion of alternative metrics, see Shine (2009) and chapter 8 in IPCC (2013)). The assumed emissions values are respectively 25, 1 and 298 gCO_{2eq}/gram (IPCC, 2007b). Table 4.16 shows the assumed energy content (*E*) and emission factors (EFs) for five types of fuel included in the model. Since these values are used to calculate on-road emissions, the values assumed for electricity and hydrogen are zero. Eq. 4.25 shows how emissions are calculated in the *Emission Factors* sub-module.

$$GHG^f = \sum_j \left(GWP_j * \left(EF_j^f * E^f \right) \right) \quad (4.25)$$

[gCO_{2eq}/unit of fuel] [gCO_{2eq}/gram] [gram/MJ] [MJ/unit of fuel]

Table 4.16: Energy content and emission factors by fuel

Fuel type	Energy content	Emission factor by type of GHG		
	[MJ/litre]	[gCH_4/MJ]	[gCO_2/MJ]	[gN_2O/MJ]
Gasoline	34.2	0.025	69.3	0.008
Diesel	38.6	0.0039	74.1	0.0039
E85	25.6	0.018	71.4	0**
Autogas	26.8	0.062	63.1	0.0002
CNG	50.0*	0.092	56.1	0.003

*The unit is [MJ/kg]. **Representative of the bioethanol market in Brazil. Source: IPCC (2006)

Figure 4.77 illustrates a summary of these calculations. Once CH_4 and N_2O emissions are taken into account, CNG supersedes diesel as the largest emitting fuel, with values close to 3,000 grams per kg and litre, respectively. Electricity and H_2 emit no direct GHG emissions. However, the information shown here is not directly related to emissions per km. For this, the corresponding car-related fuel efficiencies by powertrain need to enter the calculation. This is considered next and described for the direct CO_2 emissions of new cars by Eq. 4.26. The exception is PHEVs, which can be powered by more than one fuel.

$$CO2_{i,CO2,t}^{TTW} = \lambda_{i,t} * \left(EF_{CO2}^{TTW,f} * E^{f}\right) \tag{4.26}$$

[gram/km] [unit of fuel/km] [gram/MJ] [MJ/unit of fuel]

From the perspective of current regulation and consumer choice, only the direct CO_2 emissions of the average new passenger car are of interest. This is part of the *New Car Emissions* sub-module. The implicit assumption is that consumers only consider CO_2 emissions, as reported in manufacturers' catalogues, in their decision-making process, thereby disregarding other types of GHG emissions. Notwithstanding, calculation of CH_4 and N_2O is desirable for a more accurate picture and this is included in the model.

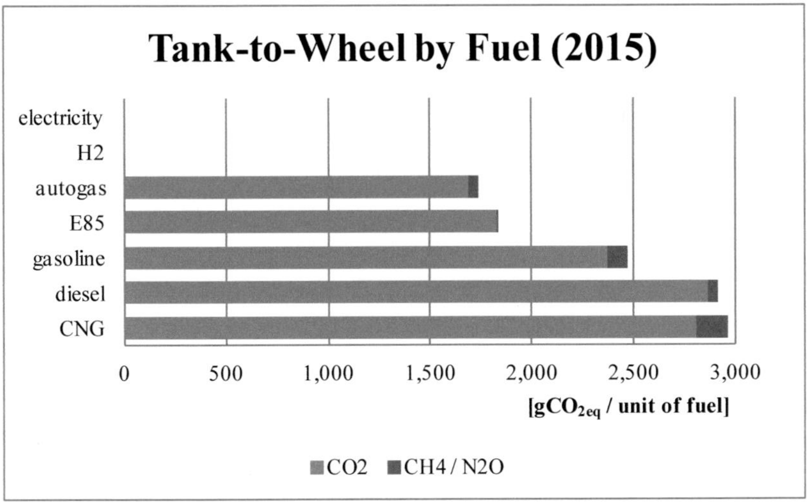

Figure 4.77: Direct GHG emissions by energy source
Source: Own work based on data shown in Table 4.16

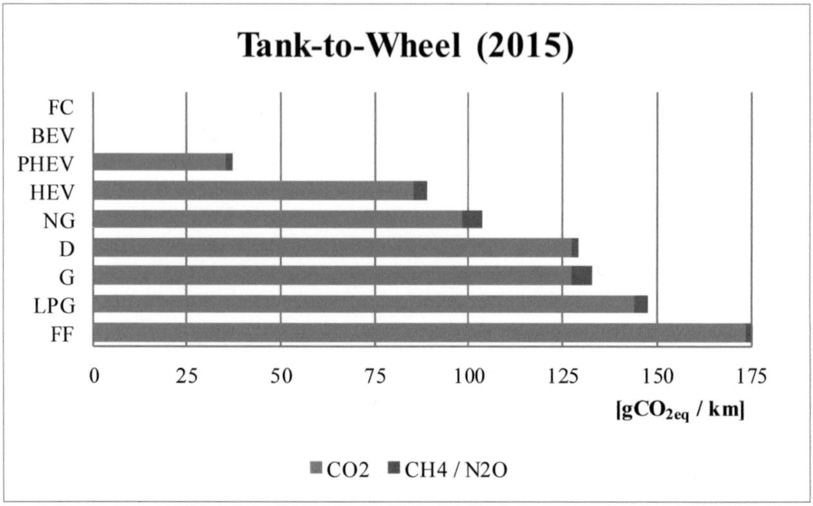

Figure 4.78: Direct emissions by powertrain in Germany
Source: Own work based on data shown in Table 4.16

In addition to direct or TTW emissions, it is of interest to provide information on indirect or WTT emissions. Based on the assumed electricity mix (section 4.2.18) and the EFs for electricity highlighted in Table 4.17, WTT emissions for this type of source of energy can be derived. The results are shown in Figure 4.79. The values originated from the *coal* and *gas* scenarios differ, as expected. The behaviour in the case of Germany and, particularly, France require a brief explanation. Since nuclear energy generation is assumed to have the lowest value, any attempt to reduce its share will inevitably lead to higher emissions, *ceteris paribus*.

Table 4.17: WTT electricity emissions by energy source

Emission factors	Oil	Coal	Natural gas	Nuclear	Renewables
gCO_{2eq}/kWh	840	1,001	469	16	27*

*Unweighted average of wind, PV and concentrated solar. Source: Edenhofer *et al.* (2011)

Overall, the resulting WTT emissions related to EVs can be treated as conservative for two main reasons. Firstly, the scenario adopted for reporting emissions in this thesis is the *coal* one. Secondly, the EF for coal found in Edenhofer *et al.* (2011) represents the value at the fiftieth percentile of a literature review that comprised 52 references. The statistical range goes from 675 to 1,689 gCO_{2eq}/kWh. Since the EFs in Table 4.17 are assumed to remain constant throughout the simulation period, efficiency gains that may occur in the future are neglected. In the particular case of coal and natural gas, the assumption of static EFs is unlikely to hold, because investments in carbon capture and storage (CCS) may be made. In Edenhofer *et al.* (2011), the EFs from coal with CCS range from a minimum of 98 to a maximum of 396 gCO_{2eq}/kWh. In contrast to other energy carriers, it is important to stress that the EF for coal is subject to uncertainty arising not only from the technology employed to burn it, but also from the product itself. Different types of coals such as anthracite (i.e. hard coal) or lignite (i.e. brown coal) possess varying grades or levels of quality that affect emissions. For an example of EFs for coal used in German power plants, see FfE (2010).

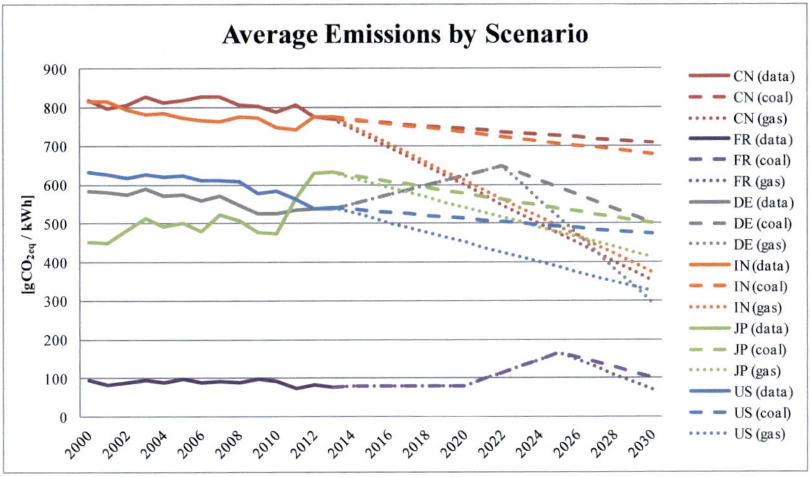

Figure 4.79: Carbon intensity of electricity generation by country
Source: Data (2000-2013) based on (IEA, 2016a) and own assumptions (2014-2030)

Taking into account WTT emissions associated with EVs is crucial. In addition, WTT emissions for the rest of fuels are required to obtain a less biased picture. The focus is on average emissions, and this reflects the implicit assumption that EVs do not affect the average carbon intensity of the grid. This is unrealistic. An increase in the number of registered EVs leads to an increase in the demand for electricity, and this has implications for the sources of energy used to supply electricity. Research on marginal vs. average emissions from electricity generation is active. As noted in section 4.2.18, capturing these feedback effects requires a more elaborate description of the electricity system than depicted here.

With regards to the WTT emissions arising from upstream H_2 and CNG production, there is also a lot of uncertainty as to which values can be plausibly assumed. What is clear is that these are different from zero. Based on Canadian values, Cetinkaya *et al.* (2012) performed an LCA using various methods and found that GHG emissions related to hydrogen production range from 970-2,412 (using respectively wind and photovoltaic electrolysis) to 11,893 as a result of natural gas steam reforming (NGSR). The latter is still the most common way of generating H_2 (Turner, 2004). In the model, the 2,412 value is selected given the expectation that electrolysis will play a greater role by 2030. Concerning CNG, for simplicity the same WTT values assumed for oil-based products are adopted for CNG. Note that differences between conventional natural gas and shale gas are to be expected. For more details, see Burnham *et al.* (2012), who used the Greenhouse gases, Regulated Emissions, and Energy use in Transportation (GREET) model.

In recent years, there has been a boom in unconventional oil extraction, with hydraulic fracturing accounting for 51% of US crude oil extraction in 2015 (EIA, 2016b). The WTT emissions of oil-based fuels are expected to differ if they are the result of conventional or unconventional oil extraction activity. To account for this possibility in the model, a stock that reflects the dynamic evolution of the share of conventional and unconventional oil was created. Throughout the modelling exercise, it shall be assumed for all the countries that the share of unconventional oil extraction and corresponding upstream emissions increases, as visible from Figure 4.80.

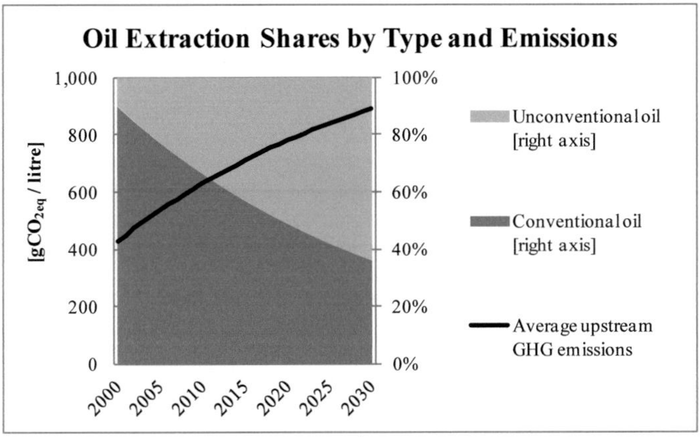

Figure 4.80: Oil extraction and upstream emissions | Source: Own assumptions

Recently, the impact of indirect land use changes (ILUC) in the context of biofuel generation has been under much discussion. First generation biofuels, also known as agrofuels, can be produced from agricultural crops with differing environmental impacts. In the model, the variable *indirect land use change CO_{2eq} from biofuel production* has a value of 34, which corresponds to 1G of ethanol production from wheat. According to Ecofys (2016), values may range from 14 (production from maize) to 231 (from palm oil). Figure 4.81 shows the upstream emission assumptions for the remaining fuels. Finally, the model has a blend of 85% ethanol and 15% gasoline for FF cars set by default.

Figure 4.82 shows the results of adding the assumed WTT GHG emissions to the numbers from Figure 4.78. Again, Germany is taken as an example and 2015 values, reported in gCO_{2eq}/km by powertrain, are derived. Based on this WTW metric, it can be deduced that FCs and BEVs are no longer zero emission technologies. But compared with the rest, these powertrains still rank as the lowest emitting. As the global trends towards greater extraction of unconventional oil and decarbonisation of the electricity grid continue, the WTW GHG emissions gap between electric and conventional cars can be expected to widen.

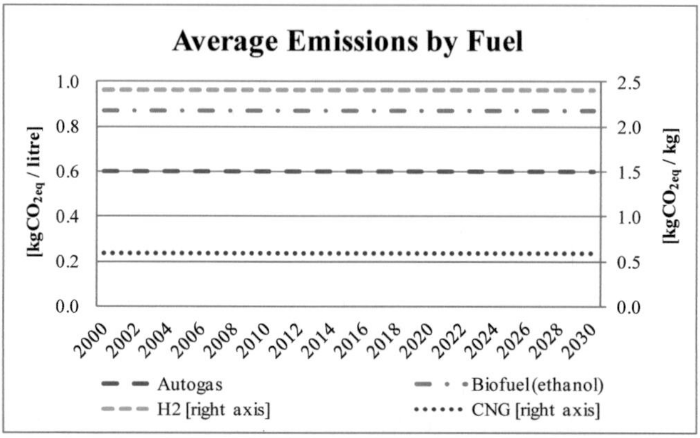

Figure 4.81: Upstream emissions by alternative fuel | Source: Own assumptions

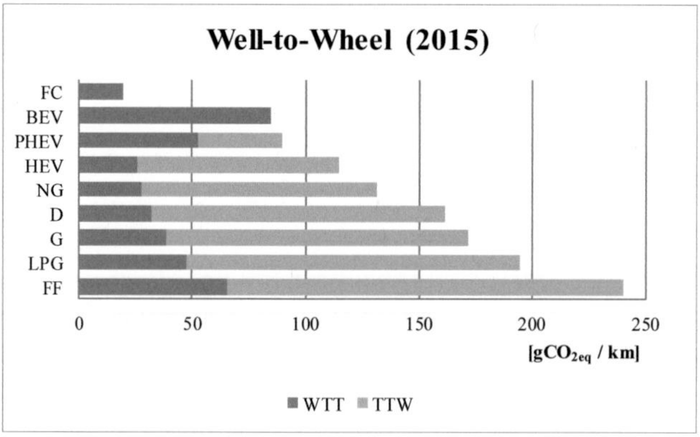

Figure 4.82: WTW emissions by powertrain in Germany
Source: Own work based on data shown in Tables 4.16-4.17 and own assumptions

Furthermore, the emissions generated by car manufacturing and scrappaging should not be entirely neglected, even if there are numerical uncertainties associated with these. The underlying assumption is that these types of emissions differ by powertrain, especially when the EVB is considered. Table 4.18 shows key assumptions. Thus it shall be assumed that electric cars have lower scrappage emissions, higher manufacturing emissions and, overall, higher manufacturing and scrappage (M&S) emissions than conventional cars.

Strictly speaking, this modelling exercise is not an example of a lifecycle assessment/analysis (LCA). Instead, the work relies on values from desk research, if readily available, and own assumptions (see e.g. Figure 4.81). Hence these are generic and not specific, average values perhaps. As Ball and Wietschel (2009) indicate, in order to reach policy conclusions on the value of alternative fuels or powertrains, a thorough LCA is not required.

Table 4.18: Car manufacturing and scrappage emissions

Variable Name	Value [Units]	Source
EV battery emissions	120 [kgCO_{2eq}/kWh]	Samaras and Meisterling (2008)
Car manufacturing emissions	8,500 [kgCO_{2eq}/car]	Samaras and Meisterling (2008)
Car scrappage emissions (ICE)	1,170 [kgCO_{2eq}/car]	Notter *et al.* (2010)
Car scrappage emissions (BEV)	1,140 [kgCO_{2eq}/car]	Notter *et al.* (2010)

4.3 Policy inputs

The set of policies available to the model user in the version of the model presented in this thesis encompasses policy options of regulatory (standards) and economic nature (taxation, subsidies and investment). In this work, the terms policy input, variable, instrument, option and measure are used interchangeably. This section concisely describes the policy inputs that are related to the module *Policy* (see Figure 4.83). For further details on the numerical values adopted in the scenarios exercise, see Table 6.1 in section 6.1). Finally, the role of budgets is illustrated. It is adventurous to ignore political realities by presuming that actual governments will devote quasi-unlimited resources to H_2 infrastructure deployment or sustain EV subsidies for many years. The basic framework is represented by means of Eq. 4.27.

$$B_h(\mathrm{t}) = \int_{t_0}^{t} [revenues_h\,(t) - expenditures_h\,(t)]dt + B_h(t_0) \qquad (4.27)$$

[currency] [currency/year] [currency/year] [currency]

where B denotes a dedicated fund, as part of the government budget.

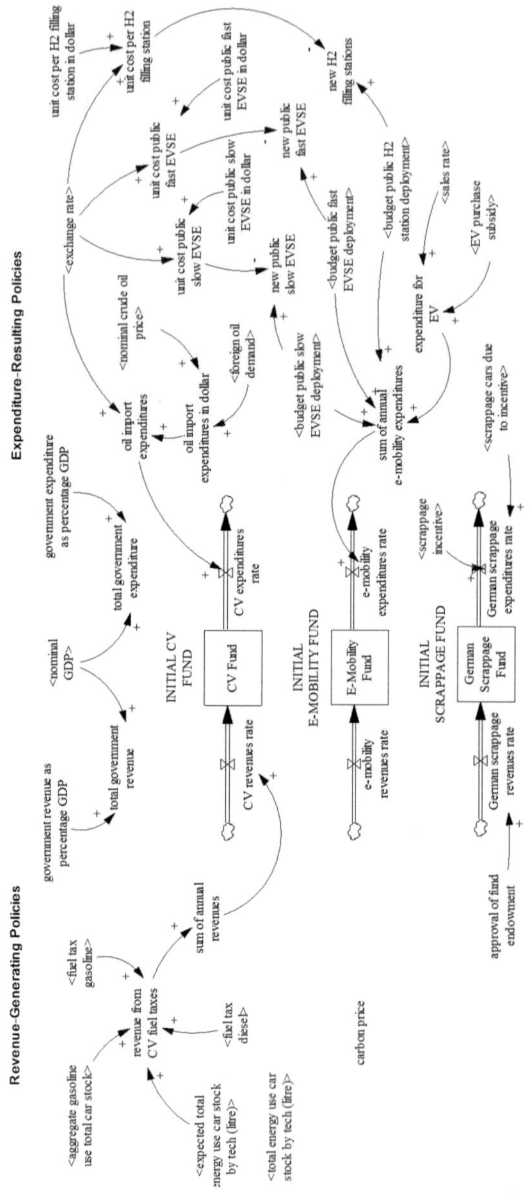

Figure 4.83: Overview of the module 'Policy' | Source: Own work using Vensim®

The implications of policies for the public budget are captured by the three stocks in that figure, namely the CV fund, the e-mobility fund and, for Germany, the scrappage fund. An example of the latter is an endowment of 5 billion euros in 2007-2008, entirely depleted in 2009 (the year the scrappage scheme was implemented in Germany).

4.3.1 Emission and efficiency standards

The only regulatory instrument examined in this work refers to emission standards. Although specifically designed in the context of reducing direct CO_2 emissions from cars, they are directly related to fuel consumption. Therefore, emission standards may be interpreted as car-related fuel efficiency or fuel economy standards. In this thesis, the goal of this policy instrument is to reduce fuel use and direct CO_2 emissions from new conventional cars. A linear relationship between litres of conventional fuel and grams of CO_2 is assumed.

4.3.2 Value added tax

The value added tax (VAT) is also known as *consumption tax* in Japan and *sales tax* in the US. Conventionally understood, the goal of this policy instrument is to generate revenues. This variable is included in the model, albeit the country-specific value of VAT (i.e. VAT rate) remains constant throughout the modelling exercise. Figure 4.84 shows the percentage of VAT in each country in 2015. Between 2000 and 2015, the values are the same with two exceptions: (i) in France, VAT was 19.6% between 2000 and 2013; in Germany, VAT was 16% over the period 2000-2006. Although different products may have differing VAT rates reflecting preferential taxation (e.g. differing VAT rates for natural gas and electricity in France (IEA, 2016b)), it is assumed for simplicity that the same VAT rate applies to all the relevant variables in each country.

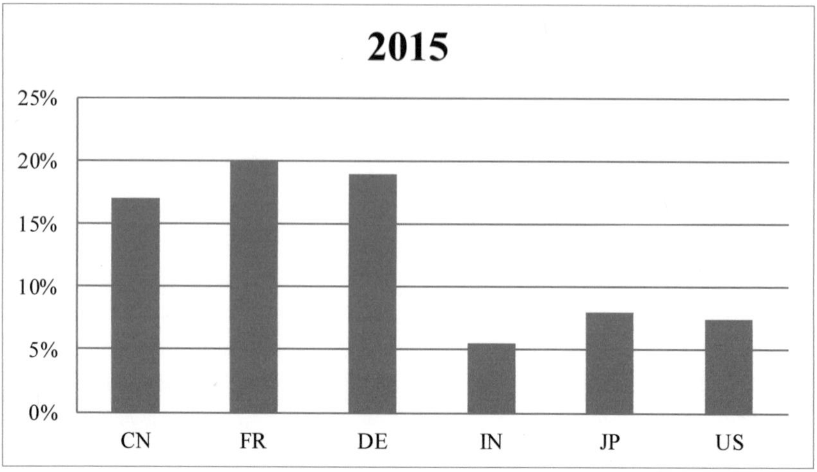

Figure 4.84: Value added tax rate by country | Source: Wikipedia (2016)

4.3.3 Energy taxation

The goal of this policy instrument is to influence energy prices. Energy taxation also provides a source of government revenue (see again Figure 4.82). Economic policy inputs are set by the model user in nominal terms, encouraging the user to reflect on the inflation assumptions. Recalling Eq. 4.6, the energy tax is expressed by $\tau_{h,t}^{nom}$. In particular, three examples of such policy input are given: *fuel tax gasoline*, *fuel tax diesel* and *electricity tax*. Throughout the modelling exercise presented here, the *electricity tax*, constrained by data availability, remains unchanged.

4.3.4 EV purchase subsidies

The goal of this policy instrument is to reduce the purchase price of EVs, thereby making them a more attractive option for prospective car purchasers. EV subsidies also represent a source of government expenditure (see again Figure 4.82). In this thesis, subsidies for only PHEVs and BEVs are examined.

4.3.5 Investment in refuelling infrastructure

The goal of investing in refuelling and recharging infrastructure is to facilitate the market uptake of AFVs and EVs. The deployment of public refuelling infrastructure represents a source of government expenditure (see again Figure 4.82). In order to invest in public refuelling infrastructure, information on deployment prices is needed. This is summarised in Table 4.19. The values are expressed in nominal terms and are assumed, for simplicity, to remain constant for the period 2015-2030. The implicit assumption is that potential reductions in deployment costs are offset by inflation. Fast EVSE is assumed to be more expensive than slow EVSE.

Table 4.19: Deployment costs of EVSE and H_2 refuelling infrastructure (2015)

[currency/station]	CN	FR	DE	IN	JP	US
Slow EVSE	59,161	8,566	8,566	609,443	1,150,000	9,500
Fast EVSE	379,877	55,000	55,000	3,913,000	7,384,000	61,000
H_2	6,227,000	901,659	901,659	64,150,000	121,040,000	1,000,000

Source: own assumptions based on DOE (2015)

Three policy inputs are available: investment in *public slow EVSE*, *public fast EVSE* and *public H_2 refuelling stations*. As indicated in section 4.2.13, the assumptions concerning E85, autogas and CNG refuelling infrastructure remain unchanged.

4.3.6 Desired car occupancy level

The policy input termed *desired car occupancy rate* is thought to affect travel demand by car. The variable of interest in this case is the *desired annual average VKT by car* ($VKT^*_{h,t}$), which complements the other two approaches described in section 4.2.12.

5 Reference scenario and testing

This chapter reports on two aspects: the results of simulating the Reference Scenario (section 5.1) and the outcomes of model testing (section 5.2). The second scenario, called the *Alternative Scenario* (AS), is introduced in chapter 6.

5.1 RS simulation

As indicated in section 1.1, the model is capable of generating more than one scenario. For this thesis, two scenarios were constructed. This section illustrates the *Reference Scenario* (RS), which can be thought of as a business-as-usual (BAU), current or base(line) scenario.

According to the SD documentation tool known as SDM-Doc (see appendix II), the version of the model presented in this thesis contains 575 variables, of which 35 are state variables. When subscripts are taken into account, the number of elements exceeds 6,000. In order to solve the system of equations of the SD model, so that the dynamic behaviour of the modelled nonlinear system can be simulated, numerical integration is executed in Vensim®. Instead of using the data functions available in the software, the dataset is directly imported and loaded into the model, which speeds up computation. Using a standard laptop and Euler integration, only a few seconds of runtime are needed to obtain the model results. To find the approximate solution to the set of ordinary differential equations, initial values are required. Key initial values are shown in Tables 5.1-5.4.

Table 5.1: Initial values for the sales rate in 2000, by country and technology

Technology	CN	FR	DE	IN	JP	US
G	475,000	1,080,849	2,349,934	285,000	4,229,674	8,627,384
D	25,000	1,046,485	1,026,002	15,000	17,698	22,823
FF	0	0	0	0	0	112,820
LPG	0	6,309	0	0	0	208
NG	0	0	0	0	0	5,138
HEV	0	0	0	0	12,500	9,350
PHEV	0	0	0	0	0	0
BEV	0	0	0	0	0	0
FC	0	0	0	0	0	0

Source: Based on information from the appendices

Table 5.2: Initial values for the new car stock (S^{new}) in 2000, by country and technology

Technology	CN	FR	DE	IN	JP	US
G	475,000	1,080,849	2,349,934	285,000	4,229,674	8,627,384
D	25,000	1,046,485	1,026,002	15,000	17,698	22,823
FF	0	0	0	0	0	112,820
LPG	0	6,309	1,181	0	0	208
NG	0	0	2,685	0	0	5,138
HEV	0	0	0	0	12,500	9,350
PHEV	0	0	0	0	0	0
BEV	0	0	0	0	0	0
FC	0	0	0	0	0	0

Source: Based on information from the appendices

Table 5.3: Initial values for the middle car stock (S^{mid}) in 2000, by country and technology

Tech-nology	CN	FR	DE	IN	JP	US
G	4,581,280	10,241,220	21,033,660	3,420,000	26,245,020	74,925,600
D	241,120	5,144,412	3,198,600	150,000	2,616,000	60,000
FF	0	0	0	0	0	48,000
LPG	0	70,015	229	0	0	108,000
NG	0	0	651	0	0	61,200
HEV	0	0	0	0	22,741	12,000
PHEV	0	0	0	0	0	0
BEV	0	0	0	0	0	0
FC	0	0	0	0	0	0

Source: Based on information from the appendices

Table 5.4: Initial values for the old car stock (S^{old}) in 2000, by country and technology

Tech-nology	CN	FR	DE	IN	JP	US
G	3,054,187	6,827,480	14,022,440	2,280,000	17,496,680	49,950,400
D	160,747	3,429,608	2,132,400	100,000	1,744,000	40,000
FF	0	0	0	0	0	32,000
LPG	0	46,676	152	0	0	72,000
NG	0	0	434	0	0	40,800
HEV	0	0	0	0	15,161	8,000
PHEV	0	0	0	0	0	0
BEV	0	0	0	0	0	0
FC	0	0	0	0	0	0

Source: Based on information from the appendices

At this stage, a collection of country-specific model output may be presented. The next charts, which show car stock under the RS, serve this purpose. Under this scenario, conventional cars continue to dominate the market until 2030.

Gasoline cars clearly dominate the Chinese market under the RS, representing 92% of the car-mix in 2030. As can be seen in Figure 5.1, HEVs rank second, with a share of 5% in 2030. Diesel retains its edge in the European countries, albeit with a declining future trend in France. Figure 5.2 shows that the number of gasoline and diesel cars in use in France under the RS is simulated to decline to ca. 6 and 12 million in 2030, respectively. Hybrid technology plays an increasing role over the simulation period.

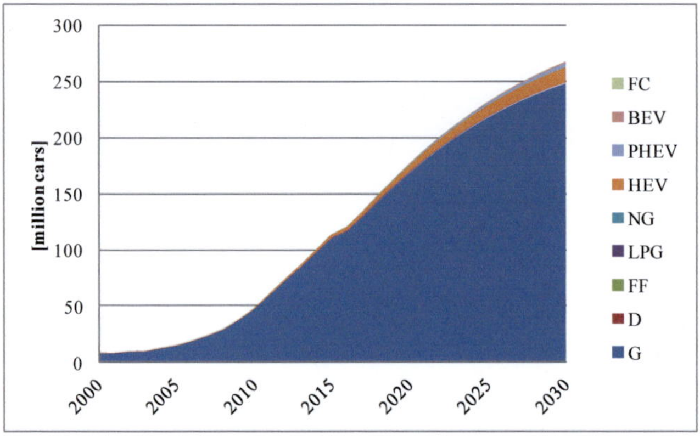

Figure 5.1: Car stock in China under the RS | Source: Own work using Vensim®

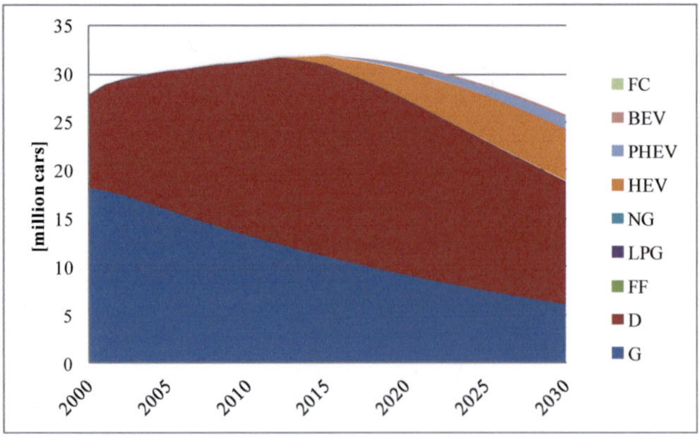

Figure 5.2: Car stock in France under the RS | Source: Own work using Vensim®

In the German market, a relatively stable stock of gasoline cars in simulated under the RS (Figure 5.3). Two powertrains exhibit visible future growth: diesel and PHEV. Whereas the former ends up accounting for over one-third of the car stock, the latter penetrates the market at a relatively slow but solid pace, reaching 4% of the car-mix in 2030.

Figure 5.4 shows that gasoline cars dominate the Indian market under the RS, followed by HEVs and, to a lesser extent, PHEVs and diesel cars.

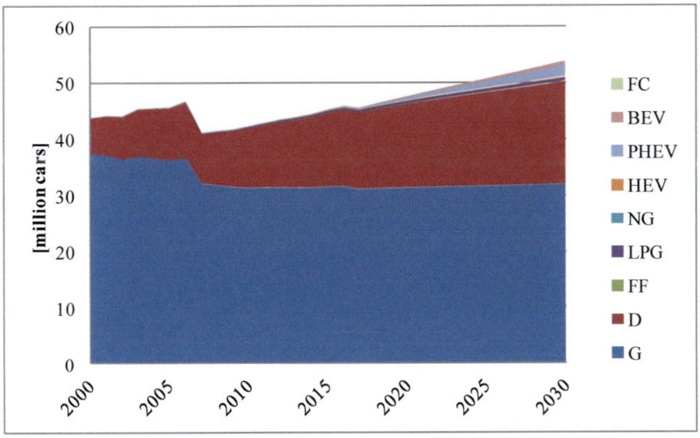

Figure 5.3: Car stock in Germany under the RS | Source: Own work using Vensim®

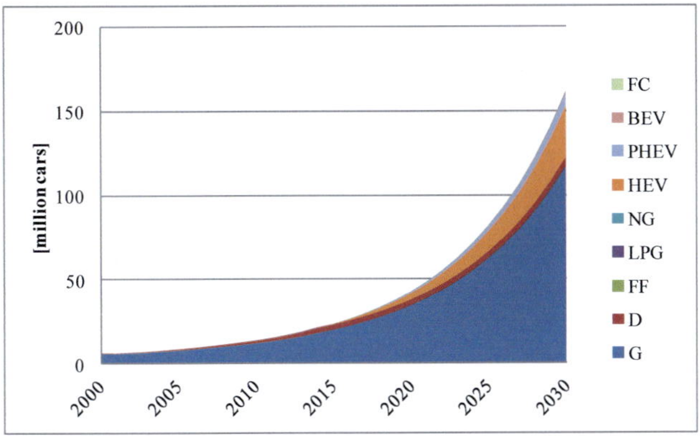

Figure 5.4: Car stock in India under the RS | Source: Own work using Vensim®

In the case of Japan, by 2030 gasoline cars account for ca. 85% of the car stock under the RS (Figure 5.5). The number of PHEVs in use is simulated to reach almost 7 million, or ca. 10% of the market, in 2030. In the US, the market position of gasoline cars is virtually uncontested under the RS (Figure 5.6). Unique to this market is the modest stock of FF cars powered by E85: 3.5 million in 2030.

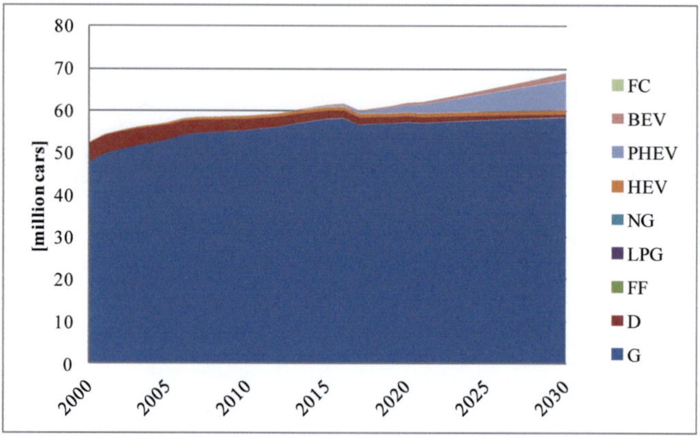

Figure 5.5: Car stock in Japan under the RS | Source: Own work using Vensim®

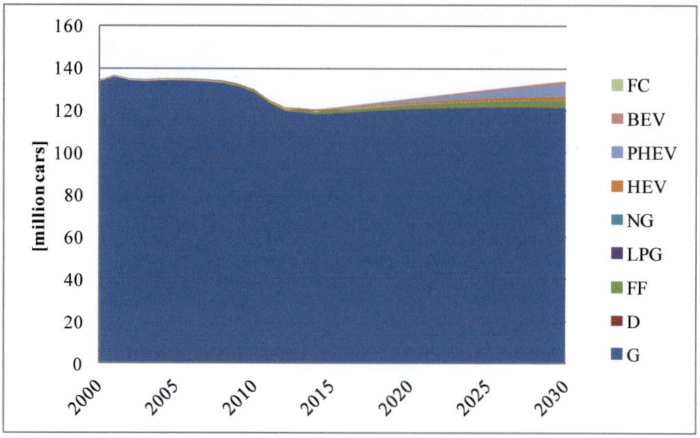

Figure 5.6: Car stock in the US under the RS | Source: Own work using Vensim®

The overall picture under the RS is that the market uptake of alternative powertrains has little reflection in the car stock until 2030. LPG and NG cars remain a niche option. In terms of electric cars, only PHEVs are simulated to gain some traction in the market under the RS.

In terms of direct CO_2 emissions, Figure 5.7 shows the results of the RS. China's emissions are simulated to exceed those of the US in this decade, clearly becoming the largest emitting country of the ones analysed by 2030. In that year, TTW CO_2 emissions in India and the US are simulated to reach a similar level. For the rest of the countries, a steady decline takes place.

In the remaining part of this chapter, key assumptions are tested, without altering the values of the policy inputs described in section 4.3. This last task shall be performed in chapter 6.

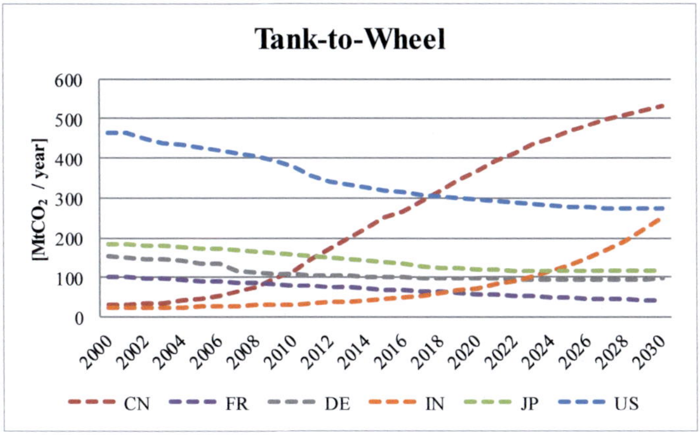

Figure 5.7: Direct CO_2 emissions from cars under the RS | Source: Own work

5.2 Testing

Under the premise that any model is wrong (Box, 1976), some attempt at validation is nevertheless desirable before model-based policy analysis is undertaken. Bossel (2007a) suggests four types of validity: structural, behavioural, empirical and application. The modelling exercise developed in the context of this thesis was particularly striving for application validity. In addition, a series of tests were conducted. Hensher *et al.* (2005) distinguish between maintained assumptions and testable assumptions. Some of the testable assumptions are checked in this section. For the methods used in this thesis, testing is important. Hendry (1980) emphasises the role of econometric testing. As a matter of fact, the number of econometric tests proposed in the literature is overwhelming. Sterman (2000) lists appropriate tests for SD models, including statistical ones (see his chapter 21). This section is divided into two broad types of model testing: pre-testing (section 5.2.1) and post-testing (section 5.2.2).

5.2.1 Pre-testing

Building the SD sub-model was a highly iterative process and some of the usual tests have been performed rather informally, such as tests on boundary adequacy and behaviour reproduction. The main pre-tests undertaken for the SD sub-model were: (i) the integration error test; and (ii) the dimensional consistency test.

SD conceptualises integral (or differential) equations. In practice, computer simulations applying numerical methods (usually Euler or Runge-Kutta), based on discrete mathematics, are used to approximate the solution. Morrison (2008) claims that 4th-order Runge-Kutta integration has the greatest versatility. But in models with random disturbances, Sterman (2000) is cautious about its use. Bossel (2007b) concludes that the Euler-Cauchy numerical integrator is generally adequate for the purposes of SD models.

The SD sub-model, which retrieves annual data (see section 3.4), uses by default a time step or delta time (DT) equal to 1 year. In order to avoid spurious dynamics arising from the DT error (Sterman, 2000), it is useful to test alternative DT values. A common procedure is to reduce DT by half and observe whether, and to what extent, the behaviour of the modelled system changes (see e.g. Ford (2010)). The numerical test is conducted by simulating the RS using the alternative DT values 0.5, 0.25, 0.125, 0.0625. For many variables the test results in no changes in values and the overall behaviour of the system is not affected. Notwithstanding, it is desirable to examine the effect of different DT values on variables that are characterised by e.g. historical jumps. For illustrative purposes, Figure 5.8 shows the outcome of this test on the variable *aggregate total car stock* for Germany. There are some differences between the behaviour using the faster DT=1, which suffices to replicate the historical data during the period of interest 2006-2008, and the rest. In addition to adjusting DT, the type of numerical integration may also be tested. The most common alternative to Euler in Vensim® is represented by 4th-order Runge-Kutta, which delivers greater accuracy. The outcome of this test is also visible in Figure 5.8. However, when discontinuities are present in SD models, this alternative may pose integration problems, as noted above. Finally, it is worth noting that there is a trade-off between the DT error and errors arising from truncation and round-off in SD models (Sterman, 2000). For the purpose of this model, Euler integration with DT=1 is judged to provide a reasonable solution.

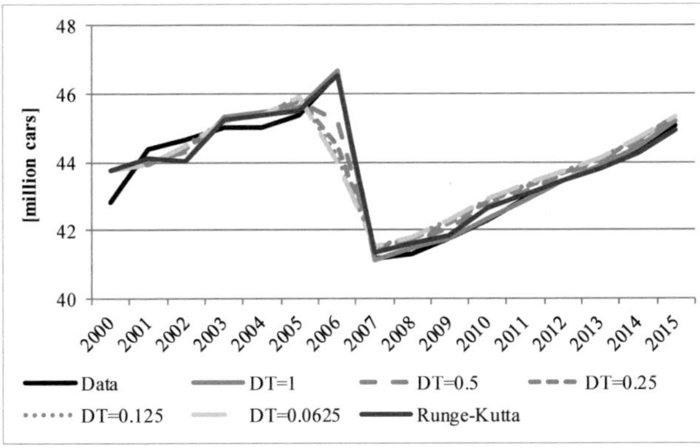

Figure 5.8: Integration error test using alternative DT values
Source: Own work using Vensim® (see appendix I for dataset sources)

The test for dimensional consistency generated positive results (i.e. not a single error was found among the units of measurement assigned to the 575 variables that the SD sub-model contains).

The remaining of the section is devoted to pre-testing for the econometric sub-model (recall section 4.2.8). Three main bodies of tests are reported: (i) unit root tests; (ii) structural break tests; and (iii) cointegration tests. Testing for unit roots is motivated by the possibility that time series follow a unit root process and by the result of the visual inspection of the data in section 4.2.8. Testing for structural breaks is considered because it can alter the conclusions derived from unit root tests, as shown by Perron (1989). If two series that are $I(1)$ are cointegrated, an ECM may be specified. The hypothesis of a cointegrated relationship can be formally tested.

The first body of tests arises from the need to investigate whether the processes under study are trend stationary (TS) (i.e. have a deterministic trend), difference stationary (DS) (i.e. have a stochastic trend) or a mix of both (Juselius, 2007). In theory, this is an important question, for the alternative remedies (detrending vs. differencing to eliminate the trend (Enders, 2014)) differ in implications (Baltagi, 2011). In practice and given the available sample, inferential errors may occur from unit root testing (Greene, 2011).

Two types of tests of unit roots are considered: (i) the augmented Dickey-Fuller (ADF) test, whose null hypothesis is that the time series process has a unit root ($H_0: y \sim I(1)$) (Dickey and Fuller, 1979); and the Kwiatkowski-Phillips-Schmidt-Shin (KPSS) test, which holds the H_0 that the series is stationary ($y \sim I(0)$) (Kwiatkowski *et al.*, 1992).

Do the series under analysis contain a single or multiple unit roots? Dickey and Pantula (1987) compare the traditional testing sequence with their alternative, concluding that the latter is more appropriate. Banerjee *et al.* (1993) and Enders (2014) also seem to endorse their alternative testing sequence for this task. To be consistent with the GETS approach, Charemza and Deadman (1997) suggest that the choice of augmentation be determined after systematically reducing the number of augmentations by imposing restrictions. For the ADF test, the lag selection is automatically determined based on the Akaike information criterion (AIC). In small T the AIC is perhaps better than the (Schwarz) Bayesian information criterion (S)BIC (Enders (2014) and Pickup (2014) citing Harvey (1993)). In some cases, a lag of order one is manually chosen for $\boldsymbol{lown}$. Whereas only the intercept is added to test for $\boldsymbol{\Delta lown}$; intercept and trend terms are included for $\boldsymbol{lown}$. The reported *t*-statistic values are based on MacKinnon (1996). The following decision rule is adopted: if the *t*-statistic is greater than the critical value (t_c) at the 5% level, then the conclusion reached is 'do not reject H_0'; if the *t*-statistic is significant at the 5% level, then the decision is 'reject H_0'. With regards to the KPSS test, the decision rule adopted is: if the test statistic is greater than t_c at the 5% level, then 'reject H_0'. The asymptotic t_c values are taken from Kwiatkowski *et al.* (1992) (see EViews (2016) for further details). Table 5.5-Table 5.10 show a summary of unit root testing for each of the countries of interest.

Table 5.5: Unit root testing for CN series

			$H_0: Series{\sim}I(1)$		$H_0: Series{\sim}I(0)$	
			ADF test		**KPSS test**	
Variable	Lag #		Intercept	Intercept + Trend	Intercept	Intercept + Trend
$\Delta lown$	0	t-stat	-6,100		0,278	
		5%	-2,954		0,463	
		p-value	0,000		–	
		conclusion	Reject		Do not reject	
$lown$	1	t-stat		-1,444		0,170
		5%		-3,553		0,146
		p-value		0,828		-
		conclusion		Do not reject		Reject
$\Delta lrinc$	1	t-stat	-4,223		0,074	
		5%	-2,954		0,463	
		p-value	0,002		–	
		conclusion	Reject		Do not reject	
$lrinc$	3	t-stat		-2,822		
		5%		-3,558		
		p-value		0,200		
		conclusion		Do not reject		

Source: Own work using EViews® (see appendix I for dataset sources)

Table 5.6: Unit root testing for FR series

			$H_0: Series \sim I(1)$ ADF test		$H_0: Series \sim I(0)$ KPSS test	
Variable	Lag #		Intercept	Intercept + Trend	Intercept	Intercept + Trend
$\Delta lown$	0	t-stat	-2,140		0,826	
		5%	-2,919		0,463	
		p-value	0,230		–	
		conclusion	Do not reject		Reject	
$\Delta lrinc$	0	t-stat	-3,783		0,336	
		5%	-2,951		0,463	
		p-value	0,007		–	
		conclusion	Reject		Do not reject	
$lrinc$	1	t-stat		-1,048		0,175
		5%		-3,548		0,146
		p-value		0,923		–
		conclusion		Do not reject		Reject

Source: Own work using EViews® (see appendix I for dataset sources)

Table 5.7: Unit root testing for DE series

			$H_0: Series \sim I(1)$ ADF test		$H_0: Series \sim I(0)$ KPSS test	
Variable	Lag #		Intercept	Intercept + Trend	Intercept	Intercept + Trend
$\Delta lown$	0	t-stat	-5,736		0,707	
		5%	-2,930		0,463	
		p-value	0,000		–	
		conclusion	Reject		Reject	
$lown$	1	t-stat		-1,031		0,216
		5%		-3,516		0,146
		p-value		0,929		–
		conclusion		Do not reject		Reject
$\Delta lrinc$	1	t-stat	-5,345		0,264	
		5%	-2,954		0,463	
		p-value	0,000		–	
		conclusion	Reject		Do not reject	
$lrinc$	1	t-stat		-2,357		0,174
		5%		-3,548		0,146
		p-value		0,394		-
		conclusion		Do not reject		Reject

Source: Own work using EViews® (see appendix I for dataset sources)

Table 5.8: Unit root testing for IN series

			H_0: $Series \sim I(1)$		H_0: $Series \sim I(0)$	
			ADF test		**KPSS test**	
Variable	Lag #		Intercept	Intercept + Trend	Intercept	Intercept + Trend
$\Delta lown$	0	t-stat	-3,710		0,473	
		5%	-2,957		0,463	
		p-value	0,009		-	
		conclusion	Reject		Reject	
$lown$	1	t-stat		0,030		0,184
		5%		-3,558		0,146
		p-value		0,995		–
		conclusion		Do not reject		Reject
$\Delta lrinc$	0	t-stat	-4,235		0,680	
		5%	-2,951		0,463	
		p-value	0,002		–	
		conclusion	Reject		Reject	
$lrinc$	1	t-stat		-0,916		0,188
		5%		-3,548		0,146
		p-value		0,942		–
		conclusion		Do not reject		Reject

Source: Own work using EViews® (see appendix I for dataset sources)

Table 5.9: Unit root testing for JP series

			$H_0\!: Series{\sim}I(1)$ ADF test		$H_0\!: Series{\sim}I(0)$ KPSS test	
Variable	Lag #		Intercept	Intercept + Trend	Intercept	Intercept + Trend
$\Delta lown$	0	t-stat	-3,541		0,662	
		5%	-2,917		0,463	
		p-value	0,011		-	
		conclusion	Reject		Reject	
$lown$	1	t-stat		-2,588		0,225
		5%		-3,495		0,146
		p-value		0,287		–
		conclusion		Do not reject		Reject
$\Delta lrinc$	0	t-stat	-4,016		0,491	
		5%	-2,951		0,463	
		p-value	0,004		–	
		conclusion	Reject		Reject	
$lrinc$	1	t-stat		-1,831		0,173
		5%		-3,548		0,146
		p-value		0,667		–
		conclusion		Do not reject		Reject

Source: Own work using EViews® (see appendix I for dataset sources)

Table 5.10: Unit root testing for US series

			$H_0\!: Series{\sim}I(1)$ ADF test		$H_0\!: Series{\sim}I(0)$ KPSS test	
Variable	Lag #		Intercept	Intercept + Trend	Intercept	Intercept + Trend
$\Delta lown$	0	t-stat	-2,732		0,821	
		5%	-2,918		0,463	
		p-value	0,075		-	
		conclusion	Do not reject		Reject	
$\Delta lrinc$	0	t-stat	-4,067		0,379	
		5%	-2,951		0,463	
		p-value	0,003		-	
		conclusion	Reject		Do not reject	
$lrinc$	1	t-stat		-1,473		0,177
		5%		-3,548		0,146
		p-value		0,819		-
		conclusion		Do not reject		Reject

Source: Own work using EViews® (see appendix I for dataset sources)

As a result of these formal tests, it can be concluded that the examined series display nonstationary properties. This is in line with the preliminary visual inspection of the data. From this analysis, the following inferences are drawn:

- CN: $lown{\sim}I(1)$ and $lrinc{\sim}I(1)$
- FR: $lown{\sim}I(2)$ and $lrinc{\sim}I(1)$
- DE: $lown{\sim}I(1)$ and $lrinc{\sim}I(1)$
- IN: $lown{\sim}I(1)$ and $lrinc{\sim}I(1)$
- JP: $lown{\sim}I(1)$ and $lrinc{\sim}I(1)$
- US: $lown{\sim}I(2)$ and $lrinc{\sim}I(1)$

This information can support the specification of both ARIMA and ADL models. Some caveats are due: (i) for China, the null of stationarity using the KPSS test for $lrinc$ could not be rejected; (ii) for Japan, the correlogram in Figure 4.44 was displayed in second differences; but ADF and KPSS unit root testing provides no evidence of $Y{\sim}I(2)$; and (iii) for France and the US, the outcomes of the unit root tests suggest $lown{\sim}I(2)$, but the presence of such series is not very usual in applied econometric work.

The second body of tests relates to structural breaks. A sudden change in structure, which may be caused by a policy regime change (Enders, 2014), is the feature of nonstationarity that is the hardest to handle (Chatfield, 2003). Nelson and Plosser (1982) argued that nonstationary economic time series are often due to unit roots. However, they did not take into account structural breaks. Perron (1989) did so by specifying a single predetermined (i.e. non-endogenous) break in the series, thereby reaching a different conclusion. Research by Zivot and Andrews (2002) using an estimated breaking point led them to a conclusion more in line with the original of Nelson and Plosser (1982). These papers highlight the importance of unit root testing that takes into account the possibility of breakpoints. In the presence of structural breaks, unit root tests have low power (Campos *et al.*, 1996).

In view of the risk of drawing erroneous inferences, it is desirable to contrast the previous outcomes of unit root testing with the results of testing for structural breaks. In EViews®, this can be examined by conducting unit root tests with a breakpoint (see EViews (2016) for details). The view that unit root testing for structural change should be performed on the full sample is accepted by Enders (2014).

The following historical events may have a priori impacted some of the series under study: oil crises and price shocks (1973-74; 1979; 1990), Japanese asset price bubble (1986-1991), German reunification (1990) and economic crises. The latter include the early 1990s recession in the US and the 2007-2009 financial crisis.

From section 4.2.8, structural breaks in the German and US series were visible. The results of breakpoint unit root testing for each country is shown below. Table 5.11 provides a summary of the test for the German series $lown$: (i) an additive outlier (AO) test was chosen, that is, with an immediate break; (ii) an intercept break (DU_t), that is a level dummy, was specified; (iii) EViews® reports the break date at the beginning of the new regime as $T_B = 1992$; and (iv) $H_0\colon y \sim I(1)$ cannot be rejected.

Table 5.11: Breakpoint unit root testing on German *lown*

Null Hypothesis: LOWN_DE has a unit root Trend Specification: Intercept only Break Specification: Intercept only Break Type: Additive outlier			
Break Date: 1992 Break Selection: Minimize Dickey-Fuller t-statistic Lag Length: 0 (Automatic - based on Schwarz information criterion, maxlag=9)			
		t-Statistic	Prob.*
Augmented Dickey-Fuller test statistic		-1.597444	> 0.99
Test critical values:	1% level	-4.949133	
	5% level	-4.443649	
	10% level	-4.193627	
*Vogelsang (1993) asymptotic one-sided p-values.			

Source: Own work using EViews® (see appendix I for dataset sources)

The results for the US series $lown$ are shown in Table 5.12: (i) the test was specified as an innovation outlier (IO), that is, with a gradual break; (ii) a trend break (DT_t), that is a trend slope change, was specified; (iii) $T_B = 2008$; and (iv) $H_0: y \sim I(1)$ cannot be rejected.

Table 5.12: Breakpoint unit root testing on US $lown$

Null Hypothesis: LOWN_US has a unit root			
Trend Specification: Trend and intercept			
Break Specification: Trend only			
Break Type: Innovational outlier			
Break Date: 2008			
Break Selection: Minimize Dickey-Fuller t-statistic			
Lag Length: 1 (Automatic - based on Schwarz information criterion, maxlag=8)			
		t-Statistic	Prob.*
Augmented Dickey-Fuller test statistic		-3.702076	0.3013
Test critical values:	1% level	-5.067425	
	5% level	-4.524826	
	10% level	-4.261048	
*Vogelsang (1993) asymptotic one-sided p-values.			

Source: Own work using EViews® (see appendix I for dataset sources)

In sum, whereas the result of testing for a breakpoint in the German series is in line with the previous unit root test; this is not the case for the US series. Here, the null of a unit root process cannot be rejected when testing for a breakpoint. Testing for multiple breakpoints could provide additional insights.

The possibility that two $I(1)$ series are cointegrated is examined. In the developed model, the dependent variable is 'car ownership' (car/population). The possibility of a cointegration relationship between 'car ownership' and 'income per capita', in logs, is investigated. Preliminary data analysis suggests that such a relationship is present in some of the countries investigated.

So far, China, Germany, India, Japan are identified as potential candidates for determining a cointegrated relationship. Testing for cointegration is therefore conducted for the series of these countries. Establishing such a relationship for France and the US becomes more complicated because of the need to include additional explanatory variables and assume future values of these.

If a cointegrated relationship is found, an arrow of causation from income to car ownership shall be established by the author on grounds of economic theory. In practice, this means that the assumption of future income per capita would determine the forecasted level of car ownership and, in turn, the projected aggregate total car stock in each of the countries examined.

With regards to the SD sub-model, an important type of pre-test is dimensional analysis. Any model equation is either dimensionally correct or incorrect. Whereas the former does not necessarily mean that the relationship is correct, the latter clearly signals a problem (Ford, 2010). Note that in the SD sub-model, *pop* is expressed in terms of passenger, not people. This is simply done to ensure dimensional consistency when this variable is related to common metrics found in transport statistics, such as passenger/km. In Vensim®, the units of all the equations of any SD model can be checked for consistency in an automated manner. When applied to the SD sub-model developed in this work, the software delivers a message of unit consistency. This is interpreted as a positive outcome in testing for dimensional consistency.

5.2.2 Post-testing

As indicated previously, there is no pretention in this work of conducting an exercise of fine forecasting accuracy. Notwithstanding, an evaluation of the car ownership projections, as shown in section 4.2.8, is informative. Optimal forecasts are defined as those yielding the lowest mean square error (MSE) (Box and Jenkins, 1976) (Pindyck and Rubinfeld, 1991). EViews® reports the root mean square error (RMSE) and the Theil inequality statistic, which can be decomposed into the bias, variance and covariance proportions. With the exception of the US, the bias proportion is high, suggesting that there is room for improvement in these forecasts, particularly for China and Japan. Concerning similar work, Table 5.13 provides a summary of selected studies and their main results.

With regards to the SD sub-module, two tasks are performed: (i) a comparison of model fit for selected results; and (ii) sensitivity analysis.

Table 5.13: Alternative 2030 projections of car stock

Million cars in year 2030, by country	CN	FR	DE	IN	JP	US
Adopted in this study	267	26	54	162	69	134
Other studies	335-390*	47	47	143-157*	NA	223-231*

*Private LDVs. Source: EC (2016c), Huo and Wang (2012) and IEA (2016c)

Figure 5.9 and 5.10 provide visual information on the data and simulated values of gasoline and diesel car stock in the European countries. Figure 5.11 illustrates the model output for HEVs in Japan and its discrepancy with available data points. Figure 5.12 shows the model output on AFVs in the US. For China and India, this type of disaggregated data is not available for the powertrains considered. Fortunately, data on EV sales and stock for all the countries investigated in this thesis is available. The model output highlighting EVs shall be shown in chapter 6. In the RS, there are no FC cars in any country, because the H_2 infrastructure is insufficient to make this technology attractive.

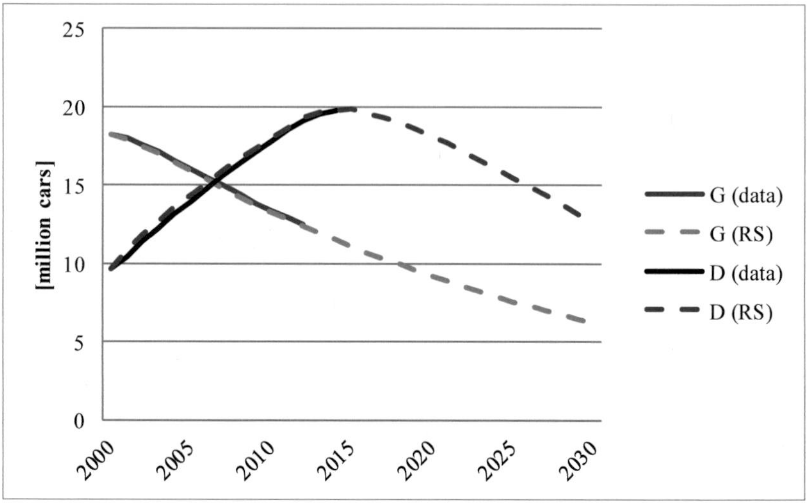

Figure 5.9: Gasoline and diesel car stock in France
Source: Own work using Vensim® (see appendix I for dataset sources)

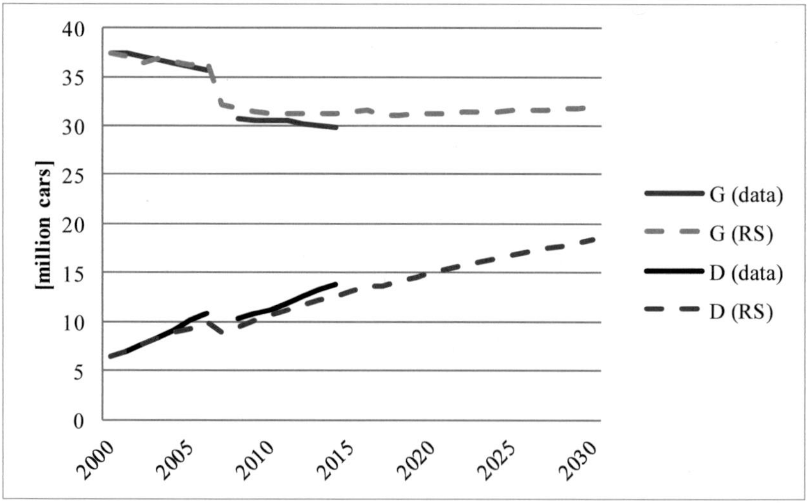

Figure 5.10: Gasoline and diesel car stock in Germany
Source: Own work using Vensim® (see appendix I for dataset sources)

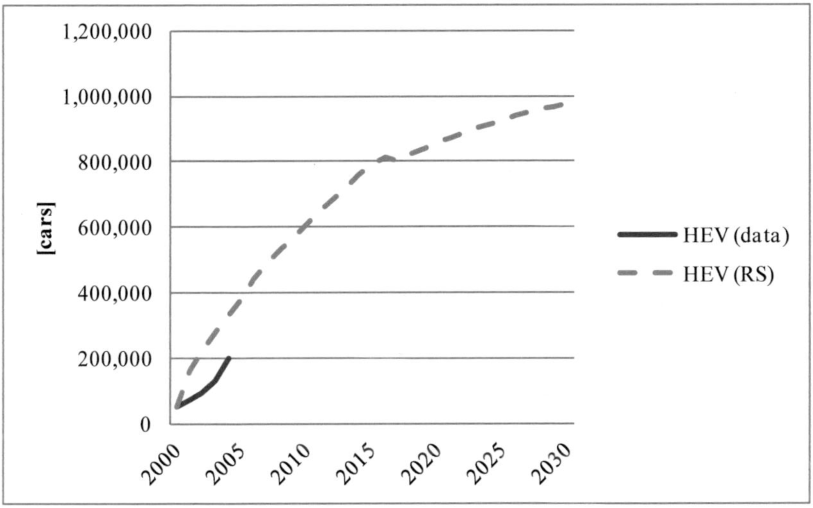

Figure 5.11: Hybrid (HEV) car stock in Japan
Source: Own work using Vensim® (see appendix for I dataset sources)

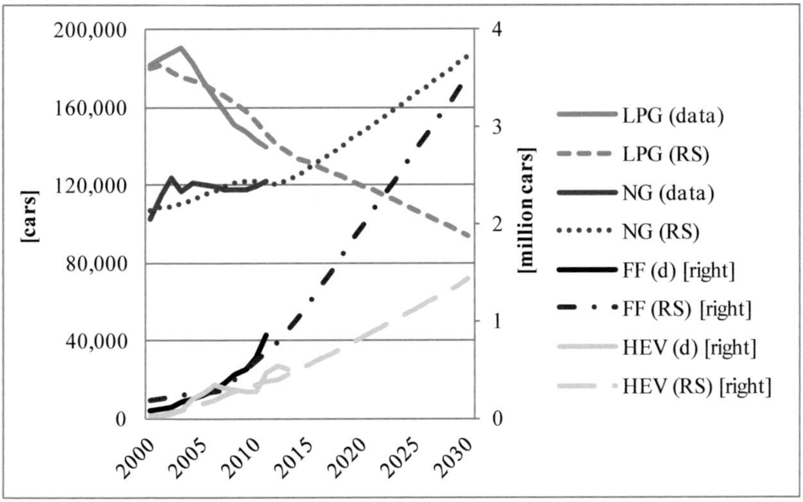

Figure 5.12: Alternative fuel car stock in the US
Source: Own work using Vensim® (see appendix I for dataset sources)

The constants of the model are readily amenable to sensitivity analysis. The assumption of the average car lifetime has implications for the speed of technology transition. The higher this value, the longer the process, *ceteris paribus*. To demonstrate this, the value of the *total average car lifetime* is lowered, from 16 years to 12 years. As a result, alternative powertrains achieve a slightly higher share in the car mix (see an example in Figure 5.13).

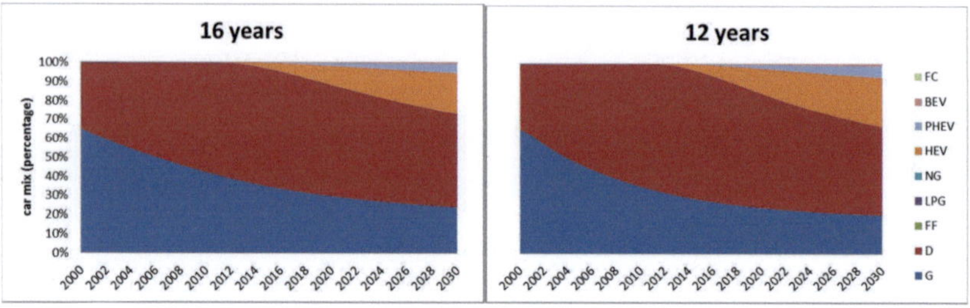

Figure 5.13: Testing a shorter average car lifetime in France | Source: Own work using Vensim®

In the model, the EVB cost is affected by the learning rate and the cumulative production of EVs. By endogenising the latter, the EVB cost can be altered. The partial endogenisation of the EVB cost is tested using several values (see Figure 5.14). As shown in the figure, the evolution of the EVB cost curve is higher in the RS, which rules out endogenisation. RS13, RS14 and RS15 refer to endogenisation for the years 2013, 2014 and 2015, respectively. This means that the experience curve no longer relies on historical data on cumulative EV production, but is instead based on the cumulative EV production simulated in the model. For instance, under RS15, the EVB cost is determined using data for the period 2000-2014 and the simulated cumulative EV production for the period 2015-2030. This formulation is adopted in both the RS and the AS. In this way, the six countries investigated in this work are jointly connected, thereby determining their future EV market evolution.

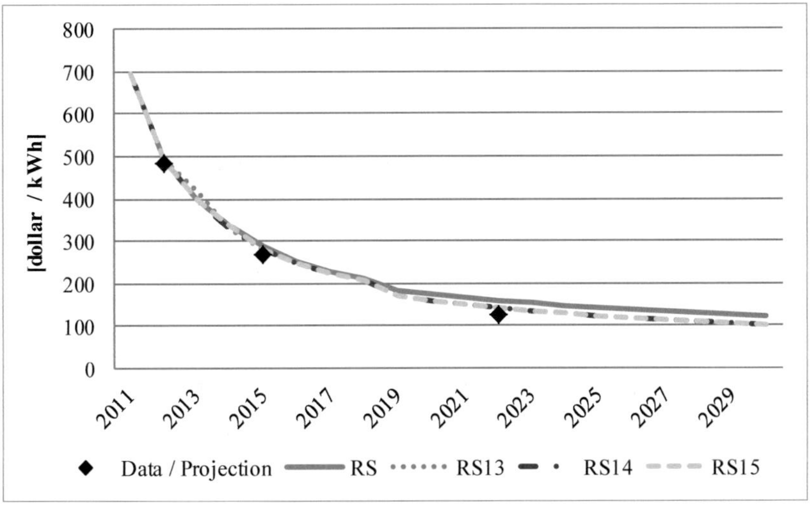

Figure 5.14: Testing for year of battery cost endogenisation
Source: Data and projection from EVI (2016b) and own simulation

A more systematic way of testing numerical values is represented by sensitivity analysis. This technique provides insights into uncertainty and policy robustness (Struben and Sterman, 2008). Vensim® facilitates performing Monte Carlo (MC) simulation to accomplish sensitivity analysis. As an example of univariate sensitivity analysis, the variable *learning rate* is chosen as a potentially critical candidate. A uniform probability distribution ranging from a minimum value of 0.05 to a maximum value of 0.2 is defined for the *cost reduction fraction*, which affects the EVB learning rate. Two hundred simulations are performed and their impact on the BEV stock in the US is plotted. Figure 5.15 is the result. As can be seen, the value of the BEV stock in the US under the RS is slightly lower than the data suggests. As time goes by, the dynamic confidence bounds widen. By 2030, MC simulations point at a possible divergence of almost 500,000 BEVs, most of it above the RS.

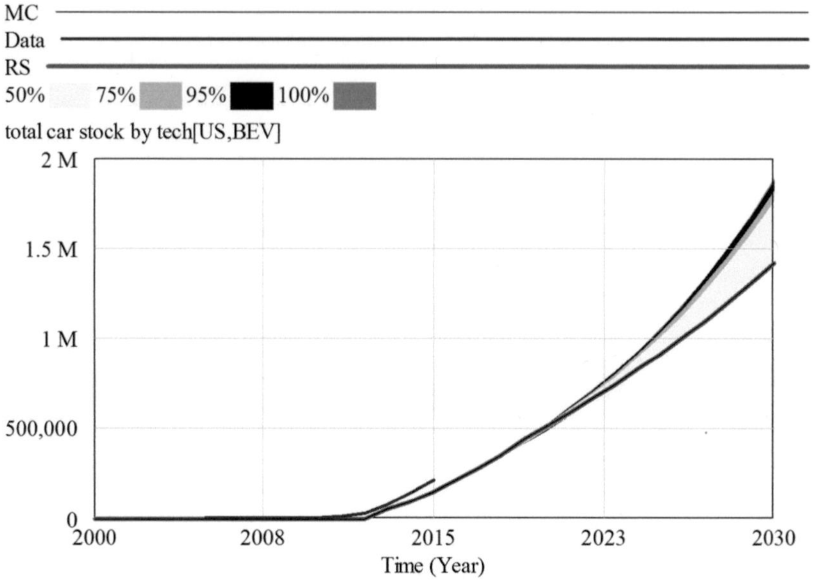

Figure 5.15: Monte Carlo simulation for battery cost reduction
Source: Own work using Vensim®

6 Alternative scenario, policy analysis and impacts

This chapter outlines the simulation of the Alternative Scenario (section 6.1) as a result of conducting policy analysis (section 6.2). Finally, the impacts on energy demand and emissions are summarised (section 6.3).

6.1 AS simulation

The RS sought to simulate, for each country, one possible future development pathway of the car-mix and its impacts (e.g. direct CO_2 emissions). The defining feature of that scenario was the absence of new policy measures. Given the policy goal (recall section 1.2) of reducing oil demand and GHG emissions from cars, success was rather limited under that scenario. To perform policy analysis and compare results with the RS, different scenarios may be constructed. As part of the development of the model, a large number of simulations were performed. By simply changing one parameter, a different scenario emerges. This thesis does not seek to illustrate the results of many scenarios, the exception being the Monte Carlo analysis from the previous section. The model is capable of generating a large number of scenarios and any potential model user may explore this possibility. In this chapter, the AS is introduced. The AS is a normative attempt to – paraphrasing Knight – make conduct more intelligent, thereby decreasing car-related oil demand and GHG emissions further. In practice, this task is entrusted to the model user, who implements a feedforward loop by altering only the policy inputs. The dotted arrows departing from the *Energy* and *Emissions* modules in Figure 4.2 denote the feedforward loop modelled under this AS. There are two practical ways to achieve this: (i) by backcasting, thereby defining policy targets and changing the policy inputs as needed to meet them; or (ii) amending the values of the policy inputs in a relatively realistic manner, as judged by the model user, and letting the dynamic behaviour to play out. An example of the first approach can be found in Haasz *et al.* (2018). The second approach is adopted in this thesis. Table 6.1 shows the differences in values between the two scenarios presented in this thesis for three policy measures. In addition, under the AS other policies are introduced: purchase subsidies for PHEVs and BEVs between 2017 and 2020 and investment in recharging and hydrogen refuelling infrastructure between 2017 and 2019. The country-specific purchase subsidy levels are ¥10,000 (CN), €3,000 (FR and DE), ₹80,000 (IN), ¥400,000 (JP) and $3,000 (US) for PHEVs and ¥15,000 (CN), €4,000 (FR and DE), ₹100,000 (IN), ¥500,000 (JP) and $4,000 (US) for BEVs. In terms of infrastructure, electric cars benefit from the following investments in recharging stations: ¥2.7 bn (CN), €95 mio (FR), €44 mio (DE), ₹59 mio (IN), ¥31 bn (JP) and $137 mio (US). The assumed investment in hydrogen refuelling stations under the AS is as follows: ¥12 mio (CN), €5.4 mio (FR), €30 mio (DE), ₹256 mio (IN), ¥9 bn (JP) and $7 mio (US).

The AS is constructed by amending the policy inputs in the data file (see appendix I). The procedure is as follows: the model user changes the values in the orange cells of the Excel file named 'Data' that accompanies the model (see Figure 6.1). Next, the data file is re-imported in Vensim®, so that the database the software is working with is up-to-date (i.e. reflects the most recent changes in the policy inputs). Then, a new simulation can be run.

Policy input	2014	2015	2016	2017	2018	2019	2020	2021
emission standard average new car[France]	114	*linear interpolation between initial and final value*						95
fuel tax gasoline[France]	0,61	0,62	0,64	0,64	0,64	0,64	0,64	0,64
fuel tax diesel[France]	0,43	0,49	0,50	0,64	0,64	0,64	0,64	0,64
EV purchase subsidy[France,PHEV]	0	0	0	3000	3000	3000	3000	0
EV purchase subsidy[France,BEV]	0	0	0	4000	4000	4000	4000	0
budget public slow EVSE deployment[France,BEV]	7E+07	0	0	7E+07	7E+07	7E+07	0	0
budget public fast EVSE deployment[France,BEV]	2E+07	0	0	2E+07	2E+07	2E+07	0	0
budget public H2 station deployment[France,FC]	5E+06	0	0	5E+06	5E+06	5E+06	0	0

Figure 6.1: Excerpt of the 'Data' spreadsheet linked to the model
Source: Own work using Excel®

Table 6.1: Comparison of policy inputs under the RS and AS

Policy [Unit]	Country	Scenario	2014	2015	2016	2017	2018	2019	2020	2021	2022	2023	2024	2025	2026	2027	2028	2029	2030
Emission standard average new car [gCO2/KM]	CN	RS	*	161	161	161	161	161	161	161	161	161	161	161	161	161	161	161	161
		AS		161	linear interpolation				117	linear interpolation									90
	FR	RS	114	114	114	114	114	114	114	114	114	114	114	114	114	114	114	114	114
		AS	114	linear interpolation						95	linear interpolation								80
	DE	RS	133	133	133	133	133	133	133	133	133	133	133	133	133	133	133	133	133
		AS	133	linear interpolation						95	linear interpolation								80
	IN	RS	*	*	130	130	130	130	130	130	130	130	130	130	130	130	130	130	130
		AS	*	*	130	linear interpolation				113	linear interpolation								90
	JP	RS	linear interpolation			119	119	119	119	119	119	119	119	119	119	119	119	119	119
		AS	linear interpolation						115	linear interpolation									90
	US	RS	165	158	151	151	151	151	151	151	151	151	151	151	151	151	151	151	151
		AS	165	158	151	142	136	131	125	119	113	108	102	97	linear interpolation				85
Gasoline tax [country currency/litre]	CN	RS	linear interpolation between last available* and final value																5.20
		AS	linear interpolation between last available* and final value																5.20
	FR	RS	0.61	0.62	0.64	0.64	0.64	0.64	0.64	0.64	0.64	0.64	0.64	0.64	0.64	0.64	0.64	0.64	0.64
		AS	0.61	0.62	0.64	0.64	0.64	0.64	0.64	0.64	0.64	0.64	0.64	0.64	0.64	0.64	0.64	0.64	0.64
	DE	RS	0.66	0.66	0.66	0.66	0.66	0.66	0.66	0.66	0.66	0.66	0.66	0.66	0.66	0.66	0.66	0.66	0.66
		AS	0.66	0.66	0.66	0.66	0.66	0.66	0.66	0.66	0.66	0.66	0.66	0.66	0.66	0.66	0.66	0.66	0.66
	IN	RS	linear interpolation between last available** and final value																46.00
		AS	linear interpolation between last available** and final value																46.00
	JP	RS	56.30	56.30	56.30	56.30	56.30	56.30	56.30	56.30	56.30	56.30	56.30	56.30	56.30	56.30	56.30	56.30	56.30
		AS	56.30	56.30	56.30	56.30	56.30	56.30	56.30	56.30	56.30	56.30	56.30	56.30	56.30	56.30	56.30	56.30	56.30
	US	RS	0.11	linear interpolation between last available and final value															0.21
		AS	0.11	linear interpolation between last available and final value															0.21
Diesel tax [country currency/litre]	CN	RS	linear interpolation between last available* and final value																4.40
		AS	linear interpolation between last available* and final value																5.20
	FR	RS	0.43	0.49	0.50	0.50	0.50	0.50	0.50	0.50	0.50	0.50	0.50	0.50	0.50	0.50	0.50	0.50	0.50
		AS	0.43	0.49	0.50	0.64	0.64	0.64	0.64	0.64	0.64	0.64	0.64	0.64	0.64	0.64	0.64	0.64	0.64
	DE	RS	0.47	0.47	0.47	0.47	0.47	0.47	0.47	0.47	0.47	0.47	0.47	0.47	0.47	0.47	0.47	0.47	0.47
		AS	0.47	0.47	0.47	0.66	0.66	0.66	0.66	0.66	0.66	0.66	0.66	0.66	0.66	0.66	0.66	0.66	0.66
	IN	RS	linear interpolation between last available** and final value																15.60
		AS	linear interpolation between last available** and final value																46.00
	JP	RS	34.60	34.60	34.60	34.60	34.60	34.60	34.60	34.60	34.60	34.60	34.60	34.60	34.60	34.60	34.60	34.60	34.60
		AS	34.60	34.60	34.60	56.30	56.30	56.30	56.30	56.30	56.30	56.30	56.30	56.30	56.30	56.30	56.30	56.30	56.30
	US	RS	0.13	linear interpolation between last available and final value															0.25
		AS	0.13	linear interpolation between last available and final value															0.21

*For interpolation, the pre-2014 values are: emission standards for CN, IN and JP are 172 gCO_2/km (2013), 136 gCO_2/km (2012) and 119 gCO_2/km (2013), respectively. The gasoline tax for CN is ¥2.60 (2012) and for IN ₹23.00 (2012). For these two countries, diesel taxes are respectively ¥2.20 (2012) and ₹7.60 (2012).

Source: Data from IEA (2017) and own scenario assumptions

Below Figures 6.2-6.7 show the simulated EV stock, with a distinction between PHEV and BEV, compared with historical data from each country. The simulated values are, until 2015, the same under the RS and the AS. As can be seen, the model underpredicts for China and the US and overpredicts for the rest, especially for India in 2015. It is worth remembering that the market evolution of electric powertrains is still at an early stage and the data covers only a few years, so it is not possible to discern a solid trend.

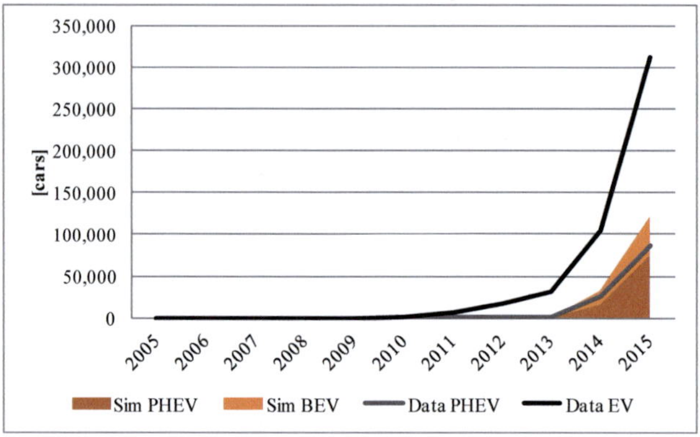

Figure 6.2: EV stock in China (2005-2015): simulation vs. data
Source: Based on EVI (2016b) and own simulation

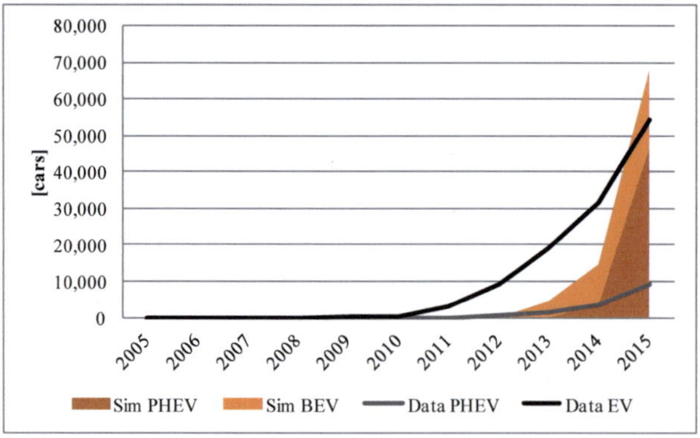

Figure 6.3: EV stock in France (2005-2015): simulation vs. data
Source: Based on EVI (2016b) and own simulation

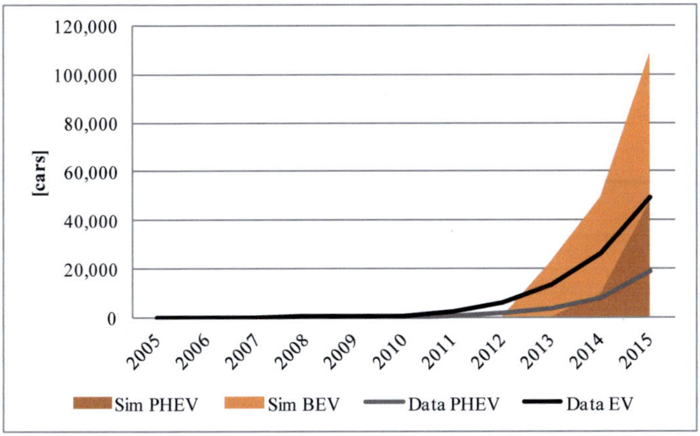

Figure 6.4: EV stock in Germany (2005-2015): simulation vs. data
Source: Based on EVI (2016b) and own simulation

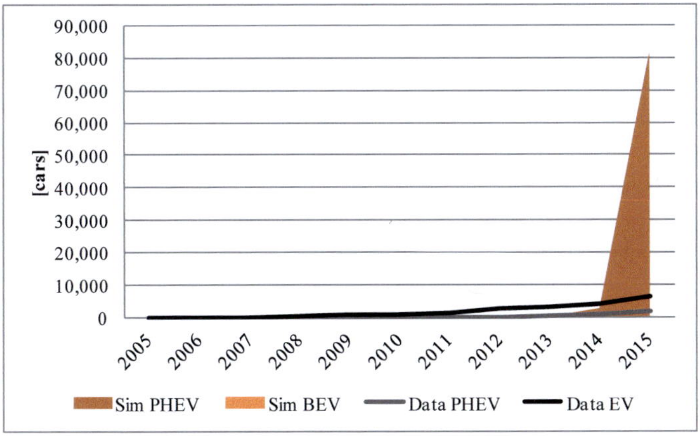

Figure 6.5: EV stock in India (2005-2015): simulation vs. data
Source: Based on EVI (2016b) and own simulation

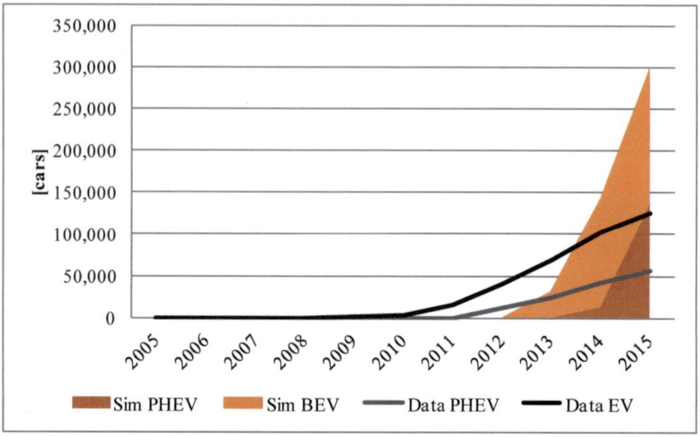

Figure 6.6: EV stock in Japan (2005-2015): simulation vs. data
Source: Based on EVI (2016b) and own simulation

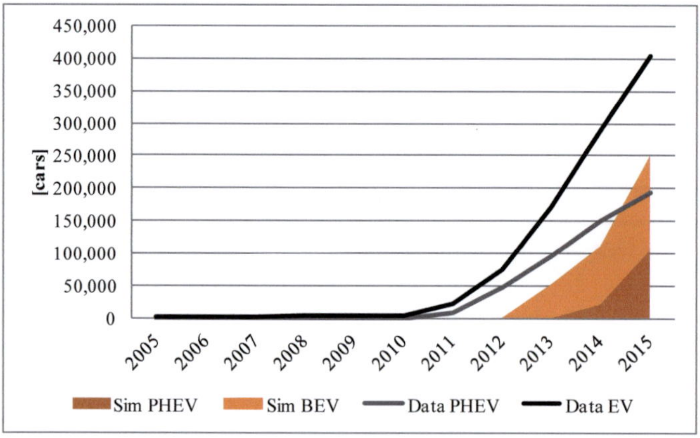

Figure 6.7: EV stock in the US (2005-2015): simulation vs. data
Source: Based on EVI (2016b) and own simulation

Furthermore, the sum of the EV stock values of the six countries analysed in this work is shown in Figure 6.8. As can be seen, EV market uptake begins later in the model but catches up by 2015. The six countries examined account for most of the electric cars in use worldwide.

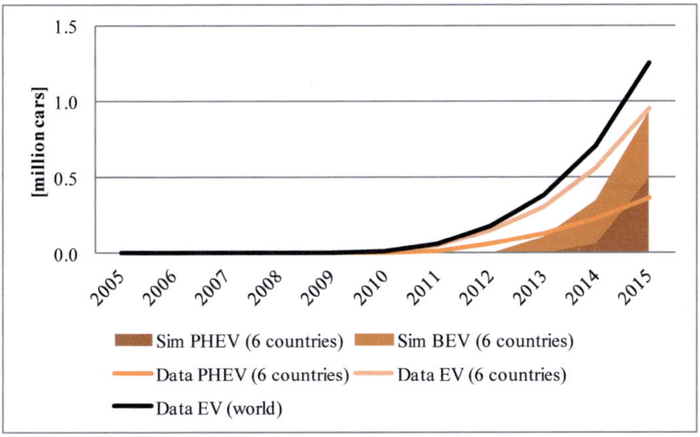

Figure 6.8: World EV stock and in analysed countries
Source: Based on EVI (2016b) and own simulation

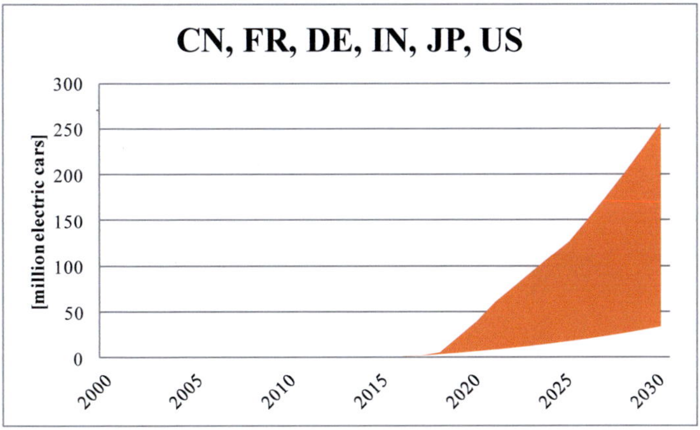

Figure 6.9: EV stock scenarios in analysed countries | Source: Own simulation

In terms of future car stock by powertrain, Figure 6.9 shows the total EV stock of the six countries analysed in this work put together, highlighting the increasingly wider spectrum of possibilities that lie between the RS and the AS. By 2030, the possibility space is defined by ca. 34 million electric cars at the lower end and over 250 million at the upper end.

By country, Figures 6.10-6.15 are the counterparts of Figures 5.1-5.6, albeit for the AS. Under this scenario, FC cars are constrained to zero, a restriction that shall be lifted in the next section.

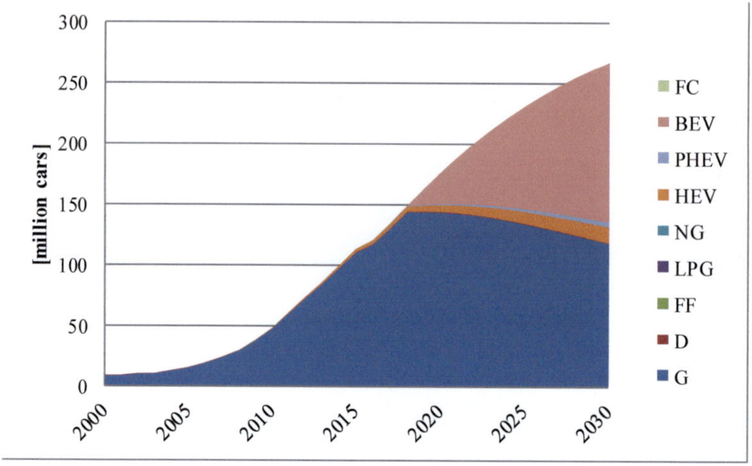

Figure 6.10: Car stock in China under the AS | Source: Own work using Vensim®

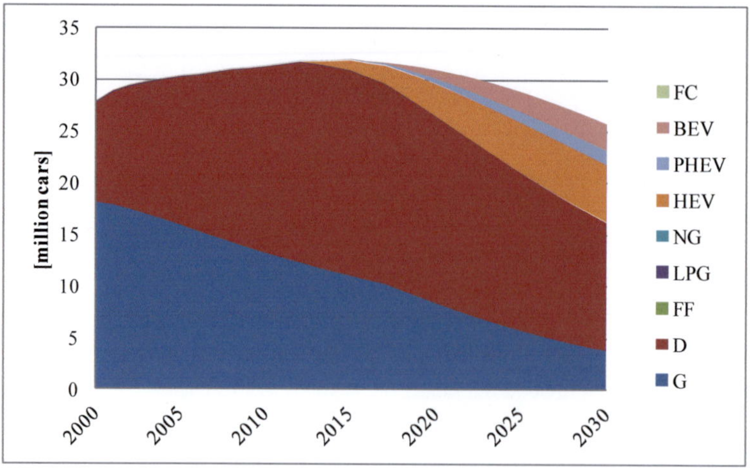

Figure 6.11: Car stock in France under the AS | Source: Own work using Vensim®

In the markets with rapid motorisation, the simulated growth in EV stock is impressive. These countries benefit from projected growth in car ownership, overcoming the conventional technology lock-in. In the mature car markets, the AS leads to the simulation of a larger BEV stock (recall that in the figures based on the RS, BEVs were not visible). Still, EVs represent a minor proportion of the car market until 2030. Nevertheless, a trend towards e-mobility begins to emerge and the importance of EVs in the simulated markets is increasing.

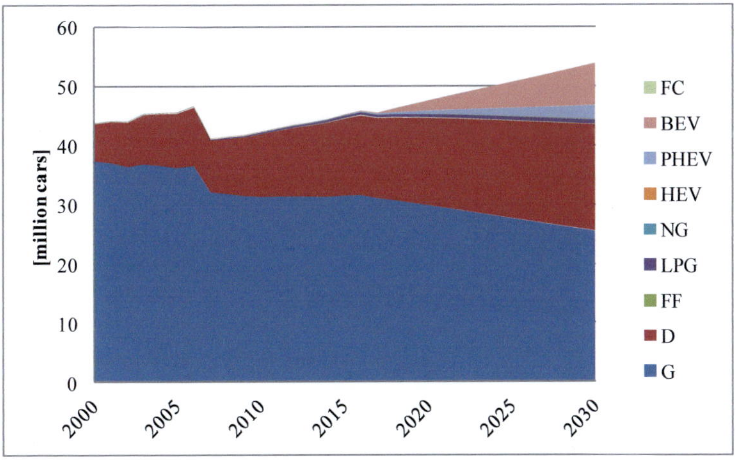

Figure 6.12: Car stock in Germany under the AS | Source: Own work using Vensim®

Remarkable kinks can be seen for China and India. This can be mainly explained by the size of the market assumed to purchase a car for the first time using a decision rule that favours low-cost technology. As soon as an alternative powertrain becomes cheaper than conventional cars, a portion of the market adjusts very fast. In this simulation, the Chinese market polarises into two powertrains (gasoline and BEV), equally important by 2030. In the case of India, the steady gasoline and diesel car stock beyond 2025 is the result, not of zero conventional car sales, but of a low sales rate virtually matching the scrappage rate of these two powertrains.

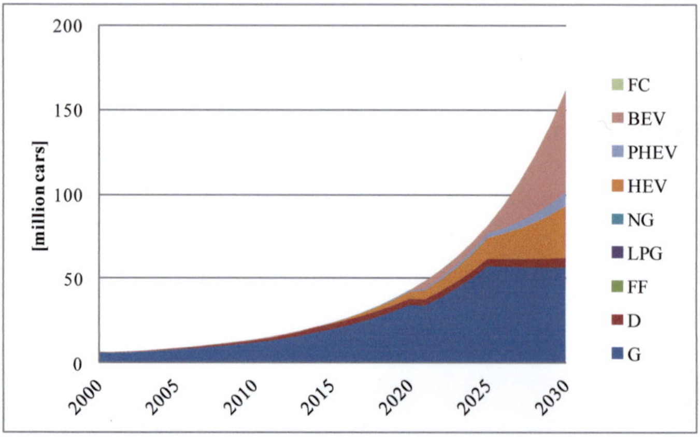

Figure 6.13: Car stock in India under the AS | Source: Own work using Vensim®

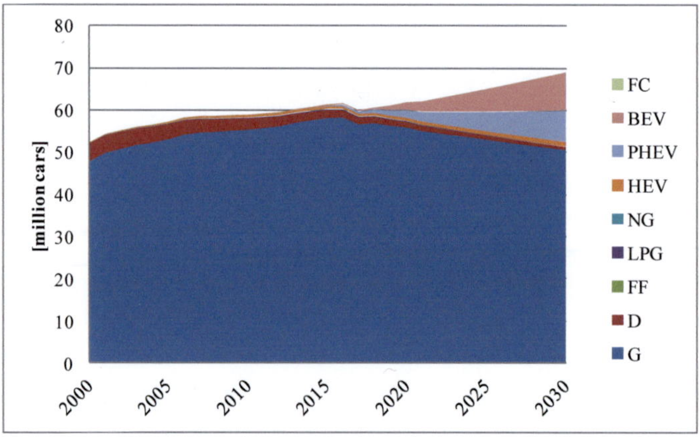

Figure 6.14: Car stock in Japan under the AS | Source: Own work using Vensim®

Unique to Japan is the fact that, under the AS, the split between PHEVs and BEVs is more equal than for the rest of the markets, where BEVs outperform PHEVs.

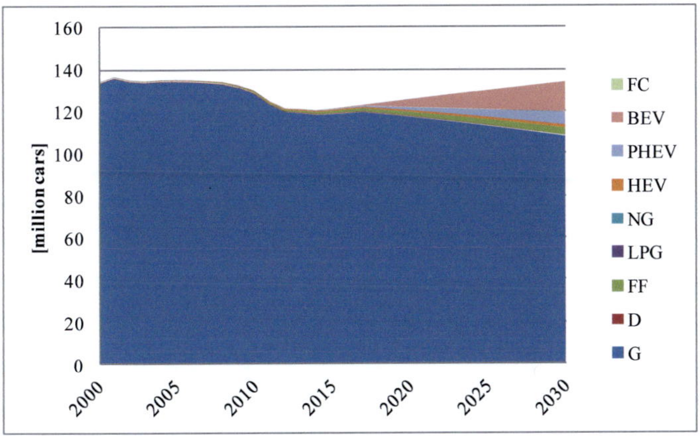

Figure 6.15: Car stock in the US under the AS | Source: Own work using Vensim®

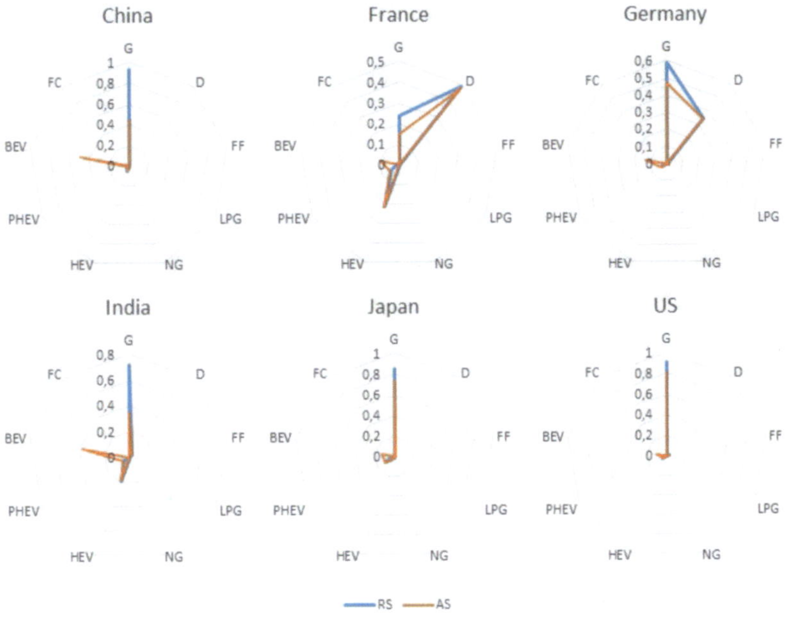

Figure 6.16: Car mix (%) in 2030: RS vs. AS | Source: Own work

To facilitate the comparison of results between both scenarios, RS and AS are plotted together in Figure 6.16 using 2030 values of the car mix in each country.

How the AS was constructed is the topic of the next section. For illustrative purposes, only one country is presented for each policy input. The chosen examples should not be mistaken as case studies examining policies under discussion.

6.2 Model-based policy analysis

In China, EVs are also known as new energy vehicles (NEVs). The promotion of NEVs is being pushed through ambitious policies, including a stringent technology quota mandate applicable to new car sales. This policy measure is not investigated in this work. Instead, the effect of changing the policy input explained in section 4.3.1 is described. Under the AS, the introduction of stricter emission standards for new cars is simulated. By assuming that it falls on conventional cars' shoulders, a decrease in the fuel intensity of the average new gasoline and diesel car can be expected (see Figure 6.17).

In the model, pushing the technical limits to improve the ICE, so that more stringent standards can be met, leads to higher manufacturing costs. This is not entirely unrealistic, given the position of OEMs on such regulation. A rise in the cost of manufacturing the powertrains that rely on the ICE (with the exceptions of HEVs and PHEVs), is modelled under the AS (see Figure 6.18), and assumed to be fully passed onto the purchase price. Mathematically, it is assumed that OEMs incur in a 20% rise in manufacturing cost when the fuel intensity of gasoline and diesel cars relative to the year 2000 falls below 0.7.

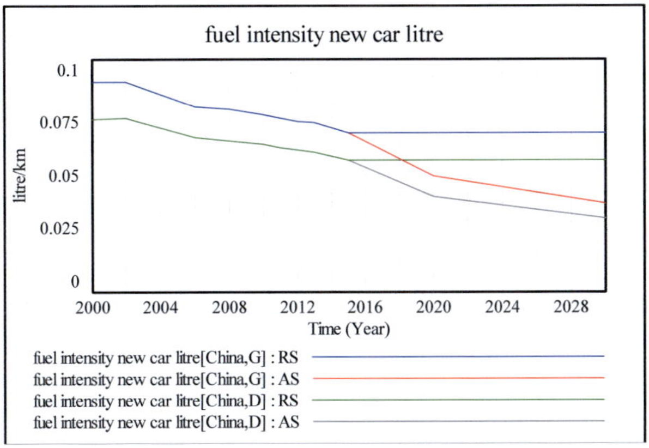

Figure 6.17: Setting stricter standards in China | Source: Own work using Vensim®

This policy measure is regarded as a cost-effective means of reducing oil use and emissions in transport (Sperling and Gordon, 2009). Figure 6.19 illustrates the simulated reduction of oil demand associated with this measure. However, its lasting success depends on potential rebound effects, which requires further examination.

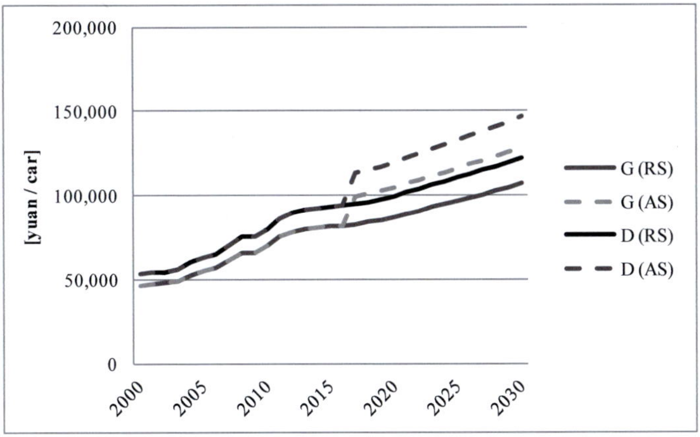

Figure 6.18: Effect of stricter standards on car prices in China
Source: Own work using Vensim®

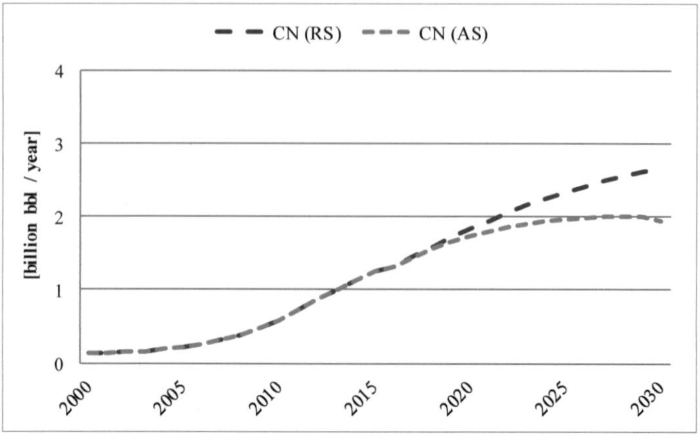

Figure 6.19: Effect of stricter standards on oil demand in China
Source: Own work using Vensim®

Among the countries analysed, diesel cars are popular only in European countries. Cames and Helmers (2013) suggest that the dieselisation process initiated in the 1980s and 1990s was motivated by the search of a market for middle distillates. Favourable taxation for diesel fuel has facilitated this process. Recent events have questioned the environmental merits of diesel cars. An increase in the tax rate for diesel fuel shall be explored. Raising this type of indirect tax can be thought of as a market-based solution to tackle an environmental externality and interpreted as a corrective or Pigouvian tax (Stiglitz and Rosengard, 2015). Below Figure 6.20 shows the pairing of the tax rate of diesel and gasoline in France the year 2017. This example illustrates the effect of changing the policy input explained in section 4.3.3.

The short-term effect of matching the level of taxation for diesel and gasoline is that the pump price for both fuels is similar and, as a result, new diesel cars become less attractive, *ceteris paribus*. Figure 6.21 illustrates the effects of this policy on the sales rate of three powertrains (diesel, HEV and PHEV), measured as the difference with respect to the tax regime in place under RS. As can be seen, the impact on diesel car sales is rather low, and most of the 'lost sales' are diverted towards conventional hybrids in 2018.

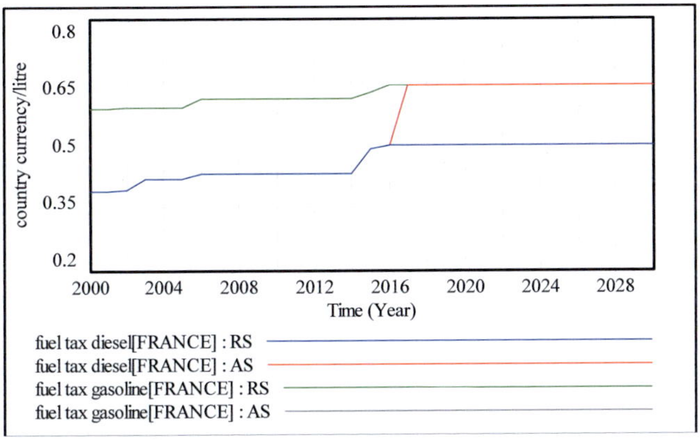

Figure 6.20: Introducing higher diesel taxation in France | Source: Own work using Vensim®

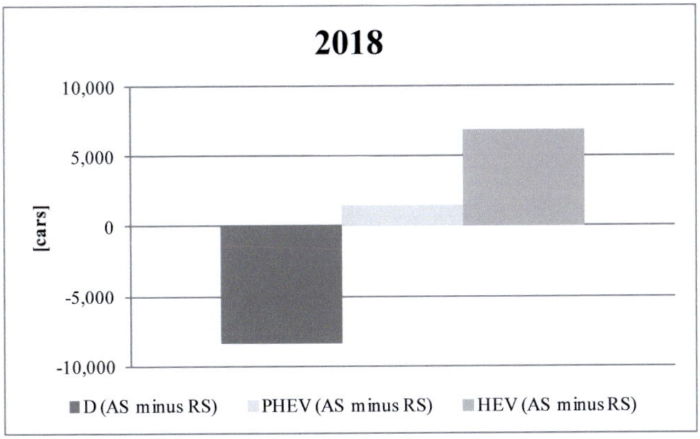

Figure 6.21: Effect of a higher diesel tax on sales rates in France | Source: Own work

The next policy measure examined is the EV purchase subsidy. This example illustrates how the policy input explained in section 4.3.4 can be applied. The introduction of EV purchase subsidies in Germany in 2017 is simulated as follows: 3,000 euros are granted for the purchase of a new PHEV and 4,000 euros per new BEV. The subsidies are temporary, running from 2017 to 2020.

The effect of the EV purchase subsidies on the EV purchase prices can be seen in Figure 6.22. The combined effect of this measure with the emission standard is not examined here. Remember that the model assumes an increase in the average EVB capacity in 2020. The simulated EV purchase subsidies help smooth the price shock associated with this increase. Despite these subsidies, the modelled EV prices are still slightly higher than the price of a new gasoline car (cf. Figure 4.64). However, thanks to the simulated temporary subsidies, BEVs beat earlier gasoline cars on a TCO basis (see Figure 6.23). Beyond 2020, the removal of EV purchase subsidies reflects the belief that the EV market may be in a good position to sustain itself.

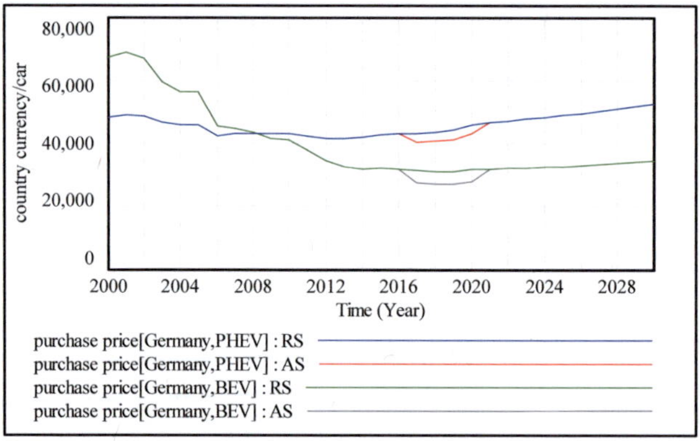

Figure 6.22: Effect of purchase subsidies on EV prices in Germany
Source: Own work using Vensim®

Does the German EV purchase subsidy have an effect on the public budget as well as on the EV market? The answer, though not directly shown, is affirmative. Notwithstanding the simulated favourable TCO for BEVs vis-à-vis gasoline cars, the shift towards electrification is far from complete, for electric range and recharging remain issues not tackled by EV purchase subsidies. Though PHEVs rank better in these aspects, their simulated TCO is higher than that of gasoline cars, even after the subsidy.

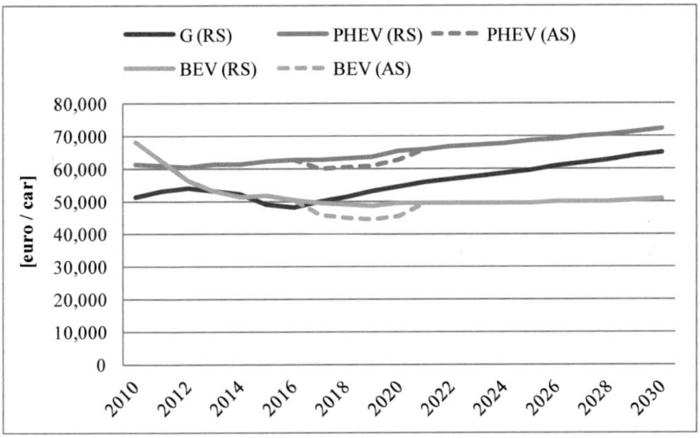

Figure 6.23: Effect of EV purchase subsidies on TCO in Germany
Source: Own work using Vensim®

Furthermore, the effect of deploying recharging infrastructure for EVs is illustrated, taking India as an example. This example shows the application of the policy input explained in section 4.3.5. Under the RS, the number of future recharging stations is stagnant. Figure 6.24 shows that investment in recharging infrastructure under the AS results in almost a doubling in re-charging stations. This number is still dwarfed by the amount of refuelling stations for conventional fuels and has little impact, *ceteris paribus*, on EV market uptake, as visible in Figure 6.25. A step further is represented by the simulation run named '*AS high infras investment*', which keeps investment constant throughout the time horizon of the model, leading to over 1,300 recharging stations deployed in 2030. Despite this extra boost, the result on the simulated BEV sales rate is still poor. Remember that because of the assumptions of the model with regards to range and recharging time, PHEVs remain basically unaltered.

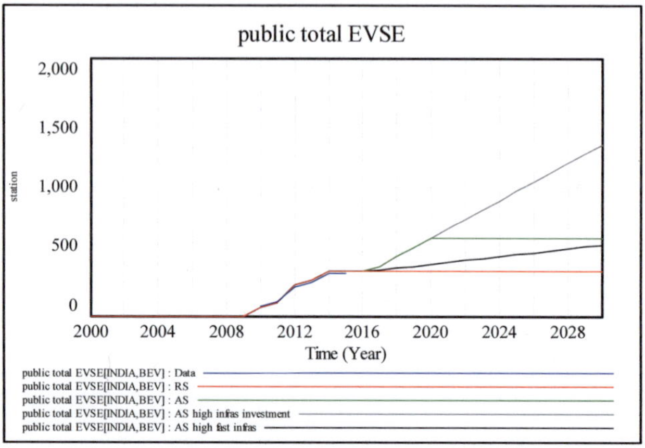

Figure 6.24: Expanding recharging infrastructure in India | Source: Own work using Vensim®

However, the situation differs depending on how the budget for recharging infrastructure deployment is allocated. So far, it has been assumed that the proportion of fast recharging stations is below 5%. Under a new simulation run named '*AS high fast infras*', the available EV budget is earmarked solely for the roll-out of fast recharging stations. As a consequence of this, the proportion of fast recharging stations jumps to over 35% by 2030 (see Figure 6.26).

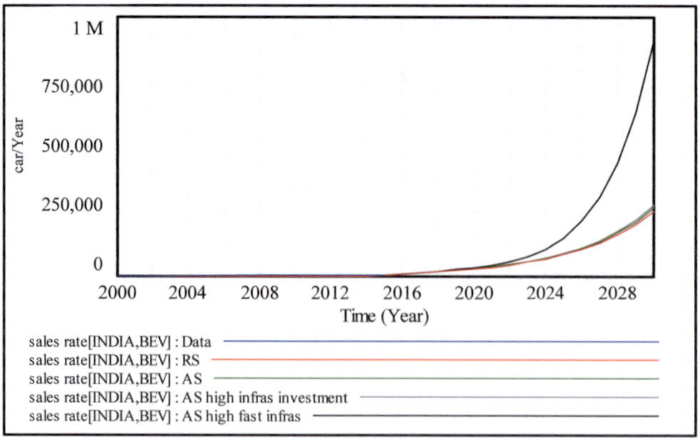

Figure 6.25: Effect of expanding infrastructure on BEV sales in India
Source: Own work using Vensim®

With this emphasis on allocating available resources to fast recharging infrastructure, the simulated BEV sales rate increases much more vigorously. Paradoxically, the effect of less recharging stations with a larger proportion of fast recharging on BEV sales is greater than having a larger number of recharging stations dominated by slow recharging.

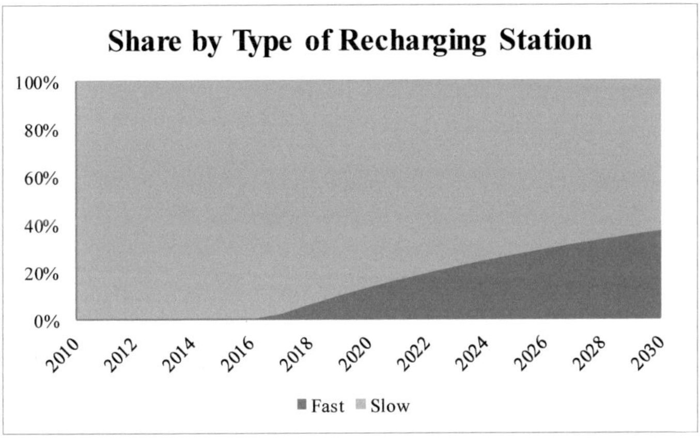

Figure 6.26: Split slow/fast recharging stations in India under 'AS high fast infras'
Source: Own work

The individual effects of four policy measures have been presented so far, using country-specific examples. These include stricter emission standards for new cars in China, higher diesel taxation in France, EV purchase subsidies in Germany and recharging infrastructure investment in India. As a matter of fact, the AS consists of the *simultaneous* introduction of these four policy measures in each of the six countries analysed in this study. In addition, two additional policy measures shall be briefly considered: (i) investment in hydrogen refuelling infrastructure; and (ii) higher average car occupancy levels.

The deployment of H_2 refuelling infrastructure shall be examined with regards to its effect on the market uptake of FC cars in Japan. Figure 6.27 shows the result of investing only in public H_2 refuelling stations.

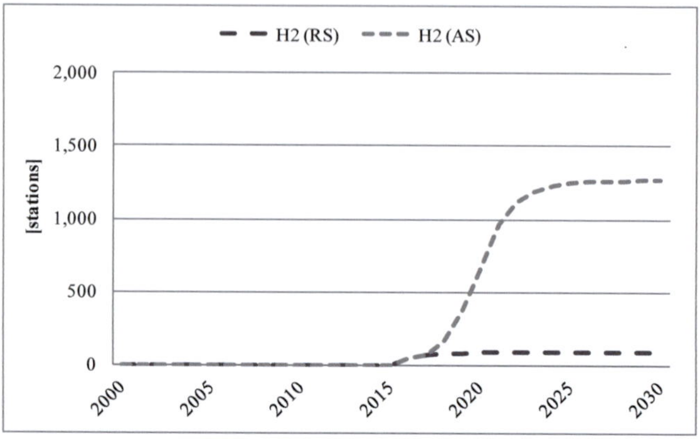

Figure 6.27: Expanding hydrogen infrastructure in Japan | Source: Own work using Vensim®

As a result of that level of investment, the simulated composition of the car stock in Japan is altered (see Figure 6.28). It can be concluded that annual sales of FC cars grow very fast between 2021 and 2024 and make a fast impact on the market. By 2030, this simulation shows that FC is becoming a widespread powertrain. Underlying these simulation results are assumptions that relate to the cost of FC technology. Figure 6.29 makes these transparent.

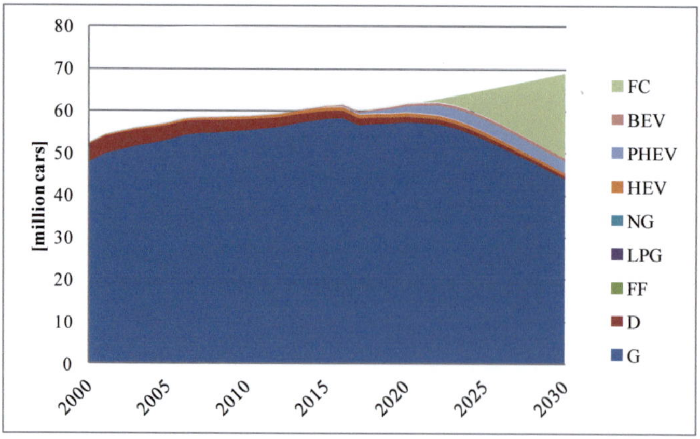

Figure 6.28: Effect of expanding hydrogen infrastructure on car stock in Japan
Source: Own work

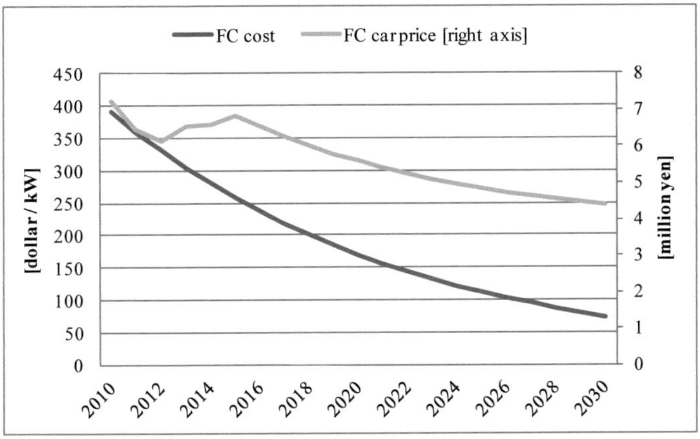

Figure 6.29: Evolution of FC cost and FC car price in Japan | Source: Own work using Vensim®

The result of changing the policy input described in section 4.3.6 is now shown taking the US as an illustrative example. Recall Figure 4.56 and the elasticity values assumed. If the model user is willing to assume that these estimated elasticities values hold over the model time horizon and attach some plausibility to the projected real GDP per capita and real gasoline price, (s)he can expect an increase in the value of the average annual VKT by car in this country. The resulting travel demand by car, measured in pkm/year, may vary depending on the simulated average car occupancy level. Figure 6.30 gives the output after assuming two different values representing the average car occupancy level: 1.2 passengers (pax) and 1.5 pax per car (assuming a linear increase from 1.2 in 2015 to 1.5 in 2030). Thus higher travel demand by car can be met with the same car stock, by defining a higher desired car occupancy level.

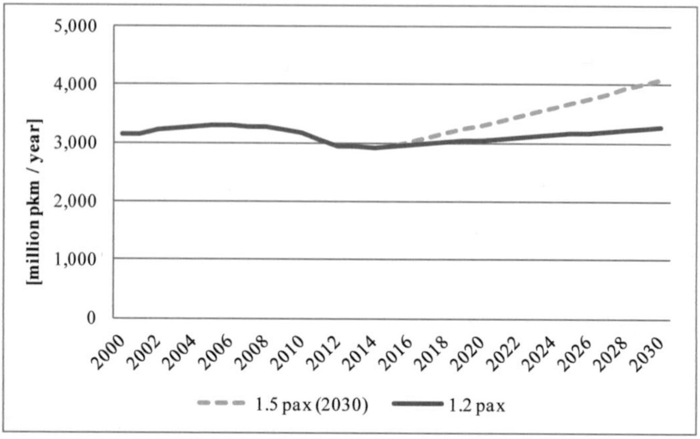

Figure 6.30: Effect of a desired car occupancy level on travel demand in the US
Source: Own work using Vensim®

In the simulations for France, car stock values in 2030 were slightly lower than in 2000, as stated in section 4.2.9. The reader may well regard that this is implausible. Since car sharing is not specifically modelled, the present model can say little about its impact. However, the projected decline in the French car stock between 2020 and 2030 does not mean that travel demand by car necessarily decreases. The point, illustrated by means of Figure 6.31, is that the average car occupancy level may rise, at least in theory.

As can be seen on the right axis, with a constant average car occupancy level of 1.2 pax, travel demand by car decreases until 2030, as a result of – *ceteris paribus* – the declining French car stock simulated. If, however, a higher level of car occupancy could be achieved, travel demand would be maintained at almost the same level in 2030. Given the simulated behaviour of the car stock, the implication of this policy measure would be reflected in the annual average VKT by car (left axis). The requirement of a higher average annual VTK by car, without reducing overall travel demand by car, could be fulfilled by e.g. car sharing units.

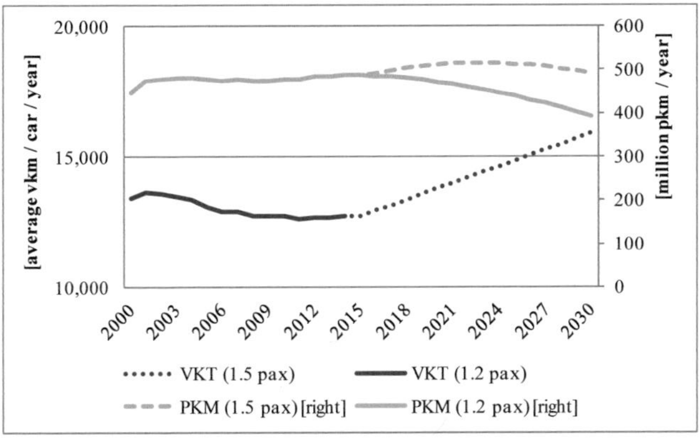

Figure 6.31: Effect of a desired car occupancy level on travel demand in France
Source: Own work using Vensim®

To conclude this section, the effect of policies on EV stock can be assessed individually or in combination (i.e. policy bundle or package). Figure 6.32 gives an example using the simulation for France. The effect of policies is measured with respect to the RS, both in 2020 (left panel) and 2030 (right panel). The four policy measures considered are: stricter efficiency standards, higher diesel taxation, EV purchase subsidies and investment in recharging infrastructure. The column on the left reflects the additive effects of simulating each policy individually (i.e. in isolation). Conversely, the column on the right is the result of simulating all the four policy measures in combination.

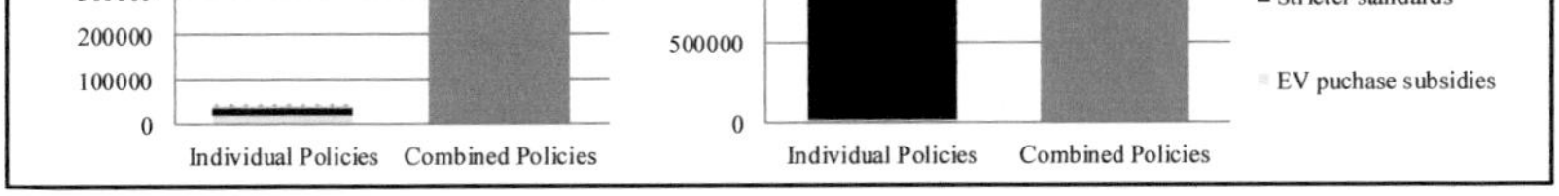

Figure 6.32: Individual policies vs. policy package: Δ EV stock w.r.t. RS in France
Source: Own work

The graph shows that the simulated policy package has positive synergies for EVs, outperforming additive individual policy measures. Over time, the differences diminish. Among the individual measures, stricter efficiency standards turn out to be the most effective policy option.

6.3 Impacts on energy demand and emissions

The final model output of both scenarios is compared in this section. In terms of energy demand, oil and electricity are examined. To facilitate the comparison among countries, the model output shown in this section is based on the VKT value assumed in Eq. 4.19. The interested reader may replicate the results by applying the two alternative metrics highlighted in section 4.2.12.

The next figures show the evolution of oil demand from car travel activity per country, highlighting the differences between scenarios. In general, oil demand is lower in the AS vis-à-vis the RS, as expected. For the fast-growing Asian markets, the difference in simulated oil demand is substantial. Oil demand is reported by taking into account the average yield by fuel (recall Figure 4.15) and refers to the sum of the demand from CVs, HEVs and PHEVs (as shown in Figure 4.1).

Figure 6.33 shows the indirect impact of electric cars on oil demand in China for both scenarios. In 2016, the simulated oil demand from cars is 1.32 bn bbl per year. With respect to this year, in 2030 demand doubles in the RS. Under the AS, oil demand is 57% lower than in the RS in 2030. This can be partially explained by the stricter emission standards (see Figure 6.17). Compare the results of Figure 6.33 with those of Figure 6.19, which relied on the setting of more stringent efficiency standards in isolation (that is, without support measures such as EV purchase subsidies or recharging infrastructure deployment). Here, oil demand from Chinese cars turns out to be lower (-42% in 2030). This is can be traced to faster BEV uptake (cf. Figure 5.1 and Figure 6.10) as a result of the policy packages simulated for the six countries under the AS.

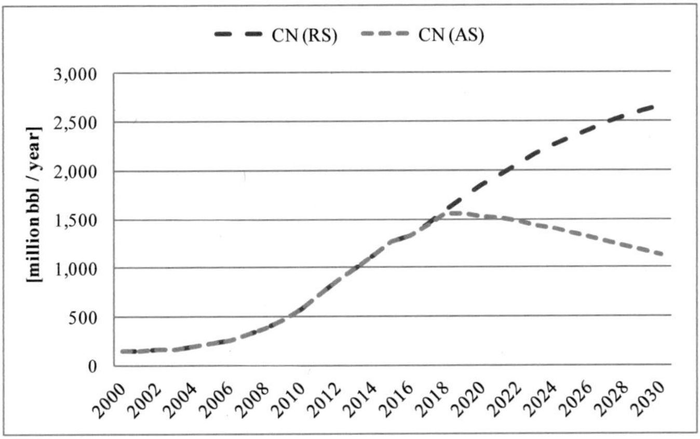

Figure 6.33: Oil demand from cars in China | Source: Own work

Annual oil demand from car travel activity in France is shown in Figure 6.34. In 2016, oil demand remains at ca. 365 million bbl. The simulated 2016-2030 reduction under the RS is 29%. In 2030, the difference between scenarios is -16% (i.e. lower in the AS).

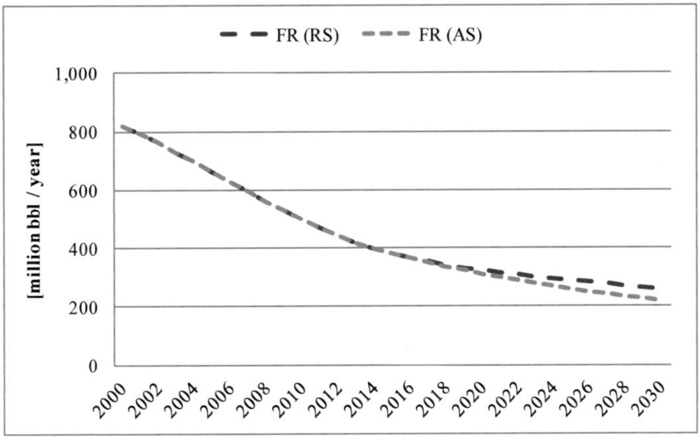

Figure 6.34: Oil demand from cars in France | Source: Own work

In Germany, annual oil demand from cars stands at 935 million bbl in the simulation. For this country, a reduction in oil demand of about 13% between 2016 and 2030 is attained for the RS (see Figure 6.35). Compared to the RS, a 29% fall in demand is simulated in the AS.

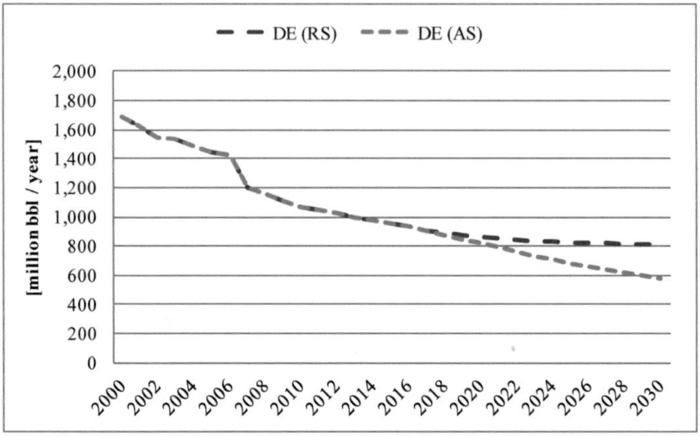

Figure 6.35: Oil demand from cars in Germany | Source: Own work

For India, oil demand from cars climbs from 215 million bbl/year in 2016 to 1.2 bn in 2030 under the RS (a 461% rise). Growth is slower under the AS, with a tripling of demand between 2016 and 2030 but a 45% reduction in 2030 in comparison with the RS (see Figure 6.36). It is worth emphasising that the projected growth in total car stock for China and India between 2016 and 2030 exceeds 400% (recall Figure 4.52).

For the Japanese market, a value of ca. 640 million bbl of oil per annum is estimated for 2016 (see Figure 6.37). Despite the projected growth in total car stock, the car-related demand for oil decreases for the period 2016-2030 in both scenarios (-12% under the RS and -24% under the AS). This has similarities with the German case. A comparison between the RS and AS in 2030 shows that annual oil demand from cars is 14% lower in the latter.

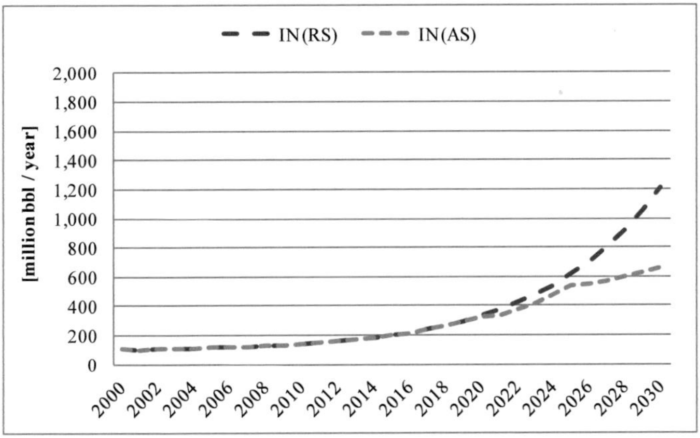

Figure 6.36: Oil demand from cars in India | Source: Own work

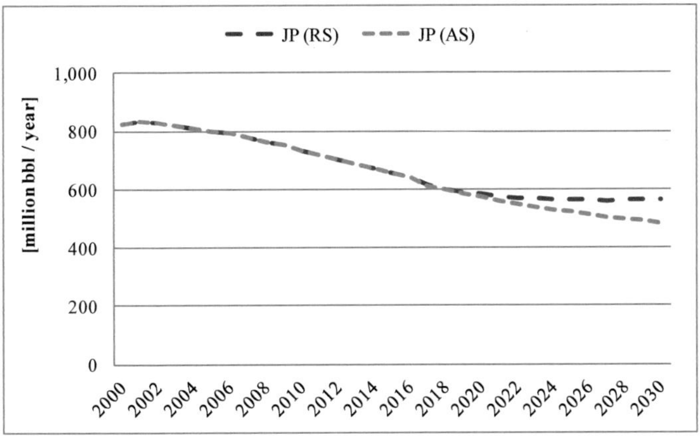

Figure 6.37: Oil demand from cars in Japan | Source: Own work

In the US, car drivers are simulated to consume 1.73 bbl of oil in 2016. For 2016-2030, oil demand is reduced 15% under the RS. Compared to this scenario, oil demand in 2030 declines by 23% in the AS (see Figure 6.38).

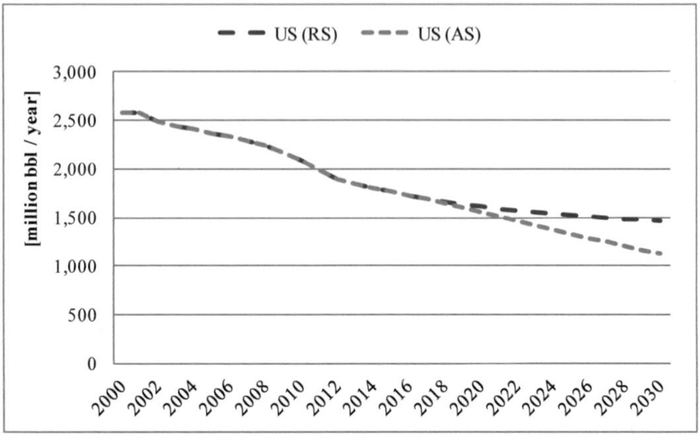

Figure 6.38: Oil demand from cars in the US | Source: Own work

Overall, the reduction in oil demand from cars is offset by the increase in electricity demand from PHEVs and BEVs. Accompanying the growth in EV stock, the demand for electricity in these countries explodes from virtually nothing under the AS. Growth in demand is much more modest under the RS.

With regards to electricity generation, Figures 6.39-6.44 contain the simulation results for RS and AS. As expected, electricity demand from EV use increases rapidly under the AS.

Relative to the amount of electricity generated in 2013 (the last year with available data in Figures 4.69-4.74), incremental demand from EVs is foreseen to be low until 2030. This does not necessarily mean that there might not be problems related to grid balancing, for EV agglomeration at the local level may pose challenges to the grid operator.

In China, the requirement for electricity generation from cars is simulated to reach 250 TWh by 2030 under the AS, compared to ca. 6 TWh in the RS (see Figure 6.39). Whereas by 2030 the demand for electricity for EVs surpasses 5 TWh in the AS in France (Figure 6.40), it rises almost linearly in Germany, approaching 16 TWh (see Figure 6.41).

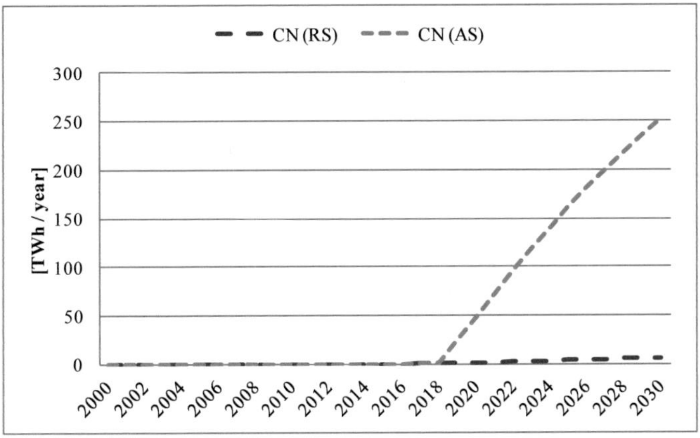

Figure 6.39: Electricity demand from cars in China | Source: Own work

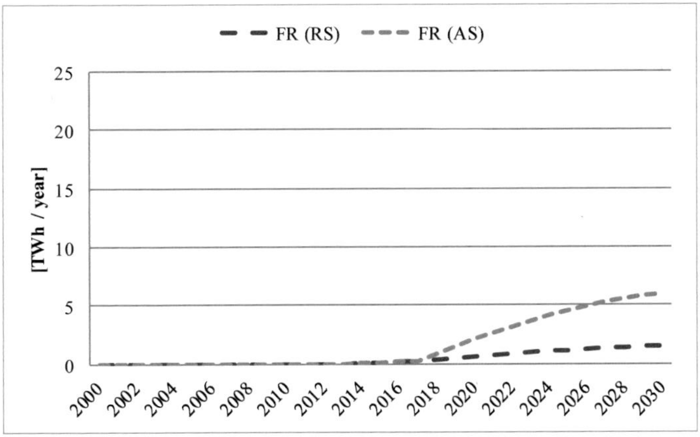

Figure 6.40: Electricity demand from cars in France | Source: Own work

The simulated demand for electricity to power Indian cars in 2030 is almost 122 TWh under the AS, up from 9 TWh in the RS (see Figure 6.42). It can be remarked that demand quickly goes up in 2021 and remains relatively flat until 2025 in the AS, only to grow strongly thereafter.

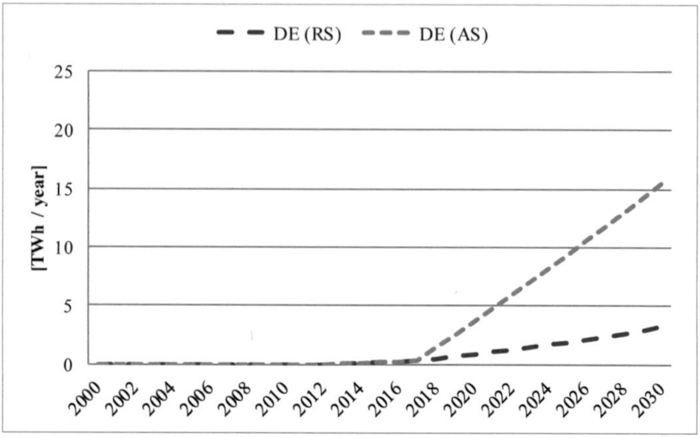

Figure 6.41: Electricity demand from cars in Germany | Source: Own work

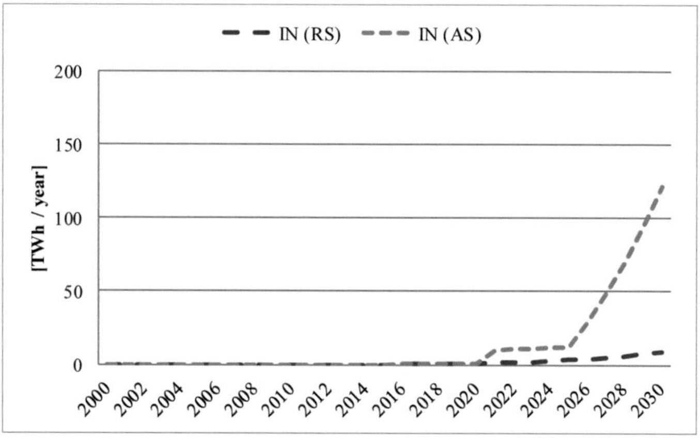

Figure 6.42: Electricity demand from cars in India | Source: Own work

In Japan, electricity generation, as demanded by EVs, is simulated to grow by a factor of 1.5 by 2030 in the AS, compared to the RS (see Figure 6.43).

Between the simulated demand for electricity arising from EV use in the RS and AS, a difference of over 24 TWh is estimated in 2030 for the US (see Figure 6.44).

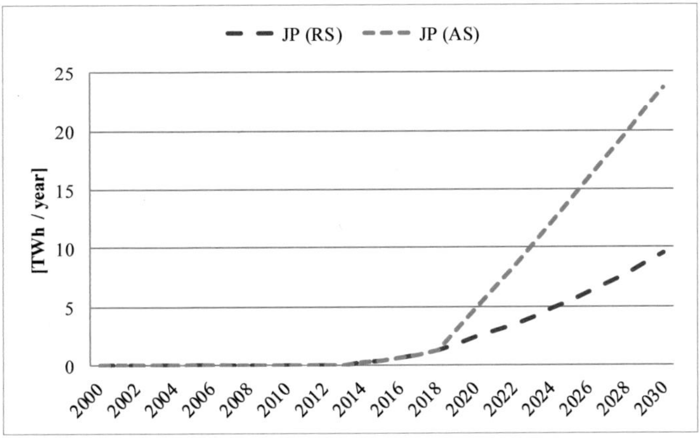

Figure 6.43: Electricity demand from cars in Japan | Source: Own work

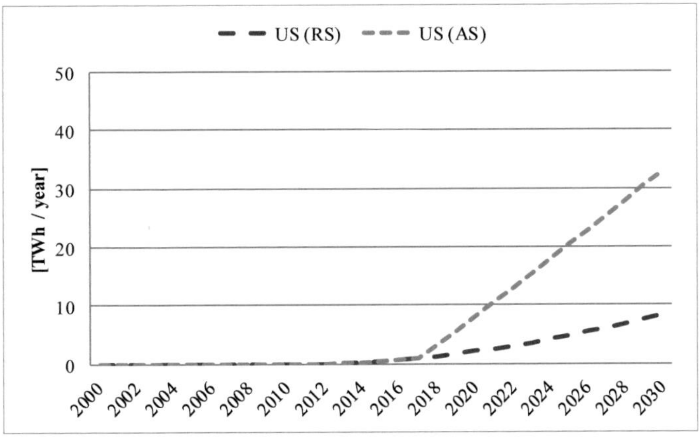

Figure 6.44: Electricity demand from cars in the US | Source: Own work

Finally, it is of interest to grasp the proportion of PHEVs within the EV stock. This also has implications for electricity demand because PHEVs are partially powered by electricity. In 2015, the simulated proportion is: 62% (CN), 69% (FR), 44% (DE), 100% (IN), 46% (JP) and 42% (US). This proportion is not constant throughout the simulation and also changes by scenario.

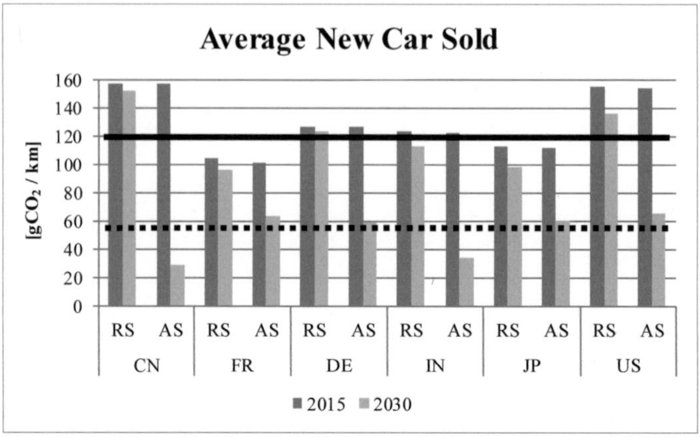

Figure 6.45: Simulated direct CO_2 emissions per km | Source: Own work

In all the countries examined, after 2017 the proportion of PHEVs within the EV stock is lower under the AS than under the RS. By 2030, the AS values range from 3% in China to 46% in Japan. The last model output of interest is GHG emissions. Figure 6.45 shows the direct CO_2 emissions per km of the average new car sold. The horizontal lines in that figure indicate the average of the six countries, simulated for the RS (solid line) and the AS (dotted line). The difference between the two scenarios is a 55% reduction in 2030, from 120 to 54 grams of CO_2 per km. Under the RS, China and the US have the largest numbers. Under the AS, the results of China and India pull down the mean value.

At the aggregate level, the simulated GHG emissions from cars under the AS are shown in the next six charts. Each time plot provides country-specific information on the dynamic behaviour of emissions by process: that is, not only TTW but also WTT plus M&S emissions are shown. For a comparison with the simulated TTW emissions under the RS, see also Figure 5.7. Figure 6.46 shows that total GHG emissions from cars are simulated to reach 733 megatonnes (Mt) of CO_{2eq} in 2030 in China, of which one-third correspond to TTW emissions. By 2027, M&S processes account for the largest source of emissions. A 12% reduction in total GHG emissions is achieved under the AS, compared to the RS.

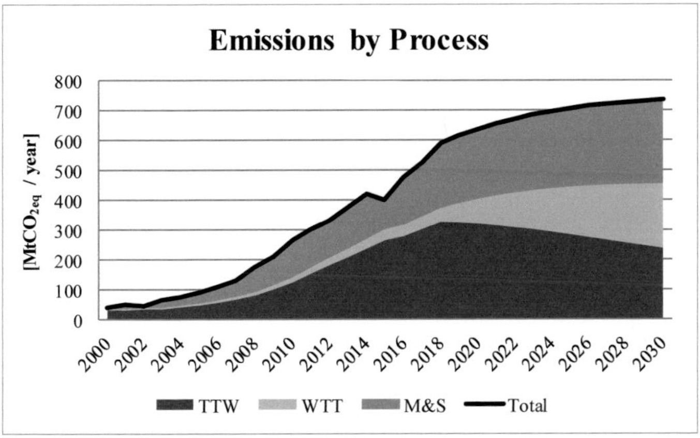

Figure 6.46: GHG emissions from cars in China under AS | Source: Own work

By 2030, cars are simulated to generate annually 57 $MtCO_{2eq}$ in France, as can be seen in Figure 6.47. The majority of these emissions can be attributed to TTW, which is about 10% lower than in the RS. Between 2016 and 2030, total GHG emissions decline 35% and 40% under the RS and AS, respectively. Compared to the RS, total GHG emissions under the AS are 7% lower.

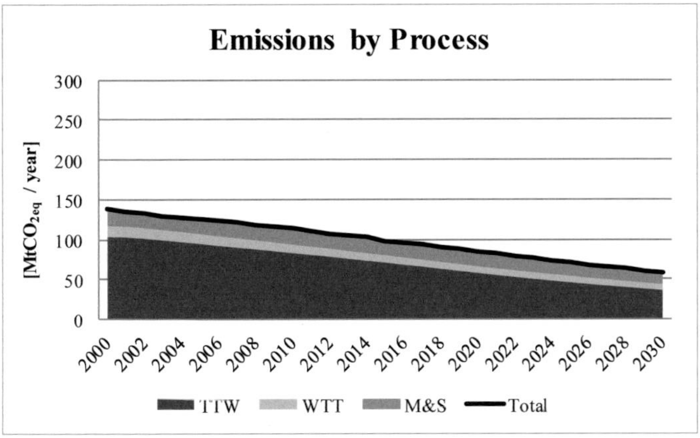

Figure 6.47: GHG emissions from cars in France under AS | Source: Own work

In Germany, a 12% fall in total GHG emissions from cars between scenarios is simulated (that is, lower in the AS). Under this scenario, in total 137 $MtCO_{2eq}$ are annually emitted by 2030: a modest 8% reduction w.r.t. 2016. Nearly half of the emissions can be attributed to TTW processes (Figure 6.48).

As expected, total GHG emissions from cars in India grow dramatically over the model time horizon (from ca. 100 $MtCO_{2eq}$ in 2016 to over 600 $MtCO_{2eq}$ in 2030 under the AS). The process mostly responsible for this growth is M&S (Figure 6.49). Interestingly, India represents the exception when it comes to differences between both scenarios: emissions are 4% higher under the AS. This can be explained by the results from Figure 6.13 and the assumptions from Table 4.18.

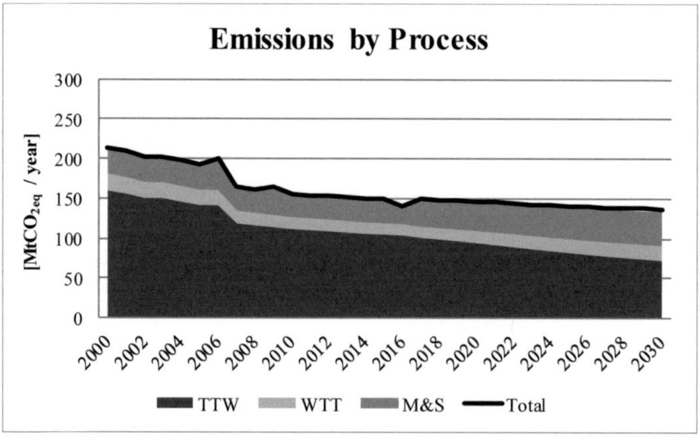

Figure 6.48: GHG emissions from cars in Germany under AS | Source: Own work

Figure 6.50 quantifies total GHG emissions from cars in Japan under the AS. In total, a value of 189 $MtCO_{2eq}$ is simulated for the year 2030. Over half of those emissions correspond to TTW. As can be seen, little mitigation in total emissions occurs, even under the more ambitious AS.

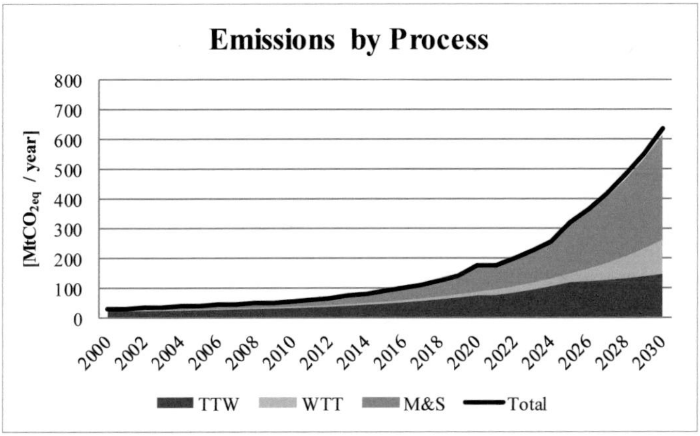

Figure 6.49: GHG emissions from cars in India under AS | Source: Own work

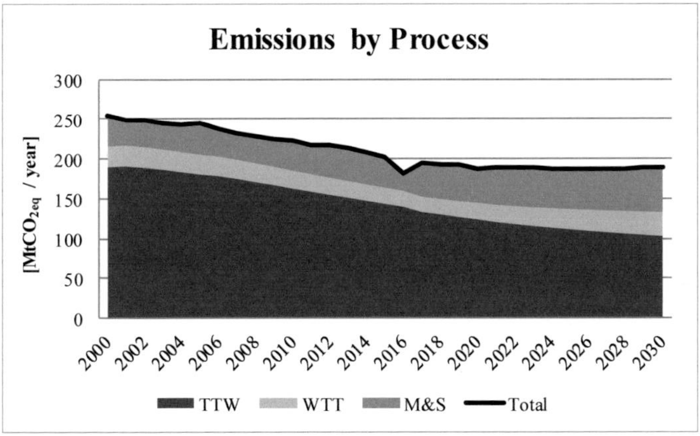

Figure 6.50: GHG emissions from cars in Japan under AS | Source: Own work

For the US, an 18% fall in total GHG emissions between 2016 and 2030 is simulated under the AS (see Figure 6.51). Compared to the RS, emissions are 13% lower in 2030, reaching ca. 375 $MtCO_{2eq}$/year.

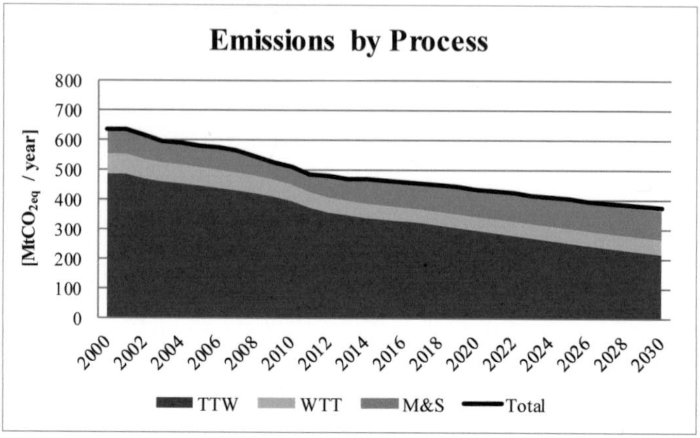

Figure 6.51: GHG emissions from cars in the US under AS | Source: Own work

To sum up, the simulated GHG emissions from car travel activity are slowly but steadily declining in the mature car markets. In these countries, the majority of GHG emissions are generated during the operation of the car (i.e. TTW). In the fast-growing markets, GHG emissions are on the rise throughout the simulation period. However, GHG emissions from cars appear to start stabilising in China by 2030. Both in China and India, a large proportion of GHG emissions are produced at the car manufacturing phase. In these two countries, indirect (i.e. WTT) GHG emissions gain importance over time.

7 Conclusions

In this final chapter, a summary is provided and conclusions drawn (section 7.1). Finally, the perceived limitations of this study are communicated and suggestions for further research offered (section 7.2).

7.1 Summary and conclusions

7.1.1 Summary

In this thesis, possible futures of the car ecosystem were explored, with nine powertrain technologies and six countries in scope. The focus lay on conventional cars (gasoline and diesel) and electric cars (plug-in hybrid electric and battery electric). Their implications for energy use and greenhouse gas emissions between the years 2000 and 2030 were considered.

The major markets analysed were China, France, Germany, India, Japan and the United States. For that, a dynamic model was developed, structured into nine interlinked modules: *Population-Gross Domestic Product, Car Stock, Travel Demand by Car, Infrastructure, Attributes, Market Behaviour, Energy, Emissions* and *Policy*. The model consisted of a time-series econometric sub-model and a system dynamics sub-model. Whereas the purpose of the former was to project aggregate car stock in each country, the purpose of the latter was to simulate and analyse the effect of policy measures.

These sub-models were soft-linked through the gasoline price and car ownership projections. The same assumptions on population, gross domestic product and crude oil price were used in both sub-models for consistency. The econometric sub-model comprised six single-equation regressions based on autoregressive integrated moving average or autoregressive distributed-lag estimation techniques. The core of the modelling exercise was the system dynamics sub-model, where endogenous feedback processes were represented. The dynamic hypothesis captured three reinforcing and two balancing feedback loops that may stimulate or suppress the market development of electric cars. The six countries were interlinked to simulate technological progress concerning the electric vehicle battery pack. In particular, its cost, price and capacity, together with the resulting electric range of the car, were investigated.

The developed model is suitable for constructing and simulating scenarios. It can provide answers to the following questions:

1. What are the projected aggregate car stock and annual sales?
2. What are the possible market shares and resulting car-mix?
3. What is the estimated demand for energy?
4. What are the corresponding greenhouse gas emissions?

Out of the numerous scenarios that were simulated during the model building process, two main scenarios were constructed and reported: the Reference Scenario and the Alternative Scenario. For each country, a given policy input was highlighted for illustrative purposes. In total, the set of policy instruments examined under the Alternative Scenario included: emission or efficiency standards, energy taxation, electric car purchase subsidies and investment in recharging infrastructure. Two further policy measures were presented: investment in hydrogen refuelling infrastructure and desired car occupancy.

In sum, compared to the Reference Scenario the diversification of the car-mix is stronger in the Alternative Scenario, with a faster market uptake of electric cars. This leads to a decline in oil demand and increase in electricity demand from cars. Consequently, the direct emissions of the average new car, measured in grams of CO_2 per km, is lower in the Alternative Scenario than in the Reference Scenario.

7.1.2 Conclusions and policy recommendations

In addition to the concluding remarks from chapter 2 and chapter 3 and as a result of this model-based study, the following main conclusions are drawn and key policy recommendations derived:

Conclusion 1: Setting stricter CO_2 emission standards for new conventional cars, which translate into higher car fuel efficiencies, leads to a reduction in oil-based energy use from car travel activity, *ceteris paribus*. To this end, this policy is the most effective of the four examined. The decline in oil demand is greater if: (i) the four policies are combined; and (ii) stricter CO_2 emission standards for new conventional cars are introduced in the other countries simultaneously.

Recommendation 1: If the primary policy goal is not to reduce vehicle-km travelled by car while reducing oil-based energy use from car travel activity, the governments of major car markets should recognise that stricter CO_2 emission standards are a key, though partial, solution towards this goal. International coordination on this policy would be beneficial.

Conclusion 2: More stringent CO_2 emission standards are expected to rise the manufacturing cost and corresponding price of conventional cars but higher fuel efficiency also lowers the operating cost faced by the drivers of conventional cars. For diesel cars, this last effect can be offset by aligning conventional fuel taxes. In this manner, a higher diesel tax increases the operating cost of diesel cars and reduces the attractiveness of this powertrain.

Recommendation 2: If the primary policy goal is not to reduce vehicle-km travelled by car while reducing diesel use from car travel activity, higher conventional fuel taxes may complement the policy on CO_2 emission standards. The governments of countries where dieselisation is high should also consider the possibility of increasing diesel taxation. The additional tax revenue could be used to temporarily cross-subsidise alternative powertrains.

Conclusion 3: If electric cars penetrate the market at the expense of conventional cars, it follows that the demand for conventional fuel and direct emissions (i.e. CO_2 emissions of the average new car sold and greenhouse gas emissions from the car stock) are, *ceteris paribus*, lowered.

Recommendation 3: If the primary policy goal is not to reduce vehicle-km travelled by car while lowering direct CO_2 emissions and oil-based energy use from car travel activity, diversification of the car-mix compared to the present situation is desirable. Combinations of conventional fuel taxes, purchase subsidies for electric cars and investment in recharging infrastructure, particularly enabling fast recharging, are needed. A bundle of coherent policies is expected to have a greater impact than isolated measures or a bundle of incoherent policies. An example of the latter would be to offer purchase subsidies for electric cars while removing gasoline and diesel taxes.

Conclusion 4: When other types of greenhouse gas emissions (CH_4 and N_2O) besides CO_2 are modelled, the reported level of emissions increases for most fuels and the a priori benefits of a fuel may be subjected to review. By further extending the model boundaries to take into account indirect greenhouse gas emissions, a more complete assessment of the relative environmental merits of each powertrain technology can be undertaken.

Recommendation 4: If the policy goal is not to reduce vehicle-km travelled by car while lowering total greenhouse gas emissions from car travel activity, policy measures that completely ignore upstream or well-to-tank as well as car manufacturing and scrappage emissions are expected to lead to policy failure. An example of this is a policy stance that promotes electric cars while favours electricity generation by coal.

Conclusion 5: Nonlinearities and adopted numerical assumptions largely determine the outcome of the simulation of powertrain choice. A simultaneous shift in battery price, battery capacity increase and cost-competitiveness of electric cars (facilitated by the effect of stricter emission standards on manufacturing prices and by temporary purchase subsidies) result in a tipping point, whereby a much larger proportion of consumers suddenly chooses this powertrain. Notwithstanding, supply-side conditions may constrain powertrain choice.

Recommendation 5: Model users are advised to complement the lessons learned from using the model presented in this work with those that can be learned by applying models that focus on the automotive industry and take into account the production process. For policy, close and regular monitoring of the evolution of key system variables (e.g. battery price) becomes a necessity. The timing of policy measures might have a noticeable effect on the market, as illustrated by the German example in section 6.2.

Overall, the analysis presented in this thesis, including the policy part in chapter 6, should be received with a healthy dose of scepticism, for it is based on the development of a formal model that is the result of the mental model of the author. Though this mental model has been enriched through the modelling process, understanding of the evolving system under investigation remains incomplete. The purpose of the model reflects different levels of ambition, ranging from a modest contribution to ongoing research to an open-source teaching tool to policy-making decision support. For the highest level of ambition, additional modelling efforts from the scientific community are welcomed.

In this thesis, a multi-method approach has been adopted and an early attempt to connect in a single modelling framework the dynamic econometrics and system dynamics methods has been made. The possible theoretical conflict between both methods has been neither completely ignored nor overemphasised, for it is concluded that researchers with skills in only one of these two methods would benefit from exposure to the other.

It is argued that the methodological linkage of econometrics and system dynamics, together with the *endogenisation* of the electric vehicle battery price evolution by explicitly modelling six major car markets, is the main contribution of this study. The key outcome of this work is the development and provision of a framework for forward-looking thinking that can be reproduced, applied, improved and extended.

7.2 Limitations and further research

7.2.1 Limitations

The conclusions and policy recommendations highlighted in the previous section need to be qualified in view of the following major limitations:

Limitation 1: Setting stricter CO_2 emission standards for new conventional cars may result in a preference for purchasing (larger) conventional cars as well as in greater annual average vehicle-km travelled. However, this work is limited by a lack of disaggregation of cars by size and insufficient analysis on the role of rebound effects.

Limitation 2: Removing the tax differential between gasoline and diesel by rising the latter as well as adjusting conventional fuel taxes to maintain real conventional fuel prices might add inflationary pressure. In the 1970s, the linkage between the oil price and inflation was revealed. Although Blanchard (2008) found that this relation diminished in recent years, the possibility that this feedback process is dormant cannot be ruled out.

Limitation 3: Analysis of the inter-temporal optimal policy package aiming at the best combination of conventional fuel taxes, purchase subsidies for electric cars and investment in recharging infrastructure has not been performed.

Limitation 4: The results on emissions are limited by the fact that (i) air pollutant emissions from cars have been excluded from this study; (ii) neither the practical implications of setting emission standards using gCO_{2eq}/km as the metric of reference nor the impact of upgrading current driving test cycles have been explored; (iii) different fuel pathways are possible and upstream greenhouse gas emissions may vary widely depending on the method of extraction and/or production employed for each fuel, which can be tested in the model through sensitivity analysis but should ideally be tackled by researchers specialised in lifecycle assessments; (iv) the prospects of battery recycling and re-use as secondary storage devices have been neglected; and

(v) annual average vehicle-km travelled by car may increase while well-to-wheel greenhouse gas emissions do not. This may happen if the use of car sharing increases sufficiently. Per each car sharing unit, up to twenty cars may be replaced (Rifkin, 2011). As a result of widespread car sharing activity, private car ownership rates are thus expected to decrease and the lower the number of private cars produced, the less car manufacturing and scrappage emissions. The emergence of car sharing (see e.g. Jackson (2011)) has not been explicitly accounted for.

Limitation 5: Uncertainty surrounds the preferences of the market as regards novel car technologies. It is important to emphasise that the current work is, at best, a crude preliminary approximation to the ideal of representative and accurate market outcomes. Understanding the complexity of human behaviour, in the context of car purchase decisions, and its mathematical representation remains a challenge. Any model assumption described in chapter 4, particularly those concerning the market segmentation and the associated decision rules (sections 4.2.10 and 4.2.11, respectively), can be challenged by theory and new evidence. Furthermore and since the market uptake of electric cars is still at an early stage, its future evolution may be either spurred or hindered by feedback processes not accounted for in this work, especially when a longer model time horizon (say, until 2050) is considered. For example, the expected increase in the price of raw materials to manufacture electric vehicle batteries as a result of increasing demand and possible trade restrictions by exporting countries, which can negatively affect the purchase price of electric cars, has not been modelled.

In addition, two specific methodological limitations are stressed:

Limitation 6: Concerning the use of econometrics, this work is adversely affected by a small sample and the invocation of asymptotic properties (see Maddala and Kim (1998)) as well as by the lack of an in-depth forecast assessment. On a different note, one may nowadays question the role, fruitful in the past, of traditional econometrics to successfully forecast future car ownership, given the prospects not only of car sharing but also of connected and automated vehicle concepts.

Limitation 7: With regards to the application of system dynamics, this work is limited by the need to conduct more comprehensive model analysis and further testing (for additional tests, see chapter 21 in Sterman (2000)). The solution to the stock management problem (recall section 4.1.3) found is adequate for the model purpose but not always ideal, as visible in the 2015-2016 dips in Figure 6.46, Figure 6.48 and Figure 6.50. It is worth remembering that the desired values arising from the econometric projections are time-variant.

7.2.2 Further research

Based on the aforementioned limitations of this study, specific lines of further inquiry are indicated below.

Expanding model boundaries:

The modelled system is non-autonomous and is largely dependent on the assumed future socio-economic (population, gross domestic product, inflation) conditions. The model boundaries can be expanded to incorporate missing feedback processes and to capture the 'endogenous point of view' (recall section 3.2.4). Three processes can be enumerated: the effect of electro-mobility on the oil price, the battery manufacturing sector and its contribution to employment and the economy. Furthermore, the inclusion of additional vehicle markets would be beneficial.

Further model disaggregation:

The concept of *average*, influentially used (see Morgan (1992)) by Belgian mathematician Adolphe Quetelet [1796-1874], is exploited in this work. Two prominent variables are: income per capita and the hypothetical average car. In contrast, Page (2010) emphasises *diversity* in complex systems and mentions quantile regression. This approach could be applied in future work to examine income distribution and how this affects car ownership in each of the countries under study. With regards to the average car, only one type of car is assumed for each powertrain technology. Although this is sufficient to derive the final model output, it represents a constraint to policy analysis. The benefits of disaggregating cars by size or segment are, however, offset by the increasing complexity in modelling powertrain choice. This means that any attempt at further disaggregating the variable *car* should take into account the implications for the technology choice sub-module.

Sophisticated time-series and discrete choice econometric analysis:

The econometric projections shown in section 4.2.8 contain high and low bounds. For China, the optimistic growth assumptions concerning gross domestic product lead to projections of car stock that are well above those found in other studies. It is worth emphasising that in China a quota system for vehicle registration is in place in various cities. As a result, the future behaviour of car stock may be less bullish than anticipated. Access to reliable longer series, thereby incorporating omitted variables, and refinements of the econometric models presented in this thesis by experienced time-series econometricians is expected to improve car ownership projections. Specifically, better statistical judgment is needed to do research on: (i) general problems of statistical inference in time-series models based on nonstationary economic data (see Yule (1926) and Banerjee *et al.* (1993)); and (ii) application of problematic unit root tests (see the strong case Maddala and Kim (1998) make against the use of well-established tests due to low-power problems). Harvey (1997) warns against misleading unit root testing and autoregressions. In a motionless world, extrapolation suffices (Hendry, 1995), but technological innovations entail randomness (Enders, 2014). As Makridakis and Hibon (2000) note, simple statistical methods may outperform sophisticated ones and more accurate forecasts are on average obtained when methods are combined.

With regards to the behavioural assumptions on choice, more sophisticated representations of technology choice by the market may be investigated and implemented in the model. The results of new country-specific discrete choice analysis, preferably based on increasingly available revealed preferences, can be embedded into the model in a relatively simple manner. Furthermore, a new module that considers the competition between public transport, car sharing and private car ownership may be created, whereby modal split is explicitly modelled. Statistical testing of various nesting frameworks may be conducted.

Contrasting alternative methods:

The fourth conclusion deserves a remark on modelling approach. Since the simulation of accurate (i.e. perfect match with real-world observations) market shares by car technology was not the goal of modelling, the model was not completely forced to replicate historical data on this by incorporating extra factors and calibration efforts were relatively modest. However, the simulated market shares remain important, for they influence the final model output. A trade-off between theoretical and empirical consistency was faced by the model builder. Basically, the path chosen was: (i) to segment the market and define decision rules for each segment; (ii) to create a pseudo discrete choice modelling framework thereby assuming that part of the market maximises utility; and (iii) to constrain the weighted values of this segment of the market by a measure of popularity. The point is that more accurate simulation of market shares is expected to improve the results. At present, it remains unclear to the author what the most successful path to achieve this in the context of dynamic modelling of car technology uptake is. The framework recently recommended by Jensen *et al.* (2016) may provide a good basis for further research. As Vroey (2016) suggests, a researcher may take an alternative path at a previous bifurcation point once a dead end is reached. In this context, agent-based modelling is a candidate worthwhile exploring, e.g. extending the work by Kieckhäfer *et al.* (2014) to other countries. This is not a suggestion that a dead end has been reached for joint system dynamics/discrete choice modelling. Instead, in the absence of a discrete choice model tailored to the requirements of system dynamics and based on comprehensive surveys regularly conducted in the key car markets, agent-based modelling may be an alternative method to contrast with.

Extending policy options:

Only a subset of available policy instruments was considered. For example, car registration taxes may be also applied, for they alter relative purchase prices. If the car insurance premium is in reality tied to the purchase price, it should also be explicitly modelled. Importantly, public investment in research and development activities can also contribute to facilitate critical transitions. It would also be interesting to model three real-world policies explicitly: the electric car mandate in China, the bonus-malus scheme in France and the top-runner programme in Japan.

Finally, further work is essentially required in two respects: (i) as a continuous process of monitoring the system under study, updating the database as new data points and other information become available; and (ii) as a one-time exercise of retrospection, to take place in about fifteen years from now. In this regard, Sampedro (1967) provides a source of inspiration and a strong motivation for revisiting in the future the work presented here. Until then…

… *discere faciendo*.

References

Abbas, K. A., & Bell, M. G. H. (1994). System dynamics applicability to transportation modeling. *Transportation Research Part A: Policy and Practice*, *28*(5), 373–390. https://doi.org/10.1016/0965-8564(94)90022-1

Acatech. (2015). *Mit Energieszenarien gut beraten. Anforderungen an wissenschaftliche Politikberatung. acatech/Leopoldina/Akademienunion* (Schriftenreihe zur wissenschaftsbasierten Politikberatung). Retrieved from http://www.acatech.de/de/publikationen/stellungnahmen/kooperationen/detail /artikel/mit-energieszenarien-gut-beraten.html

ACEA. (2016). Research and Innovation. European Automobile Manufacturers Association. Retrieved from http://www.acea.be/industry-topics/tag/category/research-and-innovation

ADAC. (2016). Entwicklung der Tankstellenanzahl seit 1965 in Deutschland. Allgemeiner Deutscher Automobil-Club (ADAC). Retrieved from https://www.adac.de/infotestrat/tanken-kraftstoffe-und-antrieb/probleme-tankstelle/anzahl-tankstellen-markenverteilung/

ADB. (2010). *Reducing Carbon Emissions from Transport Projects* (Evaluation Study). Asian Development Bank. Retrieved from http://www.oecd.org/derec/adb/47170274.pdf

AFDC. (2015). Alternative Fuels Data Center (AFDC). Energy Efficiency & Renewable Energy. U.S. Deparment of Energy (DOE). Retrieved from https://www.afdc.energy.gov/

Ahamed, L. (2009). *Lords of Finance: The Bankers Who Broke the World.* Penguin.

Ajanovic, A., Dahl, C., & Schipper, L. (2012). Modelling transport (energy) demand and policies – An introduction. *Energy Policy*, *41*, iii–xiv. https://doi.org/10.1016/j.enpol.2011.12.033

Akerlof, G. A. (1970). The Market for 'Lemons': Quality Uncertainty and the Market Mechanism. *The Quarterly Journal of Economics*, *84*(3), 488–500. https://doi.org/10.2307/1879431

Al-Alawi, B. M., & Bradley, T. H. (2013). Review of hybrid, plug-in hybrid, and electric vehicle market modeling Studies. *Renewable and Sustainable Energy Reviews*, *21*, 190–203. https://doi.org/10.1016/j.rser.2012.12.048

Alcamo, J. (2008). Chapter Six The SAS Approach: Combining Qualitative and Quantitative Knowledge in Environmental Scenarios. In J. Alcamo (Ed.), *Developments in Integrated Environmental Assessment* (Vol. 2, pp. 123-150). Elsevier. Retrieved from http://www.sciencedirect.com/science/article/pii/S1574101X08004067

Aldy, J., Pizer, W., Tavoni, M., Reis, L. A., Akimoto, K., Blanford, G., Sano, F. (2016). Economic tools to promote transparency and comparability in the Paris Agreement. *Nature Climate Change, advance online publication*. https://doi.org/10.1038/nclimate3106

Aleklett, K. (2012). *Peeking at Peak Oil*. Springer Science & Business Media.

Anderson, S. T., Parry, I. W. H., Sallee, J. M., & Fischer, C. (2011). Automobile Fuel Economy Standards: Impacts, Efficiency, and Alternatives. *Review of Environmental Economics and Policy*, *5*(1), 89–108. https://doi.org/10.1093/reep/req021

Anowar, S., Eluru, N., & Miranda-Moreno, L. F. (2014). Alternative Modeling Approaches Used for Examining Automobile Ownership: A Comprehensive Review. *Transport Reviews*, *34*(4), 441–473. https://doi.org/10.1080/01441647.2014.915440

Apel, H., Fassing, W., & Meissner, W. (1978). System Dynamics Versus Econometrics—An Approach for Synthesis. In G. J. Klir (Ed.), *Applied General Systems Research* (pp. 347–359). Springer US. https://doi.org/10.1007/978-1-4757-0555-3_25

Archibald, G. C., Simon, H. A., & Samuelson, P. A. (1963). Discussion. *The American Economic Review*, *53*(2), 227–236.

Arthur, W. B. (1999). Complexity and the Economy. *Science, 284*(5411), 107–109. https://doi.org/10.1126/science.284.5411.107

Arthur, W. B. (2014). *Complexity and the Economy*. Oxford University Press.

Auto Alliance. (2016). Patents. Auto Innovation. The Alliance of Automobile Manufacturers. Retrieved from http://www.autoalliance.org/auto-innovation/patents

Autogastanken24. (2016). Autogas Tankstellenfinder. Retrieved from https://www.autogastanken24.de/tankstellen-mit-autogas/

Avineri, E. (2012). On the use and potential of behavioural economics from the perspective of transport and climate change. *Journal of Transport Geography, 24*, 512–521. https://doi.org/10.1016/j.jtrangeo.2012.03.003

Bakker, S. (2010). The car industry and the blow-out of the hydrogen hype. *Energy Policy, 38*(11), 6540–6544. https://doi.org/10.1016/j.enpol.2010.07.019

Ball, M., & Wietschel, M. (2009). *The Hydrogen Economy: Opportunities and Challenges*. Cambridge, UK ; New York: Cambridge University Press.

Baltagi, B. H. (2011). *Econometrics*. Springer Science & Business Media.

Banerjee, A., Dolado, J., Galbraith, J. W., & Hendry, D. F. (1993). *Co-integration, Error Correction, and the Econometric Analysis of Non-stationary Data*. Oxford University Press.

Barr, N. (2012). *Economics of the Welfare State*. OUP Oxford.

Bass, F. M. (1969). A New Product Growth for Model Consumer Durables. *Management Science, 15*(5), 215–227.

Bass, F. M. (2004). Comments on "A New Product Growth for Model Consumer Durables The Bass Model". *Management Science, 50*(12_supplement), 1833–1840. https://doi.org/10.1287/mnsc.1040.0300

Batley, R. P., Toner, J. P., & Knight, M. J. (2004). A mixed logit model of U.K. household demand for alternative-fuel vehicles. *International Journal of Transport Economics / Rivista Internazionale Di Economia Dei Trasporti, 31*(1), 55–77.

Baumol, W. J. (1968). On the Social Rate of Discount. *The American Economic Review*, *58*(4), 788–802.

Baumol, W. J. (1970). *Economic Dynamics. An Introduction. Third Edition.* New York, Macmillan Publishing.

Baumol, W. J. (2000). Leontief's Great Leap Forward: Beyond Quesnay, Marx and von Bortkiewicz. *Economic Systems Research*, *12*(2), 141–152. https://doi.org/10.1080/09535310050005662

Baumol, W. J., & Oates, W. E. (1971). The Use of Standards and Prices for Protection of the Environment. In P. Bohm & A. V. Kneese (Eds.), *The Economics of Environment* (pp. 53–65). Palgrave Macmillan UK. https://doi.org/10.1007/978-1-349-01379-1_4

Baumol, W. J., & Oates, W. E. (1988). *The Theory of Environmental Policy*. Cambridge University Press.

Becker, C., Faber, M., Hertel, K., & Manstetten, R. (2005). Malthus vs. Wordsworth: Perspectives on humankind, nature and economy. A contribution to the history and the foundations of ecological economics. *Ecological Economics*, *53*(3), 299–310. https://doi.org/10.1016/j.ecolecon.2005.02.006

Becker, G. S. (1993). Nobel Lecture: The Economic Way of Looking at Behavior. *Journal of Political Economy*, *101*(3), 385–409.

Beckerman, W. (1974). *In defence of economic growth*. J. Cape.

Beggs, S., Cardell, S., & Hausman, J. (1981). Assessing the potential demand for electric cars. *Journal of Econometrics*, *17*(1), 1–19. https://doi.org/10.1016/0304-4076(81)90056-7

Bell, M. G. H., & O'Flaherty, C. A. (1997). *Transport planning and traffic engineering*. London [u.a.: Arnold. Retrieved from http://site.ebrary.com/lib/alltitles/docDetail.action?docID=10206555

Ben-Akiva, M. E., & Lerman, S. R. (1985). *Discrete Choice Analysis: Theory and Application to Travel Demand*. MIT Press.

BenDor, T., & Ford, A. (2006). Simulating a combination of feebates and scrappage incentives to reduce automobile emissions. *Energy, 31*(8–9), 1197–1214. https://doi.org/10.1016/j.energy.2005.05.024

Beran, J., Feng, Y., Ghosh, S., & Kulik, R. (2013). *Long-Memory Processes: Probabilistic Properties and Statistical Methods*. Springer Science & Business Media.

Berger, S. (2008). Circular Cumulative Causation (CCC) à la Myrdal and Kapp: 'Political' Institutionalism for Minimizing Social Costs. *Journal of Economic Issues, 42*(2), 357–365.

Bertalanffy, L. von. (2003). *General System Theory: Foundations, Development, Applications*. G. Braziller.

Bezemer, D. J. (2009). No one saw this coming: understanding financial crisis through accounting models. Faculty of Economics University of Groningen, Groningen, The Netherlands.

Blair, P. (2013). *Multiobjective regional energy planning: Application to the energy park concept*. Springer Science & Business Media.

Blanchard, O. (2008). *Macroeconomics* (5th international edition.). Upper Saddle River, N.J.; London: Prentice Hall.

Blanchard, O. J. (1983). The Production and Inventory Behavior of the American Automobile Industry. *Journal of Political Economy, 91*(3), 365-400. https://doi.org/10.1086/261154

Blaug. (2008). *Methodology of Economics 2ed: Or, How Economists Explain* (Auflage: 2). Cambridge ; New York, NY: Cambridge University Press.

Boland, L. A. (2014). *The Methodology of Economic Model Building (Routledge Revivals): Methodology after Samuelson*. Routledge.

Börjeson, L., Höjer, M., Dreborg, K.-H., Ekvall, T., & Finnveden, G. (2006). Scenario types and techniques: Towards a user's guide. *Futures, 38*(7), 723-739. https://doi.org/10.1016/j.futures.2005.12.002

Bossel, H. (2007a). *Systems and Models: Complexity, Dynamics, Evolution, Sustainability*. Norderstedt: Books on Demand.

Bossel, H. (2007b). *Systems and Models. Complexity, Dynamics, Evolution, Sustainability*. Norderstedt: BoD.

Boulding, K. E. (1956). General Systems Theory—The Skeleton of Science. *Management Science*, *2*(3), 197–208. https://doi.org/10.1287/mnsc.2.3.197

Boulding, K. E. (1988). *Economics as a Science*. University Press of America.

Boumans, M., Davis, J. B., & Blaug, M. (2010). *Economic Methodology: Understanding Economics as a Science*. Basingstoke England ; New York: Palgrave.

Box, G. E. P. (1976). Science and Statistics. *Journal of the American Statistical Association*, *71*(356), 791–799. https://doi.org/10.1080/01621459.1976.10480949

Box, G. E. P., & Jenkins, G. M. (1976). *Time series analysis: forecasting and control*. Holden-Day.

BP. (2016). Statistical Review of World Energy 2016. British Petroleum public limited company (BP plc). Retrieved from http://www.bp.com/en/global/corporate/energy-economics/statistical-review-of-world-energy.html

Brandt, P. T., & Williams, J. T. (2007). *Multiple Time Series Models*. SAGE.

Breusch, T. S. (1978). Testing for Autocorrelation in Dynamic Linear Models*. *Australian Economic Papers*, *17*(31), 334–355. https://doi.org/10.1111/j.1467-8454.1978.tb00635.x

Brown, G. S., & Campbell, D. P. (1948). *Principles of servomechanisms: dynamics and synthesis of closed-loop control systems*. J. Wiley.

Bruce, J. P., Yi, H., Haites, E. F., & III, I. P. on C. C. W. G. (1996). *Climate Change 1995: Economic and Social Dimensions of Climate Change: Contribution of Working Group III to the Second Assessment Report of the Intergovernmental Panel on Climate Change*. Cambridge University Press.

Buchanan, M. (2013). What has econophysics ever done for us? *Nature Physics*, *9*(6), 317–317. https://doi.org/10.1038/nphys2648

Bunge, M. (1964). *Critical Approaches to Science and Philosophy*. Transaction Publishers.

Bunge, M. (1979). A systems concept of society: Beyond individualism and holism. *Theory and Decision*, *10*(1–4), 13–30. https://doi.org/10.1007/BF00126329

Bunge, M. (2014). *La ciencia, su método y su filosofía*. Penguin Random House Grupo Editorial Argentina.

Bunge, M. (2015). *Economía Y Filosofía*. Pamplona: Laetoli.

Buongiorno, J. (1996). Forest sector modeling: a synthesis of econometrics, mathematical programming, and system dynamics methods. *International Journal of Forecasting*, *12*(3), 329–343. https://doi.org/10.1016/0169-2070(96)00668-1

Burnham, A., Han, J., Clark, C. E., Wang, M., Dunn, J. B., & Palou-Rivera, I. (2012). Life-Cycle Greenhouse Gas Emissions of Shale Gas, Natural Gas, Coal, and Petroleum. *Environmental Science & Technology*, *46*(2), 619–627. https://doi.org/10.1021/es201942m

Button, K. (2010). *Transport economics*. Aldershot, Hants, England; Northampton, MA: Elgar.

Button, K. J., Pearman, A. D., & Fowkes, A. S. (1982). *Car ownership modelling and forecasting*. Gower.

Caiani, A., Godin, A., Caverzasi, E., Gallegati, M., Kinsella, S., & Stiglitz, J. E. (2016). Agent based-stock flow consistent macroeconomics: Towards a benchmark model. *Journal of Economic Dynamics and Control*, *69*, 375-408. https://doi.org/10.1016/j.jedc.2016.06.001

Caiani, A., Russo, A., Palestrini, A., & Gallegati, M. (2016). *Economics with Heterogeneous Interacting Agents: A Practical Guide to Agent-Based Modeling*. Springer.

Caldwell, B. (1980). Positivist Philosophy of Science and the Methodology of Economics. *Journal of Economic Issues*, *14*(1), 53–76.

Cames, M., & Helmers, E. (2013). Critical evaluation of the European diesel car boom - global comparison, environmental effects and various national strategies. *Environmental Sciences Europe*, *25*(1), 15. https://doi.org/10.1186/2190-4715-25-15

Campos, J., Ericsson, N. R., & Hendry, D. F. (1996). Cointegration tests in the presence of structural breaks. *Journal of Econometrics*, *70*(1), 187–220. https://doi.org/10.1016/0304-4076(94)01689-5

Cao, K.-K., Cebulla, F., Gómez Vilchez, J. J., Mousavi, B., & Prehofer, S. (2016). Raising awareness in model-based energy scenario studies—a transparency checklist. *Energy, Sustainability and Society*, *6*(1). https://doi.org/10.1186/s13705-016-0090-z

Carnot, S. (1986). *Reflexions on the Motive Power of Fire*. University Press.

Carpintero, O., & Redondo, Ó. C. (2006). *La bioeconomía de Georgescu-Roegen*. Montesinos.

Carter, A. P. (1974). Energy, Environment, and Economic Growth. *The Bell Journal of Economics and Management Science*, *5*(2), 578–592. https://doi.org/10.2307/3003121

CCFA. (2016). Comité des Constructeurs Français d'Automobiles. Retrieved from http://ccfa.fr/

Cetinkaya, E., Dincer, I., & Naterer, G. F. (2012). Life cycle assessment of various hydrogen production methods. *International Journal of Hydrogen Energy*, *37*(3), 2071–2080. https://doi.org/10.1016/j.ijhydene.2011.10.064

Chang, H.-J. (2010). *Bad Samaritans: The Myth of Free Trade and the Secret History of Capitalism*. Bloomsbury Publishing.

Charemza, W., & Deadman, D. (1997). *New directions in econometric practice: general to specific modelling, cointegration, and vector autoregression*. Edward Elgar.

Charemza, W. W., & Deadman, D. F. (1997). *New Directions in Econometric Practice: General to Specific Modelling, Cointegration, and Vector Autoregression* (2 edition). Lyme, N.H: Edward Elgar Pub.

Chatfield, C. (2003). *The Analysis of Time Series: An Introduction, Sixth Edition*. Taylor & Francis.

Chen, T. D., Kockelman, K. M., & Hanna, J. P. (2016). Operations of a shared, autonomous, electric vehicle fleet: Implications of vehicle & charging infrastructure decisions. *Transportation Research Part A: Policy and Practice*, *94*, 243–254. https://doi.org/10.1016/j.tra.2016.08.020

Chertow, M. R. (2000). The IPAT Equation and Its Variants. *Journal of Industrial Ecology*, *4*(4), 13–29. https://doi.org/10.1162/10881980052541927

Chiang, A. C., & Wainwright, K. (2005). *Fundamental Methods of Mathematical Economics* (Auflage: 4. A. International Edition.). Boston, Mass.: Mcgraw-Hill Publ.Comp.

Chorus, C. (2012). Random Regret Minimization: An Overview of Model Properties and Empirical Evidence. *Transport Reviews*, *32*(1), 75–92. https://doi.org/10.1080/01441647.2011.609947

Chorus, C. G., Arentze, T. A., & Timmermans, H. J. P. (2008). A Random Regret-Minimization model of travel choice. *Transportation Research Part B: Methodological*, *42*(1), 1–18. https://doi.org/10.1016/j.trb.2007.05.004

Christ, C. F. (1994). The Cowles Commission's Contributions to Econometrics at Chicago, 1939-1955. *Journal of Economic Literature*, *32*(1), 30–59.

Clements, M., & Hendry, D. (1998). *Forecasting Economic Time Series*. Cambridge University Press.

Clô, A. (2008). *Il rebus energetico. Tra politica, economia e ambiente*. Il Mulino.

CNMC. (2016). La CNMC desmanteló 14 cárteles e impuso multas por 549 millones de euros durante 2015. Comisión Nacional de los Mercados y la Competencia. Retrieved from https://www.cnmc.es/CNMC/Prensa/TabId/254/ArtMID/6629/ArticleID/1641/La-CNMC-desmantel243-14-c225rteles-e-impuso-multas-por-549-millones-de-euros-durante-2015.aspx

Colander, D. (2006). *Post Walrasian Macroeconomics: Beyond the Dynamic Stochastic General Equilibrium Model*. Cambridge University Press.

Colander, D., & Kupers, R. (2014). *Complexity and the Art of Public Policy: Solving Society's Problems from the Bottom Up*. Princeton University Press.

Common, M. (2005). *Ecological Economics: An Introduction*. Cambridge, UK ; New York: Cambridge University Press.

Commoner, B. (2014). *The Closing Circle: Nature, Man, and Technology*. Knopf Doubleday Publishing Group.

Commoner, B., Corr, M., & Stamler, P. J. (1971). The Causes of Pollution. *Environment: Science and Policy for Sustainable Development*, *13*(3), 2–19. https://doi.org/10.1080/00139157.1971.9930577

Cooley, C. H. (1894). The Theory of Transportation. *Publications of the American Economic Association*, *9*(3), 13–148.

Costanza, R. (1989). What is ecological economics? *Ecological Economics*, *1*(1), 1–7. https://doi.org/10.1016/0921-8009(89)90020-7

Cramer, J. S. (2003). *Logit Models from Economics and Other Fields* (Auflage: 0002). Cambridge, UK ; New York: Cambridge University Press.

Creutzig, F. (2016). Evolving Narratives of Low-Carbon Futures in Transportation. *Transport Reviews*, *36*(3), 341–360. https://doi.org/10.1080/01441647.2015.1079277

Creutzig, F., Jochem, P., Edelenbosch, O. Y., Mattauch, L., Vuuren, D. P. van, McCollum, D., & Minx, J. (2015). Transport: A roadblock to climate change mitigation? *Science*, *350*(6263), 911–912. https://doi.org/10.1126/science.aac8033

Cullenward, D., Schipper, L., Sudarshan, A., & Howarth, R. B. (2010). Psychohistory revisited: fundamental issues in forecasting climate futures. *Climatic Change*, *104*(3–4), 457–472. https://doi.org/10.1007/s10584-010-9995-2

Czech, B. (2013). *Supply Shock: Economic Growth at the Crossroads and the Steady State Solution*. New Society Publishers.

Dahl, C. A. (2004). *(International Energy Markets) By Carol A. Dahl (Author) Hardcover on.*

Daly, H. E. (1991). *Steady-State Economics: Second Edition With New Essays*. Island Press.

Dargay, J. (2008). Personal Transport Choice. OECD Journal: General Papers, Vol. 2008/2.

Davidson, J. E. H., Hendry, D. F., Srba, F., & Yeo, S. (1978). Econometric Modelling of the Aggregate Time-Series Relationship Between Consumers' Expenditure and Income in the United Kingdom. *The Economic Journal*, *88*(352), 661–692. https://doi.org/10.2307/2231972

Davis, S. J., Caldeira, K., & Matthews, H. D. (2010). Future CO2 Emissions and Climate Change from Existing Energy Infrastructure. *Science*, *329*(5997), 1330–1333. https://doi.org/10.1126/science.1188566

Dawson, G. (2012). Austrian economics and climate change. *The Review of Austrian Economics*, *26*(2), 183–206. https://doi.org/10.1007/s11138-012-0174-8

de Haan, P., Mueller, M. G., & Scholz, R. W. (2009). How much do incentives affect car purchase? Agent-based microsimulation of consumer choice of new cars—Part II: Forecasting effects of feebates based on energy-efficiency. *Energy Policy*, *37*(3), 1083–1094. https://doi.org/10.1016/j.enpol.2008.11.003

de Jong, G., Fox, J., Daly, A., Pieters, M., & Smit, R. (2004). Comparison of car ownership models. *Transport Reviews*, *24*(4), 379–408. https://doi.org/10.1080/0144164032000138733

de Wolff, P. (1938). The Demand for Passenger Cars in the United States. *Econometrica*, *6*(2), 113–129. https://doi.org/10.2307/1907143

Deffeyes, K. S. (2010). *When Oil Peaked*. Macmillan.

dena. (2016). Mobilität. Deutsche Energie-Agentur (dena). Retrieved from https://www.dena.de/themen-projekte/energieeffizienz/mobilitaet/

Dewey, J. (1997). *How We Think*. Courier Corporation.

Dickey, D. A., & Fuller, W. A. (1979). Distribution of the Estimators for Autoregressive Time Series with a Unit Root. *Journal of the American Statistical Association*, *74*(366a), 427–431. https://doi.org/10.1080/01621459.1979.10482531

Dickey, D. A., & Pantula, S. G. (1987). Determining the Order of Differencing in Autoregressive Processes. *Journal of Business & Economic Statistics*, *5*(4), 455–461. https://doi.org/10.1080/07350015.1987.10509614

Dieckhoff, C. (2011). *Energieszenarien: Konstruktion, Bewertung und Wirkung - 'Anbieter' und 'Nachfrager' im Dialog*. Karlsruhe: KIT Scientific Publishing.

Dieckhoff, C., Appelrath, H.-J., Fischedick, M., Grunwald, A., Höffler, F., Mayer, C., & Weimer-Jehle, W. (2014). Zur Interpretation von Energieszenarien (Schriftenreihe Energiesysteme der Zukunft), München.

Dijk, M., Orsato, R. J., & Kemp, R. (2013). The emergence of an electric mobility trajectory. *Energy Policy*, *52*, 135–145. https://doi.org/10.1016/j.enpol.2012.04.024

DIW. (2012). *Auto-Mobilität: Fahrleistungen steigen 2011 weiter. Wochenbericht Nr. 47.2012. Deutsches Institut für Wirtschaftsforschung (DIW)*. Retrieved from https://www.diw.de/documents/publikationen/73/diw_01.c.411737.de/12-47-1.pdf

DOE. (2015). *Costs Associated with Non-residential Electric Vehicle Supply Equipment - Factors to consider in the implementation of electric vehicle charging stations. Energy Efficiency & Renewable Energy. U.S. Department of Energy (DOE)*. Retrieved from https://www.afdc.energy.gov/uploads/publication/evse_cost_report_2015.pdf

DOE. (2016a). Tesla. Loan Programs Office. U.S. Department of Energy (DOE). Retrieved from http://energy.gov/lpo/tesla

DOE. (2016b). U.S. refinery processing gain. Petroleum & other liquids. U.S. Department of Energy (DOE). Retrieved from http://www.eia.gov/dnav/pet/hist/LeafHandler.ashx?n=PET&s=MPGRYUS3&f=A

Dolan, E. G., & Studies, I. for H. (1976). *The Foundations of Modern Austrian Economics*. Sheed & Ward.

Doorman, F. (2013). *Crisis, Economics and the Emperor's Clothes*. Lulu.com.

Dorfman, R., Solow, R. M., & Samuelson, P. A. (1988). *Linear Programming and Economic Analysis* (Auflage: Revised.). New York: Dover Pubn Inc.

Dörner, D. (2003). *Die Logik des Misslingens: strategisches Denken in komplexen Situationen*. Rowohlt.

EAFO. (2017). European Alternative Fuels Observatory. Retrieved 15 May 2017, from http://www.eafo.eu/

EC. (2015). LCE-21-2015 - Modelling and analysing the energy system, its transformation and impacts. Community Research and Development Information Service (CORDIS). European Commission. Retrieved from http://cordis.europa.eu/programme/rcn/664872_en.html

EC. (2016a). Automotive industry. Growth. Sectors. European Commission. Retrieved from https://ec.europa.eu/growth/sectors/automotive_en

EC. (2016b). *COM(2016) 501. A European Strategy for Low-Emission Mobility. COMMUNICATION FROM THE COMMISSION TO THE EUROPEAN PARLIAMENT, THE COUNCIL, THE EUROPEAN ECONOMIC AND SOCIAL COMMITTEE AND THE COMMITTEE OF THE REGIONS.*

EC. (2016c). *EU Reference Scenario 2016: Energy, transport and GHG emissions - Trends to 2050. European Commission (EC)*. Retrieved from https://ec.europa.eu/energy/sites/ener/files/documents/20160713%20draft_publication_REF2016_v13.pdf

EC. (2016d). Imports and secure supplies. Energy. European Commission. Retrieved from https://ec.europa.eu/energy/en/topics/imports-and-secure-supplies

Ecofys. (2016). The land use change impact of biofuels consumed in the EU - Quantification of area and greenhouse gas impacts. A cooperation of Ecofys, IIASA and E4tech. Retrieved from https://ec.europa.eu/energy/sites/ener/files/documents/Final%20Report_GLOBIOM_publication.pdf

Edenhofer, O., Pichs-Madruga, R., Sokona, Y., Seyboth, K., Kadner, S., Zwickel, T., … Matschoss, P. (2011). *Renewable Energy Sources and Climate Change Mitigation: Special Report of the Intergovernmental Panel on Climate Change*. Cambridge University Press.

Ederer, G., & Ilgmann, G. (2014). *Deutschland im Stau: Was uns das Verkehrschaos wirklich kostet*. eBook Berlin Verlag.

EIA. (2016a). *Annual Energy Outlook 2016 - with projections to 2040. U.S. Energy Information Administration*. Retrieved from http://www.eia.gov/forecasts/aeo/

EIA. (2016b). Hydraulic fracturing accounts for about half of current U.S. crude oil production. U.S. Energy Information Administration. Retrieved from http://www.eia.gov/todayinenergy/detail.php?id=25372

Eichengreen, B. (2008). *Globalizing Capital: A History of the International Monetary System*. Princeton University Press.

Einstein, A. (2005). *Mein Weltbild*. Ullstein.

e-Mobil BW. (2011). *Strukturstudie BWe Mobil 2011 – Baden-Württemberg auf dem Weg in die Elektromobilität. Landesagentur für Elektromobilität und Brennstoffzellentechnologie Baden-Württemberg (e-mobil BW)*. Retrieved from https://www.e-mobilbw.de/files/e-mobil/content/DE/Publikationen/PDF/StrukturStudie2011_onlineversion.pdf

Enders, W. (2014). *Applied Econometric Time Series*. John Wiley & Sons.

Engle, R. F., & Granger, C. W. J. (1987). Co-Integration and Error Correction: Representation, Estimation, and Testing. *Econometrica*, *55*(2), 251–276. https://doi.org/10.2307/1913236

Engle, R. F., & Granger, C. W. J. (1991). *Long-run Economic Relationships: Readings in Cointegration*. Oxford University Press.

EPA. (2016). Evolution of the Clean Air Act, U.S. Environmental Protection Agency. Retrieved from https://www.epa.gov/clean-air-act-overview/evolution-clean-air-act

Eppstein, M. J., Grover, D. K., Marshall, J. S., & Rizzo, D. M. (2011). An agent-based model to study market penetration of plug-in hybrid electric vehicles. *Energy Policy*, *39*(6), 3789–3802. https://doi.org/10.1016/j.enpol.2011.04.007

Eurostat. (2016). Eurostat – Your key to European statistics. Database. European Commission. Retrieved from http://ec.europa.eu/eurostat/data/database

EVI. (2013). *Global EV Outlook 2013 - Understanding the Electric Vehicle Landscape to 2020. Electric Vehicles Initiative (EVI). Clean Energy Ministerial (CEM). International Energy Agency (IEA)*. Retrieved from http://www.cleanenergyministerial.org/Portals/2/pdfs/News/EVI_GEO_2013_FINAL_150dpi.pdf

EVI. (2015). *Global EV Outlook. 2015 Update. Electric Vehicles Initiative.*

EVI. (2016a). Electric Vehicles Initiative (EVI). Clean Energy Ministerial (CEM). International Energy Agency (IEA). Retrieved from http://www.iea.org/topics/transport/subtopics/electricvehiclesinitiative/

EVI. (2016b). *Global EV Outlook 2016 - Beyond one million electric cars. Electric Vehicles Initiative (EVI). Clean Energy Ministerial (CEM). International Energy Agency (IEA)*. Retrieved from https://www.iea.org/publications/freepublications/publication/Global_EV_Outlook_2016.pdf

EViews. (2016). EViews – User's Guide. Retrieved from http://www.eviews.com/help/helpintro.html#page/content%2Fpreface.html%23

Faber, M. (2008). How to be an ecological economist. *Ecological Economics*, *66*(1), 1–7. https://doi.org/10.1016/j.ecolecon.2008.01.017

Faber, M., & Manstetten, R. (2007). *Was ist Wirtschaft?: von der politischen Ökonomie zur ökologischen Ökonomie*. Alber.

Faggini, M., & Parziale, A. (2014). *Complexity in Economics: Cutting Edge Research*. Springer.

Farmer, J. D., & Foley, D. (2009). The economy needs agent-based modelling. *Nature*, *460*(7256), 685–686. https://doi.org/10.1038/460685a

FASTNED. (2017). Choose the price plan that suits you. Retrieved from https://fastned.nl/en/choose-your-priceplan

Feyerabend, P., & Hacking, I. (2010). *Against Method* (Auflage: 4th edition.). London ; New York: Verso.

FfE. (2010). Basisdaten zur Bereitstellung elektrischer Energie. Forschungsstelle für Energiewirtschaft (FfE). Retrieved from https://www.ffe.de/download/wissen/186_Basisdaten_Energietraeger/Basisdaten_von_Energietraegern_2010.pdf

FHWA. (2016). Highway Statistics Series. Office of Highway Policy Information. Federal Highway Administration (FHWA). U.S. Department of Transportation (DOT). Retrieved from https://www.fhwa.dot.gov/policyinformation/statistics.cfm

Figenbaum, E., Assum, T., & Kolbenstvedt, M. (2015). Electromobility in Norway: Experiences and Opportunities. *Research in Transportation Economics*, *50*, 29–38. https://doi.org/10.1016/j.retrec.2015.06.004

Fiorello, D., Fermi, F., & Bielanska, D. (2010). The ASTRA model for strategic assessment of transport policies. *System Dynamics Review*, *26*(3), 283–290. https://doi.org/10.1002/sdr.452

Foley, D. K. (2009). *Adam's Fallacy: A Guide to Economic Theology*. Harvard University Press.

Ford, A. (1995). Simulating the controllability of feebates. *System Dynamics Review*, *11*(1), 3–29. https://doi.org/10.1002/sdr.4260110103

Ford, A. (2010). *Modeling the environment*. Washington, DC: Island Press.

Ford, A., & Flynn, H. (2005). Statistical screening of system dynamics models. *System Dynamics Review*, *21*(4), 273–303. https://doi.org/10.1002/sdr.322

Ford, A., & Sun, H. (1995). Maintaining Control of a Feebate System. *SIMULATION*, *64*(4), 228–242. https://doi.org/10.1177/003754979506400406

Forrester, J. W. (1971). Counterintuitive behavior of social systems. *Theory and Decision*, *2*(2), 109–140. https://doi.org/10.1007/BF00148991

Forrester, J. W. (1980). Information Sources for Modeling the National Economy. *Journal of the American Statistical Association*, *75*(371), 555–566. https://doi.org/10.1080/01621459.1980.10477508

Forrester, J. W. (1985). "The" model versus a modeling "process". *System Dynamics Review*, *1*(1), 133–134. https://doi.org/10.1002/sdr.4260010112

Forrester, J. W. (2013). *Industrial Dynamics*. Martino Fine Books.

Foster, K. R., Vecchia, P., & Repacholi, M. H. (2000). Science and the Precautionary Principle. *Science*, *288*(5468), 979–981. https://doi.org/10.1126/science.288.5468.979

Friedman, M. (1953). *Essays in Positive Economics*. University of Chicago Press.

Friedman, M., & Savage, L. J. (1948). The Utility Analysis of Choices Involving Risk. *Journal of Political Economy*, *56*(4), 279–304.

Frisch, R. (1933). Editor's Note. *Econometrica*, *1*(1), 1–4.

Galbraith, J. K. (1991). *A history of economics*. London: Penguin Books.

Galbraith, J. K. (2015). *The New Industrial State*. Princeton University Press.

Gallegati, M. (2016). *Acrescita*. Giulio Einaudi Editore.

Ganser, D. (2013). *Europa im Erdölrausch: Die Folgen einer gefährlichen Abhängigkeit*. Orell Füssli Verlag.

Garrison, R. W. (1984). Time and money: The universals of macroeconomic theorizing. *Journal of Macroeconomics*, *6*(2), 197–213. https://doi.org/10.1016/0164-0704(84)90005-3

Georgescu-Roegen, N. (1971). *The Entropy Law and the Economic Process*. Harvard University Press.

Georgescu-Roegen, N. (2003). *Bioeconomia. Verso un'altra economia ecologicamente e socialmente sostenibile*. Bollati Boringhieri.

Giakoumis, E. G. (2016). *Driving and Engine Cycles*. Springer.

Gilbert, C. L. (1986). PRACTITIONERS' CORNER: Professor Hendry's Econometric Methodology. *Oxford Bulletin of Economics and Statistics*, *48*(3), 283–307. https://doi.org/10.1111/j.1468-0084.1986.mp48003007.x

Gilbert, C. L. (1989). LSE and the British Approach to Time Series Econometrics. *Oxford Economic Papers*, *41*(1), 108–128.

Gilbert, N. (2008). *Agent-Based Models*. SAGE.

Gilbert, N., & Troitzsch, K. G. (2005). *Simulation for the Social Scientist* (Auflage: 0002). Maidenhead, England ; New York, NY: Open University Press.

Gilboa, I. (2009). *Theory of Decision under Uncertainty*. Cambridge University Press.

GIZ. (2016). International fuel prices. Deutsche Gesellschaft für Internationale Zusammenarbeit (GIZ). Retrieved from https://www.giz.de/expertise/html/4282.html

Glaister, S. (1981). *Fundamentals of Transport Economics*. St. Martin's Press.

Gleick, J. (2011). *Chaos: Making a New Science*. Open Road Media.

Glimcher, P. W., & Fehr, E. (2013). *Neuroeconomics: Decision Making and the Brain*. Academic Press.

Gnann, T. (2015). *Market Diffusion of Plug-in Electric Vehicles and Their Charging Infrastructure.* Fraunhofer Verlag.

Godfrey, L. G. (1978). Testing Against General Autoregressive and Moving Average Error Models when the Regressors Include Lagged Dependent Variables. *Econometrica*, *46*(6), 1293–1301. https://doi.org/10.2307/1913829

Godley, W., & Lavoie, M. (2016). *Monetary Economics: An Integrated Approach to Credit, Money, Income, Production and Wealth*. Springer.

GoI. (2016). Total number of registered motor vehicles in India during 1951-2013. Government of India (GoI). Retrieved from https://data.gov.in/resources/total-number-registered-motor-vehicles-india-during-1951-2013

Goldberg, P. K. (1998). The Effects of the Corporate Average Fuel Efficiency Standards in the US. *The Journal of Industrial Economics*, *46*(1), 1–33. https://doi.org/10.1111/1467-6451.00059

Gómez Vilchez, J. J. (2016a). Car technologies and their impact on climate – A system dynamics approach. Presented at the 14th World Conference on Transport Research (WCTR).

Gómez Vilchez, J. J. (2016b). Linking econometrics and system dynamics. Unpublished working paper.

Gómez Vilchez, J. J., Jochem, P., & Fichtner, W. (2013a). EV market development pathways – An application of system dynamics for policy simulation. In *Proceedings of the 32nd International Association for Energy Economics (IAEE)*.

Gómez Vilchez, J. J., Jochem, P., & Fichtner, W. (2013b). The impact of electric vehicles on the global oil demand and CO2 emissions. In *Proceedings of the 13th World Conference on Transport Research (WCTR)*.

Gómez Vilchez, J., Jochem, P., & Fichtner, W. (2014). Car Technology Scenarios using System Dynamics: Exploring Market Penetration and Energy Consumption in China, Germany and US. Presented at the PhD Colloquium of the 32nd International Conference of the System Dynamics Society, Delft.

Gómez Vilchez, J., Jochem, P., & Fichtner, W. (2015). Energy Use and Emissions Impacts from Car Technologies Market Scenarios: A Multi-Country System Dynamics Model. Presented at the In: Proceedings of the 33rd International Conference of the System Dynamics Society, Cambridge, MA.

Gómez Vilchez, J., Jochem, P., & Fichtner, W. (2016). Car Technology Market Evolution and Emissions Impacts - An Example of Energy Policy Scenarios under Uncertainty. Presented at the In: Proceedings of the 34th International Conference of the System Dynamics Society, Delft.

Goodwin, P. B. (1992). A Review of New Demand Elasticities with Special Reference to Short and Long Run Effects of Price Changes. *Journal of Transport Economics and Policy*, *26*(2), 155–169.

Goodwin, R. M. (1990). *Chaotic Economic Dynamics*. Oxford : New York: Oxford University Press.

Gossen, H. H. (1854). *Entwickelung der gesetze des menschlichen verkehrs, und der daraus fliessenden regeln für menschliche handeln*. F. Vieweg.

Granger, C. W. J. (1981). Some properties of time series data and their use in econometric model specification. *Journal of Econometrics*, *16*(1), 121–130. https://doi.org/10.1016/0304-4076(81)90079-8

Granger, C. W. J., & Newbold, P. (1974). Spurious regressions in econometrics. *Journal of Econometrics*, *2*(2), 111–120. https://doi.org/10.1016/0304-4076(74)90034-7

Gravelle, H., & Rees, R. (2004). *Microeconomics* (3. A.). Harlow, England; New York: Financial Times Prent.

Gray, L. C. (1914). Rent Under the Assumption of Exhaustibility. *The Quarterly Journal of Economics*, *28*(3), 466–489. https://doi.org/10.2307/1884984

Greasley, D., & Oxley, L. (2011). *Economics and History: Surveys in Cliometrics*. John Wiley & Sons.

Greene, D. L., Patterson, P. D., Singh, M., & Li, J. (2005). Feebates, rebates and gas-guzzler taxes: a study of incentives for increased fuel economy. *Energy Policy*, *33*(6), 757–775. https://doi.org/10.1016/j.enpol.2003.10.003

Greene, W. H. (2011). *Econometric Analysis* (Auflage: 7th Revised edition.). Boston etc.: Prentice Hall.

Greenpeace. (2016). The Energy [R]evolution Scenario. Retrieved from http://www.greenpeace.org/international/en/campaigns/climate-change/energyrevolution/

Gribbin, J. (2011). *Historia de la ciencia, 1543-2001*. Barcelona: Crítica.

Griliches, Z. (1957). Hybrid Corn: An Exploration in the Economics of Technological Change. *Econometrica*, *25*(4), 501–522. https://doi.org/10.2307/1905380

Griliches, Z. (1986). Chapter 25 Economic data issues. In Zvi Griliches and Michael D. Intriligator (Ed.), *Handbook of Econometrics* (Vol. Volume 3, pp. 1465–1514). Elsevier. Retrieved from http://www.sciencedirect.com/science/article/pii/S1573441286030052

Grunwald, A. (2011). Energy futures: Diversity and the need for assessment. *Futures*, *43*(8), 820–830. https://doi.org/10.1016/j.futures.2011.05.024

Grunwald, A., & Kopfmüller, J. (2006). *Nachhaltigkeit*. Campus Verlag.

Guerci, E., & Hanaki, N. (2012). Learning Agent and Agent-Based Modeling. In P. D. N. M. Seel (Ed.), *Encyclopedia of the Sciences of Learning* (pp. 1765–1766). Springer US. https://doi.org/10.1007/978-1-4419-1428-6_545

Gujarati, D. N., & Porter, D. C. (2009). *Basic Econometrics* (Auflage: 5th edition.). Boston: Mcgraw-Hill Publ.Comp.

Haasz, T., Gómez Vilchez, J. J., Kunze, R., Deane, P., Fraboulet, D., Fahl, U., & Mulholland, E. (2018). Perspectives on decarbonizing the transport sector in the EU-28. *Energy Strategy Reviews*, *20*, 124–132. https://doi.org/10.1016/j.esr.2017.12.007

Hackbarth, A., & Madlener, R. (2016). Willingness-to-pay for alternative fuel vehicle characteristics: A stated choice study for Germany. *Transportation Research Part A: Policy and Practice, 85*, 89–111. https://doi.org/10.1016/j.tra.2015.12.005

Hahn, H., Neurath, O., & Carnap, R. (1929). *The Scientific Conception of the World: The Vienna Circle.*

Hall, D. C., & Hall, J. V. (1984). Concepts and measures of natural resource scarcity with a summary of recent trends. *Journal of Environmental Economics and Management, 11*(4), 363–379. https://doi.org/10.1016/0095-0696(84)90005-6

Hamill, L., & Gilbert, N. (2016). *Agent-Based Modelling in Economics.* John Wiley & Sons.

Hamilton, D. (1970). *Evolutionary Economics.* Transaction Publishers.

Hamilton, J. D. (1994). *Time Series Analysis.* Princeton, N.J: Princeton Univers. Press.

Hamilton, J. D. (2008). *Understanding Crude Oil Prices* (Working Paper No. 14492). National Bureau of Economic Research. Retrieved from http://www.nber.org/papers/w14492

Hamilton, W. H. (1919). The Institutional Approach to Economic Theory. *The American Economic Review, 9*(1), 309–318.

Harvey, A. (1997). Trends, Cycles and Autoregressions. *The Economic Journal, 107*(440), 192–201.

Harvey, A. C. (1990). *The Econometric Analysis of Time Series.* MIT Press.

Harvey, A. C. (1993). *Time Series Models.* Harvester Wheatsheaf.

Harvey, J. T., & Garnett, R. F. (2008). *Future Directions for Heterodox Economics.* University of Michigan Press.

Hayek, F. A. (1966). The principles of a liberal social order. *Il Politico, 31*(4), 601–618.

Heilbroner, R. L. (1999). *The Worldly Philosophers: The Lives, Times And Ideas Of The Great Economic Thinkers*. Touchstone.

Hendry, D. (1995). *Dynamic Econometrics*. Oxford; New York: Oxford Univ Pr.

Hendry, D. F. (1980). Econometrics-Alchemy or Science? *Economica*, *47*(188), 387–406. https://doi.org/10.2307/2553385

Hendry, D. F., Pagan, A. R., & Sargan, J. D. (1984). Chapter 18 Dynamic specification. In B.-H. of Econometrics (Ed.) (Vol. 2, pp. 1023–1100). Elsevier. Retrieved from http://www.sciencedirect.com/science/article/pii/S1573441284020109

Hendry, D. F., & Richard, J.-F. (1983). The Econometric Analysis of Economic Time Series. *International Statistical Review / Revue Internationale de Statistique*, *51*(2), 111–148. https://doi.org/10.2307/1402738

Hendry, D. F., & Wallis, K. F. (Eds.). (1984). *Econometrics and Quantitative Economics*. Oxford Oxfordshire ; New York, NY: Blackwell Publishers.

Hensher, D. (2010). *Applied Choice Analysis: A Primer*. Cambridge ; New York: Cambridge University Press.

Hensher, D. A., & Greene, W. H. (2003). The Mixed Logit model: The state of practice. *Transportation*, *30*(2), 133–176. https://doi.org/10.1023/A:1022558715350

Hensher, D. A., Greene, W. H., & Chorus, C. G. (2013). Random regret minimization or random utility maximization: an exploratory analysis in the context of automobile fuel choice. *Journal of Advanced Transportation*, *47*(7), 667–678. https://doi.org/10.1002/atr.188

Hensher, D. A., Rose, J. M., & Greene, W. H. (2005). *Applied Choice Analysis: A Primer*. Cambridge University Press.

Herbst, A., Toro, F., Reitze, F., & Jochem, E. (2012). Introduction to Energy Systems Modelling. *Swiss Society of Economics and Statistics*, *148*(2), 111-135.

Hicks, J. (1995). *Methods of Dynamic Economics* (Auflage: Revised.). Oxford Oxfordshire; New York: Oxford University Press.

Hill, J., Nelson, E., Tilman, D., Polasky, S., & Tiffany, D. (2006). Environmental, economic, and energetic costs and benefits of biodiesel and ethanol biofuels. *Proceedings of the National Academy of Sciences*, *103*(30), 11206–11210. https://doi.org/10.1073/pnas.0604600103

Hirschman, A. O. (2013). *The Essential Hirschman*. Princeton University Press.

Holt, R. P. F., Jr, J. B. R., & Colander, D. (2011). The Complexity Era in Economics. *Review of Political Economy*, *23*(3), 357–369. https://doi.org/10.1080/09538259.2011.583820

Holt, R. P. F., Pressman, S., & Spash, C. L. (2009). *Post Keynesian and Ecological Economics: Confronting Environmental Issues*. Edward Elgar Publishing.

Hommes, C. (2013). *Behavioral Rationality and Heterogeneous Expectations in Complex Economic Systems*. Cambridge University Press.

Hoover, K. D. (2005). The Methodology of Econometrics. In *Prepared for the Palgrave Handbooks of Econometrics, volume 1: Theoretical Econometrics*.

Hoover, K. D. (2010). Idealizing Reduction: The Microfoundations of Macroeconomics. *Erkenntnis*, *73*(3), 329–347. https://doi.org/10.1007/s10670-010-9235-1

Hotelling, H. (1931). The Economics of Exhaustible Resources. *Journal of Political Economy*, *39*(2), 137–175.

Houdry, E. J. (1956, April 17). *US2742437A*. United States. Retrieved from https://patents.google.com/patent/US2742437A/en?oq=US2742437A

Hülsmann, M., & Fornahl, D. (2013). *Evolutionary Paths Towards the Mobility Patterns of the Future*. Springer Science & Business Media.

Huo, H., & Wang, M. (2012). Modeling future vehicle sales and stock in China. *Energy Policy*, *43*, 17–29. https://doi.org/10.1016/j.enpol.2011.09.063

Hyndman, R. J., & Athanasopoulos, G. (2012). Forecasting: principles and practice. Open-access version. Retrieved from https://www.otexts.org/fpp/2/3

ICCT. (2015). Global milestone: The first million electric vehicles. The International Council on Clean Transportation. Retrieved from http://www.theicct.org/blogs/staff/global-milestone-first-million-electric-vehicles

IEA. (2016a). Energy Balances Statistics. International Energy Agency (IEA). Retrieved from http://www.iea.org/statistics/topics/energybalances/

IEA. (2016b). Energy Prices and Taxes, International Energy Agency. Retrieved from http://www.iea.org/statistics/topics/pricesandtaxes/

IEA. (2016c). Energy Technology Perspectives (ETP). International Energy Agency (IEA). Retrieved from http://www.iea.org/etp/

IEA. (2016d). Fast facts. Transport. International Energy Agency. Retrieved from https://www.iea.org/topics/transport/

IEA. (2016e). Key World Energy Statistics 2016, International Energy Agency.

IEA. (2017). *Energy Prices and Taxes, Volume 2016 Issue 4: Fourth Quarter 2016, IEA, Paris.* International Energy Agency. Retrieved from http://dx.doi.org/10.1787/energy_tax-v2016-4-en

IEA/OECD. (2009). Transport, Energy and CO2 - Moving Toward Sustainability. International Energy Agency / Organisation for Economic Co-operation and Development.

IMF. (2016). World Economic Outlook Databases. International Monetary Fund. Retrieved from http://www.imf.org/external/ns/cs.aspx?id=28

Intriligator, M. D. (1983). Chapter 3 Economic and econometric models. In B.-H. of Econometrics (Ed.) (Vol. 1, pp. 181–221). Elsevier. Retrieved from http://www.sciencedirect.com/science/article/pii/S1573441283010077

IPCC. (2000). *Scenario Driving Forces, Chapter 3 of the Special Report Emissions Scenarios. Intergovernmental Panel on Climate Change.* Geneva, Switzerland. Retrieved from http://www.ipcc.ch/ipccreports/sres/emission/index.php?idp=50

IPCC. (2006). *Guidelines for National Greenhouse Gas Inventories. Intergovernmental Panel on Climate Change.*

IPCC. (2007a). *Annex I: Glossary. Contribution of Working Group III to the Fourth Assessment Report of the Intergovernmental Panel on Climate Change.* Intergovernmental Panel on Climate Change. Retrieved from http://www.ipcc.ch/pdf/glossary/ar4-wg3.pdf

IPCC. (2007b). *Changes in Atmospheric Constituents and in Radiative Forcing. In Climate Change 2007: The Physical Science Basis. Contribution of Working Group I to the Fourth Assessment Report of the Intergovernmental Panel on Climate Change.* Intergovernmental Panel on Climate Change. Retrieved from http://www.ipcc.ch/publications_and_data/publications_ipcc_fourth_assessment_report_wg1_report_the_physical_science_basis.htm

IPCC. (2007c). *Climate Change 2007: Synthesis Report, Contribution of Working Groups I, II and III to the Fourth Assessment Report.* Intergovernmental Panel on Climate Change. Retrieved from https://www.ipcc.ch/publications_and_data/publications_ipcc_fourth_assessment_report_synthesis_report.htm

IPCC. (2013). *Climate Change 2013: The Physical Science Basis, Summary for Policymakers.* Intergovernmental Panel on Climate Change. Retrieved from https://www.ipcc.ch/report/ar5/wg1/

IPCC. (2015). *Climate Change 2014: Mitigation of Climate Change: Working Group III Contribution to the IPCC Fifth Assessment Report.* Cambridge University Press.

IRF. (2016). World Road Statistics. International Road Federation (IRF). Retrieved from https://worldroadstatistics.org/index.html

Issawi, C. (1978). The 1973 Oil Crisis and After. *Journal of Post Keynesian Economics, 1*(2), 3–26.

Jackson, T. (2011). *Prosperity Without Growth: Economics for a Finite Planet.* Routledge.

JAMA. (2016). Motor Vehicle Statistics of Japan. Japan Automobile Manufacturers Association (JAMA). Retrieved from http://www.jama.org/motor-vehicle-statistics-japan-2016/

JARI. (2016). Japan Automobile Research Institute. Retrieved from http://www.jari.or.jp/tabid/200/Default.aspx?language=en-US

Jarrett, H. (2013). *Environmental Quality in a Growing Economy: Essays from the Sixth RFF Forum*. Routledge.

Jensen, A. F., Cherchi, E., Mabit, S. L., & Ortúzar, J. de D. (2016). Predicting the Potential Market for Electric Vehicles. *Transportation Science*. https://doi.org/10.1287/trsc.2015.0659

Jevons, W. (2013). *The Theory of Political Economy* (2013th ed.). Houndmills, Basingstoke, Hampshire: Palgrave Macmillan.

Jevons, W. S. (1866). *The coal question: an enquiry concerning the progress of the Nation, and the probable exhaustion of our coal-mines*. Macmillan.

Jevons, W. S. (1874). *The Principles of Science: A Treatise on Logic and Scientific Method*. Macmillan.

Jick, T. D. (1979). Mixing Qualitative and Quantitative Methods: Triangulation in Action. *Administrative Science Quarterly*, *24*(4), 602–611. https://doi.org/10.2307/2392366

Jochem, P., Gómez Vilchez, J. J., Ensslen, A., Schäuble, J., & Fichtner, W. (2018). Methods for forecasting the market penetration of electric drivetrains in the passenger car market. *Transport Reviews*, *38*(3), 322–348. https://doi.org/10.1080/01441647.2017.1326538

Johansson. (2008). *Intro to Modern Welfare Economics* (Auflage: New.). Cambridge ; New York: Cambridge University Press.

Johansson, O., & Schipper, L. (1997). Measuring the Long-Run Fuel Demand of Cars: Separate Estimations of Vehicle Stock, Mean Fuel Intensity, and Mean Annual Driving Distance. *Journal of Transport Economics and Policy*, *31*(3), 277–292.

Johansson, P.-O. (1991). *An Introduction to Modern Welfare Economics*. Cambridge University Press.

Johnson, N. (2009). *Simply Complexity: A Clear Guide to Complexity Theory*. Oneworld Publications.

JPKE. (1978). A Statement of Purposes. The Editors. *Journal of Post Keynesian Economics*, *1*(1), 3–7.

Jr, L. G. H. (1967). The Legacy of John R. Commons. *Journal of Economic Issues*, *1*(1–2), 63–73. https://doi.org/10.1080/00213624.1967.11502739

Junges, R., & Klügl, F. (2013). Learning Tools for Agent-Based Modeling and Simulation. *KI – Künstliche Intelligenz*, *27*(3), 273–280. https://doi.org/10.1007/s13218-013-0258-z

Juselius, K. (2007). *The Cointegrated VAR Model: Methodology and Applications* (2 edition). Oxford ; New York: Oxford University Press.

Jusmet, J. R., & Martinez-Alier, J. (2013). *Economía ecológica y política ambiental*. Fondo De Cultura Economica USA.

Kahneman, D. (2013). *Thinking, Fast and Slow* (Reprint edition). New York: Farrar, Straus and Giroux.

Kahneman, D., McFadden, D., & Smith, V. L. (2012). *Critica della ragione economica*. Il Saggiatore.

Kahneman, D., & Tversky, A. (1979). Prospect Theory: An Analysis of Decision under Risk. *Econometrica*, *47*(2), 263–291. https://doi.org/10.2307/1914185

Kapp, K. W. (1978). *The Social Costs of Business Enterprise*. Spokesman.

Karlin, S., Amemiya, T., & Goodman, L. A. (2014). *Studies in Econometrics, Time Series, and Multivariate Statistics*. Academic Press.

KBA. (2016). Fahrzeuge. Statistik. Kraftfahrt-Bundesamt (KBA). Retrieved from https://www.kba.de/DE/Statistik/Fahrzeuge/fahrzeuge_node.html;jsessionid=5E94A53D6F1F17F672F42BC08B351261.live11293

Keen, S. (2011). *Debunking Economics - Revised and Expanded Edition: The Naked Emperor Dethroned?* Zed Books.

Kelly, F. J., & Zhu, T. (2016). Transport solutions for cleaner air. *Science, 352*(6288), 934–936. https://doi.org/10.1126/science.aaf3420

Kennedy, P. (2008). *A Guide to Econometrics*. Wiley.

Kettering, C. F. (1915, August 17). *US1150523A*. United States. Retrieved from https://patents.google.com/patent/US1150523/en

Keynes, J. M. (1939). Official Papers. *The Economic Journal, 49*(195), 558-577.

Keynes, J. M. (2015). *John Maynard Keynes: The General Theory of Employment, Interest, and Money (Centaur Classics)*. John Maynard Keynes.

Keynes, J. M., & Skidelsky, R. (2015). *The Essential Keynes*. Penguin Classics.

Keynes, J. N. (1891). *The Scope and Method of Political Economy*. Macmillan.

Kieckhäfer, K., Volling, T., & Spengler, T. S. (2014). A Hybrid Simulation Approach for Estimating the Market Share Evolution of Electric Vehicles. *Transportation Science, 48*(4), 651–670. https://doi.org/10.1287/trsc.2014.0526

King, J. E. (2002). *A History of Post Keynesian Economics Since 1936*. Edward Elgar Publishing.

King, J. E. (2012). *The Microfoundations Delusion: Metaphor and Dogma in the History of Macroeconomics*. Edward Elgar Publishing.

Kirchgässner, G., Wolters, J., & Hassler, U. (2012). *Introduction to Modern Time Series Analysis* (Auflage: 2nd ed. 2013). New York: Springer.

Kirman, A. (2014). Is it rational to have rational expectations? *Mind & Society, 13*(1), 29–48. https://doi.org/10.1007/s11299-014-0136-x

Kirman, A. P. (1992). Whom or What Does the Representative Individual Represent? *The Journal of Economic Perspectives, 6*(2), 117–136.

Kirman, A., & Zimmermann, J.-B. (2012). *Economics with Heterogeneous Interacting Agents*. Springer Science & Business Media.

Knight, F. H. (2012). *Risk, Uncertainty and Profit*. Courier Corporation.

Kotler, P., Armstrong, G., Wong, V., & Saunders, J. (2008). *Principles of Marketing*. Pearson Education.

Krail, M. (2009). *System-Based Analysis of Income Distribution Impacts on Mobility Behaviour*. Nomos.

Kuznets, S. (1950). [Review of *Review of On the Accuracy of Economic Observations*, by O. Morgenstern]. *Journal of the American Statistical Association*, *45*(252), 576–579. https://doi.org/10.2307/2280732

Kwiatkowski, D., Phillips, P. C. B., Schmidt, P., & Shin, Y. (1992). Testing the null hypothesis of stationarity against the alternative of a unit root. *Journal of Econometrics*, *54*(1), 159–178. https://doi.org/10.1016/0304-4076(92)90104-Y

Kwoka, J. E. (1993). The Sales and Competitive Effects of Styling and Advertising Practices in the U.S. Auto Industry. *The Review of Economics and Statistics*, *75*(4), 649–656. https://doi.org/10.2307/2110018

Lakatos, I. (1971). History of Science and its Rational Reconstructions. In R. C. Buck & R. S. Cohen (Eds.), *PSA 1970* (pp. 91–136). Springer Netherlands. Retrieved from http://link.springer.com/chapter/10.1007/978-94-010-3142-4_7

Lakatos, I., Worrall, J., & Currie, G. (1980). *The Methodology of Scientific Research Programmes: Volume 1: Philosophical Papers*. Cambridge University Press.

Lancaster, K. (1987). *Mathematical Economics* (Auflage: Revised.). New York: Dover Pubn Inc.

Larrick, R. P., & Soll, J. B. (2008). The MPG Illusion. *Science*, *320*(5883), 1593–1594. https://doi.org/10.1126/science.1154983

Laszlo, E. (1996). *The Systems View of the World: A Holistic Vision for Our Time*. Hampton Press.

Lavoie, M. (2014). *Post-Keynesian Economics: New Foundations*. Edward Elgar Publishing.

Lawson, T. (1988). Probability and Uncertainty in Economic Analysis. *Journal of Post Keynesian Economics*, *11*(1), 38–65. https://doi.org/10.1080/01603477.1988.11489724

Lawson, T. (2006). *Economics and Reality*. Routledge.

Lempert, R. J. (2003). *Shaping the Next One Hundred Years: New Methods for Quantitative, Long-Term Policy Analysis*. Rand Corporation.

Leontief, W. W. (1986). *Input-output Economics*. Oxford University Press.

Linton, C., Grant-Muller, S., & Gale, W. F. (2015). Approaches and Techniques for Modelling CO2 Emissions from Road Transport. *Transport Reviews*, *35*(4), 533–553. https://doi.org/10.1080/01441647.2015.1030004

Litman, T. (2013). Transport Elasticities: Impacts on Travel Behaviour. Retrieved from /view.aspx?id=1245895

Little, J. D. C. (1961). A Proof for the Queuing Formula: L = λW. *Operations Research*, *9*(3), 383–387. https://doi.org/10.1287/opre.9.3.383

Lovins, A. (2013). *Reinventing Fire: Bold Business Solutions for the New Energy Era*. Chelsea Green Publishing.

Lucas, R. E. (1976). Econometric policy evaluation: A critique. *Carnegie-Rochester Conference Series on Public Policy*, *1*, 19–46. https://doi.org/10.1016/S0167-2231(76)80003-6

Lucas, R. E. (1986). Adaptive Behavior and Economic Theory. *The Journal of Business*, *59*(4), S401–S426.

Luce, R. D., & Raiffa, H. (2012). *Games and Decisions: Introduction and Critical Survey*. Courier Corporation.

Lütkepohl, H. (2007). General-to-specific or specific-to-general modelling? An opinion on current econometric terminology. *Journal of Econometrics*, *136*(1), 319–324. https://doi.org/10.1016/j.jeconom.2005.11.014

Lütkepohl, H., & Krätzig, M. (2004). *Applied Time Series Econometrics*. Cambridge University Press.

MacKinnon, J. G. (1996). Numerical Distribution Functions for Unit Root and Cointegration Tests. *Journal of Applied Econometrics*, *11*(6), 601–618.

Maddala, G. S., & Kim, I.-M. (1998). *Unit Roots, Cointegration, and Structural Change*. Cambridge University Press.

Magdoff, F. (2008, July 1). The Political Economy and Ecology of Biofuels. Retrieved 6 October 2016, from http://monthlyreview.org/2008/07/01/the-political-economy-and-ecology-of-biofuels/

Magdoff, F., & Foster, J. B. (2011). *What Every Environmentalist Needs to Know About Capitalism*. NYU Press.

Mahajan, V., Muller, E., & Bass, F. M. (1991). New Product Diffusion Models in Marketing: A Review and Directions for Research. In D. N. Nakićenović & D. A. Grübler (Eds.), *Diffusion of Technologies and Social Behavior* (pp. 125–177). Springer Berlin Heidelberg. Retrieved from http://link.springer.com/chapter/10.1007/978-3-662-02700-4_6

Mahajan, V., Muller, E., & Wind, Y. (2000). *New-Product Diffusion Models*. Springer Science & Business Media.

Makridakis, S., & Hibon, M. (2000). The M3-Competition: results, conclusions and implications. *International Journal of Forecasting*, *16*(4), 451–476. https://doi.org/10.1016/S0169-2070(00)00057-1

Makridakis, S., Hogarth, R. M., & Gaba, A. (2009). Forecasting and uncertainty in the economic and business world. *International Journal of Forecasting*, *25*(4), 794–812. https://doi.org/10.1016/j.ijforecast.2009.05.012

Makridakis, S., & Taleb, N. (2009). Decision making and planning under low levels of predictability. *International Journal of Forecasting*, *25*(4), 716–733. https://doi.org/10.1016/j.ijforecast.2009.05.013

Malthus, T. (2008). *Essay on the Principle of Population*. Oxford ; New York: Oxford World's Classics.

Mandelbrot, B. B., & Hudson, R. (2010). *The (Mis)Behaviour of Markets: A Fractal View of Risk, Ruin and Reward.* Profile Books.

Manski, C. F. (2001). Daniel McFadden and the Econometric Analysis of Discrete Choice. *Scandinavian Journal of Economics, 103*(2), 217–230. https://doi.org/10.1111/1467-9442.00241

Manski, C. F. (2013). *Public Policy in an Uncertain World: Analysis and Decisions*. Harvard University Press.

Manski, C. F., & McFadden, D. (1981). *Structural analysis of discrete data with econometric applications*. MIT Press.

Mantegna, R. N., & Stanley, H. E. (1999). *Introduction to Econophysics: Correlations and Complexity in Finance*. Cambridge University Press.

Marshall, A. (2013). *Principles of Economics*. Springer.

Martinez-Moyano, I. J. (2012). Documentation for model transparency. *System Dynamics Review, 28*(2), 199–208. https://doi.org/10.1002/sdr.1471

Mas-Colell, A., Whinston, M. D., & Green, J. R. (1995). *Microeconomic Theory*. Oxford University Press.

Max-Neef, M. A., & Smith, P. B. (2014). *La economía desenmascarada : del poder y la codicia a la compasión y el bien común*. Icaria editorial.

May, R. M. (1976). Simple mathematical models with very complicated dynamics. *Nature, 261*(5560), 459–467. https://doi.org/10.1038/261459a0

Mayumi, K., & Martinez-Allier, J. (2001). *The Origins of Ecological Economics: The Bioeconomics of Georgescu-Roegen* (1 edition). London ; New York: Routledge.

Mazzucato, M. (2015). *The Entrepreneurial State: Debunking Public vs. Private Sector Myths*. PublicAffairs.

McClellan, J. E., & Dorn, H. (2006). *Science and technology in world history: an introduction*. Baltimore: Johns Hopkins University Press.

McCollum, D. L., Wilson, C., Pettifor, H., Ramea, K., Krey, V., Riahi, K., … Fujisawa, S. (n.d.). Improving the behavioral realism of global integrated assessment models: An application to consumers' vehicle choices. *Transportation Research Part D: Transport and Environment*. https://doi.org/10.1016/j.trd.2016.04.003

McFadden, D. (1999). Rationality for Economists? *Journal of Risk and Uncertainty*, *19*(1–3), 73–105. https://doi.org/10.1023/A:1007863007855

McFadden, D. (2007). The behavioral science of transportation. *Transport Policy*, *14*(4), 269–274. https://doi.org/10.1016/j.tranpol.2007.07.001

McFadden, D., & Talvitie, A. P. (1977). *Demand Model Estimation and Validation. Urban Travel Demand Forecasting Project Phase 1 Final Report Series, Vol. V*. Institute of Transportation Studies.

Meadows, D. H. (1972). *The Limits to Growth: A Report for the Club of Rome's Project on the Predicament of Mankind*. New American Library.

Meadows, D. H., & Wright, D. (2008). *Thinking in systems: a primer*. White River Junction, Vt.: Chelsea Green Pub.

MEEDM. (2016). Prix des énergies. Ministère de l'Ecologie, de l'Energie, du Développement Durable et de l'Aménagement du Territoire (MEEDM). Retrieved from http://www.statistiques.developpement-durable.gouv.fr/energie-climat/s/prix-energies.html

Menger, C., Klein, P. G., & Hayek, F. A. (2007). *Principles of Economics* (Lrg). CreateSpace Independent Publishing Platform.

Metcalfe, J. S., & Foster, J. (2007). *Evolution and Economic Complexity*. Edward Elgar Publishing.

Metz, D. (2012). *The Limits to Travel: How Far Will You Go?* Earthscan.

Meyer, P. D. B. (2005). *The Economic-Environmental model PANTA RHEI and it's Application* (GWS Discussion Paper Series No. 05-3). GWS – Institute of Economic Structures Research. Retrieved from https://ideas.repec.org/p/gws/dpaper/05-3.html

Meyers, R. A. (2009). *Encyclopedia of Complexity and Systems Science*. Springer New York.

Miller, J. H., & Page, S. E. (2009). *Complex Adaptive Systems: An Introduction to Computational Models of Social Life*. Princeton University Press.

Miller, R. E., & Blair, P. D. (2009). *Input-Output Analysis: Foundations and Extensions*. Cambridge University Press.

Mills, T. C., & Patterson, K. (Eds.). (2007). *Palgrave Handbook of Econometrics Volume 1: Econometric Theory: Econometric Theory v. 1* (2006 edition). Basingstoke: AIAA.

Minsky, H. (2008). *Stabilizing an Unstable Economy*. McGraw Hill Professional.

Miser, H. J., & Quade, E. S. (1985). *Handbook of systems analysis: overview of uses, procedures, applications, and practice*. North-Holland.

Mitchell, W. J., Borroni-Bird, C. E., & Burns, L. D. (2010). *Reinventing the Automobile: Personal Urban Mobility for the 21st Century*. MIT Press.

Mokhtarian, P. L., & Chen, C. (2004). TTB or not TTB, that is the question: a review and analysis of the empirical literature on travel time (and money) budgets. *Transportation Research Part A: Policy and Practice*, *38*(9–10), 643–675. https://doi.org/10.1016/j.tra.2003.12.004

Mom, G. (2013). *The Electric Vehicle: Technology and Expectations in the Automobile Age*. JHU Press.

Morgan, M. S. (1992). *The History of Econometric Ideas*. Cambridge University Press.

Morgenstern, O. (1963). *On the Accuracy of Economic Observations*. UMI out-of-print books on demand.

Morrison, F. (2008). *The Art of Modeling Dynamic Systems: Forecasting for Chaos, Randomness, and Determinism* (Dover.). Mineola, N.Y: Dover Pubn Inc.

Moss, R., Tzimas, E., Willis, P., Arendorf, J., & Tercero Espinoza, L. (2013). *Critical Metals in the Path towards the Decarbonisation of the EU Energy Sector: Assessing Rare Metals as Supply-Chain Bottlenecks in Low-Carbon Energy Technologies* (EUR - Scientific and Technical Research Reports). Publications Office of the European Union. Retrieved from http://publications.jrc.ec.europa.eu/repository/handle/111111111/30369

Möst, D. (2008). *New Methods for Energy Market Modelling: Proceedings of the First European Workshop on Energy Market Modelling Using Agent Based Compuational Economics*. KIT Scientific Publishing.

Mueller, M. G., & de Haan, P. (2009). How much do incentives affect car purchase? Agent-based microsimulation of consumer choice of new cars – Part I: Model structure, simulation of bounded rationality, and model validation. *Energy Policy*, *37*(3), 1072–1082. https://doi.org/10.1016/j.enpol.2008.11.002

Muth, J. F. (1961). Rational Expectations and the Theory of Price Movements. *Econometrica*, *29*(3), 315–335. https://doi.org/10.2307/1909635

MWV. (2016). Tankstellenbestand. Statistiken. Mineralölwirtschaftsverband (MWV). Retrieved from https://www.mwv.de/statistiken/

Myrdal, G. (1944). *An American Dilemma, Volume 2: The Negro Problem and Modern Democracy*. Transaction Publishers.

Myrdal, G. (1990). *Political Element in the Development of Economic theory*. Transaction Publishers.

Naredo, J. M. (2015). *La economía en evolución: historia y perspectivas de las categorías básicas del pensamiento económico*. Siglo XXI de España Editores.

Nelson, A. (1984). Some Issues Surrounding the Reduction of Macroeconomics to Microeconomics. *Philosophy of Science*, *51*(4), 573–594.

Nelson, C. R., & Plosser, C. R. (1982). Trends and random walks in macroeconmic time series: Some evidence and implications. *Journal of Monetary Economics*, *10*(2), 139–162. https://doi.org/10.1016/0304-3932(82)90012-5

Neumann, J. von, & Morgenstern, O. (2007). *Theory of Games and Economic Behavior (Commemorative Edition)*. Princeton University Press.

Newbold, P., & Granger, C. W. J. (1989). *Forecasting in Business and Economics* (Auflage: 2. Auflage.). Boston: Emerald Group Publishing Limited.

NHTS. (2009). National Household Travel Survey (NHTS) 2009, Federal Highway Administration, U.S. Department of Transportation. Retrieved from http://nhts.ornl.gov/

Nida-Rümelin, J. (2011). *Die Optimierungsfalle: Philosophie einer humanen Ökonomie*. Irisiana.

Nordhaus, W. D. (1973). World Dynamics: Measurement Without Data. *The Economic Journal*, *83*(332), 1156–1183. https://doi.org/10.2307/2230846

Nordhaus, W. D. (2013). *The Climate Casino: Risk, Uncertainty, and Economics for a Warming World*. Yale University Press.

Notter, D. A., Gauch, M., Widmer, R., Wäger, P., Stamp, A., Zah, R., & Althaus, H.-J. (2010). Contribution of Li-Ion Batteries to the Environmental Impact of Electric Vehicles. *Environmental Science & Technology*, *44*(17), 6550–6556. https://doi.org/10.1021/es903729a

Odum, H. T. (2013). *Environment, Power and Society for the Twenty-First Century: The Hierarchy of Energy*. Columbia University Press.

OECD. (1972). Recommendation of the Council on Guiding Principles concerning International Economic Aspects of Environmental Policies. 26 May 1972 – C(72)128. Decisions, Recommendations and other Instruments of the Organisation for Economic Co-Operation and Development. Retrieved from http://acts.oecd.org/Instruments/ShowInstrumentView.aspx?InstrumentID=4&InstrumentPID=255&Lang=en&Book=

O'Hara, P. A. (2008). Principle of Circular and Cumulative Causation: Fusing Myrdalian and Kaldorian Growth and Development Dynamics. *Journal of Economic Issues*, *42*(2), 375–387.

OICA. (2016). World vehicles in use 2005-2015. Organisation Internationale des Constructeurs d'Automobiles (OICA). Retrieved from http://www.oica.net/category/vehicles-in-use/

OICA. (2017). Sales statistics: Sales of new passenger cars 2005-2016. Organisation Internationale des Constructeurs d'Automobiles (OICA). Retrieved from http://www.oica.net/category/sales-statistics/

Okasha, S. (2002). *Philosophy of science: a very short introduction*. Oxford; New York: Oxford University Press.

ORNL. (2016). Transportation Energy Data Book (TEDB). Oak Ridge National Laboratory (ORNL). Retrieved from http://cta.ornl.gov/data/index.shtml

Ortúzar, J. D., & Willumsen, L. G. (2001). *Modelling transport*. Chichester: Wiley.

Pagan, A. (1987). Three Econometric Methodologies: A Critical Appraisal1. *Journal of Economic Surveys*, *1*(1–2), 3–23. https://doi.org/10.1111/j.1467-6419.1987.tb00022.x

Page, S. E. (2008). agent-based models. In S. N. Durlauf & L. E. Blume (Eds.), *The New Palgrave Dictionary of Economics* (2nd ed., pp. 47–52). Basingstoke: Nature Publishing Group. Retrieved from http://www.dictionaryofeconomics.com/article?id=pde2008_A000218

Page, S. E. (2010). *Diversity and Complexity*. Princeton University Press.

Palazuelos, E. (2000). *Contenido y método de la economía*. Ediciones AKAL.

Parry, I. W. H., Walls, M., & Harrington, W. (2007). Automobile Externalities and Policies. *Journal of Economic Literature*, *45*(2), 373–399.

Pasaoglu, G., Zubaryeva, A., Fiorello, D., & Thiel, C. (2014). Analysis of European mobility surveys and their potential to support studies on the impact of electric vehicles on energy and infrastructure needs in Europe. *Technological Forecasting and Social Change*, *87*, 41–50. https://doi.org/10.1016/j.techfore.2013.09.002

Pasinetti, L. (2010). *Keynes e i keynesiani di Cambridge*. Roma ; Bari: Gius. Laterza & Figli.

Patterson, K. D. (2000). *Introduction to Applied Econometrics: A Time Series Approach*. New York: Palgrave Macmillan.

Pearce, D. (2002). An InTellectual History of Environmental Economics. *Annual Review of Energy and the Environment*, *27*(1), 57–81. https://doi.org/10.1146/annurev.energy.27.122001.083429

Perman, R. (2011). *Natural Resource and Environmental Economics* (Auflage: 4th Revised edition.). Harlow, Essex ; New York: Financial Times Prent.

Perron, P. (1989). The Great Crash, the Oil Price Shock, and the Unit Root Hypothesis. *Econometrica*, *57*(6), 1361–1401. https://doi.org/10.2307/1913712

Petty, S. W. (1963). *The Economic Writings of Sir William Petty: Together with the Observations Upon the Bills of Mortality*. A.M. Kelley, Bookseller.

Phillips, A. W. (1957). Stabilisation Policy and the Time-Forms of Lagged Responses. *The Economic Journal*, *67*(266), 265–277. https://doi.org/10.2307/2227788

Pickup, M. (2014). *Introduction to Time Series Analysis*. SAGE Publications.

Pierenkemper, T. (2012). *Geschichte des modernen ökonomischen Denkens: Große Ökonomen und ihre Ideen*. UTB GmbH.

Pigou, A. C. (2013). *The Economics of Welfare*. Palgrave Macmillan.

Pindyck, R. S., & Rubinfeld, D. L. (1991). *Econometric models and econometric forecast*. New York [etc.: McGraw-Hill.

Polanyi, K. (2001). *The Great Transformation: The Political and Economic Origins of Our Time* (2nd ed.). Boston, MA: Beacon Press.

Ponting, C. (2011). *A New Green History Of The World: The Environment and the Collapse of Great Civilizations*. Random House.

Popper, K. R. (2007). *The logic of scientific discovery*. Cambridge: International Society for Science and Religion.

Radzicki, M. J. (1990). Methodologia oeconomiae et systematis dynamis. *System Dynamics Review*, *6*(2), 123–147. https://doi.org/10.1002/sdr.4260060202

Radzicki, M. J. (2003). Mr. Hamilton, Mr. Forrester, and a Foundation for Evolutionary Economics. *Journal of Economic Issues*, *37*(1), 133–173. https://doi.org/10.1080/00213624.2003.11506561

Radzicki, M. J., & Tauheed, L. (2009). In Defense of System Dynamics: A Response to Professor Hayden. *Journal of Economic Issues*, *43*(4), 1043-1061. https://doi.org/10.2753/JEI0021-3624430411

Raff, D. M. G., & Summers, L. H. (1987). Did Henry Ford Pay Efficiency Wages? *Journal of Labor Economics*, *5*(4), S57–S86.

Rahmandad, H., Oliva, R., Osgood, N. D., & Richardson, G. (2015). *Analytical Methods for Dynamic Modelers*. MIT Press.

Rahmandad, H., & Sterman, J. D. (2012). Reporting guidelines for simulation-based research in social sciences. *System Dynamics Review*, *28*(4), 396–411. https://doi.org/10.1002/sdr.1481

Raiffa, H. (1968). *Decision analysis: introductory lectures on choices under uncertainty*. Random House.

Randers, J. (1980). *Elements of the System Dynamics Method*. MIT Press.

Rawlinson, M., & Wells, P. (1996). Taylorism, Lean Production and the Automotive Industry. *Asia Pacific Business Review*, *2*(4), 189–204. https://doi.org/10.1080/13602389600000026

Reardon, J. (2009). *The Handbook of Pluralist Economics Education*. Routledge.

Renn, O. (2014). *Das Risikoparadox: Warum wir uns vor dem Falschen fürchten*. FISCHER Taschenbuch.

Richardson, G. P. (1991). *Feedback Thought in Social Science and Systems Theory*. University of Pennsylvania Press.

Richardson, G. P. (2011). Reflections on the foundations of system dynamics. *System Dynamics Review*, *27*(3), 219–243. https://doi.org/10.1002/sdr.462

Rifkin, J. (2003). *The Hydrogen Economy*. Penguin.

Rifkin, J. (2011). *The Third Industrial Revolution: How Lateral Power Is Transforming Energy, the Economy, and the World*. Macmillan.

Rijkee, A. G., & van Essen, H. P. (2010). *Review of projections and scenarios for transport in 2050. Task 9 Report V produced as part of contract ENV.C.3/SER2008/0053 between European Commission Directorate-General Environment and AEA Technology plc*. Retrieved from www.eutransportghg2050.eu

Rizzo, M. J. (1979). *Time, Uncertainty, and Disequilibrium: Exploration of Austrian Themes*. Lexington Books.

Robbins, L. (2007). *An Essay on the Nature and Significance of Economic Science*. Ludwig von Mises Institute.

Robinson, J. (1973). *Economic Philosophy*. Penguin Books.

Robinson, J. (1980). Time in Economic Theory. *Kyklos*, *33*(2), 219–229. https://doi.org/10.1111/j.1467-6435.1980.tb02632.x

Robson, C. (2011). *Real world research: a resource for users of social research methods in applied settings*. Chichester, West Sussex: Wiley.

Rodrik, D. (2015). *Economics Rules: The Rights and Wrongs of the Dismal Science*. W. W. Norton & Company.

Rogers, E. M. (2003). *Diffusion of Innovations, 5th Edition* (Auflage: 5th Edition). New York: Free Press.

Romilly, P., Song, H., & Liu, X. (1998). Modelling and Forecasting Car Ownership in Britain: A Cointegration and General to Specific Approach. *Journal of Transport Economics and Policy*, *32*(2), 165–185.

Romilly, P., Song, H., & Liu, X. (2001). Car ownership and use in Britain: a comparison of the empirical results of alternative cointegration estimation methods and forecasts. *Applied Economics*, *33*(14), 1803–1818. https://doi.org/10.1080/00036840011021708

Rose, A., & Casler, S. (1996). Input–Output Structural Decomposition Analysis: A Critical Appraisal. *Economic Systems Research*, *8*(1), 33–62. https://doi.org/10.1080/09535319600000003

Rose, A., & Miernyk, W. (1989). Input–Output Analysis: The First Fifty Years. *Economic Systems Research*, *1*(2), 229–272. https://doi.org/10.1080/09535318900000016

Rosser, J. B., Holt, R. P. F., & Colander, D. C. (2010). *European Economics at a Crossroads*. Edward Elgar Publishing.

Russell, B. (2004). *History of Western philosophy*. London; New York: Routledge. Retrieved from http://search.ebscohost.com/login.aspx?direct=true&scope=site&db=nlebk&db=nlabk&AN=105264

Ruth, M., & Hannon, B. M. (1997). *Modeling dynamic economic systems*. New York: Springer.

Sallee, J. M., West, S. E., & Fan, W. (2016). Do consumers recognize the value of fuel economy? Evidence from used car prices and gasoline price fluctuations. *Journal of Public Economics*, *135*, 61–73. https://doi.org/10.1016/j.jpubeco.2016.01.003

Samaras, C., & Meisterling, K. (2008). Life Cycle Assessment of Greenhouse Gas Emissions from Plug-in Hybrid Vehicles: Implications for Policy. *Environmental Science & Technology*, *42*(9), 3170–3176. https://doi.org/10.1021/es702178s

Sampedro, J. L. (1967). *Las fuerzas económicas de nuestro tiempo*. McGraw-Hill.

Sampedro, J. L. (2010). *Economía humanista: ALGO MÁS QUE CIFRAS*. DEBOLSILLO.

Schade, W. (2005). *Strategic Sustainability Analysis: Concept and Application for the Assessment of European Transport Policy*. Baden-Baden: Nomos Publishers.

Schafer, A., & Victor, D. G. (1999). Global passenger travel: implications for carbon dioxide emissions. *Energy*, *24*(8), 657–679. https://doi.org/10.1016/S0360-5442(99)00019-5

Scharlemann, J. P. W., & Laurance, W. F. (2008). How Green Are Biofuels? *Science*, *319*(5859), 43–44. https://doi.org/10.1126/science.1153103

Scheffer, M., Bascompte, J., Brock, W. A., Brovkin, V., Carpenter, S. R., Dakos, V., … Sugihara, G. (2009). Early-warning signals for critical transitions. *Nature*, *461*(7260), 53–59. https://doi.org/10.1038/nature08227

Schelling, T. C. (2006). *Micromotives and Macrobehavior*. W. W. Norton & Company.

Schipper, L., & Marie-Lilliu, C. (1999). *Transportation and CO2 emissions: Flexing the link--a path for the World Bank*. World Bank, Environment Dept.

Schumpeter, J. (1954). *History of Economic Analysis* (Auflage: 1 New). London u.a.: Routledge.

Schumpeter, J. A. (1908). *Das Wesen und der Hauptinhalt der theoretischen Nationalökonomie*. Duncker & Humblot.

Schumpeter, J. A. (2014). *Economic Doctrine and Method*. Routledge.

Schwanitz, V. J. (2013). Evaluating integrated assessment models of global climate change. *Environmental Modelling & Software*, *50*, 120–131. https://doi.org/10.1016/j.envsoft.2013.09.005

SDM-Doc. (2016). Tools for System Dynamics: SDM-Doc. Retrieved from http://tools.systemdynamics.org/sdm-doc/

SDS. (2014). System Dynamis Society. Introduction to System Dynamics. Retrieved from http://www.systemdynamics.org/what-is-s/

Sedlacek, T., & Havel, V. (2013). *Economics of Good and Evil: The Quest for Economic Meaning from Gilgamesh to Wall Street* (Auflage: Reprint). New York: Oxford University Press.

Sell, K. (2015). *Lernen aus dem Scheitern des ersten Elektroautos: General Motors EV1*. Igel Verlag RWS.

Sen, A. (1991). *On Ethics and Economics*. Wiley.

Senge, P. M. (2010). *The Fifth Discipline: The Art & Practice of The Learning Organization*. Crown Publishing Group.

Sensfuss, F. (2008). *Assessment of the Impact of Renewable Electricity Generation on the German Electricity Sector: An Agent Based Simulation Approach*. VDI-Verlag.

Serra, J. V. F. (2013). *Electric Vehicles: Technology, Policy and Commercial Development*. Routledge.

Service, R. F. (2009). Hydrogen Cars: Fad or the Future? *Science*, *324*(5932), 1257–1259. https://doi.org/10.1126/science.324_1257

Shell. (2016). Shell Scenarios. Royal Dutch Shell. Retrieved from http://www.shell.com/energy-and-innovation/the-energy-future/scenarios.html

Shepherd, S., Bonsall, P., & Harrison, G. (2012). Factors affecting future demand for electric vehicles: A model based study. *Transport Policy*, *20*, 62-74. https://doi.org/10.1016/j.tranpol.2011.12.006

Shepherd, S. P. (2014). A review of system dynamics models applied in transportation. *Transportmetrica B: Transport Dynamics*, *2*(2), 83–105. https://doi.org/10.1080/21680566.2014.916236

Shiller, R. J. (2015). *Irrational Exuberance*. Princeton University Press.

Shine, K. P. (2009). The global warming potential – the need for an interdisciplinary retrial. *Climatic Change*, *96*(4), 467–472. https://doi.org/10.1007/s10584-009-9647-6

Shmelev, S. E. (2011). *Ecological Economics: Sustainability in Practice*. Springer Science & Business Media.

Shone, R. (2002). *(ECONOMIC DYNAMICS: PHASE DIAGRAMS AND THEIR ECONOMIC APPLICATION*. Cambridge University Press.

Simon, H. A. (1959). Theories of Decision-Making in Economics and Behavioral Science. *The American Economic Review*, *49*(3), 253–283.

Simon, H. A. (1984). *Models of Bounded Rationality* (New edition). Mit University Press Group Ltd.

Sims, C. A. (1980). Macroeconomics and Reality. *Econometrica*, *48*(1), 1-48. https://doi.org/10.2307/1912017

Sismondi, J. C. L. S. de. (2011). *Sobreproducción y subconsumo*. Maia Ediciones.

Small, K. A. (2012). Energy policies for passenger motor vehicles. *Transportation Research Part A: Policy and Practice*, *46*(6), 874–889. https://doi.org/10.1016/j.tra.2012.02.017

Smith, A. (2008). *An Inquiry into the Nature and Causes of the Wealth of Nations: A Selected Edition*. OUP Oxford.

Smith, P. C., & van Ackere, A. (2002). A note on the integration of system dynamics and economic models. *Journal of Economic Dynamics and Control*, *26*(1), 1–10. https://doi.org/10.1016/S0165-1889(00)00025-7

Smith, V. L. (2007). *Rationality in Economics: Constructivist and Ecological Forms*. Cambridge University Press.

SOeS. (2016). Véhicules routiers. Service de l'Observation et des Statistiques (SOeS). Retrieved from http://www.statistiques.developpement-durable.gouv.fr/transports/i/vehicules-routiers.html

Sommer, M. (1984). The econometric challenge to system dynamics and vice versa : some future perspectives.

Soto, J. H. de. (2012). *La Escuela Austriaca, Mercado y Actividad Empresarial*. Síntesis Editorial.

Spanos, A. (1999). *Probability Theory and Statistical Inference: Econometric Modeling with Observational Data*. Cambridge University Press.

Spanos, A. (2006). Econometrics in Retrospect and Prospect. In *New Palgrave Handbook of Econometrics*. Macmillan, London.

Sperling, D., & Gordon, D. (2009). *Two Billion Cars: Driving Toward Sustainability*. Oxford University Press.

Sterman, J. D. (1987). Systems Simulation. Expectation formation in behavioral simulation models. *Behavioral Science, 32*(3), 190–211. https://doi.org/10.1002/bs.3830320304

Sterman, J. D. (2000). *Business Dynamics: Systems Thinking and Modeling for a Complex World*. McGraw-Hill/Irwin.

Stern, N. H., & Treasury, G. B. (2007). *The Economics of Climate Change: The Stern Review*. Cambridge University Press.

Stevens, S. S. (1946). On the Theory of Scales of Measurement. *Science, 103*(2684), 677–680. https://doi.org/10.1126/science.103.2684.677

Stiglitz, J. E. (2016). *The Euro: How a Common Currency Threatens the Future of Europe*. W. W. Norton.

Stiglitz, J. E., & Rosengard, J. K. (2015). *Economics of the Public Sector: Fourth International Student Edition*. W. W. Norton & Company.

Stock, J. H., & Watson, M. W. (1988). Variable Trends in Economic Time Series. *The Journal of Economic Perspectives*, *2*(3), 147–174.

Strogatz, S. H. (2014). *Nonlinear Dynamics and Chaos: With Applications to Physics, Biology, Chemistry, and Engineering*. Westview Press.

Struben, J., & Sterman, J. D. (2008). Transition Challenges for Alternative Fuel Vehicle and Transportation Systems. *Environment and Planning B: Planning and Design*, *35*(6), 1070–1097. https://doi.org/10.1068/b33022t

Sunstein, C. R., & Thaler, R. H. (2012). *Nudge: Improving Decisions About Health, Wealth and Happiness*. Penguin UK.

Swart, R. J., Raskin, P., & Robinson, J. (2004). The problem of the future: sustainability science and scenario analysis. *Global Environmental Change*, *14*(2), 137–146. https://doi.org/10.1016/j.gloenvcha.2003.10.002

Sweeney, J. L. (1993). Chapter 17 Economic theory of depletable resources: An introduction. In A. V. K. and J. L. Sweeney (Ed.), *Handbook of Natural Resource and Energy Economics* (Vol. 3, pp. 759–854). Elsevier. Retrieved from http://www.sciencedirect.com/science/article/pii/S1573443905800041

Taleb, N. N. (2010). *The Black Swan: The Impact of the Highly Improbable* (Auflage: 2nd edition.). New York: Random House Trade Paperbacks.

Tanner, J. C. (1977). CAR OWNERSHIP TRENDS AND FORECASTS. *Publication of: Transport and Road Research Laboratory*. Retrieved from /view.aspx?id=61068

Taylor, F. W. (2010). *The Principles of Scientific Management*. Cosimo, Inc.

Tesla. (2016). Tesla Repays Department of Energy Loan Nine Years Early. Tesla Motors. Retrieved from https://www.tesla.com/de_AT/blog/tesla-repays-department-energy-loan-nine-years-early

Thaler, R. H. (2015). *Misbehaving: The Making of Behavioural Economics*. Penguin UK.

Thaler, R. H., & Sunstein, C. R. (2003). Libertarian Paternalism. *The American Economic Review*, *93*(2), 175–179.

Thies, C., Kieckhäfer, K., & Spengler, T. S. (2016). Market introduction strategies for alternative powertrains in long-range passenger cars under competition. *Transportation Research Part D: Transport and Environment*, *45*, 4–27. https://doi.org/10.1016/j.trd.2015.05.002

Timms, P. (2008). Transport models, philosophy and language. *Transportation*, *35*(3), 395–410. https://doi.org/10.1007/s11116-007-9154-4

Toufflut, J.-P. (2007). *Augustin Cournot: modelling economics*. Edward Elgar.

Toyota. (2016). The 2017 Toyota Mirai.
Retrieved from https://ssl.toyota.com/mirai/fcv.html

Train, K. (1986). *Qualitative Choice Analysis: Theory, Econometrics, and an Application to Automobile Demand*. MIT Press.

Train, K. (2009). *Discrete Choice Methods with Simulation*. Cambridge University Press.

Tran, M., Banister, D., Bishop, J. D. K., & McCulloch, M. D. (2013). Simulating early adoption of alternative fuel vehicles for sustainability. *Technological Forecasting and Social Change*, *80*(5), 865–875. https://doi.org/10.1016/j.techfore.2012.09.009

Treasury. (2012). Automotive Industry Financing Program. U.S. Department of the Treasury. Retrieved from https://www.treasury.gov/initiatives/financial-stability/programs/Other%20Programs/aifp/Pages/autoprogram.aspx

Treasury. (2016). Auto Industry, Troubled Asset Relief Program (TARP). U.S. Department of the Treasury. Retrieved from https://www.treasury.gov/initiatives/financial-stability/TARP-Programs/automotive-programs/pages/default.aspx

Trutnevyte, E., Barton, J., O'Grady, Á., Ogunkunle, D., Pudjianto, D., & Robertson, E. (2014). Linking a storyline with multiple models: A cross-scale study of the UK power system transition. *Technological Forecasting and Social Change*, *89*, 26–42. https://doi.org/10.1016/j.techfore.2014.08.018

Tsang, F., Pedersen, J. S., Wooding, S., & Potoglou, D. (2012). Bringing the electric vehicle to the mass market [Product Page]. Retrieved 29 September 2016, from http://www.rand.org/pubs/working_papers/WR775.html

Tsoularis, A., & Wallace, J. (2002). Analysis of logistic growth models. *Mathematical Biosciences*, *179*(1), 21–55. https://doi.org/10.1016/S0025-5564(02)00096-2

Turner, J. A. (2004). Sustainable Hydrogen Production. *Science*, *305*(5686), 972–974. https://doi.org/10.1126/science.1103197

Turner, R. K., Pearce, D. W., & Bateman, I. J. (1994). *Environmental Economics: An Elementary Introduction*. Harvester Wheatsheaf.

Uherek, E., Halenka, T., Borken-Kleefeld, J., Balkanski, Y., Berntsen, T., Borrego, C., … Schmid, S. (2010). Transport impacts on atmosphere and climate: Land transport. *Atmospheric Environment*, *44*(37), 4772–4816. https://doi.org/10.1016/j.atmosenv.2010.01.002

UN. (2016). World Population Prospects, the 2015 Revision. United Nations. Retrieved from https://esa.un.org/unpd/wpp/

UNFCCC. (2015). Paris Declaration on Electro-Mobility and Climate Change & Call to Action, United Nations Framework Convention on Climate Change. Retrieved from http://newsroom.unfccc.int/media/521376/paris-electro-mobility-declaration.pdf

UNFCCC. (2016). Greenhouse Gas Emissions Data. Time Series. United Nations Framework Convention on Climate Change (UNFCCC). Retrieved from http://di.unfccc.int/time_series

Urban, G. L., Weinberg, B. D., & Hauser, J. R. (1996). Premarket Forecasting of Really-New Products. *Journal of Marketing*, *60*(1), 47–60. https://doi.org/10.2307/1251887

Varian, H. R. (1992). *Microeconomic Analysis*. Norton.

Veblen, T. (1898). Why is Economics not an Evolutionary Science? *The Quarterly Journal of Economics*, *12*(4), 373–397. https://doi.org/10.2307/1882952

Veblen, T., & Cuadrado, C. M. (2014). *Teoría De La Clase Ociosa* (Edición: edición). Madrid: Alianza.

Vensim. (2016). Vensim® Documentation. Retrieved from https://www.vensim.com/documentation/

VIZ. (2016). Verkehr in Zahlen 2014/2015. Bundesministerium für Verkehr und digitale Infrastrukture (BMVI). Retrieved from https://www.bmvi.de/SharedDocs/DE/Artikel/K/verkehr-in-zahlen.html

Vogelvang, B. (2004). *Econometrics: Theory & Applications With Eviews: Theory and Applications with E-Views*. Harlow: Financial Times Prentice Hall.

von Hayek, F. A. (1975). The Pretence of Knowledge. *The Swedish Journal of Economics*, *77*(4), 433–442. https://doi.org/10.2307/3439337

Vroey, M. D. (2016). *A History of Macroeconomics from Keynes to Lucas and Beyond*. Cambridge University Press.

VW. (2016). Aktionärsstruktur. Stand 31.12.2015. Volkswagen Aktiengesellschaft. Retrieved from http://www.volkswagenag.com/content/vwcorp/content/de/investor_relations/share/Shareholder_Structure.html

Wakker, P. P. (2010). *Prospect Theory: For Risk and Ambiguity*. Cambridge University Press.

Walker, W. E. (1978). *A Review of Models in the Policy Process*. Rand Corporation.

Walker, W. E., Harremoës, P., Rotmans, J., Sluijs, J. P. van der, Asselt, M. B. A. van, Janssen, P., & Krauss, M. P. K. von. (2003). Defining Uncertainty: A Conceptual Basis for Uncertainty Management in Model-Based Decision Support. *Integrated Assessment*, *4*(1), 5–17. https://doi.org/10.1076/iaij.4.1.5.16466

Walker, W. E., Lempert, R. J., & Kwakkel, J. H. (2013). Deep Uncertainty. In S. I. Gass & M. C. Fu (Eds.), *Encyclopedia of Operations Research and Management Science* (pp. 395–402). Springer US. https://doi.org/10.1007/978-1-4419-1153-7_1140

Walther, G., Wansart, J., Kieckhäfer, K., Schnieder, E., & Spengler, T. S. (2010). Impact assessment in the automotive industry: mandatory market introduction of alternative powertrain technologies. *System Dynamics Review*, *26*(3), 239–261. https://doi.org/10.1002/sdr.453

Wansart, J. (2012). *Analyse von Strategien der Automobilindustrie zur Reduktion von CO2-Flottenemissionen und zur Markteinführung Alternativer Antriebe* (Auflage: 2012). Wiesbaden: Springer Gabler.

Wards. (2016). Data & Insights. Wards Auto. Retrieved from http://wardsauto.com/data-insights

WB. (2011). *The China New Energy Vehicles Program - Challenges and Opportunities. Prepared by PRTM Management Consultants, Inc. for the World Bank.*

WB. (2016). World Bank Data. Retrieved from http://data.worldbank.org/

WBCSD. (2004). *Mobility 2030: Meeting the challenges to sustainability. The Sustainable Mobility Project. Full Report.* World Business Council for Sustainable Development. Retrieved from http://wbcsdpublications.org/project/mobility-2030-meeting-the-challenges-to-sustainability-overview-2004/

Weber, M., & Abellán, J. (2010). *Por qué no se deben hacer juicios de valor en la sociología y en la economía: (el sentido de 'no hacer juicios de valor' en la sociología y en la economía)*. Madrid: Alianza Editorial.

Weimer-Jehle, W., Buchgeister, J., Hauser, W., Kosow, H., Naegler, T., Poganietz, W.-R., … Vögele, S. (2016). Context scenarios and their usage for the construction of socio-technical energy scenarios. *Energy*, *111*, 956–970. https://doi.org/10.1016/j.energy.2016.05.073

Weitzman, M. L. (2009). On Modeling and Interpreting the Economics of Catastrophic Climate Change. *Review of Economics and Statistics*, *91*(1), 1-19. https://doi.org/10.1162/rest.91.1.1

Whalen, C. (2008). Toward 'Wisely Managed' Capitalism: Post-Keynesian Institutionalism and the Creative State. *Forum for Social Economics*, *37*(1), 43–60. https://doi.org/10.1007/s12143-008-9014-9

Wheat, I. D. (2007). The feedback method of teaching macroeconomics: is it effective? *System Dynamics Review*, *23*(4), 391–413. https://doi.org/10.1002/sdr.386

Wiener, N. (1961). *Cybernetics Or Control and Communication in the Animal and the Machine*. MIT Press.

Wikipedia. (2016). Wikipedia - the free encyclopedia. Retrieved from https://www.wikipedia.org/

Wilber, C. K., & Harrison, R. S. (1978). The Methodological Basis of Institutional Economics: Pattern Model, Storytelling, and Holism. *Journal of Economic Issues*, *12*(1), 61–89.

Wohlgemuth, N. (1997). World transport energy demand modelling: Methodology and elasticities. *Energy Policy*, *25*(14–15), 1109–1119. https://doi.org/10.1016/S0301-4215(97)00103-1

Wold, H. (1954). Causality and Econometrics. *Econometrica*, *22*(2), 162–177. https://doi.org/10.2307/1907540

Wolf, C. (1993). *Markets Or Governments: Choosing Between Imperfect Alternatives*. MIT Press.

Wolf, M. (2014). *The Shifts and the Shocks: What we've learned – and have still to learn – from the financial crisis*. Penguin UK.

Wolf, W. (2009). *Verkehr, Umwelt, Klima die Globalisierung des Tempowahns*. Wien: Promedia.

Wray, L. R. (2015a). *Modern Money Theory: A Primer on Macroeconomics for Sovereign Monetary Systems, Second Edition*. Springer.

Wray, L. R. (2015b). *Modern Money Theory: A Primer on Macroeconomics for Sovereign Monetary Systems, Second Edition*. Springer.

Yergin, D. (2011). *The Quest: Energy, Security, and the Remaking of the Modern World*. Penguin.

Yergin, D. (2012). *The Prize: The Epic Quest for Oil, Money & Power*. Simon and Schuster.

Yule, G. U. (1926). Why do we Sometimes get Nonsense-Correlations between Time-Series? – A Study in Sampling and the Nature of Time-Series. *Journal of the Royal Statistical Society*, *89*(1), 1–63. https://doi.org/10.2307/2341482

Zalewski, D. A., & Whalen, C. J. (2010). Financialization and Income Inequality: A Post Keynesian Institutionalist Analysis. *Journal of Economic Issues*, *44*(3), 757–777.

Zhang, J. shui. (2001). Iterative method for finding the balanced growth solution of the non-linear dynamic input–output model and the dynamic CGE model. *Economic Modelling*, *18*(1), 117–132. https://doi.org/10.1016/S0264-9993(00)00031-6

Zivot, E., & Andrews, D. W. K. (2002). Further Evidence on the Great Crash, the Oil-Price Shock, and the Unit-Root Hypothesis. *Journal of Business & Economic Statistics*, *20*(1), 25–44. https://doi.org/10.1198/073500102753410372

Zurek, M. B., & Henrichs, T. (2007). Linking scenarios across geographical scales in international environmental assessments. *Technological Forecasting and Social Change*, *74*(8), 1282–1295. https://doi.org/10.1016/j.techfore.2006.11.005

Appendix

Appendix I – Database

Microsoft® Excel is chosen as the type of file that contains the data employed in the modelling exercise. The data file, named *Data.xls*, divides data into six tabs (coloured in blue) used to feed EViews® and one tab (white) to feed Vensim®. This data tab includes a legend that indicates the type and level of reliability of the values shown in the cells. An empty dark brown cell indicates that historical data was not available to the modeller at the time the modelling exercise reported here took place. The cells for policy inputs that may be changed by the model user when building alternative scenarios are coloured in orange. In addition, the database has two tabs that contain, for each variable, information on the units of measurement, data source and, often, remarks. Particularly remarkable are the knowledge gaps, marked in grey. These cells quickly signal areas where data is still needed.

Table A.1 offers an overview of one of the tabs of the dataset, namely the one concerning econometric data. The data file is, with some restrictions imposed by original sources, available from the author of this thesis upon request.

Table A.1: Overview of the econometric dataset

Country	Variable	Description	Units	Period	Source	Remarks
cn	own	Car ownership	car / passenger	1980-2014	–	Own calculation based on data on car stock and population
	car	Car stock	car	1980-1996	(ORNL, 2016)	Own estimates for 81-84; 87; 89
				1997-2007	(IRF, 2016) (various)	Since the 2001 value is N/A, it was calculated by subtracting "Lorries and Vans" from "Total" in the IRF database. Vehicles in use: Passenger cars
				2008-2014	(OICA, 2016)	Vehicle in use, passenger car, estimated figures for 2010-2014
	pop	Population	passenger	1980-2030	(UN, 2016)	Total population. Future values using the middle fertility scenario
	gdp	Nominal GDP	country currency	1980-2021	(IMF, 2016)	
				2022-2030	Own	Vensim output
	def	GDP deflator	dmnl	1980-2021	(IMF, 2016)	Base year 2010
				2022-2030	Own	Vensim output
	rinc	Real GDP per cap	country currency / passenger	1980-2030	–	Own calculation based on data on real GDP and population. Base year 2010
	oil	Nominal crude oil price	dollar/bbl	1980-2030	(BP, 2016) (EIA, 2016a)	
fr	own	Car ownership	car / passenger	1960-2014	–	Own calculation based on data on car stock and population
	car	Car stock	car	1960-2010	(IRF, 2016) (various)	
				2011-2014	(CCFA, 2016)	Au 1er janvier
	pop	Population	passenger	1960-2030	(UN, 2016)	Total population. Future values using the middle fertility scenario
	Gdp	Nominal GDP	country currency	1980-2021	(IMF, 2016)	
				2022-2030	Own	Vensim output
	def	GDP deflator	dmnl	1960-1979	(WB, 2016)	Note this source uses the same base year as IMF (2016)
				1980-2021	(IMF, 2016)	Base year 2010
				2022-2030	Own	Vensim output
	rinc	Real GDP per cap	country currency / passenger	1980-2030	–	Own calculation based on data on real GDP and population. Base year 2010
	Fuel	Nominal gasoline fuel price	country currency / litre	1983-1989	(MEEDM, 2016)	Essence ordinaire
				1990-1999		Super sans plomb 95
				2000-2015	(IEA, 2016b) (various)	Premium unleaded (95 RON)
				2016-2030	Own	Vensim output

	vkt	Vehicle-km travelled	vkm/year	1990-2014	(SOeS, 2016)	Annual total cars
	avkm	Average VKT per car	km/car/year	1990-2014	Own	Calculation using vkt and car
de	own	Car ownership	car / passenger	1970-2013	–	Own calculation based on data on car stock and population
de	car	Car stock	car	1970-2004	(IRF, 2016) (various)	Missing values 1971, 1976, 1977, 1992. Own interpolation
de	car	Car stock	car	2005-2015	(KBA, 2016)	Note KBA reports stock as of 1. January
de	pop	Population	passenger	1960-2030	(UN, 2016)	Total population. Future values using the middle fertility scenario
de	gdp	Nominal GDP	country currency	1980-2021	(IMF, 2016)	Data until 1990 refers to German federation only (West Germany)
de	gdp	Nominal GDP	country currency	2022-2030	Own	Vensim output
de	def	GDP deflator	dmnl	1960-1999	(WB, 2016)	Note this source uses the same base year as IMF (2016), however discrepancies are present (not the case for FR)
de	def	GDP deflator	dmnl	2000-2021	(IMF, 2016)	Base year 2010
de	def	GDP deflator	dmnl	2022-2030	Own	Vensim output
de	rinc	Real GDP per cap	country currency / passenger	1980-2030	–	Own calculation based on data on real GDP and population. Base year 2010
de	fuel	Nominal gasoline fuel price	country currency / litre	1970-1972	(MWV, 2016)	Normalbenzin
de	fuel	Nominal gasoline fuel price	country currency / litre	1973-1999	(MWV, 2016)	Superbenzin
de	fuel	Nominal gasoline fuel price	country currency / litre	2000-2015	(IEA, 2016b) (various)	Premium unleaded (95 RON)
de	fuel	Nominal gasoline fuel price	country currency / litre	2016-2030	Own	Vensim output
de	vkt	Vehicle-km travelled	vkm/year	1990-2015	(KBA, 2016) (DIW, 2012)	
de	vkt	Vehicle-km travelled	vkm/year	2000-2001	(IRF, 2016) (various)	
de	avkm	Average VKT per car	km/car/year	1990-2015	Own	Calculation using vkt and car values
in	own	Car ownership	car / passenger	1980-2013	–	Own calculation based on data on car stock and population
in	car	Car stock	car	1980-2013	(GoI, 2016)	Cars including jeeps and taxis
in	pop	Population	passenger	1980-2030	(UN, 2016)	Total population. Future values using the middle fertility scenario
in	gdp	Nominal GDP	country currency	1980-2021	(IMF, 2016)	
in	gdp	Nominal GDP	country currency	2022-2030	Own	Vensim output
in	Def	GDP deflator	dmnl	1980-2021	(IMF, 2016)	Base year 2011
in	Def	GDP deflator	dmnl	2022-2030	Own	Vensim output
in	rinc	Real GDP per cap	country currency / passenger	1980-2030	–	Own calculation based on data on real GDP and population. Base year 2011
in	oil	Nominal crude oil price	dollar/bbl	1980-2030	(BP, 2016) (EIA, 2016a)	

jp	own	Car ownership	car / passenger	1960-2015	–	Own calculation based on data on car stock and population
	car	Car stock	car	1960-2015	(JAMA, 2016)	See also (IRF, 2016) (various), (JARI, 2016), (OICA, 2016), (ORNL, 2016), (Wards, 2016)
	pop	Population	passenger	1960-2030	(UN, 2016)	Total population. Future values using the middle fertility scenario
	Gdp	Nominal GDP	country currency	1980-2021	(IMF, 2016)	
				2022-2030	Own	Vensim output
	def	GDP deflator	dmnl	1980-2021	(IMF, 2016)	Base year 2005
				2022-2030	Own	Vensim output
	rinc	Real GDP per cap	country currency / passenger	1980-2030	–	Own calculation based on data on real GDP and population. Base year 2005
	oil	Nominal crude oil price	dollar/bbl	1980-2030	(BP, 2016) (EIA, 2016a)	
us	own	Car ownership	car / passenger	1960-2014	–	Own calculation based on data on car stock and population
	car	Car stock	car	1960-2011	(FHWA, 2016)	Car stock subject to methodological changes after 2012. Hence I used OICA data instead.
				2012-2014	(OICA, 2016)	Vehicle in use, passenger car
	pop	Population	passenger	1960-2030	(UN, 2016)	Total population. Future values using the middle fertility scenario
	gdp	Nominal GDP	country currency	1980-2021	(IMF, 2016)	
				2022-2030	Own	Vensim output
	def	GDP deflator	dmnl	1980-2021	(IMF, 2016)	Base year 2009
				2022-2030	Own	Vensim output
	rinc	Real GDP per cap	country currency / passenger	1980-2030	–	Own calculation based on data on real GDP and population. Base year 2009
	fuel	Nominal gasoline fuel price	dollar/litre	1960-1990	(EIA, 2016a)	Leaded Regular Gasoline, U.S. City Average Retail Price. Annual average price incl. Taxes. Own conversion using value = 3.78541 litre/gallon
				1991-2014	(EIA, 2016a)	Regular Motor Gasoline, All Areas, Retail Price. Annual average price incl. Taxes. Original units in US gallons. Own conversion using value = 3.78541 litre/gallon
	vkt	Vehicle-km travelled	vkm/year	1960-2006	(FHWA, 2016)	After 2006, data non comparable due to methodological changes
	avkm	Average VKT per car	km/car/year	1960-2006	Own	Calculation using vkt and car

Appendix II – Transparency Checklist for Model Reproducibility

Encouraged by the recommendations on model transparency and reproducibility made by Bossel (2007a) and Rahmandad and Sterman (2012), this section includes key aspects of model documentation. Figure 8.1 shows an excerpt of the 'model assessment results' using SDM-Doc (see Martinez-Moyano (2012)).

Model Information	Number
Total Number of Variables	575
Total Number of State Variables (Level+Smooth+Delay Variables)	35 (6.1%)
Total Number of Stocks (Stocks in Level+Smooth+Delay Variables) †	580 (100.9%)
Total Number of Macros	0
Variables with Source Information	517 (89.9%)
Variables with Dimensionless Units	150 (26.1%)
Variables without Predefined Min or Max Values	548 (95.3%)
Function Sensitivity Parameters	0
Data Lookup Tables	0
Time Unit	Year
Initial Time	2000
Final Time	2030
Reported Time Interval	1
Time Step	1
Model Is Fully Formulated	Yes
Modeler-Defined Groups	- **No** -
VPM File Available	- **No** -

Warnings	Number
Undocumented Equations	36 (6.3%)
Equations with Embedded Data (0 and 1 constants ignored)	21 (3.7%)
Equations With Unit Errors or Warnings	Unavailable
Variables Not in Any View	0
Incompletely Defined Subscripted Variables	0
Nonmonotonic Lookup Functions	0
Cascading (Chained) Lookup Functions	0
Non-Zero End Sloped Lookup Functions	0
Equations with "IF THEN ELSE" Functions	16 (2.8%)
Equations with "MIN" or "MAX" Functions	2 (0.3%)
Equations with "STEP", "PULSE", or Related Functions	1 (0.2%)

Potential Omissions	Number
Unused Variables	0
Supplementary Variables	58
Supplementary Variables Being Used	0
Complex Variable Formulations (Richardson's Rule = 3)	32
Complex Stock Formulations	0

Figure A.1: Model assessment results | Source: Own application of SDM-Doc (2016)

The main equations of the model were shown in chapter 4. The model developed in that chapter has been named TE3 (Transport, Energy, Economics, Environment) and is available from the author of this thesis upon request here: www.te3modelling.eu/model. For the complete model code, the interested reader is advised to download the SDM-Doc software, available from SDM-Doc (2016), and apply this tool to the model.

In the context of model-based energy scenario studies, Cao *et al.* (2016) propose a transparency checklist. The application of such the checklist to this modelling exercise is captured in Table A.2.

Table A.2: Application of the transparency checklist

Criterion		Evidence	
		Transparency level	Page number
General Information			
1	***Author, Institution***	Each author and corresponding institution shown on page(s):	*Title*
2	***Aim and funding***	Info included on page(s):	*xxv*
3	***Key term definitions***	A glossary is included on page(s):	*xv-xxviv*
Empirical Data			
4	***Sources***	All sources of secondary data summarised on a table on page(s):	*Appendix I*
5	***Pre-processing***	The data used had to be modified before being fed into the model. The procedure is indicated on page(s):	*Appendix I*
Assumptions			
6	***Identification of uncertain developments***	Only quantitative factors of uncertainty are considered on page(s):	*195-196*
7	***Uncertainty consideration***	Info included on page(s):	*221-227*
8	***Storyline construction***	Info included on page(s):	*197-199*
9	***Assumptions for data modification***	Info included on page(s):	*80-167*
Model			
10	***Model fact sheet***	The key features of the model are described verbally on page(s):	*71-79*
11	***Model specific properties***	Model strengths and weaknesses are shown on page(s):	*64-70; 238-240*
12	***Model interaction***	Linkages between submodels and/or models described on page(s):	*79-80*
13	***Model documentation***	The model code is available elsewhere, as stated on page(s):	*Appendix II (see weblink)*
14	***Output data access***	Access to model output data is facilitated, as indicated on page(s):	*Appendix II (see weblink)*
15	***Model validation***	The validation method applied is shown on page(s):	*179-194*
Results			
16	***Post-processing***	There was no need to modify the model output	*If applicable, insert number*
17	***Sensitivity analysis***	Info included on page(s):	*194-196*
18	***Robustness***	Info not included	*If applicable, insert number*
Conclusions and Recommendations			
19	***Results - recommendation - relationship***	Info included on page(s):	*235-237*
20	***Uncertainty communication***	Info included on page(s):	*195-196; 239*

Source: Cao *et al.* (2016)

PRODUKTION UND ENERGIE

Karlsruher Institut für Technologie (KIT)
Institut für Industriebetriebslehre und Industrielle Produktion
Deutsch-Französisches Institut für Umweltforschung

ISSN 2194-2404

Band 1 **National Integrated Assessment Modelling zur Bewertung umweltpolitischer Instrumente.**
Entwicklung des otello-Modellsystems und dessen Anwendung auf die Bundesrepublik Deutschland. 2012
ISBN 978-3-86644-853-7

Band 2 **Erhöhung der Energie- und Ressourceneffizienz und Reduzierung der Treibhausgasemissionen in der Eisen-, Stahl- und Zinkindustrie (ERESTRE).** 2013
ISBN 978-3-86644-857-5

Band 3 Frederik Trippe
Techno-ökonomische Bewertung alternativer Verfahrenskonfigurationen zur Herstellung von Biomass-to-Liquid (BtL) Kraftstoffen und Chemikalien. 2013
ISBN 978-3-7315-0031-5

Band 4 Dogan Keles
Uncertainties in energy markets and their consideration in energy storage evaluation. 2013
ISBN 978-3-7315-0046-9

Band 5 Heidi Ursula Heinrichs
Analyse der langfristigen Auswirkungen von Elektromobilität auf das deutsche Energiesystem im europäisschen Energieverbund. 2013
ISBN 978-3-7315-0131-2

Band 6 Julian Stengel
Akteursbasierte Simulation der energetischen Modernisierung des Wohngebäudebestands in Deutschland. 2014
ISBN 978-3-7315-0236-4

Band 7 Sonja Babrowski
Bedarf und Verteilung elektrischer Tagesspeicher im zukünftigen deutschen Energiesystem. 2015
ISBN 978-3-7315-0306-4

Band 8 Marius Wunder
Integration neuer Technologien der Bitumenkalthandhabung in die Versorgungskette. 2015
ISBN 978-3-7315-0319-4

Band 9 Felix Teufel
Speicherbedarf und dessen Auswirkungen auf die Energiewirtschaft bei Umsetzung der politischen Ziele zur Energiewende. 2015
ISBN 978-3-7315-0341-5

Band 10 D. Keles, L. Renz, A. Bublitz, F. Zimmermann, M. Genoese, W. Fichtner, H. Höfling, F. Sensfuß, J. Winkler
Zukunftsfähige Designoptionen für den deutschen Strommarkt: Ein Vergleich des Energy-only-Marktes mit Kapazitätsmärkten. 2016
ISBN 978-3-7315-0453-5

Band 11 Patrick Breun
Ein Ansatz zur Bewertung klimapolitischer Instrumente am Beispiel der Metallerzeugung und -verarbeitung. 2016
ISBN 978-3-7315-0494-8

Band 12 P. Ringler, H. Schermeyer, M. Ruppert, M. Hayn, V. Bertsch, D. Keles, W. Fichtner
Decentralized Energy Systems, Market Integration, Optimization. 2016
ISBN 978-3-7315-0505-1

Band 13	Marian Hayn **Modellgestützte Analyse neuer Stromtarife für Haushalte unter Berücksichtigung bedarfsorientierter Versorgungssicherheitsniveaus.** 2016 ISBN 978-3-7315-0499-3
Band 14	Frank Schätter **Decision support system for a reactive management of disaster-caused supply chain disturbances.** 2016 ISBN 978-3-7315-0530-3
Band 15	Robert Kunze **Techno-ökonomische Planung energetischer Wohngebäudemodernisierungen: Ein gemischt-ganzzahliges lineares Optimierungsmodell auf Basis einer vollständigen Finanzplanung.** 2016 ISBN 978-3-7315-0531-0
Band 16	A. Kühlen, J. Stengel, R. Volk, F. Schultmann, M. Reinhardt, H. Schlick, S. Haghsheno, A. Mettke, S. Asmus, S. Schmidt, J. Harzheim **ISA: Immissionsschutz beim Abbruch - Minimierung von Umweltbelastungen (Lärm, Staub, Erschütterungen) beim Abbruch von Hoch-/Tiefbauten und Schaffung hochwertiger Recyclingmöglichkeiten für Materialien aus Gebäudeabbruch.** 2018 ISBN 978-3-7315-0534-1
Band 17	Konrad Zimmer **Entscheidungsunterstützung zur Auswahl und Steuerung von Lieferanten und Lieferketten unter Berücksichtigung von Nachhaltigkeitsaspekten.** 2016 ISBN 978-3-7315-0537-2
Band 18	Kira Schumacher, Wolf Fichtner and Frank Schultmann (Eds.) **Innovations for sustainable biomass utilisation in the Upper Rhine Region.** 2017 ISBN 978-3-7315-0423-8

Band 19 Sophia Radloff
Modellgestützte Bewertung der Nutzung von Biokohle als Bodenzusatz in der Landwirtschaft. 2017
ISBN 978-3-7315-0559-4

Band 20 Rebekka Volk
Proactive-reactive, robust scheduling and capacity planning of deconstruction projects under uncertainty. 2017
ISBN 978-3-7315-0592-1

Band 21 Erik Merkel
Analyse und Bewertung des Elektrizitätssystems und des Wärmesystems der Wohngebäude in Deutschland. 2017
ISBN 978-3-7315-0636-2

Band 22 Rebekka Volk (Hrsg.)
Entwicklung eines mobilen Systems zur Erfassung und Erschließung von Ressourceneffizienzpotenzialen beim Rückbau von Infrastruktur und Produkten („ResourceApp"): Schlussbericht des Forschungsvorhabens. 2017
ISBN 978-3-7315-0653-9

Band 23 Thomas Kaschub
Batteriespeicher in Haushalten unter Berücksichtigung von Photovoltaik, Elektrofahrzeugen und Nachfrage-steuerung. 2017
ISBN 978-3-7315-0688-1

Band 24 Felix Hübner, Rebekka Volk, Oktay Secer, Daniel Kühn, Peter Sahre, Reinhard Knappik, Frank Schultmann, Sascha Gentes, Petra von Both
Modellentwicklung eines ganzheitlichen Projektmanagementsystems für kerntechnische Rückbauprojekte (MogaMaR): Schlussbericht des Forschungsvorhabens. 2018
ISBN 978-3-7315-0762-8

Die Bände sind unter www.ksp.kit.edu als PDF frei verfügbar oder als Druckausgabe zu bestellen.

Band 25 Karoline Fath
Technical and economic potential for photovoltaic systems on buildings. 2018
ISBN 978-3-7315-0787-1

Band 26 Ann-Kathrin Müller
Decision Support for Biomass Value Chains for the Production of Biochemicals Considering Uncertainties. 2018
ISBN 978-3-7315-0820-5

Band 27 Jonatan J. Gómez Vilchez
The Impact of Electric Cars on Oil Demand and Greenhouse Gas Emissions in Key Markets. 2019
ISBN 978-3-7315-0914-1